Data Structures and Algorithms
Using Python and C++

David M. Reed
Capital University

John Zelle
Wartburg College

Franklin, Beedle & Associates Incorporated
22462 SW Washington St.
Wilsonville, Oregon 97140
www.fbeedle.com

President and Publisher   Jim Leisy (jimleisy@fbeedle.com)
Project Manager   Tom Sumner
Editor   Stephanie Welch

Printed in the U.S.A.

ISBN 978-1-59028-233-5

Library of Congress Cataloging-in-Publication Data

Reed, David M.
  Data structures and algorithms using Python and C++ / David M. Reed, John Zelle.
      p. cm.
  ISBN 978-1-59028-233-5 (alk. paper)
 1. Python (Computer program language) 2. C++ (Computer program language) 3.
Data structures (Computer science) 4. Computer algorithms. I. Zelle, John M. II. Title.
  QA76.73.P98R44 2009
  005.1--dc22

                          2008053540

Contents

Preface

This book is intended for use in a traditional college-level data structures course (commonly known as CS2). The authors have found that Python is an excellent language for an introductory course. Its relatively simple syntax allows students to focus on problem solving more so than the more complicated syntax of languages such as Java, C++, and Ada. Python's built-in data structures and large standard library also allow students to write more interesting programs than can easily be written with other languages. This book assumes that students have learned the basic syntax of Python and been exposed to the use of existing classes. Most traditional CS1 courses that use Python will have covered all the necessary topics, and some may have covered a few of the topics covered in this book.

Python's object-oriented features make it an elegant language for starting a data structures course. We have found that most students successfully completing a CS1 course know how to use classes, but many of them need more experience to learn how to design and write their own classes. This is not surprising given the limited amount of time that is typically spent designing classes in a CS1 course. We address this issue by including a number of examples of class design in the first few chapters of this book.

Starting with Python in a CS2 course allows students to continue expanding their skills and gain experience designing and writing classes in a simple, familiar language. Python also makes it relatively easy to learn about linked structures. Every name in Python is a reference, so there is no additional syntax that needs to be learned in order to write linked structures. These advantages allow topics to be covered more quickly than is possible using more complex languages.

One potential drawback of Python for a data structures course is that it hides the complexity of memory management. This is a benefit in a first course, but we think that in a second course it is important that students begin to understand some of these low-level details that the Python interpreter hides from them. Since we can cover the basic data structures in less time using Python, there is time to learn a second language, even in a single-semester CS2 course. After the students have continued to improve their Python programming skills while covering the first few chapters of the book, it is relatively easy for them to learn a second object-oriented language. By using C++ as the second language, the students are exposed to a lower-level, compiled language. The syntax of C++ is more complicated than Python, but that is a relatively small hurdle once students have mastered fundamental programming concepts using Python. For example, now that they understand the basic concepts of programming and the semantics of statements such as conditional statements and looping statements, they can focus on learning the C++ syntax for these statements.

Once the students have learned fundamental C++ syntax, we cover the concepts of dynamic memory management by rewriting linked structures in C++. This reinforces the basic data structure concepts while focusing on the memory management issues. This book is not intended to provide complete coverage of the C++ language; instead, it is designed to introduce a large subset of the C++ language so students can understand the low-level details of memory management and write object-oriented code in C++. After covering the basics of the C++ language, we also introduce some of the more advanced data structures by providing Python implementations and leaving the student to write them in C++. In effect, Python becomes an executable pseudocode for presenting key algorithms and data structures.

Coverage Options

Since Python allows coverage of topics more quickly than other languages, a five semester-hour CS2 course can cover most, if not all, of this book. One of the authors covers the entire book over two courses that are three semester-hours each. In the three semester-hour CS2 course, the first seven chapters are covered in eight weeks and then the first three C++ chapters are covered in seven weeks, allowing plenty of time for the students to write a significant amount of C++ code. The final five chapters are covered in detail in the second three semester-hour course. This allows a week of review at the beginning of the course and more time to discuss the advanced algorithms and data structures in the last three chapters.

Depending on the amount of experience students have with object-oriented programming, the first three chapters of the book may be covered fairly quickly or may require more detailed coverage. We introduce the asymptotic run-time analysis of algorithms in the first chapter so that we can analyze the running time of all the data structure implementations. We also introduce one of Python's unit-testing frameworks early on so the students can formally test their code. After completing the discussion of linked structures in Chapter 4, the basic concepts of stacks and queues can be covered quickly, or the example applications can be used to continue developing algorithm and design skills. Some CS1 courses cover recursion, although in the our experiences, most students do not fully understand recursion the first time they study it. Since the study of tree data structures requires recursion, a chapter on recursion (Chapter 6) is included before trees (Chapter 7).

After the chapter on trees, the book switches to C++. Chapter 8 provides an introduction to C++ assuming the reader knows Python. Chapter 9 covers the details of writing and using classes in C++. Chapters 10 and 11 cover the issues of dynamic memory and writing linked structures in C++. We strongly recommend that you cover chapters 8 through 11 in order. Chapter 12 covers the basics of using and writing template code, but is not intended to provide complete coverage of templates. Chapter 12 may be skipped as none of the remaining chapters require an understanding of templates. The last three chapters cover some of the advanced data structures and algorithms. These three chapters can be covered in any order although there are a few references to topics in the other chapters.

Acknowledgments

We would like to thank Nancy Saks and Steve Bogaerts at Wittenberg University for comments on early drafts of the C++ chapters. We also thank Franklin, Beedle & Associates, especially Jim Leisy and Tom Sumner. We also need to thank our editor, Stephanie Welch, who found numerous minor mistakes, helping us improve the quality of this book.

David thanks Capital University for their support through a sabbatical, which allowed him to start the book. David would also like to thank his students who used early drafts and provided suggestions for improvements. The following Capital University students deserve special recognition for their many suggestions: Kyle Beal, Michael Herold, Jeff Huenemann, John Larison, and Brenton Wolfe. Finally, David would like to thank his wife, Sherri, for her support and understanding during the countless hours required to complete this book.

John extends thanks to his departmental colleagues at Wartburg College who have always been supportive of his writing endeavors and his students who have helped "test drive" some of the material. Most importantly, John thanks his family, especially his wife Elizabeth Bingham; for the love, support, and understanding that makes projects like this possible.

Chapter 1 — Abstraction and Analysis

Objectives

- To understand how programming "in the large" differs from programming "in the small."

- To understand the motivation and use for pre- and postconditions.

- To develop design and decomposition skills.

- To understand the importance of algorithm efficiency and learn how to analyze the running time of simple algorithms.

1.1 Introduction

Believe it or not, a first course in computer programming covers all the tools strictly necessary to solve any problem that can be solved with a computer. A very famous computer scientist named Alan Turing conjectured, and it is now widely accepted, that any problem solvable with computers requires only the basic statements that all computer programming languages include: decision statements (e.g., `if`), looping statements (e.g., `for` and `while`) and the ability to store and retrieve data. Since you already know about these, you may wonder what else there is to learn. That's a good question.

Programming in the Large

If you think of computer programming as a process similar to constructing a building, right now you have the knowledge equivalent to how to use a few tools such as a hammer, screwdriver, saw, and drill. Those might be all the tools necessary to build a house, but that does not mean you can build yourself a habitable home, let alone one that meets modern building codes. That's not to say that you can't do some useful things. You are probably capable of building benches or birdhouses, you're just not yet ready for the challenges that come with a larger project.

In programming, just as in house construction, tackling bigger projects requires additional knowledge, techniques, and skills. This book is intended to give you a solid foundation of this additional knowledge that you can build on in future courses and throughout your career. As you work your way through this material, you will be making a transition from programming "in the small" to programming "in the large."

Software projects can vary in difficulty in many ways. Obviously, they may range from the very small (e.g., a program to convert temperatures from Celsius to Fahrenheit) to the very large (e.g., a computer operating system) to anything in-between. Projects also differ widely in how mission-critical the developed systems are. A web-based diary need not be designed to the same exacting specifications as, say, an online banking system, and neither is as critical as the software controlling a medical life-support device.

There is no single property that makes any particular project "large" or "difficult." In general, though, there are a number of characteristics that distinguish real-world programming from the simpler academic exercises that you have probably seen so far. Here are some of them:

program size So far you may have written programs that comprise up to hundreds (perhaps thousands) of lines of code. It is not uncommon for real applications to have hundreds of thousands or millions of lines. For example, the Linux operating system kernel contains around six million lines of code.

single programmer vs. programming team Most of the programs you have worked on so far have probably been your own projects. However, most software today is produced by teams of developers working together. No single programmer has complete knowledge of every facet of the system.

working from scratch vs. existing code base You have probably written most of your programs pretty much starting from scratch. In real-world projects, programming happens in the context of existing applications. Existing systems may be extended, borrowed from, superseded, or used in concert with new software.

system lifetime When you are first learning to program, you may write many programs just for practice. Once your program has been graded, it may not ever be looked at again. Most real software projects have extended lifetimes. While they are in use, they continue to be refined, improved, and updated.

environment complexity A small project may be written in a single programming language using a small set of standard libraries. Larger projects tend to use many languages and a vast array of supporting development tools and software libraries.

1.1.2 The Road Ahead

The fundamental problem of programming in the large is managing the associated complexity. Humans are good at keeping track of only a few things at a time. In order to deal with a complex software system, we need ways of limiting the number of details that have to be considered at any given moment. The process of ignoring some details while concentrating on those that are relevant to the problem at hand is called *abstraction*. Effective software development is an exercise in building appropriate abstractions. Therefore, we will visit the idea of abstraction frequently throughout this book.

Another important technique in coping with complexity is to reuse solutions that have been developed before. As a programmer, you will need to learn how to use various *application programming interfaces* (APIs) for the tools/libraries you will use. An API is the collection of classes and functions that a library of code provides and an explanation of how to use them (i.e., what the parameters and return types are and what they represent). For example, you have already learned some simple APIs such as the functions provided in the Python `math` module and methods for built-in data structures such as the list and dictionary. Another common example of an API is a graphical user interface (GUI) toolkit.

Most languages provide APIs for accomplishing many common tasks. APIs will vary from language to language and from one operating system to another. This book cannot possibly begin to cover even a small fraction of the APIs that you will learn and use during your career. However, by learning a few APIs and, more importantly, by learning to develop your own APIs, you will acquire the skills that will make it easy for you to master new APIs in the future.

Just as important as being able to reuse existing code through APIs is the ability to leverage existing *knowledge* of good design principles. Over the years, computer scientists have developed algorithms for solving common problems (e.g., searching and sorting) and ways of structuring data collections that are used as the basic building blocks in most programs. In this course, you will be learning how these algorithms and data structures work so that you can write larger, more complicated programs that are well designed and maintainable using these well-understood components. Studying these existing algorithms and data structures will also help you learn how to create your own novel algorithms and data structures for the unique problems you will face in the future.

Computer scientists have also developed techniques for analyzing and classifying the efficiency of various algorithms and data structures so that you can predict whether or not a program using them will solve problems in a reasonable amount of time and within the memory constraints you have. Naturally, you will also need to learn algorithm analysis techniques so that you can analyze the efficiency of the algorithms you invent.

This book covers abstraction and data structures using two different programming languages. Getting experience in more than one language is important for a number of reasons. Seeing how languages differ, you can start to gain an appreciation of how different tools available to the developer are suitable for different tasks. Having a larger toolkit at your disposal makes it easier to solve a wider variety of problems. However, the most important advantage is that you will also see how the underlying ideas of abstraction, reuse, and analysis are applied in both languages. Only by seeing different approaches can you really appreciate what are underlying principles versus what are just details of a particular language. Rest assured, those underlying principles will be useful no matter what languages or environments you may have in your future.

Speaking of programming languages, at about the time this book is going to press, a new version of Python is coming out (Python 3.0). The new version includes significant redesign and will not be backward compatible with programs written for the 2.x versions of Python. The code in this book has been written in Python 2.x style. As much as possible, we have tried to use conventions and features that are also compatible with Python 3.0, and the conversion to 3.0 is straightforward. To make the code run in Python 3.0, you need to keep the following changes in mind.

- `print` becomes a function call. You must put parentheses around the sequence of expressions to print.

- The `input` function acts like the old `raw_input`. If you want to evaluate user input, you must do it yourself explicitly (`eval(input("Enter a number: ")))`).

- **range** no longer produces a list. You can still use it as before in **for** loops (e.g., **for i in range(10):**), but you need to use something like **nums = list(range(10))** to produce an explicit list.

- The single slash operator, **/**, always produces floating point division. Use the double slash, **//**, for integer division (this also works in Python 2.x).

We have provided both Python 2.x and Python 3.0 versions of all the code from the text in the online resources, so you should be able to use this book comfortably with any modern version of Python.

1.2 Functional Abstraction

In order to tackle a large software project, it is essential to be able to break it into smaller pieces. One way of dividing a problem into smaller pieces is to decompose it into a set of cooperating functions. This is called *functional (or procedural) abstraction*.

1.2.1 Design by Contract

To see how writing functions is an example of abstraction, let's look at a simple example. Suppose you are writing a program that needs to calculate the square root of some value. Do you know how to do this? You may or may not actually know an algorithm for computing square roots, but that really doesn't matter, because you know how to use the square root function from the Python **math** library.

```
import math
...
answer = math.sqrt(x)
```

You can use the **sqrt** function confidently, because you know *what* it does, even though you may not know exactly *how* it accomplishes that task. Thus, you are focusing on some aspects of the **sqrt** function (the what) while ignoring certain details (the how). That's abstraction.

This separation of concerns between what a component does and how it accomplishes its task is a particularly powerful form of abstraction. If we think of a function in terms of providing a service, then the programs that use the function are called *clients* of the service, and the code that actually performs the function is said to *implement* the service. A programmer working on the client needs to know

only what the function does. He or she does not need to know any of the details of
how the function works. To the client, the function is like a magical black box that
carries out a needed operation. Similarly, the implementer of the function does not
need to worry about how the function might be used. He or she is free to concentrate
only on the details of how the function accomplishes its task, ignoring the larger
picture of where and why the function is actually called.

In order to accomplish this clean separation, the client and implementer must
have a firm agreement about what the function is to accomplish. That is, they
must have a common understanding of the *interface* between the client code and
the implementation. The interface forms a sort of abstraction barrier that separates
the two views of the function. Figure 1.1 illustrates the situation for the Python
string split method (or the equivalent split function in the string module). The
diagram shows that the function/method accepts one required parameter that is a
string and one optional parameter that is a string and returns a list of strings. The
client using the split function/method does not need to be concerned with how the
code works (i.e., what's *inside* the box), just how to use it. What we need is a
careful description of what a function will do, without having to describe how the
function will accomplish the task. Such a description is called a *specification*.

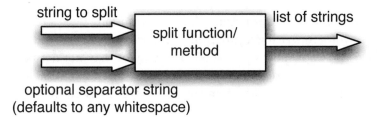

Figure 1.1: Split function as black box with interface

Obviously, one important part of a specification is describing how the function
is called. That is, we need to know the name of the function, what parameters
are required, and what if anything the function will return. This information is
sometimes called the *signature* of a function. Beyond the signature, a specification
also requires a precise description of what the function accomplishes. We need
to know how the result of calling the function relates to the parameters that are
provided. Sometimes, this is done rather informally. For example, suppose you are
writing a `math` library function for square root. Consider this specification of the
function:

```
def sqrt(x):
    """Computes the square root of x"""
```

This doesn't really do the job. The problem with such informal descriptions is that they tend to be incomplete and ambiguous. Remember, both the client and the implementer (even if they're one and the same person) should be able to fulfill their roles confidently based *only* on the specification. That's what makes the abstraction process so useful. What if the implementation *computes* the square root of x, but does not return the result? Technically, the specification is met, but the function will not be useful to the client. Is it OK if sqrt(16) returns -4? What if the implementation works only for floating-point numbers, but the client calls the function with an integer parameter? Whose fault is it then if the program crashes? What happens if the client calls this function with a negative number? Perhaps it returns a complex number as a result, or perhaps it crashes. What happens if the client calls this function with a string parameter? The bottom line is that the simple, informal description just does not tell us what to expect.

Now this may sound like nitpicking, since everyone generally "understands" what the square root function should do. If we had any questions, we could just test our assumptions by either looking at the code that implements the function or by actually trying it out (e.g., try computing sqrt(-1) and see what happens). But having to do either of these things breaks the abstraction barrier between the client and the implementation. Forcing the client coder to understand the actual implementation means that he or she has to wrestle with all the details of that code, thus losing the benefit of abstraction. On the other hand, if the client programmer simply relies on what the code actually does (by trying it out), he or she risks making assumptions that may not be shared by the implementer. Suppose the implementer discovers a better way of computing square roots and changes the implementation. Now the client's assumptions about certain "fringe" behavior may be incorrect. If we keep the abstraction barrier firmly in place, both the client code and the implementation can change radically; the abstraction barrier ensures that the program will continue to function properly. This desirable property is called *implementation independence*.

Hopefully you can see how precise specification of components is important when programming in the large. In most situations, careful specification is an absolute necessity; real disaster can loom when specifications are not clearly spelled out and adhered to. In one notorious example, NASA's 1999 Mars Climate Orbiter mission crashed at a loss of $125 million due to a mismatch in assumptions: a module was being given information in imperial units, but was expecting them in metric units.

Clearly, we need something better than an informal comment to have a good specification. Function specifications are often written in terms of preconditions and postconditions. A precondition of a function is a statement of what is assumed to be true about the state of the computation at the time the function is called. A postcondition is a statement about what is true after the function has finished. Here is a sample specification of the `sqrt` function using pre- and postconditions:

```
def sqrt(x):
    """Computes the square root of x.

    pre: x is an int or a float and x >= 0
    post: returns the non-negative square root of x"""
```

The job of the precondition is to state any assumptions that the implementation makes, especially those about the function parameters. In doing so, it describes the parameters using their formal names (`x` in this case). The postcondition describes whatever the code accomplishes as a function of its input parameters. Together, the pre- and postconditions describe the function as a sort of contract between the client and the implementation. If the client guarantees that the precondition is met when the function is called, then the implementation guarantees the postcondition will hold when the function terminates. For this reason, using pre- and postconditions to specify the modules of a system is sometimes called *design by contract*.

Pre- and postconditions are specific examples of a particular kind of documentation known as program *assertions*. An assertion is a statement about the state of the computation that is true at a specific point in the program. A precondition must be true just before a function executes, and the postcondition must be true immediately after. We will see later that there are other places in a program where assertions can also be extremely valuable for documentation.

If you are reading very carefully, you might be a bit uneasy about the postcondition from the `sqrt` example above. That postcondition describes what the function is supposed to do. Technically speaking, an assertion should not state what a function does, but rather what is now true at a given point in a program. It would be more correct to state the postcondition as something like `post:  RETVAL ==` $\sqrt{x}$, where `RETVAL` is a name used to indicate the value that was just returned by the function. Despite being less technically accurate, most programmers tend to use the less formal style of postcondition presented in our example. Given that the informal style is more popular and no less informative, we'll continue to use the "returns this, that, and the other thing" form of postcondition. Those who are sticklers for honest-to-goodness assertions can, no doubt, do the necessary translation.

This brings up an important point about pre- and postconditions in particular, and specifications in general. The whole point of a specification is that it provides a succinct and precise description of a function or other component. If the specification is ambiguous or longer or more complicated than the actual implementation code, then little has been gained. Mathematical notations tend to be succinct and exact, so they are often useful in specifications. In fact, some software engineering methods employ fully formal mathematical notations for specifying all system components. The use of these so-called *formal methods* adds precision to the development process by allowing properties of programs to be stated and proved mathematically. In the best case, one might actually be able to prove the correctness of a program, that is, that the code of a program faithfully implements its specification. Using such methods requires substantial mathematical prowess and has not been widely adopted in industry. For now, we'll stick with somewhat less formal specifications but use well-known mathematical and programming notations where they seem appropriate and helpful.

Another important consideration is where to place specifications in code. In Python, a developer has two options for placing comments into code: regular comments (indicated with a leading #) and docstrings (string expressions at the top of a module or immediately following a function or class heading). Docstrings are carried along with the objects to which they are attached and are inspectable at run-time. Docstrings are also used by the internal Python help system and by the PyDoc documentation utility. This makes docstrings a particularly good medium for specifications, since API documentation can then be created automatically using PyDoc. As a rule of thumb, docstrings should contain information that is of use to client programmers, while internal comments should be used for information that is intended only for the implementers.

1.2.2   Testing Preconditions

The basic idea of design by contract requires that if a function's precondition is met when it is called, then the postcondition must be true at the end of the function. If the precondition is not met, then all bets are off. This raises an interesting question. What should the function do when the precondition is not met? From the standpoint of the specification, it does not matter what the function does in this case, it is "off the hook," so to speak. If you are the implementer, you might be tempted to simply ignore any precondition violations. Sometimes, this means executing the function body will cause the program to immediately crash; other times the code might run, but produce nonsensical results. Neither of these outcomes seems particularly good.

A better approach is to adopt defensive programming practices. An unmet precondition indicates a mistake in the program. Rather than silently ignoring such a situation, you can detect the mistake and deal with it. But how exactly should the function do this? One idea might be to have it print an error message. The `sqrt` function might have some code like this:

```
def sqrt(x):
    ...
    if x < 0:
        print 'Error: can't take the square root of a negative'
    else:
        ...
```

The problem with printing an error message like this is that the calling program has no way of knowing that something has gone wrong. The output might appear, for example, in the middle of a generated report. Furthermore, the actual error message might go unnoticed. In fact, if this is a general-purpose library, it's very possible that the `sqrt` function is called within a GUI program, and the error message will not even appear anywhere at all.

Most of the time, it is simply not appropriate for a function that implements a service to print out messages (unless printing something is part of the specification of the method). It would be much better if the function could somehow signal that an error has occurred and then let the client program decide what to do about the problem. For some programs, the appropriate response might be to terminate the program and print an error message; in other cases, the program might be able to recover from the error. The point is that such a decision can be made only by the client.

The function could signal an error in a number of ways. Sometimes, returning an out-of-range result is used as a signal. Here's an example:

```
def sqrt(x):
    ...
    if x < 0:
        return -1
    ...
```

Since the specification of `sqrt` clearly implies that the return value cannot be negative, the value -1 can be used to indicate an error. Client code can check the result to see if it is OK. Another technique that is sometimes used is to have a *global* (accessible to all parts of the program) variable that records errors. The client code checks the value of this variable after each operation to see if there was an error.

Of course, the problem with this ad hoc approach to error detection is that a client program can become riddled with decision structures that constantly check to see whether an error has occurred. The logic of the code starts looking something like this:

```
x = someOperation()
if x is not OK:
    fix x
y = anotherOperation(x)
if y is not OK:
    abort
z = yetAnotherOperation(y)
if z is not OK:
    z = SOME_DEFAULT_VALUE
```

The continual error checking with each operation obscures the intent of the original algorithm.

Most modern programming languages now include *exception handling* mechanisms that provide an elegant alternative for propagating error information in a program. The basic idea behind exception handling is that program errors don't directly lead to a "crash," but rather they cause the program to transfer control to a special section called an *exception handler*. What makes this particularly useful is that the client does not have to explicitly check whether an error has occurred. The client just needs to say, in effect, "here's the code I want to execute should any errors come up." The run-time system of the language then makes sure that, should an error occur, the appropriate exception handler is called.

In Python, run-time errors generate *exception objects*. A program can include a `try` statement to catch and deal with these errors. For example, taking the square root of a negative number causes Python to generate a `ValueError`, which is a subclass of Python's general `Exception` class. If this exception is not handled by the client, it results in program termination. Here is what happens interactively:

```
>>> sqrt(-1)
Traceback (most recent call last):
  File "<stdin>", line 1, in ?
ValueError: math domain error
>>>
```

Alternatively, the program could "catch" the exception with a `try` statement:

```
>>> try:
...     sqrt(-1)
... except ValueError:
...     print "Ooops, sorry."
...
Ooops, sorry.
>>>
```

The statement(s) indented under `try` are executed, and if an error occurs, Python sees whether the error matches the type listed in any `except` clauses. The first matching `except` block is executed. If no `except` matches, then the program halts with an error message.

To take advantage of exception handling for testing preconditions, we just need to test the precondition in a decision and then generate an appropriate exception object. This is called *raising an exception* and is accomplished by the Python `raise` statement. The `raise` statement is very simple: `raise <expr>` where `<expr>` is an expression that produces an exception object containing information about what went wrong. When the `raise` statement executes, it causes the Python interpreter to interrupt the current operation and transfer control to an exception handler. If no suitable handler is found, the program will terminate.

The `sqrt` function in the Python library checks to make sure that its parameter is non-negative and also that the parameter has the correct type (either `int` or `float`). The code for `sqrt` could implement these checks as follows:

```
def sqrt(x):
    if x < 0:
        raise ValueError('math domain error')
    if type(x) not in (type(1), type(1l), type(1.0)):
        raise TypeError('number expected')

    # compute square root here
```

Notice that there are no `else`s required on these conditions. When a `raise` executes, it effectively terminates the function, so the "compute square root" portion will only execute if the preconditions are met.

Oftentimes, it is not really important what specific exception is raised when a precondition violation is detected. The important thing is that the error is diagnosed as early as possible. Python provides a statement for embedding assertions directly into code. The statement is called `assert`. It takes a Boolean expression and raises an `AssertionError` exception if the expression does not evaluate to `True`. Using `assert` makes it particularly easy to enforce preconditions.

```
def sqrt(x):
    assert x >= 0 and type(x) in (type(1), type(11), type(1.0))
    ....
```

As you can see, the `assert` statement is a very handy way of inserting assertions directly into your code. This effectively turns the documentation of preconditions (and other assertions) into extra testing that helps to ensure that programs behave correctly, that is, according to specifications.

One potential drawback of this sort of defensive programming is that it adds extra overhead to the execution of the program. A few CPU cycles will be consumed checking the preconditions each time a function is called. However, given the ever-increasing speed of modern processors and the potential hazards of incorrect programs, that is a price that is usually well worth paying. That said, one additional benefit of the `assert` statement is that it is possible to turn off the checking of assertions, if desired. Executing Python with a -O switch on the command line causes the interpreter to skip testing of assertions. That means it is possible to have assertions on during program testing but turn them off once the system is judged to be working and placed into production.

Of course, checking assertions during testing and then turning them off in the production system is akin to practising a tightrope act 10 feet above the ground with a safety net in place and then performing the actual stunt 100 feet off the ground on a windy day—without the net. As important as it is to catch errors during testing, it's even more important to catch them when the system is in use. Our advice is to use assertions liberally and leave the checking turned on.

1.2.3   Top-Down Design

One popular technique for designing programs that you probably already know about is *top-down design*. Top-down design is essentially the direct application of functional abstraction to decompose a large problem into smaller, more manageable components. As an example, suppose you are developing a program to help your instructor with grading. Your instructor wants a program that takes a set of exam scores as input and prints out a report that summarizes student performance. Specifically, the program should report the following statistics about the data:

high score This is the largest number in the data set.

low score This is the smallest number in the data set.

mean This is the "average" score in the data set. It is often denoted $\bar{x}$ and calculated using this formula:

$$\bar{x} = \frac{\sum x_i}{n}$$

That is, we sum up all of the scores (x_i denotes the ith score) and divide by the number of scores (n).

standard deviation This is a measure of how spread out the scores are. The standard deviation, s, is given by the following formula:

$$s = \sqrt{\frac{\sum (\bar{x} - x_i)^2}{n - 1}}$$

In this formula $\bar{x}$ is the mean, x_i represents the ith data value, and n is the number of data values. The formula looks complicated, but it is not hard to compute. The expression $(\bar{x} - x_i)^2$ is the square of the "deviation" of an individual item from the mean. The numerator of the fraction is the sum of the deviations (squared) across all the data values.

As a starting point for this program, you might develop a simple algorithm such as this.

```
Get scores from the user
Calculate the minimum score
Calculate the maximum score
Calculate the average (mean) score
Calculate the standard deviation
```

Suppose you are working with a friend to develop this program. You could divide this algorithm up into parts and each work on various pieces of the program. Before going off and working on the pieces, however, you will need a more complete design to ensure that the pieces that each of you develops will fit together to solve the problem. Using top-down design, each line of the algorithm can be written as a separate function. The design will just consist of the specification for each of these functions.

One obvious approach is to store the exam scores in a list that can be passed as a parameter to various functions. Using this approach, here is a sample design:

```
# stats.py
def get_scores():
    """Get scores interactively from the user

    post: returns a list of numbers obtained from user"""

def min_value(nums):
    """ find the minimum

    pre: nums is a list of numbers and len(nums) > 0
    post: returns smallest number in nums"""

def max_value(nums):
    """ find the maximum

    pre: nums is a list of numbers and len(nums) > 0
    post: returns largest number in nums"""

def average(nums):
    """ calculate the mean

    pre: nums is a list of numbers and len(nums) > 0
    post: returns the mean (a float) of the values in nums"""

def std_deviation(nums):
    """calculate the standard deviation

    pre: nums is a list of numbers and len(nums) > 1
    post: returns the standard deviation (a float) of the values
          in nums"""
```

With the specification of these functions in hand, you and your friend should easily be able to divvy up the functions and complete the program in no time. Let's implement one of the functions just to see how it might look. Here's an implementation of `std_deviation`.

```
def std_deviation(nums):

    xbar = average(nums)
    sum = 0.0
    for num in nums:
        sum += (xbar - num)**2
    return math.sqrt(sum / (len(nums) - 1))
```

Notice how this code relies on the **average** function. Since we have that function specified, we can go ahead and use it here with confidence, thus avoiding duplication of effort. We have also used the "shorthand" `+=` operator, which you may not have seen before. This is a convenient way of accumulating a sum. Writing `x += y` produces the same result as writing `x = x + y`.

The rest of the program is left for you to complete. As you can see, top-down design and functional specification go hand in hand. As necessary functionality is identified, a specification formalizes the design decisions so that each part can be worked on in isolation. You should have no trouble finishing up this program.

$\boxed{1.2.4}$ Documenting Side Effects

In order for specifications to be effective, they must spell out the expectations of both the client and the implementation of a service. Any effect of a service that is visible to the client should be described in the postcondition. For example, suppose that the `std_deviation` function had been implemented like this:

```
def std_deviation(nums):
    # This is bad code. Don't use it.
    xbar = average(nums)
    n = len(nums)
    sum = 0.0
    while nums != []:
        num = nums.pop()
        sum += (xbar - num)**2
    return math.sqrt(sum / (n - 1))
```

This version uses the `pop()` method of Python lists. The call to `nums.pop()` returns the last number in the list and also *deletes that item from the list*. The loop continues until all the items in the list have been processed. This version of `std_deviation` returns the correct value, so it would seem to meet the contract specified by the pre- and postconditions. However, the list object `nums` passed as a parameter is mutable, and the changes to the list will be visible to the client. The user of this code is likely to be quite surprised when they find out that calling `std_deviation(examScores)` causes all the values in `examScores` to be deleted!

These sorts of interactions between function calls and other parts of a program are called *side effects*. In this case, the deletion of items in `examScores` is a side effect of calling the `std_deviation` function. Generally, it's a good idea to avoid side effects in functions, but a strict prohibition is too strong. Some functions are designed to have side effects. The `pop` method of the list class is a good example. It's used in the case where one wants to get a value and also, as a side effect, remove the value from the list. What is crucial is that any side effects of a function should be indicated in its postcondition. Since the postcondition for `std_deviation` did not say anything about `nums` being modified, an implementation that does this is implicitly breaking the contract. The *only* visible effects of a function should be those that are described in its postcondition.

By the way, printing something or placing information in a file are also examples of side effects. When we said above that functions should generally not print anything unless that is part of their stated functionality, we were really just identifying one special case of (potentially) undocumented side effects.

1.3 Algorithm Analysis

When we start dealing with programs that contain collections of data, we often need to know more about a function than just its pre- and postconditions. Dealing with a list of 10 or even 100 exam scores is no problem, but a list of customers for an online business might contain tens or hundreds of thousands of items. A programmer working on problems in biology might have to deal with a DNA sequence containing millions or even billions of nucleotides. Applications that search and index web pages have to deal with collections of a similar magnitude. When collection sizes get large, the efficiency of an algorithm can be just as critical as its correctness. An algorithm that gives a correct answer but requires 10 years of computing time is not likely to be very useful.

Algorithm analysis allows us to characterize algorithms according to how much time and memory they require to accomplish a task. In this section, we'll take a first look at techniques of algorithm analysis in the context of searching a collection.

1.3.1 Linear Search

Searching is the process of looking for a particular value in a collection. For example, a program that maintains the membership list for a club might need to look up the information about a particular member. This involves some form of a search process. It is a good problem for us to examine because there are numerous algorithms that can be used, and they differ in their relative efficiency.

Boiling the problem down to its simplest essence, we'll consider the problem of finding a particular number in a list. The same principles we use here will apply to more complex searching problems such as searching through a customer list to find those who live in Iowa. The specification for our simple search problem looks like this:

```
def search(items, target):
    """Locate target in items

    pre: items is a list of numbers
    post: returns non-negative x where items[x] == target, if target in
          items; returns -1, otherwise"""
```

Here are a couple interactive examples that illustrate its behavior:

```
>>> search([3, 1, 4, 2, 5], 4)
2
>>> search([3, 1, 4, 2, 5], 7)
-1
```

In the first example, the function returns the index where 4 appears in the list. In the second example, the return value -1 indicates that 7 is not in the list.

Using the built-in Python list methods, the `search` function is easily implemented:

```
# search1.py
def search(items, target):
    try:
        return items.index(target)
    except ValueError:
        return -1
```

The `index` method returns the first position in the list where a target value occurs. If `target` is not in the list, `index` raises a `ValueError` exception. In that case, we catch the exception and return -1. Clearly, this function meets the specification; the interesting question for us is how efficient is this method?

One way to determine the efficiency of an algorithm is to do empirical testing. We can simply code the algorithm and run it on different data sets to see how long it takes. A simple method for timing code in Python is to use the `time` module's `time` function, which returns the number of seconds that have passed since January 1, 1970. We can just call that method before and after our code executes and print the difference between the times. If we placed our search function in a module named `search1.py`, we could test it directly like this:

```
# time_search.py
import time
from search1 import search

items = range(1000000) # create a big list

start = time.time()
search(items, 999999) # look for the last item
stop = time.time()
print stop - start

start = time.time()
search(items, 499999) # look for the middle item
stop = time.time()
print stop - start

start = time.time()
search(items, 10)      # look for an item near the front
stop = time.time()
print stop - start
```

Try this code on your computer and note the time to search for the three numbers. What does that tell you about how the **index** method works? By the way, the Python library contains a module called **timeit** that provides a more accurate and sophisticated way of timing code. If you are doing much empirical testing, it's worth checking out this module.

Let's try our hand at developing our own search algorithm using a simple "be the computer" strategy. Suppose that I give you a page full of numbers in no particular order and ask whether the number 13 is in the list. How will you solve this problem? If you are like most people, you simply scan down the list comparing each value to 13. When you see 13 in the list, you quit and tell me that you found it. If you get to the very end of the list without seeing 13, then you tell me it's not there.

This strategy is called a *linear search*. You are searching through the list of items one by one until the target value is found. This algorithm translates directly into simple code.

```
# search2.py
def search(items, target):
    for i in range(len(items)):
        if items[i] == target:
            return i
    return -1
```

You can see here that we have a simple **for** loop to go through the valid indexes for the list (**range(len(items))**). We test the item at each position to see if it is the target. If the target is found, the loop terminates by immediately returning the index of its position. If this loop goes all the way through without finding the item, the function returns -1.

One problem with writing the function this way is that the **range** expression creates a list of indexes that is the same size as the list being searched. Since an **int** generally requires four bytes (32 bits) of storage space, the index list in our test code would require four megabytes of memory for a list of one million numbers. In addition to the memory usage, there would also be considerable time wasted creating this second large list. Python has an alternative form of the **range** function called **xrange** that could be used instead. An **xrange** is used only for iteration, it does not actually create a list. However, the use of **xrange** is discouraged in new Python code.[1]

If your version of Python is 2.3 or newer, you can use the **enumerate** function. This elegant alternative allows you to iterate through a list and, on each iteration, you are handed the next index along with the next item. Here's how the search looks using **enumerate**.

```
# search3.py
def search(items, target):
    for i,item in enumerate(items):
        if item == target:
            return i
    return -1
```

Another approach would be to avoid the whole **range/xrange/enumerate** issue by using a **while** loop instead.

```
# search4.py
def search(items, target):
    i = 0
    while i < len(items):
        if items[i] == target:
            return i
        i += 1
    return -1
```

---

[1]In Python 3.0, the standard **range** expression behaves like **xrange** and does not actually create a list.

Notice that all of these search functions implement the same algorithm, namely linear search. How efficient is this algorithm? To get an idea, you might try experimenting with it. Try timing the search for the three values as you did using the list `index` method. The only code you need to change is the import of the actual `search` function, since the parameters and return values are the same. Because we wrote to a specification, the client code does not need to change, even when different implementations are mixed and matched. This is implementation independence at work. Pretty cool, huh?

1.3.2 Binary Search

The linear search algorithm was not hard to develop, and it will work very nicely for modest-sized lists. For an unordered list, this algorithm is as good as any. The Python `in` and `index` operations both implement linear searching algorithms.

If we have a very large collection of data, we might want to organize it in some way so that we don't have to look at every single item to determine where, or if, a particular value appears in the list. Suppose that the list is stored in sorted order (lowest to highest). As soon as we encounter a value that is greater than the target value, we can quit the linear search without looking at the rest of the list. On average, that saves us about half of the work. But if the list is sorted, we can do even better than this.

When a list is ordered, there is a much better searching strategy, one that you probably already know. Have you ever played the number guessing game? I pick a number between 1 and 100, and you try to guess what it is. Each time you guess, I will tell you if your guess is correct, too high, or too low. What is your strategy?

If you play this game with a very young child, they might well adopt a strategy of simply guessing numbers at random. An older child might employ a systematic approach corresponding to linear search, guessing $1, 2, 3, 4$, and so on until the mystery value is found.

Of course, virtually any adult will first guess 50. If told that the number is higher, then the range of possible values is 50–100. The next logical guess is 75. Each time we guess the middle of the remaining numbers to try to narrow down the possible range. This strategy is called a *binary search* Binary means two, and at each step, we are dividing the remaining numbers into two parts.

We can employ a binary search strategy to look through a sorted list. The basic idea is that we use two variables to keep track of the endpoints of the range in the list where the item could be. Initially, the target could be anywhere in the list, so we start with variables `low` and `high` set to the first and last positions of the list, respectively.

The heart of the algorithm is a loop that looks at the item in the middle of the remaining range to compare it to x. If x is smaller than the middle item, then we move high, so that the search is narrowed to the lower half. If x is larger, then we move low, and the search is narrowed to the upper half. The loop terminates when x is found or there are no longer any more places to look (i.e., low > high). The code below implements a binary search using our same search API.

```python
# bsearch.py
def search(items, target):
    low = 0
    high = len(items) - 1
    while low <= high:          # There is still a range to search
        mid = (low + high) // 2 # position of middle item
        item = items[mid]
        if target == item :     # Found it! Return the index
            return mid
        elif target < item:     # x is in lower half of range
            high = mid - 1      #     move top marker down
        else:                   # x is in upper half
            low = mid + 1       #     move bottom marker up
    return -1                   # no range left to search,
                                # x is not there
```

This algorithm is quite a bit more sophisticated than the simple linear search. You might want to trace through a couple of sample searches to convince yourself that it actually works.

1.3.3   Informal Algorithm Comparison

So far, we have developed two very different algorithms for our simple searching problem. Which one is better? Well, that depends on what exactly we mean by better. The linear search algorithm is much easier to understand and implement. On the other hand, we expect that the binary search is more efficient, because it doesn't have to look at every value in the list. Intuitively, then, we might expect the linear search to be a better choice for small lists and binary search a better choice for larger lists. How could we actually confirm such intuitions?

One approach would be to do an empirical test. We could simply code both algorithms and try them out on various-sized lists to see how long the search takes. These algorithms are both quite short, so it would not be difficult to run a few experiments. When this test was done on one of our computers (a somewhat dated laptop), linear search was faster for lists of length 10 or less, and there was not much noticeable difference in the range of length 10–1,000. After that, binary search was a clear winner. For a list of a million elements, linear search averaged 2.5 seconds to find a random value, whereas binary search averaged only 0.0003 seconds.

The empirical analysis has confirmed our intuition, but these are results from one particular machine under specific circumstances (amount of memory, processor speed, current load, etc.). How can we be sure that the results will always be the same?

Another approach is to analyze our algorithms abstractly to see how efficient they are. Other factors being equal, we expect the algorithm with the fewest number of "steps" to be the more efficient. But how do we count the number of steps? For example, the number of times that either algorithm goes through its main loop will depend on the particular inputs. We have already guessed that the advantage of binary search increases as the size of the list increases.

Computer scientists attack these problems by analyzing the number of steps that an algorithm will take relative to the size or difficulty of the specific problem instance being solved. For searching, the difficulty is determined by the size of the collection. Obviously, it takes more steps to find a number in a collection of a million than it does in a collection of ten. The pertinent question is how many steps are needed to find a value in a list of size n. We are particularly interested in what happens as n gets very large.

Let's consider the linear search first. If we have a list of 10 items, the most work our algorithm might have to do is to look at each item in turn. The loop will iterate at most 10 times. Suppose the list is twice as big. Then we might have to look at twice as many items. If the list is three times as large, it will take three times as long, etc. In general, the amount of time required is linearly related to the size of the list n. This is what computer scientists call a *linear time* algorithm. Now you really know why it's called a linear search.

What about the binary search? Let's start by considering a concrete example. Suppose the list contains 16 items. Each time through the loop, the remaining range is cut in half. After one pass, there are eight items left to consider. The next time through there will be four, then two, and finally one. How many times will the loop execute? It depends on how many times we can halve the range before running out of data. This table might help you to sort things out:

List Size	Halvings
1	0
2	1
4	2
8	3
16	4

Can you see the pattern here? Each extra iteration of the loop allows us to search a list that is twice as large. If the binary search loops i times, it can find a single value in a list of size 2^i. Each time through the loop, it looks at one value (the middle) in the list. To see how many items are examined in a list of size n, we need to solve this relationship: $n = 2^i$ for i. In this formula, i is just an exponent with a base of 2. Using the appropriate logarithm gives us this relationship: $i = \log_2 n$. If you are not entirely comfortable with logarithms, just remember that this value is the number of times that a collection of size n can be cut in half.

OK, so what does this bit of math tell us? Binary search is an example of a *log time* algorithm. The amount of time it takes to solve a given problem grows as the log of the problem size. In the case of binary search, each additional iteration doubles the size of the problem that we can solve.

You might not appreciate just how efficient binary search really is. Let's try to put it in perspective. Suppose you have a New York City phone book with, say, 12 million names listed in alphabetical order. You walk up to a typical New Yorker on the street and make the following proposition (assuming their number is listed): "I'm going to try guessing your name. Each time I guess a name, you tell me if your name comes alphabetically before or after the name I guess." How many guesses will you need?

Our analysis above shows the answer to this question is $log_2 12{,}000{,}000$. If you don't have a calculator handy, here is a quick way to estimate the result. $2^{10} = 1{,}024$ or roughly 1,000, and $1{,}000 \times 1{,}000 = 1{,}000{,}000$. That means that $2^{10} \times 2^{10} = 2^{20} \approx 1{,}000{,}000$. 2^{20} is approximately one million. So, searching a million items requires only 20 guesses. Continuing on, we need 21 guesses for two million, 22 for four million, 23 for eight million, and 24 guesses to search among sixteen million names. We can figure out the name of a total stranger in New York City using only 24 guesses! By comparison, a linear search would require (on average) 6 million guesses. Binary search is a phenomenally good algorithm!

We said earlier that Python uses a linear search algorithm to implement its built-in searching methods. If a binary search is so much better, why doesn't Python use it? The reason is that the binary search is less general; in order to work, the list must be in order. If you want to use binary search on an unordered list, the first thing you have to do is put it in order or *sort* it. This is another well-studied problem in computer science, and one that we will return to later on.

1.3.4 Formal Analysis

In the comparison between linear and binary searches we characterized both algorithms in terms of the number of abstract steps required to solve a problem of a certain size. We determined that linear search requires a number of steps directly proportional to the size of the list, whereas binary search requires a number of steps proportional to the (base 2) log of the list size. The nice thing about this characterization is that it tells us something about these algorithms *independent of any particular implementation.* We expect binary search to do better on large problems because it is an inherently more efficient algorithm.

When doing this kind of analysis, we are not generally concerned with the exact number of instructions an algorithm requires to solve a specific problem. This is extremely difficult to determine, since it will vary depending on the actual machine language of the computer, the language we are using to implement the algorithm, and in some cases, as we saw with the searching algorithms, the specifics of the particular input. Instead, we abstract away many issues that affect the exact running time of an implementation of an algorithm; in fact, we can ignore all the details that do not affect the relative performance of an algorithm on inputs of various sizes. Always keep in mind that our goal is to determine how the algorithm will perform on large inputs. After all, computers are fast; for small problems, efficiency is unlikely to be an issue.

To summarize, in performing algorithm analysis, we can generally make the following simplifications.

- We ignore the differences caused by using different languages and different machines to implement the algorithm.

- We ignore the differences in execution speed of various operations (i.e., we do not care that a floating-point division calculation may take longer than an integer division); we assume all "basic operations" (assignment, comparison, most mathematical operations, etc.) take the same amount of time.

- We assume all constant time operations that are independent of the input size are equivalent (i.e., we do not care if it takes 10 operations, 100 operations, or even 1,000 operations as long as those operations will solve the problem no matter what the input size is).

Obviously, each of these simplifications could make a significant difference in comparing the actual running time of two algorithms, or even two implementations of the same algorithm, but the result still shows us what to expect *as a function of the input size.* Hence, the results do tell us what kind of relative performance to expect for larger problems. Computer scientists use a notation known both as *big O* or *asymptotic* notation to specify the efficiency of an algorithm based on these simplifications.

Before looking at the details of big O notation, let's look at a couple simple mathematical functions to gain some intuition. Consider the function $f(n) = 3n^2 + 100n + 50$. Suppose you are trying to estimate the value of this function as n grows very large. You would be justified in only considering the first term. Although for smaller values of n the $100n$ term dominates, when n gets large, the contributions of the second and third term are insignificant. For example at $n = 1{,}000{,}000$ using only the first term gives a result that is within 0.01 percent of the true value of the function.

To see why the first term dominates as n increases, you just have to look at the "shape" of the graphs for the first and second terms (see Figure 1.2). Even though x is larger than x^2 over the interval from 0 to 1, x^2 overtakes it for $n > 1$. Even when we multiply x by some constant, say 100, that would change the slope of the line, since the function x^2 curves upward, it will still overtake the line for $100 * x$ (at $x = 100$). No matter what constants we multiply these functions by, the shape of the two graphs dictates that for sufficiently large values, the curve for x^2 will eventually dominate.

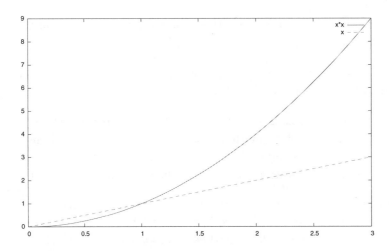

Figure 1.2: x^2 is less than x between 0 and 1, but for larger values, x^2 is greater

The idea of a dominating function is formalized in big O notation. For example, when an algorithm is said to be $O(n^2)$, it means the number of steps for the algorithm with input size n is $< cn^2$ for all $n > n_0$ for some constants c and n_0. To prove an algorithm is $O(n^2)$ we would have to find those two constants. In most cases, it is pretty obvious (as in the examples above). What constants could we pick for the function $3n^2 + 100n + 50$? We do not need to care about having a *tight* bound. We could pick 1,000,000 for both constants since $3n^2 + 100n + 50 < 1,000,000n^2$ for every $n > 1,000,000$. If an algorithm is $2n^3$, can we find two constants to prove it is $O(n^3)$? In practice we generally do not worry about finding the constants. In most cases, it is fairly easy to convince ourselves of the relative growth rate. It should be clear that for any polynomial, it is the largest degree that matters so any polynomial of degree x is $O(n^x)$.

Now that you've seen the mathematical details, let's look at some short examples and determine the running time.

```
n = input('enter n: ')
for i in range(n):
    print i
```

This code fragment is $O(n)$. The input size, n, determines how many operations occur. The `print` statement will be executed n times. The `input` statement will be executed once. If we think about how the `for` statement works, we realize that the `range` statement generates a list of n items that itself takes at least n steps. Each time through the `for` statement, i is assigned to the next item in the list, so we can easily convince ourselves that there are around $2n + 1$ basic steps to execute this code. This should be enough to convince you that the algorithm is $O(n)$. We still have ignored the fact that the Python code needs to determine when the end of the list is reached, but in practice we normally do not need to go into all the details we did to convince ourselves of the running time of short code fragments.

Consider this short fragment. Can you determine its running time?

```
n = input('enter n: ')
for i in range(100):
    print i
```

With a quick look, you might be tempted to say this code is also $O(n)$ since you see a `for` loop. In this case, however, the `for` loops executes 100 times no matter what the input is. This is essentially no different than 100 `print` statements, and that is 100 constant-time operations. This code fragment runs in the same constant time regardless of the input, and we refer to all constant operations as simply $O(1)$.

Here's an example with two loops in it:

```
n = input('enter n: ')
for i in range(n):
    print i
for j in range(n):
    print j
```

These two loops execute sequentially, one right after the other. So the total running time is $O(n+n)$, which is still $O(n)$. If you find that surprising, just think of it as $O(2n)$ and remember that constant multipliers do not affect the big O notation. In general when adding sequential sections of an algorithm together, the big O for the overall algorithm is the maximum of the big Os of the individual parts. That means you just need to find the part of the algorithm that executes the most steps and analyze it.

Let's try another example with two loops.

```
n = input('enter n: ')
for i in range(n):
    for j in range(n):
        print i, j
```

In this fragment, the loops are nested. Notice that the second loop executes n times *for each iteration* of the first loop. This means the **print** statement executes a total of n^2 times, and so the code has $O(n^2)$ running time. Frequently, when you have nested loops, the running time is the product of the number of times each loop executes.

Now consider this example:

```
n = input('enter n: ')
total = 0
for i in range(n):
    for j in range(10):
        print i, j
        total = total + 1
```

Since this example also has two nested loops, you might think it is $O(n^2)$, but note that the one loop always executes 10 times no matter what the value of **n** is. We can still apply the rule of multiplying the number of times each loop executes; the result is $10 * n$ and that tells us this fragment is $O(n)$ (remember, constant multipliers are ignored in asymptotic analysis).

Let's try a slightly trickier case of nested loops.

```
n = input('enter n: ')
for i in range(n):
    for j in range(i, n):
        print i, j
```

Here again we have two loops nested, but the inner loop executes a different number of times during each iteration of the outer loop. Our simple multiplication rule won't work, but fortunately, the analysis is not too difficult. Remember we want to know for an input of size n, how many times does the **print** statement execute? Let's think it through. The first time through the outer loop, the inner loop executes n times. The second time it executes $n - 1$ times, and so forth, until finally, on the last iteration of the outer loop, the inner loop executes 1 time. To get the total number of iterations of the inner loop, we just add these all up: $1 + 2 + \cdots + n$.

You may have seen a formula for this sum in one of your math courses. If not, here is one way to figure it out. Suppose we add this value to itself lined up in this way:

```
    (1   +    2   +   3   + ... + n)
 +  (n   + (n-1) + (n-2) + ... + 1)
```

Each column sums to $n + 1$ and there are n columns. The total of all the columns is $n(n + 1)$. That sum is just double the original, so dividing by 2 gives use this formula: $n(n + 1)/2$. Expanding this produces a quadratic polynomial, so we can conclude this code fragment has running time $O(n^2)$.

Finally, here's a little example using a **while** loop.

```
n = input('enter n: ')
while n > 1:
    n = n // 2  # // is integer division
```

This code is a little different from all the other code fragments. We have a loop, but it does not execute n times. Each time through the loop, n is divided by 2 so we need to determine how many times it will take to reach 1. This is the same problem we examined with the "guess a number game" and binary search. The number of iterations increases by 1 each time the size of the input doubles. So the number of steps for an input of size n is represented as x in the equation $2^x = n$. The answer is $x = log_2 n$. In many algorithms, the input is divided in half and we end up with $O(log_2)$ in asymptotic notation.

Now returning to the search functions, you have all the tools you need to formally analyze the code we wrote. Our linear search uses a **for** loop that executes n times, so it is $O(n)$. This is the reason it is referred to as a *linear search*; the running time of the function is a linear function (i.e., a polynomial of degree 1). And, as discussed earlier, the binary search algorithm for sorted lists is $O(log_2 n)$. The loop executes (at most) $log_2 n$ times and the number of operations executed each time through the loop is a constant.

Asymptotic notation tells us how efficient we can expect our algorithm to be for large data sets. For small cases or code that is only going to be executed once or twice, efficiency is often not a significant concern. Of course, if your program will take two years to solve the problem, then it is. The big O notation allows us to extrapolate and determine how long our program will take to run on a larger data set. If we want to know how long our program will take to run with an input twice as large, we can plug $2n$ in for n in our function. For example, if the analysis of an algorithm is $O(n^2)$ and we double the input, we can expect it to take four times as long, since $(2n)^2$ is $4n^2$. If it takes one minute for our algorithm to execute on an input of size one million we can expect it to take four minutes on an input of size two million.

1.3.5 Big O Notation vs. Theta Notation

Technically, big O notation gives us only an upper bound on the efficiency of an algorithm. Look back at the definition of big O. If an algorithm is $O(n)$, then it is also $O(n^2)$, $O(n^3)$, etc. In fact, we can say that most algorithms are $O(2^n)$, but that is not very useful when we want to compare two specific algorithms. Usually when we do a big O analysis of an algorithm we are trying to find a "tight" upper bound. For example, we *know* that a linear search will take twice as long to discover that a number is not in a list when the size of the list doubles. It would be more informative to say that the asymptotic growth rate of linear search is not just bounded by n, but it *is* n.

Θ is used to describe situations where we have a tight upper (and lower) bound. To formally prove an algorithm is $\Theta(f(n))$ we must find constants c_1, c_2, and n_0 such that the number of steps for the algorithm is greater than $c_1 f(n)$ and the number of steps is less than $c_2 f(n)$ for all $n > n_0$. By bounding it between two multiples of $f(n)$ we show that the number of steps grows *at the same rate as* $f(n)$ so the number of steps in the algorithm is essentially equal to some multiple of $f(n)$ (for large values of n). In practice, we will not actually find the constants unless analyzing the algorithm is particularly difficult. See Figure 1.3 for an example of bounding a function.

The growth rates of some functions that commonly appear in the analysis of algorithms are shown in Figure 1.4. Note how important the order of the algorithm

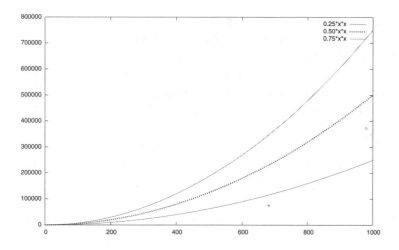

Figure 1.3: $0.5x^2$ is between $0.25x^2$ and $0.75x^2$

n	$log_2(n)$	$\sqrt{n}$	$n\log_2(n)$	n^2	n^3	2^n
100	6.6	10	660	10,000	1,000,000	10^{30}
1,000	10	32	10,000	1,000,000	10^9	10^{301}
10,000	13	100	130,000	10^8	10^{12}	10^{3010}
100,000	17	320	1,700,000	10^{10}	10^{15}	10^{30103}
1,000,000	20	1,000	$2*10^7$	10^{12}	10^{18}	10^{301029}

Figure 1.4: Approximate growth rate of common functions

is for making the problem solvable in a reasonable amount of time. Algorithms that have exponential growth (e.g., 2^n) cannot be used to solve problems of even modest sizes. How long would it take an exponential algorithm to complete with an input of size 100 if we can perform one billion operations per second? Using the information in Figure 1.4, we see that 2^{100} is about 10^{30} (i.e., one followed by 30 zeros); this is a very large number. Dividing it by one billion operations per second tells us it will take 10^{21} seconds or over 10^{13} years to run our algorithm on an input of size 100. The universe is thought to be between 10 and 20 billion years old so this is thousands of times longer than the universe has existed!

If we know how long it takes to solve a problem of a certain size, we can use the theta classification to approximate how long it will take to solve problems of larger sizes. For example, if we have a $\Theta(n^2)$ sorting algorithm that takes 25 seconds to sort one million items on our computer, we can estimate how long it will take to sort two million items on our computer with the same code. This information gives us the equation $c(1{,}000{,}000)^2 = 25$ seconds. Remember that theta notation (like big O) hides the constant multiplier in front of the largest term. When setting up a specific equation, we need to include that multiplier term. We can solve for c and get $c = 2.5(10^{-11})$. We can now calculate $2.5(10^{-11})(2{,}000{,}000)^2$ and we get 100 seconds.

As you might have determined already, we do not even need to solve for c in this case. We know our algorithm is $\Theta(n^2)$ and now we want to know what happens when our input size is twice as large. We can just plug in $2n$ for n and expand: $(2n)^2 = 4n^2$. This tells us it should take four times as long to solve a problem that is twice as large when using a $\Theta(n^2)$ algorithm. This matches our earlier answer (i.e., $25(4) = 100$).

Obviously, we will try to use Θ notation whenever possible to state the performance of an algorithm. For some complicated algorithms it can be difficult to prove a tight bound and then we might just prove an upper bound (big O notation). We will also usually only analyze the worst-case running time of an algorithm. You might argue that the average case is more useful, but that is sometimes difficult to determine. For our linear search, we found the best case was $\Theta(1)$ and the worst case was $\Theta(n)$, and it is not too difficult to convince ourselves that the average case is also $\Theta(n)$. If we search once for each item in a list of unique items, the value will be found once in the first position, once in the second position, once in the third position, and so on through the last position. We know that sum is $n(n+1)/2$ and for the average case we need to divide that by the n searches we did, resulting in $\Theta(n)$. For the binary search, determining the average case is more complicated.

1.4   Chapter Summary

This chapter introduced basic concepts that are vital for writing larger software systems:

- Programming in the large varies from programming in the small along numerous dimensions. The fundamental problem in designing and implementing larger programs is how to control complexity.

- Abstraction is used to simplify and reduce the amount of information a programmer needs to understand at any given moment when writing software. One particularly useful type of abstraction (functional abstraction) allows the separation of "what" from "how" and facilitates design by contract.

- Program assertions document a program by stating what must be true at a given point of execution. Pre- and postconditions are special kinds of assertions that provide a convenient way to specify the behavior of a function or method.

- Larger problems can be broken down into smaller problems through top-down design. Specification of functional decompositions allows multiple programmers to work on a project together.

- For larger data sets, the efficiency of algorithms is important. Asymptotic analysis is used to classify the efficiency of algorithms. Big O notation is used to indicate upper bounds, while theta notation is used to characterize a more exact growth rate.

1.5   Exercises

True/False Questions

1. To use functions/classes/methods defined in a library correctly, you must understand the API (i.e., what the parameters and return values are).

2. Assuming the pre- and postconditions and code are correct, the post condition is guaranteed to be true after the code is executed if the precondition is met before the code is executed.

3. A function that detects a violation of its precondition should print out an error message.

4. A function's signature provides a complete specification of its behavior.

5. A well-designed function/method often has undocumented side effects.

6. Using the same computer, programming language, and input data, executing an algorithm that is $\Theta(n)$ must be faster than executing an algorithm that is $\Theta(n^2)$.

7. A function with more lines of code can be faster than a function with fewer lines.

8. Theta notation is an effective measure of algorithm efficiency when the expected input size for the algorithm is small.

9. All $O(n^2)$ algorithms are $\Theta(n^2)$.

10. All $\Theta(n^2)$ algorithms are $O(n^2)$.

Multiple Choice Questions

1. Which of the following is not part of the *signature* of a function?

   a) the name of the function
   b) how the function works
   c) the parameters
   d) the return value

2. Which of these actions inside a function would produce a side effect?

   a) setting an immutable parameter to a new object
   b) setting a mutable parameter to a new object
   c) modifying a mutable parameter
   d) returning a value

3. Which of the following indicates that a function's precondition was met?

   a) the function does not crash
   b) the function returns a value
   c) the function raises an exception
   d) none of the above

4. In general what will have the biggest effect on how long your algorithm takes to execute on a large data set?

   a) the efficiency of your algorithm
   b) the computer language used to implement the algorithm
   c) the number of lines of code in your algorithm
   d) the speed of the hard disk on the computer

5. A function with two loops has an asymptotic running time of

   a) $\Theta(log_2 n)$
   b) $\Theta(n)$
   c) $\Theta(n^2)$
   d) not enough information to determine

6. If a $\Theta(n^2)$ algorithm requires 3 seconds to execute on an input of one million elements, approximately how long should it take on an input of two million elements?

a) 6 seconds   b) 9 seconds   c) 12 seconds   d) 18 seconds

7. If a $\Theta(n^3)$ algorithm requires 4 seconds to execute on an input of one million elements, approximately how long should it take on an input of two million elements?

a) 8 seconds   b) 16 seconds   c) 32 seconds   d) 64 seconds

8. If a $\Theta(log_2 n)$ algorithm requires 20 seconds to execute on an input of one million elements, approximately how long should it take on an input of two million elements?

a) 21 seconds   b) 25 seconds   c) 30 seconds   d) 40 seconds

9. If a $\Theta(2^n)$ algorithm requires 10 seconds to execute on an input of 10 elements, approximately how long should it take on an input of 20 elements?

a) 20 seconds   b) 100 seconds   c) 1,000 seconds   d) 10,000 seconds

10. If a computer is capable of performing one billion operations per second, approximately how long would it take to execute an algorithm that requires n^2 operations on an input of two million elements.

a) 400 seconds
b) 2,000 seconds   1,000,000,000
c) 4,000 seconds
d) 20,000 seconds

Short-Answer Questions

1. What is a side effect of a function/method?

2. Describe the basic approach of top-down design and how it relates to design by contract.

3. If you need to repeatedly search a random list of 20 items for different values that are input by the user, what search method should you use? Should you create another list that contains the same items but is sorted and search it? Why or why not?

4. If you need to repeatedly search a random list of 2,000,000 items for different values that are input by the user, what search method should you use? Should you create another list that contains the same items but is sorted and search it? Why or why not?

5. For the preceding problems is a Python list the most appropriate data type to store the numbers? If not, what Python data type would you use?

6. If a computer is capable of performing one billion operations per second, how long would it take to execute an algorithm that requires 2^n operations for an input of $n = 100$ elements?

7. If a computer is capable of performing one billion operations per second, how long would it take to execute an algorithm that requires n^2 operations on an input of $n = 1,000,000$. How long would it take if the algorithm requires n^3 operations?

8. Give a theta analysis of the time efficiency of the following code fragments.

   a)
```
n = input('enter n: ')
for i in range(n):
    x = 2 * n
    while x > 1:
        x = x / 2
```
   $log_2(n)$

   b)
```
n = input('enter n: ')
total = 0
for i in range(n):
    for j in range(10000):
        total += j
print total
```

   c)
```
total = 0
n = input('enter n: ')
for i in range(2 * n):
    for j in range(i, n):
        total += j
for j in range(n):
    total += j
print j
```

9. Our first version of the linear search algorithm used the Python `index` method and did not have any loops. Yet we said that the linear search algorithm is $\Theta(n)$. Generally, an algorithm without any loops is $\Theta(1)$. Explain the (apparent) discrepancy.

Programming Exercises

1. Create a list of one million integers numbered 0 to 999,999. Time (using the `time.time` function as we did in the examples in this chapter) the worst and best cases for the list `index` method version of the linear search, the linear search code written using a `for` statement, and the binary search code. In comments list the specifications of your computer (CPU chip and clock speed, operating system, and Python version) along with the worst and best times for each of the three searches.

2. Create a random list of 10,000, 100,000, and 1,000,000 integers with each number between 1 and 10 million. Measure how long it takes to sort each list using the built-in list's `sort` method. In comments, list the specifications of your computer (CPU chip and clock speed, operating system, and Python version) along with how long it took to sort each list. Also include comments that indicate what you think the Θ classification is for the `sort` method based on the running times.

3. The selection sort algorithm sorts a list by finding the smallest element and swapping it with the element in position zero of the list. It then finds the next smallest element and swaps it with the element in position one of the list. This process repeats until we have found the $n-1$th smallest element and put it in position $n-2$. At this point, the largest element is in position $n-1$. Implement this algorithm in Python and indicate what its Θ classification is in comments. Also time your code for the three lists described in the previous question.

4. Design your own experiment to compare the behavior of linear search and binary search on lists of various sizes. Plot your results on a graph and see if you can find a "crossover" point where linear search actually beats binary search on your computer. Since the searches will be very quick for smaller lists, you will need to be somewhat clever in how you time the searches in order to get valid data. (Hint: get larger timing intervals by timing how long it takes to do a given search many times.) Write up a complete lab report explaining your experimental set-up, methods, data, and analysis.

5. Complete the implementation of the simple statistics program in subsection 1.2.3. Be sure to thoroughly test your program on some data sets with known results.

6. Add a function to the example in subsection 1.2.3 that returns five integers: the number of scores in the 90s, in the 80s, in the 70s, in the 60s, and below

60. Be sure to provide a complete specification of your new function including appropriate pre- and postconditions along with the implementation code.

7. Whenever the average value of a set of data is needed, it is usually also appropriate to calculate the standard deviation. The current API for the simple statistics program of section subsection 1.2.3 is somewhat inefficient in this regard, as asking for both the average and the standard deviation results in the former being computed twice (why?). Redesign the API for this simple library to overcome this issue. Your new design should allow the user to efficiently calculate just the average, just the standard deviation, or both.

8. Design and implement a quiz program. The program should read question and answer information from a file. For example, a state capital quiz would contain the state and its capital on each line (e.g., `Ohio:Columbus`). Your program should ask a fixed number of questions and output the number of correct answers. Create at least three separate functions in your design.

9. Write a specification and implementation for a function that "squeezes" the duplicates out of a sorted list. For example:

```
>>> x = [1, 1, 3, 3, 3, 4, 5, 5, 8, 9, 9, 9, 9, 10]
>>> squeeze(x)
>>> x
[1, 3, 4, 5, 8, 9, 10]
```

Test your function thoroughly and analyze its theta efficiency.

Chapter 2　　　　　　　　　　Data Abstraction

Objectives

- To learn how abstract data types are used in software design.

- To review the basic principles and techniques of object-oriented design.

- To learn about unit testing and how to write unit tests in Python.

- To learn about operator overloading and how to overload operators in Python.

2.1　Overview

Algorithms are one fundamental building block of programs. In Chapter 1, we saw the benefits that come from separating the idea of what a function does from the details of how it is implemented. In this chapter, we'll take a look at the data that our programs process. Separating behavior from implementation is even more powerful when we consider data objects. This process of *data abstraction* is a foundational concept that must be mastered in order to build practical software systems. Computer scientists formalize the idea of data abstraction in terms of *abstract data types* (ADTs). Abstract data types, in turn, are the foundation for object-oriented programming, which is the dominant development method for large systems.

We'll start out by examining ADTs and how they relate to object-oriented programming. Along the way we'll show how object-oriented programming can be used to extend a programming language with new data types that can make it more suitable for solving problems in new domains. In languages that support a special technique known as *operator overloading*, new data types can be made to look and act just like the language's own built-in types.

Using ADTs and objects, program design becomes a process of breaking a problem into smaller pieces: a set of cooperating objects that provide most of the program's functionality. As these smaller pieces are implemented, they can be tested in isolation so that developers have confidence in their correctness before the parts are combined into a larger system. Learning how to do effective testing is another important piece of the software development puzzle.

2.2 Abstract Data Types

One important property of any value stored in a computer is its *data type*. The type of an object determines both what values it can have and what we can do with it (i.e., what operations it supports). For example, on a 32-bit computer the built-in type int can represent integers in the range from -2^{31} to $2^{31} - 1$ and can be used with operations such as addition (+), subtraction (-), multiplication (*) and division(/). Knowing this information, you can write programs that use ints without having to know how such numbers are actually stored on the computer. Using our terminology from last chapter, we would say that a program that manipulates int values is a client of the int data type.

Of course, in order for a data type to actually be useful, there must be some underlying implementation of that type. The implementation consists of both a way to represent all the possible values of the type and a set of functions that manipulate the underlying representation. Consider again the int data type. It is typically stored on today's computers as a 32-bit binary number. Algorithms for operations such as addition and subtraction are defined in the underlying machine hardware, and functions for input and output of ints are built into most programming languages.

2.2.1 From Data Type to ADT

Applying the idea of abstraction, we can separate the concerns of how data is represented from how it is used. That is, we can provide a specification for a data type that is independent of any actual implementation. Such a specification describes abstract data type . A precise and complete description allows client programs to be written without worrying about how an ADT is realized in the computer. In this way, data abstraction extends the advantages of implementation independence. We can delay decisions about how data should be represented in our programs until we have sufficient information about how that data is going to be used. We can also go in and change a representation, and the abstraction barrier ensures that the rest of the program will not be adversely affected.

Data abstraction is particularly important for those parts of a program that are likely to change. Major design decisions can be encapsulated in ADTs, and the implementation of the ADTs can be adjusted as necessary without affecting the rest of the program. As you will see, it is often the case that changing how data is represented can have a major impact on the efficiency of the associated operations; so, having the freedom to modify representations is a big win when trying to tune a program's efficiency.

Another advantage of ADTs is that they promote reuse. Once a relevant abstraction has been implemented, it can be used by many different client programs. Those clients are freed from the hassle of having to reinvent the data type. This allows programmers to extend programming languages with new data objects that are useful in their particular area of programming. After the ADT has been thoroughly tested, it can be used with confidence and the implementation details never have to be revisited.

2.2.2 Defining an ADT

You can think of an ADT as a collection of functions or methods that manipulate an underlying representation. The representation is really just some collection of data. To specify an ADT we just describe what the operations supported by the ADT do. We can apply the same techniques we used for specifying functions. The only difference is that a single ADT is described by a *collection* of functions.

Let's look at a simple example. Suppose we are writing some programs dealing with card games, say bridge or Texas hold 'em. A playing card could be modeled as a simple ADT. Here's a description of the ADT:

```
ADT Card:
    A simple playing card. A Card is characterized by two components:
    rank: an integer value in the range 1-13, inclusive (Ace-King)
    suit: a character in 'cdhs' for clubs, diamonds, hearts, and
        spades.

Operations:

    create(rank, suit):
        Create a new Card
        pre: rank in range(1,14) and suit in 'cdhs'
        post: returns a Card of the given rank and suit

    suit():
        Card suit
        post: Returns Card's suit as a single character
```

```
rank():
    Card rank
    post: Returns Card's rank as an int

suitName():
    Card suit name
    post: Returns one of ('clubs', 'diamonds', 'hearts',
          'spades') corrresponding to Card's suit.

rankName():
    Card rank name
    post: Returns one of ('ace', 'two', 'three', ..., 'king')
          corresponding to Card's rank.

toString():
    String representation of Card
    post: Returns string naming the Card, e.g. 'Ace of Spades'
```

Notice how this specification describes a **Card** in terms of some abstract attributes (**rank** and **suit**) and the things that we can do with a card. It does not describe how a **Card** is actually represented or how the operations are achieved. In fact, the specification doesn't even explicitly refer to any card object or parameter; it is implicit that these are the operations that can *somehow* be applied to any card.

In the process of designing an ADT, our goal is to include a complete set of operations necessary to make the ADT useful. Of course, there are many different design choices that could be made for the **Card** ADT. For example, we could have different names for the operations; some designers prefer to use names starting with "get" for accessing components of an ADT. Thus, they might use **getSuit** and **getRank** in place of **suit** and **rank**. Other designers might choose different types for the parameters of the various operations. Perhaps suits might be represented with **int**s instead of **string**s. Another approach is to "hide" the exact representation of suits and ranks by simply providing a set of variables representing the suits and ranks. For example, an identifier named **CLUBS** might be assigned to some value representing that suit, similar to the way the identifier **None** refers to Python's special **None** object. The ranks could be represented using names like **ACE**, **TWO**, **THREE**, etc.

As you gain experience working with ADTs, you will develop your own design sense. The most important thing to keep in mind is implementation independence. An ADT describes only a set of operations, not how those operations are implemented. One good way of "testing" the design for an ADT is to try writing some client algorithms that use it. For example, here is an algorithm that prints out the rank, suit, and "name" of all the cards in a standard deck:

```
for s in 'cdhs':
    for r in range(1,14):
        card = create(r, s)
        print 'Suit:', suit(card)
        print 'Rank:', rank(card)
        print toString(card)
```

Notice how this algorithm is expressed using a Python-like syntax, but makes use of the abstract functions of the ADT presented above. The algorithm shows us that our set of operations would be sufficient to create and print out all 52 possible cards.

2.2.3 | Implementing an ADT

It is possible to design and reason about ADTs in a language-independent fashion, but once we get down to the point of implementing and using an ADT in a program, we need to fill in some details that are specific to the particular programming environment. There are numerous ways that a programmer could go about translating an ADT into a particular programming language. Virtually all languages provide the ability to define new functions, so one way of implementing an ADT is simply to write an appropriate set of functions. For example, in Python we could write a function for each **Card** operation and place them together in a module file.

Of course, in writing the functions we will need to decide how a **Card** will be represented on the computer. The abstract type has components for rank and suit. In Python, a simple representation would be to package the rank and suit together as a pair of values in a tuple. A Python tuple is an immutable (unchangeable) sequence of values. A tuple literal is indicated by enclosing a comma-separated sequence in parentheses. Using tuples, the ace of clubs would be represented by the tuple (1,'c') and the king of spades would be (13,'s').

The underlying representation of an ADT is called the *concrete representation*. We would say that the tuple (5,'d') is the concrete representation of the abstract **Card** known as the five of diamonds.

Now that we have a representation for our **Card** ADT, writing the implementation code is straightforward. Here is one version:

```
# cardADT.py
#    Module file implementing the card ADT with functions

_SUITS = 'cdhs'
_SUIT_NAMES = ['clubs', 'diamonds', 'hearts', 'spades']
```

```
_RANKS = range(1,14)
_RANK_NAMES = ['Ace', 'Two', 'Three', 'Four', 'Five', 'Six',
               'Seven', 'Eight', 'Nine', 'Ten',
               'Jack', 'Queen', 'King']

def create(rank, suit):
    assert rank in _RANKS and suit in _SUITS
    return (rank,suit)

def rank(card):
    return card[0]

def suit(card):
    return card[1]

def suitName(card):
    index = _SUITS.index(suit(card))
    return _SUIT_NAMES[index]

def rankName(card):
    index = _RANKS.index(rank(card))
    return _RANK_NAMES[index]

def toString(card):
    return rankName(card) + ' of ' + suitName(card)
```

Take a look at the **create** function. It uses an **assert** to check that the preconditions for creating a card are met, and then it simply returns a rank-suit tuple. In this way, the function returns a single value that represents all the information about a particular card.

The **rank** and **suit** operations simply unpackage the appropriate part of the card tuple. Tuple components are accessed through indexing, so **card[0]** gives the first component, which is the rank, and **card[1]** gives the suit. These two operations are so simple, you might even wonder if they are necessary. Couldn't a client using the **Card** ADT simply access the suit directly by doing something like **myCard[1]**? The answer is that the client *could* do this, but it *shouldn't*. The whole point of an ADT is to uncouple the client from the implementation. If the client accesses the representation directly, then changing the representation later will break the client code. Remember this rule: clients may use an ADT only through the provided operations.

One other point worth noting about this code is the use of some special values: **_RANKS**, **_SUITS**, **_RANK_NAMES**, and **_SUIT_NAMES**. The **suitName** and **rankName** methods could have been written as large multi-way **if** statements. Instead, we have employed a *table-driven* approach. We use the **index** method to find the position of a rank or suit, and then use it to look up the corresponding name. This shortens the code and makes it much easier to modify. For example, we could easily add a fifth suit by simply adding another item to the end of _SUITS and _SUIT_NAMES.

Just in case you were wondering, there's a reason for the funny-looking variable names used for the lookup tables. The use of uppercase is a programming convention often employed for constants, that is, things that are assigned once and never changed. The leading underscore is a Python convention indicating that these names are "private" to the module. If the client imports the module via

```
from cardADT import *
```

the identifiers beginning with an underscore are not imported into the local program. This keeps implementation details, such as the use of lookup tables, from cluttering up the client's namespace (the set of defined identifiers).

Now that we have the **Card** ADT implementation, we can actually code up our program that prints out cards using this card module.

```
# test_cardADT.py
import cardADT

def printAll():
    for suit in 'cdhs':
        for rank in range(1,14):
            myCard = cardADT.create(rank, suit)
            print cardADT.toString(myCard)

if __name__ == '__main__':
    printAll()
```

To summarize, one way of implementing an ADT is to choose a concrete representation and then write a set of functions that manipulate that representation. If our implementation language includes modules (a la Python), we can place the implementation in a separate module so that it has its own independent namespace.

If the implementation language does not support the idea of separate modules, then we could run into trouble with the names of operations between ADTs "clashing." For example, if we were writing a program to play a card game, we might also have a **deckADT** representing a deck of cards. Of course, the **deckADT** would have its own **create** method. Without modules, we'd have to rely on naming conventions to keep the operations straight. For example, all of the operations on cards might begin with **card_** while those for decks would start with **deck_**. Thus, we would have separate functions, **card_create** and **deck_create**.

2.3 ADTs and Objects

As we have seen, an ADT comprises a set of operations that manipulate some underlying data representation. This should sound familiar to you. If you are working in an object-oriented language (such as Python), then it is natural to think of implementing an ADT as an object, since objects also combine data and operations. Simply put, an object "knows stuff (data) and does stuff (operations)." The data in an object is stored in instance variables, and the operations are its methods. We can use the instance variables to store the concrete representation of an ADT and write methods to implement the operations.

As you know, new object types are defined using the `class` mechanism. As the Python language has evolved, it has come to support two different kinds of classes sometimes called the *classic* and *new-style* classes. For our examples, classic and new-style classes behave exactly the same. We will use Python's new-style classes throughout this book as they are strongly recommended for new code. A new-style class is indicated simply by having the class inherit from the built-in class `object`. You do not need to know any details about inheritance in order to use new-style classes; you just need to change the class heading slightly. For example, to create a `Card` class with new-style classes, we write `class Card(object):` instead of `class Card:`.[1]

2.3.1 Specification

In object-oriented languages, new object data types can be created by defining a new class. We can turn an ADT description directly into an appropriate class specification. Here is a class specification for our `Card` example:

```
class Card(object):
    """A simple playing card. A Card is characterized by two components.
     rank: an integer value in the range 1-13, inclusive (Ace-King)
     suit: a character in 'cdhs' for clubs, diamonds, hearts, and
           spades."""

    def __init__(self, rank, suit):
        """Constructor
        pre: rank in range(1,14) and suit in 'cdhs'
        post: self has the given rank and suit"""
```

---

[1]In Python 3.0, support for classic classes has been dropped and either class heading form will produce a new-style class.

```
    def suit(self):
        """Card suit
        post: Returns the suit of self as a single character"""

    def rank(self):
        """Card rank
        post: Returns the rank of self as an int"""

    def suitName(self):
        """Card suit name
        post: Returns one of ('Clubs', 'Diamonds', 'Hearts',
              'Spades') corrresponding to self's suit."""

    def rankName(self):
        """Card rank name
        post: Returns one of ('Ace', 'Two', 'Three', ..., 'King')
              corresponding to self's rank."""

    def __str__(self):
        """String representation
        post: Returns string representing self, e.g. 'Ace of Spades' """
```

Basically, this specification is just the outline of a **Card** class as it would look in Python. The docstring for the class gives an overview, and the docstrings for the methods specify what each one does. Following Python conventions, the method names that begin and end with double underscores (__init__ and __str__) are special. Python recognizes __init__ as the constructor, and the __str__ method will be called whenever Python is asked to convert a **Card** object into a string. For example:

```
>>> c = Card(4,'c')
>>> print c
Four of Clubs
```

We have now translated our ADT into an object-oriented form. Clients of this class will use dot notation to perform operations on the ADT. Here's the code that prints out all 52 cards translated into its object-based form:

```
# printcards.py
#     Simple test of the Card ADT

from Card import Card

def printAll():
    for suit in 'cdhs':
        for rank in range(1,14):
            card = Card(rank, suit)
            print 'Rank:', card.rank()
            print 'Suit:', card.suit()
            print card

if __name__ == '__main__':
    printAll()
```

Notice that the constructor is invoked by using the name of the class, **Card**, and the
`__str__` method is implicitly called by Python when it is asked to print the card.

2.3.2   Implementation

We can translate our previous implementation of the card ADT into our new class-
based implementation. Now the rank and suit components of a card can just be
stored in appropriate instance variables:

```
# Card.py
class Card(object):
    """A simple playing card. A Card is characterized by two components:
    rank: an integer value in the range 1-13, inclusive (Ace-King)
    suit: a character in 'cdhs' for clubs, diamonds, hearts, and
    spades."""

    SUITS = 'cdhs'
    SUIT_NAMES = ['Clubs', 'Diamonds', 'Hearts', 'Spades']

    RANKS = range(1,14)
    RANK_NAMES = ['Ace', 'Two', 'Three', 'Four', 'Five', 'Six',
                  'Seven', 'Eight', 'Nine', 'Ten',
                  'Jack', 'Queen', 'King']

    def __init__(self, rank, suit):
        """Constructor
        pre: rank in range(1,14) and suit in 'cdhs'
        post: self has the given rank and suit"""

        self.rank_num = rank
        self.suit_char = suit
```

```
    def suit(self):
        """Card suit
        post: Returns the suit of self as a single character"""

        return self.suit_char

    def rank(self):
        """Card rank
        post: Returns the rank of self as an int"""

        return self.rank_num

    def suitName(self):
        """Card suit name
        post: Returns one of ('clubs', 'diamonds', 'hearts',
            'spades') corresponding to self's suit."""

        index = self.SUITS.index(self.suit_char)
        return self.SUIT_NAMES[index]

    def rankName(self):
        """Card rank name
        post: Returns one of ('ace', 'two', 'three', ..., 'king')
            corresponding to self's rank."""

        index = self.RANKS.index(self.rank_num)
        return self.RANK_NAMES[index]

    def __str__(self):
        """String representation
        post: Returns string representing self, e.g. 'Ace of Spades' """

        return self.rankName() + ' of ' + self.suitName()
```

Notice that the lookup tables from the previous version have now been implemented as variables that are assigned inside of the `Card` class but outside of any of the methods of the class. These are *class variables*. They "live" inside the class definition, so there is one copy shared by all instances of the class. These variables are accessed just like instance variables using the `self.<name>` convention. When Python is asked to retrieve the value of an object's attribute, it first checks to see if the attribute has been assigned directly for the object. If not, it will look in the object's class to find it. For example, when the `suitName` method accesses `self.SUITS`, Python sees that `self` does not have a SUIT attribute, so the value from the `Card` class is used (because `self` is a `Card`).

You now have three different kinds of variables for storing information in programs: regular (local) variables, instance variables, and class variables. Choosing the right kind of variable for a given piece of information is an important decision when implementing ADTs. The first question you must answer is whether the data needs to be remembered from one method invocation to another. If not, you should use a local variable. The `index` variable used in `rankName()` is a good example of a local variable; its value is no longer needed once the method terminates. Notice that there is also a local variable called `index` in the `suitName` method. These are two completely independent variables, even though they happen to have the same name. Each exists only while the method where they are used is executing. We could have written this code using an instance variable `self.index` in these two methods. Doing so would be a misleading design choice, because we have no reason to hang onto the value of index from the last execution of `rankName` or `suitName`. Reusing an instance variable in this case would imply a connection where none exists.

Data that does need to be remembered from one method invocation to another should be stored in either instance variables or class variables. The decision about which to use in this case depends on whether the data may be different from one object to the next or whether it is the same for all objects of the class. In our card example, `self.rank_num` and `self.suit_char` are values that will vary among cards. They are part of the intrinsic state of a particular card, so they have to be instance variables. The suit names, on the other hand will be the same for all cards of the class, so it makes sense to use a class variable for that. Constants are often good candidates for class variables, since, by definition, they are the same from one object to the next. However, there are also times when non-constant class variables make sense. Keeping these simple rules in mind should help you turn your ADTs into working classes.

As you can see there is a natural correspondence between the notion of an ADT and an object-oriented class. When using an object-oriented language, you will usually want to implement an ADT as a class. The nice thing about using classes is that they naturally combine the two facets of an ADT (data and operations) into a single programming structure.

2.3.3   Changing the Representation

We have emphasized that the primary strength of using ADTs to design software is implementation independence. However, the playing card example that we've discussed so far has not really illustrated this point. After all, we said that a card has a rank that is an `int` and a suit that is a character, then we simply stored these values as instance variables. Isn't the client directly using the representation when it manipulates suits and ranks?

The reason it *seems* that the client has access to the representation in this case is simply because the concrete representation that we've chosen directly mirrors the data types that are used to pass information to and from the ADT. However, since access to the data takes place through methods (like `suit` and `rank`) we can actually change the concrete representation without affecting the client code. This is where the independence comes in.

Suppose we are developing card games for a handheld device such as a PDA or cell phone. On such a device, we might have strict memory limitations. Our current representation of cards requires two instance variables for each card; the rank, which is a 32-bit `int`; and the suit, which is a character. An alternative way to think about cards is simply to number them. Since there are 52 cards, each can be represented as a number from 0 to 51. Think of putting the cards in order so that all the clubs come first, diamonds second, etc. Within each suit, put the cards in rank order. Now we have a complete ordering where the first card in the deck is the ace of clubs, and the last card is the king of spades.

Given a card's number, we can calculate its rank and suit. Since there are 13 cards in each suit, dividing the card number by 13 (using integer division) produces a value between 0 and 3 (inclusive). Clubs will yield a 0, diamonds a 1, etc. Furthermore, the remainder from the division will give the relative position of the card within the suit (i.e., its rank). For example, if the card number is 37, $37//13 = 2$ so the suit is hearts, and $37\%13 = 11$ which corresponds to a rank of queen since the first card in a suit (the ace) will have a remainder of 0. So card 37 is the queen of hearts. Using this approach, the concrete representation of our `Card` ADT can be a single number. We leave it as an exercise for the reader to complete an implementation of the `Card` class using this more-memory-efficient alternative representation.

2.3.4 Object-Oriented Design and Programming

As you have seen, there is a close correspondence between the ideas of ADTs and object-oriented programming. But there is more to object-orientation (OO) than just implementing ADTs. Most OO gurus talk about three features that together make development truly object-oriented: encapsulation, polymorphism, and inheritance.

Encapsulation

As you know, objects know stuff and do stuff. They combine data and operations. This process of packaging some data along with the set of operations that can be performed on the data is called *encapsulation*.

Encapsulation is one of the major attractions of using objects. It provides a convenient way to compose solutions to complex problems that corresponds to our intuitive view of how the world works. We naturally think of the world around us as consisting of interacting objects. Each object has its own identity, and knowing what kind of object it is allows us to understand its nature and capabilities. When you look out your window, you see houses, cars, and trees, not a swarming mass of countless molecules or atoms.

From a design standpoint, encapsulation also provides the critical service of separating the concerns of "what" vs. "how." The actual implementation of an object is independent of its use. Encapsulation is what gives us implementation independence. Encapsulation is probably the chief benefit of using objects, but alone it only makes a system *object-based*. To be truly objected-*oriented*, the approach must also have the characteristics of polymorphism and inheritance.

Polymorphism

Literally, the word *polymorphism* means "many forms." When used in object-oriented literature, this refers to the fact that what an object does in response to a message (a method call) depends on the type or class of the object. Consider a simple example. Suppose you are working with a graphics library for drawing two-dimensional shapes. The library provides a number of primitive geometric shapes that can be drawn into a window on the screen. Each shape has an operation that actually draws the shape. We have a collection of classes something like this:

```
class Circle(object):
    def draw(self, window):
        # code to draw the circle

class Rectangle(object):
    def draw(self, window):
        # code to draw the rectangle

class Polygon(object):
    def draw(self, window):
        # code to draw the polygon
```

Of course, each of these classes would have other methods in addition to its `draw` method. Here we're just giving a basic outline for illustration.

Suppose you write a program that creates a list containing a mixture of geometric objects: circles, rectangles, polygons, etc. To draw all of the objects in the list, you would write code something like this:

```
for obj in objects:
    obj.draw(win)
```

Now consider the single line of code in the loop body. What function is called when `obj.draw(win)` executes? Actually, this single line of code calls several distinct functions. When `obj` is a circle, it executes the `draw` method from the circle class. When `obj` is a rectangle, it is the `draw` method from the rectangle class, and so on. The `draw` operation takes many forms; the particular one used depends on the type of `obj`. That's the polymorphism.

Polymorphism gives object-oriented systems the flexibility for each object to perform an action just the way that it should be performed for that object. If we didn't have objects that supported polymorphism we'd have to do something like this:

```
for obj in objects:
    if type(obj) is Circle:
        draw_circle(...)
    elif type(obj) is Rectangle:
        draw_rectangle(...)
    elif type(obj) is Polygon:
        draw_polygon(...)
    ...
```

Not only is this code more cumbersome, it is also much less flexible. If we want to add another type of object to our library, we have to find all of the places where we made a decision based on the object type and add another branch. In the polymorphic version, we can just create another class of geometric object that has its own `draw` method, and all the rest of the code remains exactly the same. Polymorphism allows us to extend the program without having to go in and modify the existing code.

Inheritance

The third important property for object-oriented development is *inheritance*. As its name implies, the idea behind inheritance is that a new class can be defined to borrow behavior from another class. The new class (the one doing the borrowing) is called a *subclass*, and the existing class (the one being borrowed from) is its *superclass*.

For example, if we are building a system to keep track of employees, we might have a class `Employee` that contains the general information and methods that are common to all employees. One sample attribute would be a `homeAddress` method that returns the home address of an employee. Within the class of all employees, we might distinguish between `SalariedEmployee` and `HourlyEmployee`. We could make these subclasses of `Employee`, so they would share methods like `homeAddress`; however, each subclass would have its own `monthlyPay` function, since pay is computed differently for these different classes of employees. Figure 2.1 shows a simple class diagram depicting this situation. The arrows with open heads indicate inheritance; the subclasses inherit the `homeAddress` method defined in the `Employee` class, but each defines its own implementation of the `monthlyPay` method.

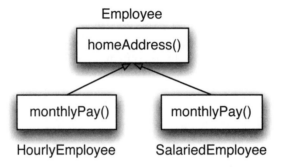

Figure 2.1: Simple example of inheritance with subclasses inheriting one shared method and each separately implementing one method

Inheritance provides two benefits. One is that we can structure the classes of a system to avoid duplication of operations. We don't have to write a separate `homeAddress` method for the `HourlyEmployee` and `SalariedEmployee` classes. A closely related benefit is that new classes can often be based on existing classes, thus promoting code reuse.

2.4 An Example ADT: Dataset

Now that we've covered ADTs and object-oriented principles, let's go back and look at the simple statistics problem introduced in Chapter 1. This time, we're going to tackle the problem using an object-oriented approach.

2.4.1 The Process of OOD

The essence of design is describing a system in terms of "black boxes" and their interfaces. Each component provides a service or set of services through its interface. In top-down design, functions serve the role of our black boxes. A client program can use a function as long as it understands what the function does. The details of how the task is accomplished are encapsulated in the function definition. In *object-oriented design* (OOD) , the black boxes are objects.

If we can break a large problem into a set of cooperating classes, we drastically reduce the complexity that must be considered to understand any given part of the program. Each class stands on its own. Object-oriented design is the process of finding and defining a useful set of classes for a given problem. Like all design, it is part art and part science.

There are many different approaches to OOD, each with its own special techniques, notations, gurus, and textbooks. Probably the best way to learn about design is to do it. The more you design, the better you will get. Just to get you started, here are some intuitive guidelines for object-oriented design:

1. *Look for object candidates.* Your goal is to define a set of objects that will be helpful in solving the problem. Start with a careful consideration of the problem statement. Objects are usually described by nouns. You might underline all of the nouns in the problem statement and consider them one by one. Which of them will actually be represented in the program? Which of them have "interesting" behavior? Things that can be represented as primitive data types (numbers or strings) are probably not important candidates for objects. Things that seem to involve a grouping of related data items (e.g., coordinates of a point or personal data about an employee) probably are.

2. *Identify instance variables.* Once you have uncovered some possible objects, think about the information that each object will need to do its job. What kinds of values will the instance variables have? Some object attributes will have primitive values; others might themselves be complex types that suggest other useful objects/classes. Strive to find good "home" classes for all the data in your program.

3. *Think about interfaces.* When you have identified a potential object/class and some associated data, think about what operations would be required for objects of that class to be useful. You might start by considering the verbs in the problem statement. Verbs are used to describe actions—what must be done. List the methods that the class will require. Remember that all manipulation of the object's data should be done through the methods you provide.

4. *Refine the nontrivial methods.* Some methods will look like they can be accomplished with a couple of lines of code. Other methods will require considerable work to develop an algorithm. Use top-down design and stepwise refinement to flesh out the details of the more difficult methods. As you go along, you may very well discover that some new interactions with other classes are needed, and this might force you to add new methods to other classes. Sometimes you may discover a need for a brand new kind of object that calls for the definition of another class.

5. *Design iteratively.* As you work through the design, you will bounce back and forth between designing new classes and adding methods to existing classes. Work on whatever seems to be demanding your attention. No one designs a program top to bottom in a linear, systematic fashion. Make progress wherever it seems progress needs to be made.

6. *Try out alternatives.* Don't be afraid to scrap an approach that doesn't seem to be working or to follow an idea and see where it leads. Good design involves a lot of trial and error. When you look at the programs of others, you are seeing finished work, not the process they went through to get there. If a program is well designed, it probably is not the result of a first try. Fred Brooks, a legendary software engineer, coined the maxim: "Plan to throw one away." Often you won't really know how a system should be built until you've already built it the wrong way.

7. *Keep it simple.* At each step in the design, try to find the simplest approach that will solve the problem at hand. Don't design in extra complexity until it is clear that a more complex approach is needed.

2.4.2 Identifying an ADT

Recall that in the statistics problem our goal was to report some simple statistics for a set of exam scores. What are the likely candidates for objects in this program?

Looking at the problem description, we are going to have to manipulate scores (a noun). Should a score be an object? Since a score is just a number, it looks like one of the built-in numeric types can be used for this, probably `float`. What else is there? In order to compute the required statistics, we need to keep track of an entire set of scores. In statistics, we would call these scores a *dataset*. Collections are often good candidates for ADTs; let's try specifying a `Dataset` class. It's obvious that we want methods that return the minimum value, maximum value, mean, and standard deviation of the values in the dataset, since those are the statistics called for in the original problem.

The only remaining question is how we get the numbers into the `Dataset` in the first place. Once simple approach is to have an `add` method that places another number in the dataset. We can construct an initially empty set and then add the numbers one at a time. Here's a sample specification:

```python
# Dataset.py
class Dataset(object):
    """Dataset is a collection of numbers from which simple
    descriptive statistics can be computed."""

    def __init__(self):
        """post: self is an empty Dataset"""

    def add(self, x):
        """add x to the data set
        post: x is added to the data set"""

    def min(self):
        """find the minimum
        pre: size of self >= 1
        post: returns smallest number in self"""

    def max(self):
        """find the maximum
        pre: size of self >= 1
        post: returns largest number in self"""

    def average(self):
        """calculate the mean
        pre: size of self >= 1
        post: returns the mean of the values in self"""

    def std_deviation(nums):
        """calculate the standard deviation
        pre: size of self >= 2
        post: returns the standard deviation of the values in self"""
```

Examining this specification immediately suggests one more operation that we should add to the ADT. Since various operations have preconditions based on how many values are in the dataset, we really should have an operation that returns this. It's always a good idea to ensure that the preconditions of ADT operations are testable. This allows the client to make sure it is using an ADT properly and also allows the implementation to easily check the preconditions. Let's add one more method:

```
def size(self):
    """
    post: returns the size of self (number of values added)
    """
```

As before, we can "test" our design by writing some code that makes use of it. In this case, we can actually write the main program for our application, relying on the Dataset ADT to do the hard work. All we need is a sentinel loop to input the data:

```
# test_Dataset.py
def main():
    print 'This is a program to compute the min, max, mean and'
    print 'standard deviation for a set of numbers.\n'
    data = Dataset()
    while True:
        xStr = raw_input('Enter a number (<Enter> to quit): ')
        if xStr == '':
            break
        try:
            x = float(xStr)
        except ValueError:
            print 'Invalid Entry Ignored: Input was not a number'
            continue
        data.add(x)
    print 'Summary of', data.size(), 'scores.'
    print 'Min:', data.min()
    print 'Max:', data.max()
    print 'Mean:', data.average()
    print 'Standard Deviation:', data.std_deviation()

if __name__ == '__main__':
    main()
```

2.4.3 Implementing the ADT

To implement our Dataset ADT, we need to come up with a concrete representation for the set of numbers. One obvious approach would be to use a list of numbers, just as we did in the original version developed using top-down design. In this approach, the `add` method would simply append another number to the list. Each of the statistics methods could then loop through the list of numbers to perform their calculations.

Of course, as with virtually any ADT, there are other possible concrete representations. Do we really need to store a list of all the numbers in the `Dataset`? Actually, none of the methods really needs to know the specific numbers in the collection, they just need some summary information about the numbers. Clearly, for the `min` and `max` methods, we just need to know the smallest and largest values, respectively, that have been added to the set so far. For `average` we just need to know the sum of the values and the size of the dataset. We could store summary information such as the size, minimum, maximum, and sum of the data as instance variables. These instance variables would be updated in the `add` method when a new number is added to the `Dataset`. The actual number would not need to be stored separately.

There is still a problem in figuring out the standard deviation. Our original formulation of standard deviation required us to compute the difference of each value with the mean. Of course, we can't know the mean until we have all the data values, so calculating the individual differences appears to require iterating back through the collection of numbers after the mean is known. It turns out, however, that there is an equivalent formulation of standard deviation, sometimes called the "shortcut formula," that is computed as follows:

$$s = \sqrt{\frac{\sum x_i^2 - \frac{(\sum x_i)^2}{n}}{n-1}}$$

This formula does not require us to know each x_i, instead we just need the sum of the values and the sum of the squares of the values. To use this formula, we just need one additional instance variable for the sum of the squares.

So, we have two possible concrete representations for the `Dataset` class. The first version, based on the original design, maintains a single instance variable (say `self.data`) containing a list of all the numbers. The second version maintains instance variables (`self._size`, `self._min`, `self._max`, `self._sum`, `self._sum_squares`) representing summary information of the data.[2]

You should have little difficulty implementing the `Dataset` class using either of these concrete representations. Writing the actual code is left as an exercise. Even

---

[2]The use of leading underscores in the instance variable names is a common convention both to "mark" them as instance variables and to keep them from conflicting with similarly named methods (`max`, the method, vs. `_max`, the instance variable).

without the code, however, it's possible to analyze the relative efficiency of these two representations. The second representation has several advantages over the version originally developed with top-down design. Obviously, it is more efficient in terms of storage space, since it does not have to remember the list of values that have been added to the set. In fact, the memory footprint of this more-efficient `Dataset` object does not even change when more data is added.

Interestingly, the second representation is also more efficient in terms of execution time. In the first version, each of the statistical operations has to loop over the list of numbers and thus has $\Theta(n)$ efficiency where n is the size of the dataset. The second version needs no loops, and all the operations are constant time, $\Theta(1)$.

2.5   An Example ADT: Rational

Hopefully, you're getting the hang of designing and implementing ADTs using objects. New classes allow us to extend our available vocabulary for solving new kinds of problems. In this section, we're going to take a look at some practical techniques to extend Python with a new numeric data type.

As you know, numbers with fractional values are generally represented using the `float` data type. One disadvantage of using `float`s is that the underlying representations are only approximations. The number is first converted into binary (base 2) so any fractions having denominators that are not powers of 2 will translate into a quotient with an infinitely repeating pattern. When the quotient is truncated to fit into a finite memory location, some precision is lost. For some applications, it would be nice to have a data type that manipulated the fractions directly so that values such as $\frac{1}{10}$ can be stored and used accurately. Let's extend the language with a new `Rational` class to represent rational numbers (fractions).

2.5.1   Operator Overloading

Abstractly, our rational class should behave just like rational numbers in mathematics. A rational number has a numerator and a denominator that are integers and supports the usual numeric operations. Concretely, we'll implement the rational number ADT in a `Rational` class.

In building the `Rational` class, we'd like to make it behave as much as possible like the existing numeric types. We generally use mathematical operators such as +, −, *, and / to perform functions on integers and floating-point numbers. Technically, these operators are said to be *overloaded* in Python (and many other languages) in that each can be used to indicate a number of different operations. For example, the

+ sign is used for both integer and floating-point addition. The type of operation carried out depends on the data types of the operands. We don't notice this much with addition, but it makes a big difference when using the division operator.[3]

Sometimes when we design our own classes, it makes sense to use existing operators in the context of our new data type. Some object-oriented languages such as Python and C++ support a mechanism that allows programmers to invoke new functions with existing operators, thus extending operator overloading to new programmer-defined types. Other languages, Java for example, do not.

If we were implementing `Rational`s in a language without operator overloading, we might write code for a method `add` and call it using the syntax `r3 = r1.add(r2)` to add two rational numbers and store the result in `r3`. There is nothing wrong with this, but it is more familiar and readable if addition can be written as `r3 = r1 + r2`. As you can see, operator overloading is not necessary but it can lead to enhanced readability when used properly. Of course, it can also lead to decreased readability if used sloppily. Think about what would happen if someone wrote code that caused the plus operator to subtract the two objects or do some completely unrelated function.

In Python, certain built-in operators can be overloaded in a new class by defining methods having special names that begin and end with two underscores. The *Python Reference Manual* specifies the complete list of operators that may be extended. Table 2.1 is a partial list of the methods you can write to provide operator functionality for your own classes.. This table shows us that if we want to be able to write `c = a + b` for instances of a class, we need to write the method `__add__(self, other)` for the class. Once we do this, the code `c = a + b` is equivalent to writing `c = a.__add__(b)`. In Python it is not necessary that `a` and `b` are the same data type, but in most cases, it makes sense for that to be the case.

2.5.2 The Rational Class

Using Python's operator overloading, it's quite easy to write a class for rational numbers. The following code shows the start of a `Rational` class; it implements the `__mul__` and `__str__` methods along with a constructor that supports zero, one, or two parameters in addition to the `self` parameter. As usual, the preconditions and postconditions for each method are specified as part of the documentation strings. This example has two instance variables, `num` and `den`. Note that the `__mul__` method creates a new `Rational` object and does not modify the instance variables

---

[3]In Python 3.0 the slash (/) always produces floating-point division, and the double slash (//) is used for integer division.

Method	Returns
__add__(self, other)	self + other
__sub__(self, other)	self - other
__mul__(self, other)	self * other
__div__(self, other)	self / other
__neg__(self)	-self
__and__(self, other)	self & other
__or__(self, other)	self | other
__iadd__(self, other)	self += other
__isub__(self, other)	self -= other
__imul__(self, other)	self *= other
__idiv__(self, other)	self /= other
__lt__(self, other)	self < other
__le__(self, other)	self <= other
__gt__(self, other)	self > other
__ge__(self, other)	self >= other
__eq__(self, other)	self == other
__ne__(self, other)	self != other

Table 2.1: Some operator methods that can be overloaded in Python classes.

for self or other. When overloading operators, it's important to preserve the "standard" semantics of operators, which is that they produce new values without modifying the originals. When we see c = a + b, we do not expect the values of a and b to be changed!

```python
# Rational.py
# demonstrates operator overloading

class Rational(object):

    def __init__(self, num = 0, den = 1):

        """creates a new Rational object
        pre: num and den are integers
        post: creates the Rational object num / den"""

        self.num = num
        self.den = den
```

```
    def __mul__(self, other):

        """* operator
        pre: self and other are Rational objects
        post: returns Rational product: self * other"""

        num = self.num * other.num
        den = self.den * other.den
        return Rational(num, den)

    def __str__(self):

        """return string for printing
        pre: self is Rational object
        post: returns a string representation of self"""

        return str(self.num) + '/' + str(self.den)
```

Of course, a complete `Rational` class would have to implement methods for all of the basic numeric operations. You're probably itching to dig in and finish out this class. That's a great idea, but we suggest looking at the material in the next section before you tackle the completion of this class.

2.6   Incremental Development and Unit Testing

Once we break the development of a program into separate classes, it's nice to be able to test each class once it's developed. In fact, it's very convenient if we can test the class *as* it's being developed. In Python, one good way of testing an evolving class is to use the Python shell to try it out interactively. For example, we could test out the multiplication method for our `Rational` class:

```
>>> from Rational import Rational
>>> r1 = Rational(1,2)
>>> r2 = Rational(1,3)
>>> print r1 * r2
1/6
```

Testing a component in isolation like this is known as *unit testing*. By testing a single component, we can easily isolate where errors are occurring. Once we have confidence in the individual components, then we can start combining them into a system.

One disadvantage of interactive unit testing is that each time we change a component, we have to go back and re-create the tests. Suppose our multiplication test had given us an incorrect result; we would go back, locate the error, and fix the code. After making the fix, we would have to retype the four lines of testing code again. This is OK for small tests, but it becomes very tedious when the tests are more sophisticated.

An alternative to interactive unit testing is to write unit tests as actual programs that can be run whenever needed. This is such a common task that numerous frameworks have been developed to make writing unit tests easier. The Python library includes two different frameworks for unit testing: `unittest` and `doctest`. The Python `unittest` module is based on a popular framework (generically called `xUnit`) that has been ported to many object-oriented languages. We'll use this framework in our unit testing examples. Here is some code, using the `unittest` module, that tests our simple `Rational` class.

```python
# test_Rational.py
# unittest example

import sys
import unittest

sys.path.insert(0, '..')
from Rational import *

class RationalTest(unittest.TestCase):

    def testConstructorOneInt(self):

        r = Rational(-3)
        self.assertEqual(str(r), '-3/1')

    def testConstructorTwoInt(self):

        r = Rational(3, 4)
        self.assertEqual(str(r), '3/4')

    def testMul(self):

        r1 = Rational(2, 3)
        r2 = Rational(3, 4)
        r3 = r1 * r2
        self.assertEqual(str(r3), '6/12')
```

```
def main(argv):
    unittest.main()

if __name__ == '__main__':
    main(sys.argv)
```

Although there's not much code in this example, there are several things that you may not have seen before, starting right near the top with the `sys.path.insert`. Many programmers follow the convention of creating a subdirectory named `test` containing the code for tests. This keeps the production code for the program separated from the code that is written just for testing. Following this convention, we're assuming that `test_rational.py` is placed in a subdirectory a level below the directory where the code for the `Rational` class (`Rational.py`) is placed.

One issue with putting the testing code in its own directory is that Python will not know where to look when the testing code asks to import the `Rational` module. The sequence of directories that Python searches to find a module is called the *path*. Normally, the path contains Python's system directories where all the standard library modules are located and also the local directory wherever Python is executing. So there is no problem as long as we are importing either system-wide modules or modules that are in the same folder as the running program. In order for the testing code to import the `Rational` module, however, we need to modify the standard path. Python makes the path available to programmers as a list in the system module, `sys.path`. This is just a list of strings specifying the various directories where Python modules live. Executing `sys.path.insert(0,'..')` puts `".."` at the front of the path list. The `".."` is a convention to indicate the parent of the current directory (which is represented with `"."`, by the way). This allows the test code to search the parent directory for the `Rational.py` file when the line `from Rational import *` is executed.

The heart of the testing code is a class named `RationalTest` defined using the line `class RationalTest(unittest.TestCase):`. This declaration indicates that the `RationalTest` class inherits from the `TestCase` class in the `unittest` module. Another way to state this is the `RationalTest` class *subclasses* the `TestCase` class defined in the `unittest` module. By virtue of inheritance, any instance of `RationalTest` will also be an instance of the superclass `TestCase`. You can think of a `TestCase` instance as a set of tests that we want to run.

The `TestCase` superclass defines a number of very useful methods for unit tests. The two most commonly used are `assertEqual` (also known as `failUnlessEqual`) and `assertNotEqual` (also known as `failIfEqual`). Each method takes two additional parameters that are tested for equality and an optional third parameter that is a message to be displayed if the test fails. The `assertEqual` test fails if the two parameters are not equal, and the `assertNotEqual` fails if the two parameters are equal. The `TestCase` class supports many additional methods that you can learn about by consulting the `unittest` documentation.

Within our `RationalTest` class, each of the methods that start with the four letters `test` will be called automatically by the `unittest` framework when the testing code runs. The idea of unit testing is to write methods that test all the code you have written. You will notice in this case there are more test methods than methods in the `Rational` class. This is common since one test is often not enough to ensure that a function/method works correctly. To run the tests, we just need to issue a call to the `main` function in the `unittest` module. This function will automatically create instances of all the test classes in the file (those that are subclasses of `unittest.TestCase`) and then execute each of the testing methods. Note that each test method is run with a "fresh" test case, so that each test is independent and the order in which the tests run does not matter.

Here is the output of the `test_Rational.py` test code when all the tests pass:

```
...
----------------------------------------------------------------------
Ran 3 tests in 0.001s

OK
```

The three dots show the results of our three test methods. A dot indicates successful completion of the test. If the testing code raises an unhandled exception, the result is an "E" and a failed check results in an "F."

Of course, the results are more interesting when a test fails. If the `__mul__` method is changed so the one line contains `den = self.den * other.num` and the test program is executed again, we get the the following output.

```
..F
======================================================================
FAIL: testMul (__main__.RationalTest)
----------------------------------------------------------------------
Traceback (most recent call last):
  File "./test_Rational.py", line 39, in testMul
    self.assertEqual(str(r3), '6/12')
  File "/usr/lib/python2.2/unittest.py", line 286, in failUnlessEqual
    raise self.failureException, \
AssertionError: '6/9' != '6/12'


----------------------------------------------------------------------
Ran 3 tests in 0.004s

FAILED (failures=1)
```

Notice that the status line at the top of the output shows that the third test failed, and a traceback is printed stating exactly which line caused the failure.

Coding unit tests in this way provides numerous benefits. Obviously, it allows the tests to be run easily when we go back and modify the code. In fact, we can save all of our tests, and any time we make changes to the code we can easily rerun all of the tests, even the ones that passed previously. Running a modified program against the previously successful tests is called *regression testing*. It helps to ensure that the program continues to improve as it is developed (i.e., that new modifications haven't broken the previous functionality).

Another benefit of writing unit tests while writing the class is that they help us work out the design of a class. The testing code shows how a class is to be used, and writing the tests helps us determine if our class is well-designed and useful. In fact, some modern approaches to software development advocate *test-driven development*. With test-driven development, tests are always written before any actual production code is added to the system. That way, as each function/method is added, it is immediately testable. You can determine if it works correctly (i.e., passes your tests for that code) before writing the next function/method.

We think test-driven development is a very good technique. We recommend that you write the original class with each method containing just a `pass` statement. Next, write the test code for a method and then implement enough of the class to get the test to pass. Keep repeating this process of writing a test and modifying the class until the class is complete and passes all of the tests. Being able to run all the tests each time you make a change to the class will give you the confidence you need to try out new design ideas as they arise. A testing framework such as this helps make the promise of implementation independence a practical reality. And you'll be amazed at how quickly coding goes when coding and testing are done in tandem.

2.7 Chapter Summary

This chapter has covered the fundamental ideas of data abstraction and object-oriented programming. Here is a quick summary of some of the key ideas.

- An abstract data type (ADT) defines an API for manipulating data independent of the implementation; in object-oriented languages, ADTs are commonly implemented using classes.

- Encapsulation, polymorphism, and inheritance are the defining techniques used in objected-oriented code.

- Designing classes and programs is both art and science. A general rule is to study the problem statement and identify nouns as classes and verbs as methods.

- Operator overloading allows programmers to define methods to be called when the built-in operators such as +, -, <, >, etc. are used with instances of the programmer-defined class.

- Unit tests allow parts of a program to be tested in isolation. A unit-testing framework makes it convenient to write automated unit tests and facilitates the testing of code as it is written. Regression testing helps ensure that code changes do not "break" previously working components of a program.

- Test-driven development is a common technique that involves writing test code for each new feature before writing the production code that implements the feature.

2.8 Exercises

True/False Questions

1. To implement an ADT in Python, you must use classes.

2. If the programming language supports classes, you should usually use them when implementing an ADT.

3. Class variables can be shared by all instances of a class.

4. When designing a program, one way of locating potential objects is by looking for verbs in the system description.

5. *Encapsulation* refers to combining the data and methods into one syntactic unit.

6. With polymorphism, a programmer writes multi-way `if` statements to check the type of an object and determine which method to call.

7. Subclasses inherit methods defined in their superclasses.

8. Operator overloading allows programs to compute results that could not be computed without operator overloading.

9. To do operator overloading in Python, you must use classes.

10. Unit tests should be executed whenever you make a change to a class.

Multiple Choice Questions

1. When developing large software systems, you should:

    a) immediately sit down at the computer and start writing code

    b) design some of the system, write some code, possibly redesign it, and test the components as you write them

    c) design the entire system before you write any code

    d) implement the entire system before you test any of the code

2. Which parts of the program description will be most helpful in identifying possible objects for a system design?

    a) adjectives

    b) nouns

    c) verbs

    d) all of the above

3. Which parts of the program description will be most helpful in identifying possible methods in a system design?

    a) adjectives

    b) nouns

    c) verbs

    d) all of the above

4. How do you distinguish between instance variables and local variables for a method?

    a) instance variables are part of the data for a particular object and are needed in multiple methods while local variables are needed only within that method

    b) a class should never use local variables; all variables used in methods should be instance variables

    c) a class should never use instance variables; all variables used in methods should be local variables

    d) instance variables should be used for constants only

5. If you are examining a Python class that someone else wrote, how do you determine if a variable is a local variable or an instance variable?

   a) the same variable name is used in more than one method
   b) the variable is accessed by placing `self.` before the variable name
   c) the variable is used in the `__init__` method
   d) instance variables are always preceded by an underscore

6. When should you use class variables?

   a) when each instance of the class needs its own copy of the data
   b) when each instance of the class can share the same copy of the data
   c) when the data is constant
   d) b and c

7. If you are designing a class to represent a polynomial, which of the following should be instance variables?

   a) the coefficients
   b) a value to evaluate with the polynomial
   c) the result of evaluating the polynomial with a specific value
   d) all of the above

8. If you are designing a class to represent a polynomial, which of the following should be class variables?

   a) the coefficients
   b) a value to evaluate with the polynomial
   c) the result of evaluating the polynomial with a specific value
   d) none of the above

9. When writing unit tests using the Python `unittest` framework the test code is written as

   a) a number of functions
   b) a separate class that subclasses your class
   c) a separate class that subclasses `unittest.TestCase`
   d) part of the class you are testing

10. What is the purpose of unit testing?

   a) to help you to think about your design
   b) to help you find errors in your code
   c) to allow you to easily test your code each time you change it
   d) all of the above

Short-Answer Questions

1. What is the difference between the *interface* of a class and the *implementation* of a class?

2. What are some reasons for writing the unit testing code before writing the class code?

3. What are some reasons for intermixing the writing of the unit testing code and the class code?

4. What are some reasons for writing unit testing code after you write the class code?

5. What happens in Python if you use the same name for an instance variable and a method? Write a short example to try it.

6. Give two different specifications (i.e., list the instance variables and method names, but not the implementation of the methods) for a Deck class that simulates an entire deck of cards including methods you would want if you were going to simulate card games with this class.

7. What class or classes might be useful in a program that plays tic-tac-toe? What instance variables and what methods would your class(es) use?

8. What are the benefits of writing unit tests?

9. What is the purpose of operator overloading?

Programming Exercises

1. Write unit testing code for the Card class of section 2.3.

2. Implement the Card class using the alternative representation discussed in subsection 2.3.3. Test it using your unit tests from the previous exercise.

3. Write a simple implementation of a card deck to deal cards out randomly. Your Deck class will contain a list of card objects. Initially, the deck will contain one instance of each of the 52 possible cards. Your deck should implement a deal() method that chooses a random location from the list and "pops" that card. You should also implement a cardsLeft method that tells how many cards are left in the deck. Note: a more sophisticated Deck class is implemented in Chapter 3; using that design does not count.

4. Using the `Deck` class from the previous exercise, write a program that plays blackjack with two players.

5. Using the `Deck` class from exercise 3, write a program that plays a simple solitaire game. The game starts by dealing several cards from the deck face-up. If two of the cards have the same rank, two more cards are dealt from the deck face-up on top of them. The process continues until all of the cards have been dealt or there are no cards with matching ranks showing. A player "wins" if all the cards have been dealt. Your program should allow the user to choose the number of piles to use for the game and then simulate the dealing until the game is over.

6. Modify the previous exercise so that it calculates the probability of winning for any given number of piles.

7. Implement the `DataSet` class using each of the two concrete representations suggested in the chapter. Include code to test all of the methods.

8. Write a program to allow two players to play the game Othello (also known as Reversi) on the computer. If you are not familiar with the game, search the Internet for the rules of the game. Design your program by creating a class that keeps track of the pieces on the board and provides methods for determining if a move is legal, updating the board based on a legal move, and displaying the board (either as text or graphically). Also provide methods for determining what piece is at each position on the board.

9. Write a unit test for your Othello/Reversi class to test the methods that check for a legal move and update the board based on the move.

10. Complete the `Rational` class with the operators for the plus, minus, divide, and six comparison operators and write a unit testing class to test all the methods. The comparison operators should return `True` or `False`. For bonus points, have your class always store the fraction in reduced form. (Hint: use Euclid's GCD algorithm in the class constructor.)

11. Use your `Rational` class to write a program that investigates Egyptian fractions. An Egyptian fraction is formed as a sum of unit fractions (the numerator is 1) having unique denominators. For example $\frac{7}{8}$ can be represented as the sum: $\frac{1}{2} + \frac{1}{3} + \frac{1}{24}$. Your program should allow a user to enter an arbitrary fraction and then print out an equivalent Egyptian fraction. If necessary, do a bit of research to come up with an algorithm for the conversion.

12. Write a class to represent a polynomial. The class should store a list of the coefficients and the degree of the polynomial. Write the methods for the addition, subtraction, and multiplication methods. Write the `__str__` method that returns a string representation of the polynomial. Also provide a method for evaluating the polynomial at a specific value. Write a unit test for your polynomial class.

Chapter 3   Container Classes

———————————————

Objectives

- To understand the list ADT as a general container class for manipulating sequential collections.

- To understand how lists are implemented in Python and the implications this has for the efficiency of various list operations.

- To develop intuition about collection algorithms such as selection sort and use Python operator overloading to make new sortable classes.

- To learn about Python dictionaries as an implementation of a general mapping and understand the efficiency of various dictionary operations.

3.1   Overview

Program design gets more interesting when we start considering programs that manipulate large data sets. Typically, we need more efficient algorithms to operate on large collections. Oftentimes the key to an efficient algorithm lies in how the data is organized, that is, the so-called *data structures* on which the algorithms operate. Object-oriented programs often use *container classes* to manage collections of objects. An instance of a container class manages a single collection. Objects can be inserted into and retrieved from the container object at run-time. Python includes a number of container classes as built-in types. You are probably familiar with lists and dictionaries, which are the two main container classes in Python.

In this chapter, we review the basics of Python lists and dictionaries and also take a look at how these containers are implemented in Python. Knowing how a collection is implemented is often crucial to understanding the efficiency of the supported operations.

3.2   Python Lists

Lists are one of the main workhorse data structures in the Python language. Just about every program makes use of lists in some form. A thorough understanding of lists is essential for anyone writing in Python. Given their usefulness, it is not surprising that containers similar to Python lists are provided by virtually every high-level programming language.

Informally, a list is a collection of objects that is stored in sequential order. For example, a list might be used to represent the students in a class or a deck of cards. Because a list has an ordering, it is meaningful to talk about things such as the first object in a list or the next object in a list.

Using our new terminology from last chapter, we can think of a Python list as implementing an ADT for a sequential collection. Python provides quite a number of operations on lists. Some operations are supported by built-in functions and operators, whereas others are list methods. Here is a specification for some of the operations provided:

Concatenation (*list1* + *list2*) Returns a new list that contains the elements of *list1* followed by the elements of *list2*.

Repetition (*list1* * *int1* or *int1* * *list1*) Returns a new list corresponding to the list of elements obtained by concatenating *list1* with itself *int1* times.

Length (len(*list1*)) Returns the number of items in *list1*.

Index (*list1*[*int1*]) Returns the item at position *int1* in *list1*. The first item in the list is at index 0 and the last item is at index len(*list1*)-1.

Slice (*list1*[*int1* : *int2*]) Returns a new list containing the items in *list1* starting at position *int1* up to, but not including, *int2*. If $int2 \leq int1$ the resulting list is empty (assuming *int1* and *int2* are non-negative).

Check membership (*item* in *list1*) Returns **True** if *item* occurs in *list1* and **False** otherwise.

Add at end (*list1*.append(*obj1*)) Modifies *list1* by adding *obj1* to the end.

Add anywhere (*list1*.insert(*int1*,*obj1*)) Modifies *list1* by adding *obj1* at position *int1*. The original items from position *int1* on are "shifted" to make room.

Delete index (*list1*.pop(*int1*)) Returns the item at *list1*[*int1*] and modifies *list1* by deleting this item from the list. Items in position *int1*+1 on are shifted down one index to "fill the gap." If *int1* is not supplied, the last item in the sequence is the one deleted.

Remove object (*list1*.remove(*obj1*)) Deletes the first occurrence of *obj1* in *list1*.

You probably used descriptions similar to this when you first learned how to use Python lists. Notice that the description says nothing about how a Python list is actually implemented in the computer; that's the hallmark of an ADT. A little later on, we'll take a look under the hood to see how lists can be implemented. Right now, we're taking a client's point of view and looking only at how lists are used.

3.3 A Sequential Collection: A Deck of Cards

Since Python provides an implementation of lists, it is common to make use of this built-in type to implement various collection abstractions. Continuing our card-game example from last chapter, let's try implementing a collection to represent a deck of cards. As a starting point, we need to determine the set of operations that will be useful for a deck of cards. Obviously, we will need a way to create a new (full) deck of cards. Usually, the deck is shuffled and used to deal cards into hands. If we are modeling the ADT using a Python class, we might try something along these lines:

```
class Deck(object):

    def __init__(self):
        """post: Create a 52-card deck in standard order"""

    def shuffle(self):
        """Shuffle the deck
        post: randomizes the order of cards in self"""

    def deal(self):
        """Deal a single card
        pre:  self is not empty
        post: Returns the next card in self, and removes it from self."""
```

A quick inspection of this specification shows a shortcoming of our design so far. Notice that the `deal` method contains a precondition, since we can't deal any card from an empty deck. For completeness, we should add a way for client code to check this precondition. We could add something like an `isEmpty` method that tells when the deck is exhausted. More generally, we might have a `size` method that gives the number of cards left in the deck. In many card games, it's important to know how many cards are left, so the latter approach seems a bit more useful. Let's add it to the specification.

```python
def size(self):
    """Cards left
    post: Returns the number of cards in self"""
```

Adding this operation to the ADT also allows us to state the precondition for the `deal` method more precisely. Here's the improved specification:

```python
def deal(self):
    """Deal a single card
    pre:  self.size() > 0
    post: Returns the next card in self, and removes it from self."""
```

Having thought out the interface for our ADT, we're now ready to start implementing. Obviously, a deck is a sequence of cards, so a natural choice of representation is to use a Python list to hold the cards in the deck. Here's a constructor for our `Deck`.

```python
# Deck.py
from random import randrange
from Card import Card

class Deck(object):

    def __init__(self):
        cards = []
        for suit in Card.SUITS:
            for rank in Card.RANKS:
                cards.append(Card(rank,suit))
        self.cards = cards
```

Notice how this code uses nested loops to produce every possible combination of rank and suit. Each subsequent card is appended to the list of cards, and the resulting list is stored away as an instance variable of the `Deck` object.

Once we have created a `Deck` object, checking its size and dealing cards from the deck can be accomplished with simple list operations.

```
def size(self):
    return len(self.cards)

def deal(self):
    return self.cards.pop()
```

The `deal` method returns cards in order from the end of the list. Using this approach the ordering imposed by the Python list data structure determines the order in which the cards are dealt.

Now all we need is a method to shuffle a deck (i.e., put it into a random order). This gives us a chance to exercise our algorithm development skills. You probably know some ways of shuffling a deck of cards, but the usual methods don't transfer very well into code. One way to think about the problem is to consider the task of putting the cards into a specific arrangement. The shuffle operation should ensure that any of the 52! possible arrangements of the deck is equally likely. That means that every card in the deck has to have an equal chance of being the first card, and each of the remaining cards has an equal chance of being the second card, etc.

We can implement a shuffle algorithm by building a new list out of the cards in the original list. We start with an empty list and repeatedly transfer a card chosen at random from the old list to the new list. Here's how the algorithm looks in code:

```
def shuffle(self):
    cards0 = self.cards
    cards1 = []
    while cards0 != []:
        # delete a card at random from those in original list
        pos = randrange(len(cards0))
        card = cards0.pop(pos)

        # transfer the card to the new list
        cards1.append(card)

    # replace old list with the new
    self.cards = cards1
```

We can improve this algorithm slightly by doing the shuffle in place. Rather than going to the trouble of building a second list, we could choose a card at random and move it to the front of the existing list. Then we ccould pick a card from locations 1 through n and move it to position 1, etc. There is one subtlety in this approach; when we place a random card into a given position, we have to be careful not to clobber the card that is currently in that position. That is, we need to save the card that is being replaced somewhere so that it is still part of the pool for subsequent placement. The easiest way to do this is to simply swap the positions of the two cards. Here's the in-place version of our shuffle algorithm:

```python
def shuffle(self):
    n = self.size()
    cards = self.cards
    for i,card in enumerate(cards):
        pos = randrange(i,n)
        cards[i] = cards[pos]
        cards[pos] = card
```

Notice that in this code it is not necessary to do `self.cards = cards` at the end of the method. The assignment statement immediately before the loop sets `cards` to be a reference to the same list as `self.cards`. Therefore, the changes made to this list (swapping cards) are changing `self.cards`. The local variable `cards` is used for convenience (so we don't have to keep typing `self.cards`) and efficiency (retrieval of local variable values is more efficient than retrieval of instance variables).

We now have a complete `Deck` class. Let's take it for an interactive test drive.

```
>>> d = Deck()
>>> print d.deal()
King of Spades
>>> print d.deal()
Queen of Spades
>>> print d.deal()
Jack of Spades
>>> d.shuffle()
>>> d.size()
49
>>> print d.deal()
Seven of Hearts
>>> print d.deal()
Nine of Diamonds
```

Notice how the initial deck deals cards out from the standard ordering. After shuffling, the cards come out randomly, just as we expect.

3.4 A Sorted Collection: Hand

In the previous section, we used a Python list as a container class to implement a deck of cards. A deck has an implicit ordering of cards, namely the order in which the cards are dealt, and so it made sense to use a list to store the cards. Of course, the particular order that the deck is in is supposed to be random; that's why we shuffle a deck. Sometimes we want the objects in a container to be in a specific order according to the value of each item. The process of putting a collection in order by value is called *sorting*. In this section, we'll look at an example of a sorted collection.

3.4.1 Creating a Bridge Hand

Let's put our `Deck` class to work in an actual application. Suppose we are writing a program to play the popular card game bridge. Building such a program incrementally, our first task might be to deal four 13-card hands from a shuffled deck. We'd also like to display the hands nicely so that we can analyze them. For example, newspapers that carry bridge columns often show hands arranged by suit (in the order spades, hearts, diamonds, clubs) with cards in each suit arranged by decreasing rank (ace, king, queen, ..., 2). Note that aces are considered higher than kings in bridge.

Our task is to deal cards into hands and then to arrange those hands into the specified order. This suggests the invention of a new kind of collection, a `Hand` class. A `Hand` is initially empty, and cards are added to it one by one as they are dealt. Considering our `Hand` as an ADT, we need operations to create a hand, add a card, put the hand in order (sort it), and display the cards in the hand. An initial specification of the class looks like this:

```
# Hand.py
class Hand(object):

    """A labeled collection of cards that can be sorted"""

    def __init__(self, label=""):
        """Create an empty collection with the given label."""

    def add(self, card):
        """ Add card to the hand """

    def sort(self):
        """ Arrange the cards in descending bridge order."""

    def dump(self):
        """ Print out contents of the Hand."""
```

We have added to our initial description the ability to give each hand a name or label to identify it. Traditionally, bridge hands are identified with the compass points north, east, south and west. Notice that we have also added a `dump` method to display the contents of the hand. This is useful for testing and debugging purposes.

Since hands are ordered, a Python list is again the container of choice for implementing the new collection. Most of the operations are trivial to implement. The constructor must store away the label and create an empty collection. Let's store it in an instance variable called `cards`:

```python
# Hand.py
class Hand(object):

    def __init__(self, label=""):
        self.label = label
        self.cards = []
```

The `add` operation takes a card as a parameter and puts it into the collection. A simple `append` suffices:

```python
    def add(self, card):
        self.cards.append(card)
```

To dump the contents of the hand, we just need to print out a heading and then loop through the list to print each card.

```python
    def dump(self):
        print self.label + "'s Cards:"
        for c in self.cards:
            print "   ", c
```

Let's try out what we've got so far.

```python
>>> from Hand import Hand
>>> from Card import Card
>>> h = Hand("North")
>>> h.add(Card(5,"c"))
>>> h.add(Card(10,"d"))
>>> h.add(Card(13,"s"))
>>> h.dump()
North's Cards:
    Five of Clubs
    Ten of Diamonds
    King of Spades
>>>
```

That looks good. Notice how the listing of the cards is indented under the hand heading.

Comparing Cards

That leaves us with the problem of putting the hand in order. The sorting problem is an important and well-studied one in computer science. We'll take a quick look at it here and revisit it again in later chapters. If we want to put some things in a particular order, the first problem we have to solve is what exactly the ordering should be.

In the case of our bridge program, we want to order our **Card** objects, grouping them first by suit and then ordering by rank within suit. Usually orderings are determined by a relation such as "less than." For example, if we say that a list of numbers is in increasing order, that means that for any two numbers x and y in the list, if $x < y$ then x must precede y in the list. Similarly, we need a way of comparing cards so that we can order them in our **Hand**. In Chapter 2, we saw how Python operator overloading allows us to build new classes that "act like" existing classes. Here, we would like our cards to behave like numbers so that we can compare them using the standard Python operators such as $<$, $==$, $>$, and so on.

We can do this by defining methods for these operations in the **Card** class. Here are the definitions of the "hook" functions for these operators.

```python
def __eq__(self, other):

    return (self.suit_char == other.suit_char and
            self.rank_num == other.rank_num)

def __lt__(self, other):

    if self.suit_char == other.suit_char:
        return self.rank_num < other.rank_num
    else:
        return self.suit_char < other.suit_char

def __ne__(self, other):

    return not(self == other)

def __le__(self, other):

    return self < other or self == other
```

Notice that we've given "primitive" definitions for **__eq__** and **__lt__**; the rest of the necessary operators can easily be defined in terms of these two. We have not bothered to write definitions for **__gt__** and **__ge__** because Python gives us these for free. In an expression such as **x > y**, when the **>** operator is not implemented

for x, Python will try the symmetric operation y < x. Similarly, x >= y invokes y
<= x.

Now that our Card objects are comparable, there's one last detail to clean up.
When we originally created the Card class, we used a rank of 1 to represent an ace,
but in bridge aces are the highest card, coming right after the king. Right now, our
comparison method will put aces at the low end, since the rank is 1.

We can handle this issue in a couple of ways. One approach would be to code
a special case for aces into the comparison methods. Another solution is to simply
modify the Card class to use ranks that run from 2 to 14 with 14 representing the
ace. Taking the latter approach, the start of our modified Card class would now
look like this:

```
class Card(object):
    """A simple playing card. A Card is characterized by two
    components:
    rank: an integer value in the range 2-14, inclusive (Two-Ace)
    suit: a character in "cdhs" for clubs, diamonds, hearts, and
    spades."""

    SUITS = "cdhs"
    SUIT_NAMES = ["Clubs", "Diamonds", "Hearts", "Spades"]

    RANKS = range(2,15)
    RANK_NAMES = ["Two", "Three", "Four", "Five", "Six",
                  "Seven", "Eight", "Nine", "Ten",
                  "Jack", "Queen", "King", "Ace"]
...
```

Recall that our Deck class actually has to generate every possible card to create
the initial deck. As such, the Deck class depends on the Card class, and changing the
interface to the Card class might break the Deck class, since it might not know that
14 is now a legal rank but 1 isn't. Fortunately, when we originally coded up Deck we
used Card.RANKS to generate all the possible ranks rather than using a hard-coded
range such as range(1,14). By changing this constant in the Card class, we still
are playing with a full deck. This illustrates the design advantage of using named
constants rather than filling your code with "magic values." In this case, use of the
constant helps us maintain the abstraction barrier between Card and Deck.

Given these modifications to our Card class, we can now compare cards just as
if they were numbers using the relational operators:

```
>>> Card(14,"c") < Card(2,"d")
True
>>> Card(8,"s") > Card(10,"s")
False
>>> Card(6,"c") == Card(6,"c")
True
>>>
```

Notice how the ace of clubs is "less than" the two of diamonds, since we have said that all clubs proceed any diamond.

3.4.3 Sorting Cards

Now that we can compare cards, we just need to come up with an algorithm to put them in order. Perhaps surprisingly, we can use an algorithm very similar to the one we used to shuffle the deck. Instead of choosing a card at random to become the first card in the hand, we choose the biggest card. Then we choose the biggest of the remaining cards to be the next one, and so on. This algorithm is known as a selection sort. As we'll see later, it's not the most efficient way of sorting a list, but it's an easy algorithm to develop and analyze.

In Python, a particularly simple way to implement the selection sort algorithm is to use two lists. The "old" list is the original hand, and the "new" list will be the ordered hand, which starts out empty. As long as there are cards in the old list, we simply find the largest one, remove it from the old list, and place it at the back of the new list. When the old list is empty, the new list contains the cards in descending order. Here's an implementation:

```python
def sort(self):
    cards0 = self.cards
    cards1 = []
    while cards0 != []:
        next_card = max(cards0)
        cards0.remove(next_card)
        cards1.append(next_card)
    self.cards = cards1
```

Notice how the step of finding the largest card in the old list (`cards0`) is accomplished using the Python built-in function `max`. This is a nice side effect of implementing the comparison operators. Now that `Card` objects can be compared, any existing Python sequence operations that rely on comparing elements can be used on collections of `Card` objects. That certainly simplifies things, doesn't it?

Notice that we have developed a general sorting algorithm. It should work for sorting lists of any type of object. Right now, it sorts by creating a brand new list that is in sorted order. However, just like the shuffling algorithm we did earlier, the selection sort can easily be converted to sort a list in place. Performing this conversion is left as an exercise.

Actually, we have done more work than necessary to sort our hands. Since our Card objects are now comparable, we can let Python do the sorting of the cards for us by using the sort method that is built into the Python list type. Of course, the built-in sort will put the cards into ascending order. To get the cards into descending order, we'll need to reverse them after sorting. Here's a version of the sort method using this approach.

```
def sort(self):
    self.cards.sort()
    self.cards.reverse()
```

That's certainly easiest, but if we had jumped to this solution right away, we would have missed out on the excitement of developing our own sorting algorithm.

How efficient is the selection sort algorithm that we developed? Obviously the main work of the function is being done inside the while loop. Notice that the loop continues until the cards0 list is empty. Each time through the loop, exactly one item is removed from cards0, so it's clear that this loop will execute n times, where n is the number of items in the original list. Each time through the loop, we need to find the largest card in cards0. In order to find the largest card, the Python max function must look at each card in the list in turn and keep track of which is the largest. That's a $\Theta(c)$ operation, where c is the number of items in the list being analyzed. The first time through the while loop, max examines n cards. The next time through, it only has $n-1$ cards to consider, then $n-2$, etc. So the total work done in all the iterations of the while loop is $n + (n-1) + (n-2) + \ldots + 1$. As we discussed in subsection 1.3.4, this sum is given by the formula $\frac{n(n+1)}{2}$. That makes our selection sort at least an n^2 algorithm. While it can be no better than $\Theta(n^2)$, it could even be worse, depending on the efficiencies of the remove and insert methods, which are also executed in the body of the while loop. We'll consider those operations in section 3.5.

By contrast, the built-in sort method in Python is a $\Theta(n \log n)$ algorithm, which is much more efficient. For our simple hands of 13 cards, that doesn't make much difference, but for a large list, it can mean the difference between sorting the collection in seconds vs. hours or days. We'll see how to design more efficient sorting algorithms in section 6.5.

3.5 Python List Implementation

When we analyzed the selection sort above, we concentrated on the `max` operation, which turned out to be $\Theta(n)$, but we ignored the `insert` and `remove` methods for lists. It turns out that both of these methods have the same time complexity as `max`. How do we know that? Just as the choice of using a Python list to implement our collection classes `Deck` and `Hand` determines the relative efficiency of the methods in these classes, the choice of data structures in the implementation of Python lists determines the efficiency of various list operations. Therefore, understanding the true efficiency of various operations requires some understanding of Python's underlying data structures.

3.5.1 Array-based Lists

So how can we efficiently store and access a collection of objects in computer memory? Recall that computer memory is simply a sequence of storage locations. Each storage location has a number associated with it (much like an index) called its *address*. A single data item may be stored across a number of contiguous memory locations. To retrieve an item from memory, we need a way to either look up or compute the starting address of the object. If we want to store a collection of objects, we need to have some systematic method for figuring out where each object in the collection is located.

Consider the case when all of the objects in a collection are the same size, that is they all require the same number of bytes to be stored. This would be the case with a homogeneous (all the same type) collection. A simple method for storing the collection would be to allocate a single contiguous area of memory sufficient to hold the entire collection. The objects could then be stored one after the next. For example, suppose an integer value requires 4 bytes (32 bits) of memory to store. A collection of 100 integers could be stored sequentially into 400 bytes of memory. Let's say the collection of integers starts at the memory location with the address 1024. This means the number at index 0 in the list starts at address 1024, index 1 is at 1028, index 2 is at 1032, etc. The location of the ith item can be computed simply using the formula $address\_of\_ith = 1024 + 4 * i$.

What we have just described is a data structure known as an *array*. Arrays are a common data structure used for storing collections, and many programming languages use arrays as a basic container type. Arrays are very memory efficient and support quick random access (meaning we can "jump" directly to the item we want) via the address calculation we just discussed. By themselves, however, they are somewhat restrictive. One issue is the fact that arrays must generally be homogeneous. For example, it's usually not possible to have an array that contains both integers and strings. In order for the address calculations to work, all elements must be the same size.

Another shortcoming of arrays is that the size of the array is determined when memory is allocated for it. In programming language terminology, arrays are said to be *static*. When we allocate an array for 100 items, the underlying operating system grants us an area of memory sufficient to hold that collection. The memory around the array will be allocated to other objects (or even other running programs). There is no way for the array to grow, should more elements be added later. Programmers can work around this limitation to some extent by creating an array large enough to hold some theoretical maximum collection size. By keeping track of how many slots of the array are actually in use, the programmer can allow the collection to grow and shrink up to that maximum size. However, this negates the memory efficiency of arrays, since it forces the programmer to request more memory than might actually be needed. And, of course, we're still out of luck if the size of the collection needs to grow beyond the anticipated maximum.

In contrast to arrays, Python lists are heterogeneous (they can mix objects of different types) and dynamic (they grow and shrink). Underneath, Python lists are actually implemented using arrays. Remember that Python variables store references to the actual data objects. Don't worry too much if you are not familiar with or do not fully understand the concept of references; we will discuss them in detail in the next chapter. The point here is that what is stored in the consecutive memory locations of the Python list array are the *addresses* of actual data objects. Each address is the same length (typically 32 or 64 bits on modern CPUs). To retrieve a value from a list, the Python interpreter first uses the indexing formula to find the location of the reference (address) to the object and then uses the reference to retrieve the object. So an array with fixed-sized elements can be used to store the addresses that are then used to retrieve arbitrarily sized objects.

Of course, Python lists can also grow by calling methods such as `insert` and `append`. Internally, Python allocates a fixed-sized array for a list and keeps track of this maximum fixed size and the current size of the list. When an attempt is made to add elements beyond the current maximum size, a new contiguous section of memory large enough to store all the elements must be allocated. The references stored in the old array are then copied to the new larger array, and finally the memory for storing the old list is deallocated (given back to the operating system). Using this trick of dynamic array allocation, Python lists can continue to grow as long as enough system memory is available to hold the new list.

3.5.2   Efficiency Analysis

Knowing that Python lists are implemented as dynamically resizing arrays, we are now in a position to analyze the run-time efficiency of various list operations.

Allocating a new larger array is a relatively expensive operation, so the new array that is allocated is typically significantly larger. Allocating a much larger array prevents the resize operation from being necessary until quite a number of additional items have been added to the array. This means appending onto the end of a Python list will occasionally require $\Theta(n)$ computation (to allocate a new array and copy the existing items over), but most of the time it is a $\Theta(1)$ operation. If the size of the array is doubled each time it needs to be made larger, then the $\Theta(n)$ resize operation only needs to be executed every n appends. Amortizing the cost of creating the new larger array over the n appends that can be performed without the resize operation results in the average cost of an append being $\Theta(1)$.

The situation for arbitrary insertion operations anywhere in the list is a little different. Because the elements of an array are in contiguous memory locations, to insert into the middle of an array we have to first create a "hole" by shifting all of the following items one place to the right. When the insertion is at the very front of the list, the Python interpreter has to move all n elements currently in the array. So the insertion operation is still $\Theta(n)$ even if the size doubling trick is used when the array is full.

Python lists also support a method to delete elements from an existing list. The analysis for deletion is the same as for insertion. If we delete the element in position four, all the elements in positions five and above must be shifted down one location. So deletion, like insertion, is a $\Theta(n)$ operation. When deleting elements, we do not need to change the maximum size of the list; however, if a list grows very large for a short time period and then shrinks and stays much smaller for the rest of the program, the memory allocated to store the largest size will always be in use.

3.6   Python Dictionaries (Optional)

Python lists are an example of a sequential data structure. There is an inherent ordering of the data. Even in our implementation of the randomly shuffled deck, the items in the underlying list are still indexed by the natural numbers (0, 1, 2, ...), which gives the collection a natural ordering. In fact, one can view lists abstractly as just a kind of *mapping* from indexes to items in the list. That is, each valid index is associated with (maps to) a particular list item.

The idea of mapping is very general and need not be restricted to using numbers as the indexes. If you think about it a bit, you can probably come up with all sorts of useful collections that involve other sorts of mappings. For example, a phone book is a mapping from names to phone numbers. Mappings pop up everywhere in programming, and that is why Python provides an efficient built-in data structure for managing them, namely a dictionary.

3.6.1 A Dictionary ADT

You have probably run across Python dictionaries before, but perhaps not given them much thought. A dictionary is a data structure that allows us to associate keys with values, that is, it implements a mapping. Abstractly, we can think of a dictionary as just a set of ordered (`key, value`) pairs. Viewed as an ADT, we just need a few operations in order to have a useful container type.

`Create`
>   post: Returns an empty dictionary.

`put(key,value)`
>   post: The value `value` is associated with `key` in the dictionary. (`key,value`) is now the one and only pair in the dictionary having the given key.

`get(key)`
>   pre: There is an `X` such that (`key,X`) is in the dictionary.
>   post: Returns `X`.

`delete(key)`
>   pre: There is an `X` such that (`key,X`) is in the dictionary.
>   post: (`key,X`) is removed from the dictionary.

There are many programming situations that call for dictionary-like structures. Some programming languages such as Python and Perl provide built-in implementations of this important ADT. Other languages such as C++ and Java provide them as part of a standard collection library.

3.6.2 Python Dictionaries

A Python dictionary provides a particular implementation of the dictionary ADT. Let's start with a simple example. Remember in our `Card` example we needed to be able to turn characters representing suits into full suit names. That's a perfect job for a dictionary. We could define a suitable Python dictionary like this:

```
suits = { "c":"Clubs", "d":"Diamonds", "h":"Hearts", "s":"Spades" }
```

As you can see, the syntax for a dictionary literal resembles our abstract description of a dictionary being a set of pairs. In Python, the key-value pairs are joined with a colon. In this case, we are saying that the string `"c"` maps to the string `"Clubs"`, `"d"` maps to `"Diamonds"`, etc.

Values can be retrieved from a Python dictionary via a `get` method, but Python also allows dictionaries to be indexed in a manner similar to lists. Here are some interactive examples:

```
>>> suits
{"h": "Hearts", "c": "Clubs", "s": "Spades", "d": "Diamonds"}
>>> suits.get("c")
'Clubs'
>>> suits["c"]
'Clubs'
>>> suits["s"]
'Spades'
>>> suits["j"]
Traceback (most recent call last):
  File "<stdin>", line 1, in ?
KeyError: "j"
>>> suits.get("j")
>>> suits.get("x", "Not There")
'Not There'
```

Notice that when `suits` was evaluated, the key-value pairs did not print out in the same order as when the dictionary was created. Dictionaries do not preserve the ordering of items, only the mapping. The last interactions show a subtle difference between indexing and the `get` operation. Trying to index into a dictionary using a nonexistent key raises a `KeyError` exception. However, the `get` method simply returns `None` as a default value in this case. As illustrated in the last interaction, `get` also allows an optional second parameter to provide an alternative default value, should the key lookup fail.

The abstract `put` operation for changing entries in a dictionary or extending it with new entries is implemented via assignment in Python. Again, this makes the syntax for working with dictionaries very similar to that of lists. Here are a few examples:

```
>>> suits["j"] = "Joker"
>>> suits
{'h': 'Hearts', 'c': 'Clubs', 'j': 'Joker', 's': 'Spades', 'd': 'Diamonds'}
>>> suits["j"]
'Joker'
>>> suits["c"] = "Clovers"
>>> suits["s"] = "Shovels"
>>> suits
{'h': 'Hearts', 'c': 'Clovers', 'j': 'Joker', 's': 'Shovels', 'd': 'Diamonds'}
```

To remove items, Python dictionaries understand the `del` function, just as Python lists do. You can also remove all the entries from a dictionary using the `clear` method.

```
>>> suits
{'h': 'Hearts', 'c': 'Clovers', 'j': 'Joker', 's': 'Shovels', 'd':
'Diamonds'}
>>> del suits['j']
>>> suits
{'h': 'Hearts', 'c': 'Clovers', 's': 'Shovels', 'd': 'Diamonds'}
>>> suits.clear()
>>> suits
{}
```

In addition to these basic operations, Python provides a number of conveniences for working with dictionaries. For example, we often want to do something to every item in a dictionary. For that, it's useful to deal with the dictionary in a sequential fashion. Python dictionaries support three methods for producing list representations of dictionary components: `keys` returns a list of keys, `values` returns a list of values, and `items` returns a list of (`key,value`) pairs.[1] You can also directly iterate through the keys of a dictionary using a `for` loop and check whether a given key is in the dictionary using the `in` operator.

---

[1]In Python 3.0, these methods return iterator objects (see Chapter 4). They can easily be converted to lists, for example `list(myDictionary.items())`.

```
>>> suits.keys()
['h', 'c', 's', 'd']
>>> suits.values()
['Hearts', 'Clovers', 'Shovels', 'Diamonds']
>>> suits.items()
[('h', 'Hearts'), ('c', 'Clovers'), ('s', 'Shovels'), ('d', 'Diamonds')]
>>> for key in suits:
...     print key, suits[key]

h Hearts
c Clovers
s Shovels
d Diamonds
>>> 'c' in suits
True
>>> 'x' in suits
False
```

3.6.3 Dictionary Implementation

As with virtually any ADT, there are numerous ways one could go about implementing dictionaries. The choice of implementation will determine how efficient the various operations will be. One simple representation would be to store the dictionary entries as a list of key-value pairs. A `get` operation would involve some form of lookup on the list to find the pair with the specified key. Other operations could also be performed using simple list manipulation. Unfortunately, this approach will not be very efficient, as some of the operations will require $\Theta(n)$ effort. (An exact analysis of the situation is left as an exercise.)

Python uses a more efficient data structure called a *hash table*. Hash tables are covered in-depth in section 13.5. Here we just want to give you some intuition so that you can understand the efficiency of various dictionary operations. That will enable you to judge the efficiency of algorithms that use Python dictionaries.

The heart of a hash table is a *hashing function*. A hashing function takes a key as a parameter and performs some simple calculations on it to produce a number. Since all data on the computer is ultimately stored as bits (binary numbers), it's pretty easy to come up with hashing functions. Python actually has a built-in function `hash` that does this. You can try it out interactively.

```
>>> hash(2)
2
>>> hash(3.4)
-751553844
>>> hash("c")
-212863774
>>> hash("hello")
-1267296259
>>> hash(None)
135367456
>>> hash((1,"spam",4,"U"))
40436063
>>> hash([1,"spam",4,"U"])
Traceback (most recent call last):
  File "<stdin>", line 1, in ?
TypeError: list objects are unhashable
```

Feeding anything that is "hashable" to hash produces an int result. Take a close look at the last two interactions. A tuple is hashable, but a list is not. One requirement of a hash function is that whenever it is called on a particular object, it must always produce the exact same result. Since the hash function relies on the underlying representation of the object to produce a hash value, the value is guaranteed to be valid only for objects whose underlying representations are not subject to change. In other words, we can only hash immutable objects. Numbers, strings, and tuples are all immutable and, hence, hashable. Lists can be changed, so Python does not allow them to be hashed.

With a suitable hash function in hand, it's easy to create a hash table to implement a dictionary. A hash table is really just a large list that stores (key,value) pairs. However, the pairs are not just stored sequentially one right after another. Instead they are stored in the list at an index determined by hashing the key. For example, suppose we allocate a list of size 1000 (this is our "table"). To store the pair ("c","Clubs") we compute hash("c") % 1000 = 226. Thus, the item will be stored in location 226. Notice that the remainder operation guarantees we get a result in range(1000), which will be a valid index for our table. With a good hashing function, items will be distributed across the table in a relatively uniform way.

As long as no two keys in the dictionary hash to the exact same location, this implementation will be very efficient. Inserting a new item takes constant time, since we just apply the hash function and assign the item to a location in the list. Lookup has similar complexity; we just compute the hash and then we know where to go grab the item. To delete an item we can just put a special marker (e.g., None) into the appropriate slot. So all basic dictionary operations can be accomplished in constant ($\Theta(1)$) time.

But what happens when two keys hash to the same spot? This is called a *collision*. Dealing with collisions is an important issue that is covered in section 13.5. For now it suffices to note that there are good techniques for dealing with this problem. Using these techniques and ensuring a table of adequate size yields data structures that, in practice, allow for constant time operations. Python dictionaries are very efficient and can easily handle thousands, even millions of entries, provided you have enough memory available. The Python interpreter itself relies heavily on the use of dictionaries to maintain namespaces, so the dictionary implementation has been highly optimized.

3.6.4 An Extended Example: A Markov Chain

Let's put our new knowledge of dictionaries to use in a program that combines several Python container classes to build Markov models. A Markov model is a statistical technique for modelling systems that change over time. One application of Markov models is in the area of systems for natural language understanding. For example, a speech recognition system can use predictions about what word is likely to come next in a sentence in order to decide among homonyms such as "their," "they're," and "there."

Our task is to develop a Markov class that could be used in such applications. We will demonstrate our class by using it to construct a program that can generate "random" language of a particular style. For example, if we train the program by feeding it mystery novels, it will generate gibberish that sounds like it came from a (really) bad mystery novel.

The basic idea behind a Markov model of language is that one can make predictions about the next word of an utterance by looking at some small sequence of preceding words. For example, a trigram model looks at the preceding two words to predict the next (third) word in a sequence. More or fewer words could be used as a "window" depending on the application. For example, a bigram model would predict the probabilities for the next word based only on the immediately preceding word. Our initial design will be for a trigram model; extending the program to arbitrary length prefixes is left as an exercise.

Here is a quick specification of our Markov class.

```
class Markov(object):

    """A simple trigram Markov model.  The current state is a sequence
        of the two words seen most recently. Initially, the state is
        (None, None), since no words have been seen. Scanning the
        sentence "The man ate the pasta" would cause the
        model to go through the sequence of states: [(None,None),
        (None, 'The'), ('The', 'man'), ('man','ate'), ('ate','the'),
        ('the','pasta')]"""

    def __init__(self):

        """post: creates an empty Markov model with initial state
                (None, None)."""

    def add(self, word):

        """post: Adds word as a possible following word for current
                state of the Markov model and sets state to
                incorporate word as most recently seen.

            ex: If state was ("the", "man") and word is "ate" then
                "ate" is added as a word that can follow "... the man" and
                the state is now ("man", "ate")"""

    def randomNext(self):

        """post: Returns a random choice from among the possible choices
                of next words, given the current state, and updates the
                state to reflect the word produced.

            ex: If the current state is ("the", "man"), and the known
                next words are ["ate", "ran", "hit", "ran"], one of
                these is selected at random. Suppose "ran" is selected,
                then the new state will be: ("man", "ran"). Note the
                list of next words can contain duplicates so the
                relative frequency of a word in the list represents its
                probability of being the next word."""

    def reset(self):

        """post: The model state is reset to its initial
                (None, None) state.

            note: This does not change the transition information that
                has been learned so far (via add()), it
                just resets the state so we can start adding
                transitions or making predictions for a "fresh"
                sequence."""
```

Reading this specification closely reveals a number of container structures that we must weave together to produce a working class. An instance of the `Markov` class must always know its current state, which is a sequence of the last two words encountered. We could represent this sequence as either a list or a tuple. Given the current state, we need some sort of model that allows us to retrieve a collection of possible next words. That's just a mapping, so we can use a dictionary to implement the model. The keys for the dictionary will be pairs of words, and the values will be lists of possible next words. Note we must use a tuple to represent the word pair, since Python lists are not hashable.

We are now in a position to write the code for this class.

```python
import random

class Markov(object):

    def __init__(self):
        self.model = {}  # maps states to lists of words
        self.state = (None, None)  # last two words processed

    def add(self, word):
        if self.state in self.model:
            # we have an existing list of words for this state
            # just add this new one (word).
            self.model[self.state].append(word)
        else:
            # first occurrence of this state, create a new list
            self.model[self.state] = [word]
        # transition to the next state given next word
        self._transition(word)

    def reset(self):
        self.state = (None, None)

    def randomNext(self):
        # get list of next words for this state
        lst = self.model[self.state]
        # choose one at random
        choice = random.choice(lst)
        # transition to next state, given the word choice
        self._transition(choice)
        return choice

    def _transition(self, next):
        # help function to construct next state
        self.state = (self.state[1], next)
```

You should read this code carefully to make sure that you understand how the class makes use of Python dictionaries, lists, and tuples.

All that remains to complete our gibberish-generating program is to write some code to "train" a model on a large sample of input text and then use the resulting model to generate a stream of output. Here are a couple of functions that fit the bill.

```
# test_Markov.py
def makeWordModel(filename):
    # creates a Markov model from words in filename
    infile = open(filename)
    model = Markov()
    for line in infile:
        words = line.split()
        for w in words:
            model.add(w)
    infile.close()
    # Add a sentinel at the end of the text
    model.add(None)
    model.reset()
    return model

def generateWordChain(markov, n):
    # generates up to n words of output from a model
    words = []
    for i in range(n):
        next = markov.randomNext()
        if next is None: break  # got to a final state
        words.append(next)
    return " ".join(words)
```

Here is an example of the output obtained by training a model on Lewis Carroll's *Alice's Adventures in Wonderland*:

> Alice was silent. The King looked anxiously at the mushroom for a rabbit! 'I suppose I ought to have it explained,' said the Caterpillar angrily, rearing itself upright as it was written to nobody, which isn't usual, 'Oh, don't talk about cats or dogs either,' if you want to go nearer till she got up and down in an encouraging opening for a minute or two. 'They couldn't have wanted it much,' said Alice, swallowing down her anger as well as she did not get dry again: they had a little before she made it out to sea. So they began solemnly dancing round and round Alice, every now and then treading on her face brightened up at the Caterpillar's making such a curious appearance in the middle of one!

As you can see, parts of this output are tantalizingly close to coherent sentences. In contrast, here is sample output from a program that just chooses words at random from the text:

of cup,' sort!' forehead you However, house the went to me unhappy up impossible settled We had help the always in see, forgot tree of you 'for night? because hadn't her ear. all confused sit took the care went quite do up, 'How three An Turtle, the was soldiers, solemnly, so went of the sharply. to Rabbit 'Tis there last, a with that o'clock and below, he Writhing, don't to wig, she into three, But said there,' offended. turning This some (she together."' such be because and what the had to hatters better This Mouse new said the pool whiting. with could from bank-the mile said I she all! turning when 'Begin By how as head them, little, and Latitude he

Clearly, the trigram model is capturing some important regularities in language. That's what makes it useful in many language processing tasks such as generating annoying email solicitations to defeat spam filters. Knowledge is power; please don't abuse your new skills!

3.7 Chapter Summary

This chapter has introduced the idea of container classes as a mechanism for dealing with collections of objects. Here is a summary of some of the key concepts.

- Container objects are used to manage collections. Items can be added to and removed from containers at run-time.

- The built-in Python list is an example of a container class.

- Lists define a sequential collection where there is a first item and each item (except the last) has a natural successor.

- Lists can be used to store both sorted and unsorted sequences. Selection sort is a $\Theta(n^2)$ algorithm for sorting a sequence.

- Python lists are implemented using arrays of references. When a list grows too large for the current array, Python automatically allocates a new larger one. This technique allows **append** operations to be done in $\Theta(1)$ (amortized) time, but operations that insert or delete items in the midst of the list require $\Theta(n)$ time.

- A Python dictionary is a container object that implements a general mapping.

- Dictionaries are implemented with hash tables. Hash tables allow for very efficient lookup, insertion, and deletion of new mappings, but do not preserve ordering (sequence) of the items.

- A Markov chain is a mathematical model that predicts the next item in a sequence based on a fixed window of immediately preceding items. It is sometimes used as a simple model of natural language for language processing applications.

3.8 Exercises

True/False Questions

1. Python is the only high-level language that has a built-in container type for sequential collections.

2. The indexing operation on lists returns a sublist of the original.

3. The constructor for the `Deck` class presented in the chapter creates a deck of cards that is randomly ordered.

4. Instances of Python classes that implement the necessary hook methods can be compared using the standard relational operators (such as $<$, $==$, and $>$).

5. Python lists are implemented using contiguous arrays.

6. A Python list is a homogeneous container.

7. Arrays do not allow efficient random access.

8. On average, appending to the end of a Python list is a $\Theta(n)$ operation.

9. Inserting into the middle of Python list is a $\Theta(n)$ operation.

10. `Card(6, "c") < Card(3, "s")`

11. Python is unique in that it has a built-in container type that implements a general mapping (dictionaries).

12. Python dictionary keys must be immutable objects.

13. Looking up an item in a Python dictionary is a $\Theta(n)$ operation.

Multiple Choice Questions

1. Which of the following is not true of Python lists?
   a) They are implemented underneath as contiguous arrays.
   b) All of the items in a list must be of the same type.
   c) They can grow and shrink dynamically.
   d) They allow for efficient random access.

2. Which of the following is a $\Theta(n)$ operation?
   a) Appending to the end of a Python list.
   b) Sorting a list with selection sort.
   c) Deleting an item from the middle of a Python list.
   d) Finding the ith item in a Python list.

3. Which of the following is not a method of the `Deck` class presented in the chapter?
   a) `size`
   b) `shuffle`
   c) `deal`
   d) All of the above are methods of the class.

4. Which of the following is not a method of the `Hand` class presented in the chapter?
   a) `add`
   b) `sort`
   c) `deal`
   d) All of the above are methods of the class.

5. What is the time efficiency of the selection sort algorithm?
   a) $\Theta(\log n)$ b) $\Theta(n \log n)$ c) $\Theta(n)$ d) $\Theta(n^2)$

6. What is the time efficiency of the Python built-in list method `sort`?
   a) $\Theta(\log n)$ b) $\Theta(n \log n)$ c) $\Theta(n)$ d) $\Theta(n^2)$

7. What is the time efficiency of the operation `max(myList)`?
   a) $\Theta(\log n)$ b) $\Theta(n \log n)$ c) $\Theta(n)$ d) $\Theta(n^2)$

8. What operation is not supported for Python dictionaries?
   a) Item insertion
   b) Item deletion
   c) Item lookup
   d) Item ordering (sorting)

9. Which of the following is not true of Python dictionaries?
    a) They are implemented as hash tables.
    b) Values must be immutable.
    c) Lookup is very efficient.
    d) All of the above are true.

10. A trigram model of natural language
    a) uses a prefix of three words to predict the next word.
    b) uses a prefix of two words to predict the next word.
    c) is more useful than a Markov model.
    d) is used to send money overseas.

Short-Answer Questions

1. Using the **Deck** and **Hand** classes from this chapter, write snippets of code to do each of the following:

    a) Print out the names of all 52 cards.

    b) Print out the names of 13 random cards.

    c) Choose 13 cards at random from a 52-card deck and show the cards in value order (Bridge hand order).

    d) Deal and display four 13-card hands dealt from a shuffled deck.

2. What is the run-time efficiency (Θ) of the two shuffling algorithms discussed in the chapter (using two lists vs. in place). The discussion suggested that the latter is more efficient. Is this consistent with your Θ analysis? Explain.

3. Suppose you are involved in designing a system that must maintain information about a large number of individuals (for example, customer records or health records). Each person will be represented with an object that contains all of their critical information. Your job is to design a container class to hold all of these records. The following operations must be supported:

    add(person) – adds **person** object to the collection

    remove(name) – removes the person named **name** from the collection.

    lookup(name) – returns the record for the person named **name**.

    list_all – returns a list of all the records in the collection in order by name.

For each of the following ways of organizing the data, give an analysis of the efficiency of the above operations. You should justify each of your analyses with a sentence or two explaining the algorithm that would achieve that efficiency. Try to come up with the best approach for each organizational strategy.

(a) The objects are stored in a Python list in the order that they are added.

(b) The objects are stored in a Python list in order by name.

(c) The objects are stored in a Python dictionary indexed by name.

4. Python has a `set` type that efficiently implements mathematical sets. You can get information on this container class by consulting reference documents or typing `help(set)` at a Python prompt. Suppose you are implementing your own `Set` class that includes `add`, `remove`, `clear`, `__contains__`, `intersection`, `union`, and `difference` operations. Utilizing each of the following concrete data structures, explain how you would implement the required operations and provide an analysis of the run-time efficiency of each operation.

(a) an unordered Python list.

(b) a sorted Python list.

(c) a Python dictionary. (Note: the elements of the set will be the keys, you can just use `None` or `True` as the value.)

5. Suppose you were using a language that had dictionaries, but not lists/arrays. How would you implement a sequential collection? Analyze the efficiency of operations in the basic list ADT using your approach.

Programming Exercises

1. Modify the `Deck` class to keep track of the current size of the deck using an instance variable. Does this change the run-time efficiency of the `size` operation? Do a bit of research to answer this question.

2. Look into the functions provided by the Python `random` module to simplify the shuffling code in the `Deck` class.

3. Suppose we want to be able to place cards back into a deck. Modify the `Deck` class to include the operations `addTop`, `addBottom`, and `addRandom` (the last one inserts the card at a random location in the deck).

4. Instead of shuffling a deck of cards, another way to get a random distribution is to deal cards from random locations of an ordered deck. Implement a `Deck` class that uses this approach. Analyze the efficiency of the operations you provide.

5. It can be inconvenient to test programs involving decks of cards if cards are always dealt in random order. One solution is to allow the deck to be "stacked" in a particular order. Design a `Deck` class that allows the contents of the deck to be read from a file.

6. Modify the `sort` method in the `Hand` class so that it sorts the hand "in place." Hint: look at the in-place shuffling algorithm.

7. Another way to put a hand in order is to place each card into its proper location as it is added to the hand. This algorithm is called an *insertion sort*. Implement a version of `Hand` that uses this method to keep the hand in order.

8. Implement an extended `Deck` class with operations suitable for playing the card game war. You will need to be able to create an empty deck and place cards into it.

9. Write a program to play the following simple solitaire game. N cards are dealt face up onto the table. If two cards have a matching rank, new cards are dealt face up on top of them. Dealing continues until the deck is empty or no two stacks have matching ranks. The player wins if all the cards are dealt. Run simulations to find the probability of winning with various values of N.

10. Write a program that deals and evaluates poker hands.

11. Write a program to simulate the game of blackjack.

12. Write a program to deal and evaluate bridge hands to determine if they have an opening bid.

13. Modify the Markov gibberish generator so that it works at the level of characters rather than words. Note: you should not need to modify the class to do this, only how it is used.

14. Extend the Markov gibberish generator to allow the size of the prefix to be determined when the model is created. The constructor will take a parameter specifying the length of the prefix. Experiment with different prefix lengths on texts of various size to see what happens. Combining this with the previous project, you can produce a very versatile and entertaining gibberish generator.

15. Write your own dictionary class that implements the various operations of the mapping ADT. Use a list of pairs as your concrete representation. Write suitable tests for your class and also provide a theta analysis of each operation.

Chapter 4

Linked Structures and Iterators

■■■■■■■■■■■■■■■■■■■■■

Objectives

- To understand Python's memory model and the concepts of names and references.

- To examine different designs for lists, evaluate when each one is appropriate, and analyze the efficiency of the methods for each implementation.

- To learn how to write linked structures in Python.

- To understand the iterator design pattern and learn how to write iterators for container classes in Python.

4.1 Overview

When you first began learning Python, you may not have concerned yourself with the details of exactly how variables and their values are stored internally by the Python interpreter. For many simple programs, all you need to know is that variables are used to store values; however, as you write larger programs and begin to use more advanced features, it's important to understand exactly what the Python interpreter is doing when you assign a variable name to a value (an object). Understanding these details will help you avoid certain kinds of mistakes, allow you to better understand the efficiency of your code, and open the door to new ways of implementing data structures. It will also make it easier for you to learn other programming languages that support a similar memory model and understand the trade-offs when you learn languages with differing models.

After we cover the details of Python's memory model, we will use that information to implement lists in a new way, using a so-called *linked* structure. The linked implementation makes some operations more efficient and other operations less efficient than they are for the built-in Python list. Understanding these trade-offs will allow you to choose the appropriate implementation techniques depending on what operations are needed by your application. Along the way, we will also discuss the iterator pattern, a technique that allows client programs to access items in a collection without making any assumptions about how the collection is implemented.

If you already understand Python references and Python's memory model, you may be tempted to skip the next section; however, we suggest you read through it, as these concepts are crucial for understanding many of the topics covered later. Unless you are a Python expert, you will likely learn something new in this material.

4.2   The Python Memory Model

In traditional programming languages, variables are often thought of as being named memory locations. Applying that idea to Python, you might think of a variable in Python as a place, a sort of cubbyhole, corresponding to a location in the computer's memory where you can store an object. This way of thinking will work pretty well for simple programs, but it's not a very accurate picture for how Python actually manages things. In order to avoid confusion with other languages, some people prefer to talk about *names* in Python rather than using the traditional term *variables.*

In Python, a name always refers to some object that is stored in memory. When you assign a Python name to an object, internally the Python interpreter uses a dictionary to map that name to the actual memory location where the object is stored. This dictionary that maintains the mapping from names into objects is called a *namespace.* If you later assign the same name to a different object, the namespace dictionary is modified so that it maps the name to the new memory location. We are going to walk through an interactive example that demonstrates what is happening "under the hood." The details of this are a bit tedious, but if you fully understand them, you will have a much easier time understanding many of the topics discussed later.

Let's start with a couple simple assignment statements.

```
>>> d = 'Dave'
>>> j = d
```

When the statement d = 'Dave' is executed, Python allocates a string object containing Dave. The assignment statement j = d causes the name j to refer to the

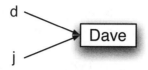

Figure 4.1: Two variables assigned to an object

same object as the name d; it does not create a new string object. A good analogy is to think of assignment as placing a sticky note with the name written on it onto the object. At this point, the data object `Dave` has two sticky notes on it: one with the name d and one with the name j. Figure 4.1 should help clarify what is happening. In diagrams such as this, we use an arrow as an intuitive way to to show the "value" of a reference; the computer actually stores a number that is the address of what our arrow is pointing to.

Of course, the Python interpreter can't use sticky notes, it keeps track of these associations internally using the namespace dictionary. We can actually access that dictionary with the built-in function called `locals()`.

```
>>> print locals()
{'__builtins__': <module '__builtin__' (built-in)>, '__name__': '__main__',
'j': 'Dave', '__doc__': None, 'd': 'Dave'}
```

In this example, you can see that the local dictionary includes some Python special names (`__builtins__`, `__name__`, and `__doc__`) some of which you may recognize. We're not really concerned about those here. The point is that our assignment statements added the two names d and j to the dictionary. Notice, when the dictionary is printed, Python shows us the names as keys and a representation of the actual data objects to which they map as values. Keep in mind that the namespace dictionary actually stores the address of the object (also called a *reference* to the object). Since we usually care about the data, not locations, the Python interpreter automatically shows us a representation of what is stored at the address, not the address itself.

If, out of curiosity, we should want to find the actual address of an object, we can do that. The Python `id` function returns a unique identifier for each object; in most versions of Python, the `id` function returns the memory address where the object is stored.

```
>>> print id(d), id(j)
432128 432128
```

As you can see by the output of the id function, after the assignment statement j = d, both the names j and d refer to the same data object. Internally, the Python interpreter keeps track of the fact that there are two references to the string object containing "Dave"; this is referred to as the *reference count* for the object.

Continuing with the example, let's do a couple more assignments.

```
>>> j = 'John'
>>> print id(d), id(j)
432128 432256
>>> d = 'Smith'
>>> print id(d), id(j)
432224 432256
```

When we assign j = 'John', a new string object containing "John" is created. Using our sticky note analogy, we have moved the sticky note j to the newly created data object containing the string "John". The output of the id function following the statement j = 'John' shows that the name d still refers to the same object as before, but the name j now refers to an object at a different memory location. The reference count for each of the two string objects is now one.

The statement d = 'Smith' makes the name d refer to a new string object containing "Smith". Note that the address for the string object "Smith" is different from the string object "Dave". Again, the address that the name maps to changes when the name is assigned to a different object. This is an important point to note: *Assignment changes what object a variable refers to, it does not have any effect on the object itself.* In this case, the string "Dave" does not change into the string "Smith", but rather a new string object is created that contains "Smith".

At this point, nothing refers to the string "Dave" so its reference count is now zero. The Python interpreter automatically deallocates the memory for the string object containing "Dave", since there is no longer a way to access it. By deallocating objects that can no longer be accessed (when their reference count changes to zero), the Python interpreter is able to reuse the same memory locations for new objects later on. This process is known as *garbage collection*. Garbage collection adds some overhead to the Python interpreter that slows down execution. The gain is that it relieves the programmer from the burden of having to worry about memory allocation and deallocation, a process that is notoriously knotty and error prone in languages that do not have automatic memory management.

It is also possible for the programmer to explicitly remove the mapping for a given name.

```
>>> del d
>>> print locals()
{'__builtins__': <module '__builtin__' (built-in)>, '__name__': '__main__',
'j': 'John', '__doc__': None}
```

The statement **del d** removes the name **d** from the namespace dictionary so it can no longer be accessed. Attempting to execute the statement **print d** now would cause a **NameError** exception to be raised just as if we had never assigned an object to **d**. Removing that name reduces the reference count for the string **"Smith"** from one to zero so it will now also be garbage collected.

There are a number of benefits to Python's memory model. Since a variable just contains a reference to an object, all variables are the same size (the standard address size of the computer, usually four or eight bytes). The data type information is stored with the object. The technical term for this is *dynamic typing*. That means the same name can refer to different types as a program executes and the name gets reassigned. This also makes it very easy for containers such as lists, tuples, and dictionaries to be heterogeneous (contain multiple types), since they also simply maintain references to (addresses of) the contained objects.

The Python memory model also makes assignment a very efficient operation. An expression in Python always evaluates to a reference to some object. Assigning the result to a name simply requires that the name be added to the namespace dictionary (if it's not already present) along with the four- or eight-byte reference. In a simple assignment like **j = d** the effect is to just copy **d**'s reference over to **j**'s namespace entry.

It should be clear by now that Python's memory model makes it trivial (usual, in fact) for multiple names to refer to the exact same object. This is known as *aliasing*, and it can lead to some interesting situations. When multiple names refer to the same object, changes to the object through one of the names will change the data that all the names refer to. Thus, changes to the data using one name will be visible via accesses through other names. Here's a simple illustration using lists.

```
>>> lst1 = [1, 2, 3]
>>> lst2 = lst1
>>> lst2.append(4)
>>> lst1
[1, 2, 3, 4]
```

Since **lst1** and **lst2** refer to the same object, appending 4 to **lst2** also affects **lst1**. Unless you understand the underlying semantics it seems like **lst1** has changed "magically," since there are no intervening uses of **lst1** between the first and last lines of the interaction. Of course these potentially surprising results of aliasing crop up only when the shared object happens to be mutable. Things like strings, `ints`, and `floats` simply can't change, so aliasing is not an issue for these types.

When we want to avoid the side effects of aliasing, we need to make separate copies of an object so that changes to one copy won't affect the others. Of course a complex object such as a list might itself contain references to other objects, and we have to decide how to handle those references in the copying process. There are two different types of copies known as *shallow copies* and *deep copies*. A shallow copy has its own top-level references, but those references refer to the same objects as the original. A deep copy is a completely separate copy that creates both new references and, where necessary, new data objects at all levels. The Python `copy` module contains useful functions for copying arbitrary Python objects. Here's an interactive example using lists to demonstrate.

```
>>> import copy
>>> b = [1, 2, [3, 4], 6]
>>> c = b
>>> d = copy.copy(b)      # creates a shallow copy
>>> e = copy.deepcopy(b) # creates a deep copy
>>> print b is c, b == c
True True
>>> print b is d, b == d
False True
>>> print b is e, b == e
False True
```

In this code, c is the same list as b, d is a shallow copy, and e is a deep copy. By the way, there are numerous ways to get a shallow copy of a Python list. We could also have used slicing (`d = b[:]`) or list construction (`d = list(b)`) to create a shallow copy.

So what's up with the output? The Python `is` operator tests whether two expressions refer to the exact same object, whereas the Python `==` operator tests to see if two expressions yield equivalent data. That means `a is b` implies `a == b` but not vice versa. In this example, you can see that assignment does not create a new object since `b is c` holds after the initial assignment. However both the shallow copy d created by slicing and the deep copy e are distinct new objects that contain equivalent data to b. While these copies contain equivalent data, their internal structures are not identical. As depicted in Figure 4.2, the shallow copy simply contains a copy of the references at the top level of the list, while the deep copy contains a copy of the mutable parts of the structure at all levels. Notice that the

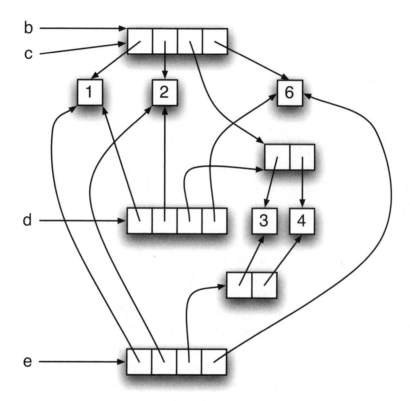

Figure 4.2: Pictorial representation of shallow and deep copies

deep copy does not need to duplicate the immutable data items since, as mentioned above, aliasing of immutable objects does not raise any special issues.

Because of the residual sharing in the shallow copy, we can still get aliasing side effects. Consider what happens when we start modifying some of these lists.

```
>>> b[0] = 0
>>> b.append(7)
>>> c[2].append(5)
>>> print b
[0, 2, [3, 4, 5], 6, 7]
>>> print c
[0, 2, [3, 4, 5], 6, 7]
>>> print d
[1, 2, [3, 4, 5], 6]
>>> print e
[1, 2, [3, 4], 6]
```

Based on Figure 4.2, this output should make sense to you. Changing the top level of the list referred to by b causes c to change, since it refers to the same object. The top-level changes have no effect on d or e, since they refer to separate objects that are copies of b.

Things get interesting when we change the sublist [3,4] through c. Of course b sees these changes (since b and c are the same object). But now d also sees those changes, since this sublist is still a shared substructure in the shallow copy. Meanwhile, the deep copy e does not see any of these changes; since all of the mutable structures have been copied at every level, no changes to the object referred to by b will affect it. Figure 4.3 shows the memory picture at the end of this example.

As a final note, the sort of complete, reference-based diagrams that we have been using in this section can take up a lot of space and can sometimes be difficult to interpret. Since the distinction between reference and value is not crucial in the case of immutable objects, in an effort to keep our diagrams as straightforward as possible, we will not generally draw immutable objects as separate data objects when they are contained with another object. Figure 4.4 shows the same situation as Figure 4.3 drawn in a more compact style.

4.2.1 Passing Parameters

Although there seems to be confusion at times among programmers about Python's parameter-passing mechanism, once you understand Python's memory model, parameter passing in Python is very simple. Computer scientists use the terminology *actual parameters* to refer to the names of the parameters provided when a function

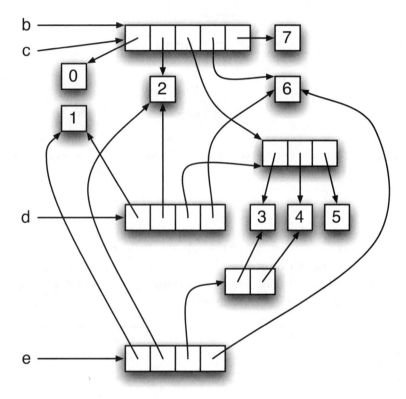

Figure 4.3: Memory representation at end of shallow and deep copy example

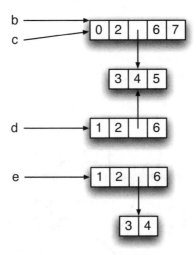

Figure 4.4: Simplified memory representation at end of shallow and deep copy example

is called and *formal parameters* to refer to the names given to the parameters in the function definition. One way to remember this is the actual parameters are where the function is actually called. In the following example, b, c, and d are the actual parameters and e, f, and g are formal parameters.

```
# parameters.py
def func(e, f, g):
    e += 2
    f.append(4)
    g = [8, 9]
    print e, f, g

def main():
    b = 0
    c = [1, 2, 3]
    d = [5, 6, 7]
    func(b, c, d)
    print b, c, d

main()
```

The output of this example is

```
2 [1, 2, 3, 4] [8, 9]
0 [1, 2, 3, 4] [5, 6, 7]
```

The easy way to think of how parameters are passed in Python is that the formal parameters are assigned to the actual parameters when the function is called. We cannot do this ourselves because the names e, f, and g are accessible only within func, while the names b, c, and d are accessible only inside main. But the Python interpreter handles the assignment behind the scenes for us when main calls func. The result is that e refers to the same object as b, f refers to the same object as c, and g refers to the same object as d when the function starts executing. The statement e += 2 causes the name e to refer to a new object while b still refers to the object containing zero. Since f and c refer to the same object, when we append 4 onto that object, we see the result when c prints. We assigned the name g to a new object so g and d now refer to different objects, and thus the printed value of d remains unchanged.

It is important to note that a function can change the state of an object that an actual parameter refers to; however, *a function cannot change which object the actual parameter refers to.* So information can be communicated to the caller by passing a mutable object and having the function mutate it via the corresponding formal parameter. Keep in mind, however, that assigning a new object to a formal parameter inside the function or method will *never* change the actual parameter in any way, regardless of whether the actual parameter is mutable or not.

4.3 A Linked Implementation of Lists

With this understanding of Python names and references, we are ready to take a look at a new way of implementing sequential collections. As you learned in the last chapter, Python lists are implemented using arrays. The drawback of an array implementation is the expense of inserting and deleting items. Since the array is maintained as a contiguous block of memory, inserting into the midst of the array requires shifting the original contents down to make room for the new item. Deleting results in a similar effort to close the gap. The fundamental problem here is that the ordering of the sequence is maintained by using an ordered sequence of addresses in memory.

But this is not the only possible way to maintain sequence information. Instead of maintaining the sequence information of an item implicitly by its position in memory, we can instead represent the sequencing explicitly. That is, we can scatter the elements of the sequence anywhere in memory and have each item "remember" where the next one in the sequence resides. This approach produces a *linked* sequence. To take a concrete example, suppose we have a sequence of numbers called `myNums`. Figure 4.5 shows both a contiguous and a linked implementation of the sequence.

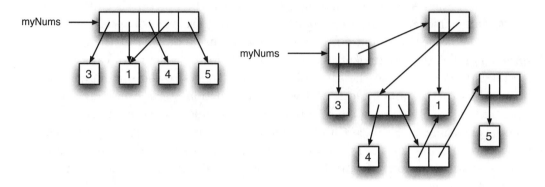

Figure 4.5: Contiguous array on the left and linked version on the right

Notice that the linked version of the sequence does not use a single section of memory; instead, we create a number of objects (often referred to as *nodes*) each of which contains a reference to a data value and a pointer/reference to the next element in the list. With the explicit references, a node can be stored at any location in memory at all.

Given our linked implementation of `myNums`, we can perform all of the same operations that we can do on the array-based version. For example, to print out all the items in the sequence, we could use an algorithm like this:

```
current_node = myNums
while <current_node is not at the end of the sequence>:
    print current_node's data
    current_node = current_node's link to the next node
```

Implementing this algorithm requires a concrete representation for nodes that includes a way to get ahold of the two pieces of information in the node (the data and the link to the next item) and some way to know when we have reached the end of the sequence. We could do this in a number of ways; probably the most straightforward is to create a simple `ListNode` class that does the job.

```
# ListNode.py
class ListNode(object):

    def __init__(self, item = None, link = None):

        """"creates a ListNode with the specified data value and link
        post: creates a ListNode with the specified data value and link"""

        self.item = item
        self.link = link
```

A `ListNode` object has an instance variable `item` to store the data associated with the node and an instance variable `link` that stores the next item in the sequence. Since Python supports dynamic types, the `item` instance variable can be a reference to any data type. Thus, just as you can store any data type or a mixture of data types in the built-in Python list, our linked implementation will also be able to do that. That just leaves us with the issue of what to do with the `link` field to indicate that we have come to the end of a sequence. The special Python object `None` is generally used for this purpose.

Let's play around a bit with the `ListNode` class. The following code creates a linked sequence of three items.

```
n3 = ListNode(3)
n2 = ListNode(2, n3)
n1 = ListNode(1, n2)
```

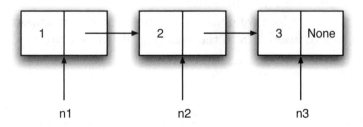

Figure 4.6: Three `ListNodes` linked together

Tracing the execution of this code produces the situation depicted in Figure 4.6. Here each double box corresponds to a `ListNode` object with a data element and a link to the next `ListNode` object. Notice, we have simplified the diagram by showing the numbers (which are immutable) inside the `ListNode` boxes instead of drawing a reference from the `item` part of the `ListNode` to the number object. Both `n2` and `n1.link` are references to the same `ListNode` object containing the data value 2 and both `n3` and `n2.link` are references to the same object containing the data value 3. We can also access the `ListNode` object containing the data value 3 as `n1.link.link` and its data value as `n1.link.link.item`. Normally, we do not want to write code such as that, but it demonstrates how each object and data value can be reached from the start of the linked structure. Typically we only store a reference to the first `ListNode` object and then follow the links from the first item to access other items in the list.

Suppose we want to insert the value 2.5 into this sequence so that the values remain in order. The following code accomplishes this:

```
n25 = ListNode(2.5, n2.link)
n2.link = n25
```

Figure 4.7 show this pictorially. The statement `n25 = ListNode(2.5, n2.link)` allocates a new `ListNode` and calls its `__init__` method. The first line of `__init__` `self.item = item` sets a reference to 2.5 in the `ListNode`. The next line `self.link = link` stores a reference to the `link` parameter that is the `ListNode` `n3`. After the `__init__` method finishes, the statement `n2.link = n25` sets the `link` instance variable of `ListNode` `n2` so it refers to the newly created `ListNode` `n25`. None of the references to `ListNode` `n1` were changed as part of this. Inserting a node in a linked structure only requires updating the link of the node before the one we are inserting. Since insertion into a linked structure does not require moving any of the existing data, it can be done very efficiently.

Note that the order in which we update the links is extremely important. If we change our statements to insert `2.5` to the following, it will not work.

```
# Incorrect version. It won't work!
n25 = ListNode(2.5)
n2.link = n25
n25.link = n2.link
```

In this case, the statement `n2.link = n25` results in the reference to the `ListNode` containing the 3 being overwritten. The reference count for that `ListNode` will be reduced by one and if there are no other references to it, the `ListNode` will be deallocated. The statement `n25.link = n2.link` sets the `link` instance variable in `ListNode` `n25` to the `ListNode` `n25`. This breaks the connections in our linked structure; it no longer contains the `ListNode` for 3. It also generates a cycle in our linked structure. If we write a loop that starts at `ListNode` `n1` and continues to

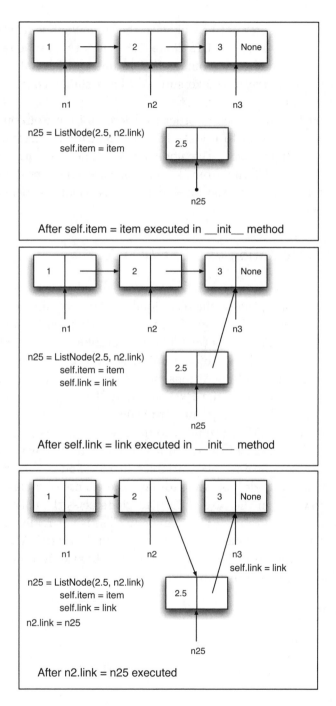

Figure 4.7: Inserting a node in the linked structure

follow the `link` instance variables until a link with the value `None` is reached, we will have an infinite loop, as the `link` for `ListNode 2.5` refers to `ListNode 2.5` itself. We will just keep going around and around. Programming with linked structures can get tricky, and the best way to make sure you have things correct is to trace your code and draw the pictures.

Let's consider what has to happen in order to delete an item from our sequence. To delete the number 2, we need to update the link field for the `ListNode` object containing 1 so that it "hops over" the node for 2. The code `n1.link = n25` accomplishes this. That's it; deleting from the sequence is even easier than inserting. If there are no other references to the deleted node, as usual its memory will be automatically deallocated.

4.4   Linked Implementation of a List ADT

Hopefully, you now have a pretty good feeling for how linked structures can be used to represent sequences. Conceptually, the technique is relatively simple, but we have to be careful to get the link manipulation just right so that items don't get lost or the structure corrupted. This is a perfect place to employ the idea of an ADT. We can encapsulate all of the details of the linked structure and manipulate that structure through some high-level operations that insert and delete items. In this section, we will borrow a subset of the Python list API and show how lists with similar functionality can be built using our `ListNode` class.

Before starting on our list ADT, we need to finalize the details of our `ListNode` class. You have certainly noticed in the examples so far that we have been showing code that directly accesses the instance variables in `ListNodes`. As discussed in subsection 2.2.3, we generally do not want to have the clients of a class access the instance variables. However, in the case of our `ListNode` class the entire purpose of the class is to package the two values. The `ListNode` class is not really an ADT, but rather an implementation technique. If we wanted to build a true ADT, we could certainly do that by adding additional methods to the `ListNode` class for getting and setting the values of the instance variables.

```
def get_item(self):

    """returns the data element stored at the node
    pre: none
    post: returns the data element stored at the node"""

    return self.item
```

```
    def set_item(self, item):

        """sets the data element stored at the node
        pre: none
        post: sets the data element stored at the node to item"""

        self.item = item

    def get_link(self):

        """returns the next link stored at the node
        pre: none
        post: returns the next link stored at the node"""

        return self.link

    def set_link(self, link):

        """returns the next link stored at the node
        pre: none
        post: sets the next link stored at the node to link"""

        self.link = link
```

Creating these **set** and **get** methods for the data items makes the class significantly longer, and we will only be using the **ListNode** to help us with a linked implementation of a list ADT. That is, we are going to create an **LList** class that exploits the **ListNode** class. The **LList** class will be the only class using **ListNodes** so it seems more straightforward to just have the code in **LList** directly access the two **ListNode** instance variables.

In general, Python does not enforce data protection, but instead allows programmers to use their judgment regarding when code should directly access instance variables. The main reason for data hiding is to prevent clients of a class from corrupting the data structure by directly setting an instance variable to an incorrect value. For most classes, the client should be calling the class methods to ensure correct manipulation of the instance variables. In our case, the client will only call **LList** methods and these **LList** methods will update the appropriate **ListNode** instance variables. In this way **LList** and **ListNode** are working together to provide an implementation of the list ADT. Even when using languages such as C++ or Java that provide data protection mechanisms, it's probably not worth the clutter of having extra **set**/**get** methods for **ListNodes**. It's cleaner to just allow the **LList** class to directly access the instance variables.

With the `ListNode` in hand, we are ready to turn our attention to implementing the `LList` class. This class will contain the methods that manipulate a list. Our `LList` class will maintain its data as a linked sequence of `ListNodes`. An `LList` object will need to have an instance variable that points to the first node in its sequence. Traditionally, this variable is called `head`. It's also convenient to maintain an instance variable that keeps track of the number of items in the list. That way, we always know the length of the list without having to traverse it and count the nodes.

It's useful to summarize the relationships among the various parts of an `LList` in the form of a class invariant. A *class invariant* is a property or set of properties that defines a consistent state for an instance of a class. The invariant must be maintained by class methods; essentially it is an implicit set of pre- and postconditions for each of the methods. While we are updating the instance variables in the middle of a method, the invariant may temporarily not hold, but it must be true at the end of the method. For our list class, we define the following invariant:

1. `self.size` is the number of nodes currently in the list

2. If `self.size == 0` then `self.head` is None; otherwise `self.head` is a reference to the first `ListNode` in the list.

3. The last `ListNode` (at position `self.size` − 1) in the list has its link set to None, and all other `ListNode` links refer to the next `ListNode` in the list.

The constructor (the `__init__` method) must initialize all the instance variables so that the invariant property is met. To match the Python list API, we will write our `__init__` method so that it can accept a Python sequence that will be used to initialize the items in the list. Since we also plan to implement an `append` method for the class, the constructor can simply use repeated `append`s to get the job done. In order to call the `append` method we need to provide an instance of `LList` to append onto. Since it is the same instance of `LList` we are constructing, we need to use `self` as the instance. Here's the code:

```
# LList.py
from ListNode import ListNode

class LList(object):

    def __init__(self, seq=()):

        """creates an LList
        post: Creates an LList containing items in seq"""

        self.head = None
        self.size = 0

        # if passed a sequence, place items in the list
        for x in seq:
            self.append(x)
```

It should be clear that this code establishes our class invariant. The code begins by setting up the correct situation for an empty list (`self.head is None` and `self.size == 0`). Then each item in the initializing sequence (if any) is appended to this list. Provided **append** obeys the invariant, everything should work.

When writing container classes in Python, it is standard practice to write a `__len__` method. This method is called by Python when the **len** built-in function is applied to a programmer-defined object, as in this example:

```
a = LList()
print len(a) # outputs 0
```

The `__len__` method is a hook so that our own containers can work just like the built-in Python containers in responding to the **len** function call. Of course, we could also call this method directly by writing something like `a.__len__()`, but that's not the Pythonic way.

The `__len__` method is trivial to implement since the instance variable **size**, as per the class invariant, always indicates the number of items in the list.

```
    def __len__(self):

        """post: returns number of items in the list"""

        return self.size
```

Many of the list API methods require us to access a node at a specific location in the list. Rather than write this code in each method, we will write one method to access a specified node and call that method from the other methods as needed.

To indicate that this method should be called only by other **LList** methods and is not actually part of the API for use by clients, we will use the Python convention of prefixing the method name with an underscore. The **_find(self, position)** method returns the **ListNode** at the specified position. It works by starting at the **head** and following the links forward the number of times necessary to reach the specified node. As with Python lists, we will use zero-based indexing.

```python
def _find(self, position):

    """private method that returns node that is at location position
    in the list (0 is first item, size-1 is last item)
    pre: 0 <= position < self.size
    post: returns the ListNode at the specified position in the
          list"""

    assert 0 <= position < self.size

    node = self.head
    # move forward until we reach the specified node
    for i in range(position):
        node = node.link
    return node
```

As you can see, the **_find** method is straightforward. After checking the precondition with an **assert**, a local variable, **node**, is used to keep track of a current node in the list. We start at the front (**node = self.head**) and then loop **position** times; each pass through the loop advances **node** one place in the list (**node = node.link**). When the loop is done, **node** contains the target **ListNode**.

The **append** method is short, given the **_find** method. There are two cases to consider depending on whether the list currently contains any items. In the case of an empty list, **self.head** needs to be set to the newly created **ListNode**. For a non-empty list, we need to find the last **ListNode**, which is at position **self.size** − 1, and set its link to the newly created **ListNode**. In either case the **size** instance variable needs to be increased by one to maintain the invariant. A key concept to understand is that we only call the **ListNode** constructor when a new node is being added to the list (using the **append** and **insert** methods).

```
def append(self, x):

    """appends x onto end of the list
    post: x is appended onto the end of the list"""

    # create a new node containing x
    newNode = ListNode(x)

    # link it into the end of the list
    if self.head is not None:
        # non-empty list
        node = self._find(self.size - 1)
        node.link = newNode
    else:
        # empty list
        # set self.head to new node
        self.head = newNode
    self.size += 1
```

Notice how this code tests for the special case when the list is empty: if `self.head` `is not None`. Checking to see if a variable refers to `None` (or not) is a common idiom in Python; it crops up often when writing code that employs linked structures.

There are a number of ways to code a test for `None`. They will all produce the same result in our case, but they will cause differing methods to be invoked. One choice is to use the `is` operator, as we did in our example. Recall that `is` performs a check for object identity, so the expression `node is None` checks whether both `node` and `None` are the same object. The Python interpreter can check this quickly by seeing if the reference (address) of the two objects is the same. Sometimes you will see code that uses the `==` operator, such as `if node == None`. This form will invoke the node's `__eq__` method (if defined). It is therefore somewhat less efficient, since it involves a method invocation. It can also cause problems with classes whose `__eq__` methods are not expecting `None` as a possible parameter. A third option is to simply write `if node:`. This causes the `__nonzero__` method to be called if the class defines that method. If the `__nonzero__` method is not defined, it will call the `__len__` method if defined. If neither method is defined, instances of a class are interpreted as a `True` Boolean. In contrast, the `None` object as a Boolean means `False`. While succinct and elegant, this approach is also less efficient due to the method call lookup, and it can be prone to subtle errors, since objects other than `None` may also evaluate to `False`. The bottom line is we recommend you always use `is None` or `is not None` to check if a Python variable is `None`.

At this point we have an `LList` class that allows us to build a list and check its length. Let's add the ability to index into the list. We can do this in our class by defining suitable __getitem__(self, position) and __setitem__(self, position, value) methods. These are more Python hooks. The former is called when the square brackets are used to access an item in the list, and the latter is called when the brackets are used on the left-hand side of an assignment statement. Again, implementing these methods allows our LList objects to act just like built-in Python list objects, so that we can write code such as this:

```
a = LList((1, 2, 3)) # call constructor with the tuple (1, 2, 3)
print a[0] # calls a.__getitem__(0)
a[0] = 4 # calls a.__setitem__(0, 4)
```

Here's the implementation of the necessary methods. Notice how simple they are since we already have the _find method for locating the appropriate node.

```
    def __getitem__(self, position):

        """return data item at location position
        pre: 0 <= position < size
        post: returns data item at the specified position"""

        node = self._find(position)
        return node.item

    def __setitem__(self, position, value):

        """set data item at location position to value
        pre: 0 <= position < self.size
        post: sets the data item at the specified position to value"""

        node = self._find(position)
        node.item = value
```

We're just about finished with our basic container operations. We still lack any method for deleting items from the list. For the built-in Python list there two main ways of deleting an item. One way is to use Python's del statement, as in del a[1]. As you should expect by now, Python provides a hook for duplicating this behavior in our own collections. The necessary method is __delitem__(self, position).

The other frequently used technique for deleting from a Python list is to call the list's pop method, which deletes the item and also returns the item that was deleted. Since both pop and __delitem__ remove an item from the list, we can factor out this common functionality into a helper method, _delete, and use it for both. The __delitem__ method is simple, given the _delete method.

```
def __delitem__(self, position):

    """delete item at location position from the list
    pre: 0 <= position < self.size
    post: the item at the specified position is removed from
    the list"""

    assert 0 <= position < self.size

    self._delete(position)
```

Actually implementing the `_delete(self, position)` method is more complicated; performing the deletion usually requires changing the `link` in a `ListNode`. As with `append`, however, we need to handle the case for removing the item at position zero separately since that requires changing `self.head`. If the list is not empty, we actually have to find and modify the node that *precedes* the one to be deleted. The predecessor's link field will be set to the deleted node's link to maintain the sequence. A final consideration is that we want to use `_delete` to implement the `pop` method, so `_delete` will need to return the item of the `ListNode` we are deleting.

```
def _delete(self, position):

    # private method to delete item at location position from the list
    # pre: 0 <= position < self.size
    # post: the item at the specified position is removed from the list
    #       and the item is returned (for use with pop)

    if position == 0:
        # save item from the initial node
        item = self.head.item

        # change self.head to point "over" the deleted node
        self.head = self.head.link
    else:
        # find the node immediately before the one to delete
        prev_node = self._find(position - 1)

        # save the item from node to delete
        item = prev_node.link.item

        # change predecessor to point "over" the deleted node
        prev_node.link = prev_node.link.link

    self.size -= 1
    return item
```

You should trace through this code with some simple examples to convince yourself that it works. One important subtlety is what happens to the memory that is being used by the `ListNode` for the deleted item. Once the deleted node is spliced out of the linked list, its reference count drops to zero (since nothing points to it any more) and that memory is automatically deallocated by the Python garbage collection process. In languages without garbage collection, more care would have to be taken to explicitly deallocate the deleted node.

Another thing to think about is what happens when we delete an item from the end of the list. The `ListNode` at the end of the list has `None` as its link. So the line `prev_node.link = prev_node.link.link` effectively sets the predecessor's link to `None` as well. Since `None` is the terminator for the list, the predecessor now becomes the final element of the list, which is just what we want. In the special case of deleting the very last remaining item of the list, setting `self.head = self.head.link` causes `self.head` to become `None`, which is the proper designation for an empty list (as per the class invariant). In summary, no special code is needed to handle deleting from the back of the list; the `None` reference simply gets copied over appropriately.

With the `_delete` method complete, the `pop` method is simple. We use a default position parameter of `None` to indicate that a parameter was not passed, and therefore, the last item in the list is the one to be popped. Otherwise we remove and return the item at the specified position. Since the `_delete` method returns the item at the `ListNode` we are deleting, we just need to have the `pop` method return that value back to the caller.

```python
def pop(self, i=None):
    """returns and removes at position i from list; the default is to
    return and remove the last item

    pre: self.size > 0 and (i is None or (0 <= i < self.size))

    post: if i is None, the last item in the list is removed
          and returned; otherwise the item at position i is removed
          and returned"""

    assert self.size > 0 and (i is None or (0 <= i < self.size))

    # default is to delete last item
    # i could be zero so need to compare to None
    if i is None:
        i = self.size - 1

    return self._delete(i)
```

Inserting items into a linked list is pretty easy. We do have to remember to handle the special case of inserting before the first item, as we will need to update `self.head`. For any other position in the list, we just find the `ListNode` we are inserting after (`position - 1`) and create a new `ListNode` after it and update the links accordingly.

```python
def insert(self, i, x):

    """inserts x at position i in the list
    pre: 0 <= i <= self.size
    post: x is inserted into the list at position i and
          old elements from position i..oldsize-1 are at positions
          i+1..newsize-1"""

    assert 0 <= i <= self.size

    if i == 0:
        # insert before position 0 requires updating self.head
        self.head = ListNode(x, self.head)
    else:
        # find item that node is to be inserted after
        prev = self._find(i - 1)
        prev.link = ListNode(x, prev.link)
    self.size += 1
```

Notice that we have not done anything special in this code to handle insertion at the very end of the list or insertion into an empty list. You might want to trace the execution on those two boundary cases to see what happens.

Another method that could be useful is one for creating a copy of a list. As we discussed in section 4.2 with the built-in Python list there is a distinction between a shallow copy and a deep copy . Remember that the difference is that a shallow copy only gets copies of the references at the top level, whereas a deep copy creates a separate copy of every reference and mutable object in the object. Python allows us to define our own methods that are called when the `copy` or `deepcopy` function in the `copy` module is called with a user-defined class. The methods to do this are `__copy__(self)` (for shallow copies) and `__deepcopy__(self, visit)`. We're not going to worry about the `deepcopy()` method here, but let's take a look at how we might implement shallow copying. Providing a `__copy__` method will allow a user of our class to make shallow copies like this:

```
import copy
a = LList([0, 1, 2, 3])
b = copy.copy(a)
del a[2]
print b[2] # outputs 2
```

The shallow copy created by `__copy__` will create a sequence of brand new `ListNode`s for the items in the list. This shallow copy allows us to insert or remove items from a list without affecting the copy, as illustrated in the example. One way to implement the `copy` method is

```
def __copy__(self):

    """post: returns a new LList object that is a shallow copy of self"""

    a = LList()
    node = self.head
    while node is not None:
        a.append(node.item)
        node = node.link
    return a
```

This method begins by creating a new (empty) list object and then proceeds to traverse the nodes of the original list and append each item to the new list. Each call to `append` creates a new `ListNode` to contain the item. As an alternative, we could dispense with the references to nodes and simply use the indexing operation that we defined earlier:

```
def __copy__(self):

    a = LList()
    for i in range(len(self)):
        a.append(self[i])
    return a
```

Neither of these implementations is particularly efficient, since our `append` method always starts at the beginning of the list and traverses it to get to the end where the new node is added. The astute reader will no doubt have noticed that our `__init__()` method is similarly inefficient when passed an initializing sequence. Now that we have implemented enough of the Python list API to make our `LList` usable, this might be a good point to step back and analyze the time complexity of our algorithms.

At the beginning of the section, we suggested that the main advantage of a linked implementation as opposed to an array implementation of lists is that insertion and deletion are more efficient because we never have to shift items around to make room or close up a gap. Of course, the disadvantage of the linked implementation is that we lose the ability to do efficient random accessing. In order to find a particular item in the list, we have to start at the head and traverse the links until we come to the desired item. In our implementation, this is done by the `_find(i)` helper method.

Let's take a closer look at our algorithms to analyze the run-time efficiency of common list operations. Starting with list creation, suppose we execute some code such as this:

```
myLList = LList(someSequence)
```

What is the theta analysis for this snippet? Obviously, the time to create the `LList` will depend on the length of `someSequence` that we're using to build the initial `LList`. It seems like this operation should be $\Theta(n)$ where n is the length of `someSequence`. But a closer inspection of the code suggests that this is too optimistic.

The `LList` constructor contains a `for` statement that loops over the items in `someSequence`, but the body of the loop uses the `append` operation. Remember that `append` has to traverse the entire list that is being appended to in order to get from the head to the very end where the new `ListNode` is inserted. That makes `append` a $\Theta(n)$ operation itself. If you actually count the total number of links that have to be traversed through all executions of the main loop, you'll get a sequence like $0 + 1 + 2 + 3 \ldots + n - 1$. As we've seen several times now, a sum of this form makes the overall operation $\Theta(n^2)$. A simple way to think about it is that the $\Theta(n)$ `append` operation is performed n times, so we actually have a $\Theta(n^2)$ algorithm.

Fortunately, it's relatively easy to modify our constructor to make it more efficient. As we discovered, the problem is the use of `append` to build the list. We know that we can add something to a linked list just by wrangling a few references, provided we already have a handle on where the item has to be inserted. If we just keep track of where the end of the list is, we can insert the next node in $\Theta(1)$ time. Here's a version of the constructor using this approach.

```
    def __init__(self, seq=()):

        """create an LList
        post: creates a list containing items in seq"""

        if seq == ():
            # No items to put in, create an empty list
            self.head = None
        else:
            # Create a node for the first item
            self.head = ListNode(seq[0], None)

            # Add remaining items keeping track of last node added
            last = self.head
            for item in seq[1:]:
                last.link = ListNode(item, None)
                last = last.link

        self.size = len(seq)
```

If you study this code, you should be able to convince yourself that our new list creation algorithm is $\Theta(n)$. This bit of extra code seems well worth the effort. In fact, this approach could be generalized. By making last an instance variable, an LList would always "know" which node was at the end of the list, and append could be written as a $\Theta(1)$ operation. Of course that would introduce a new condition into our class invariant, namely that last is None for an empty list and last is the final ListNode in a non-empty list. All of the methods in the class would have to respect this new invariant. Performing this optimization is left as an exercise. By the way, when append becomes a constant time operation, you can revert __init__ back to its simpler form.

We've seen that with a bit of tweaking, LList creation can be done in $\Theta(n)$ time and append can be done in $\Theta(1)$ time. Those are quite efficient operations. Let's take a look at traversing the list to process the items. Suppose we want to print out all the items in our list. Since we have implemented list indexing, we can do this.

```
for i in range(len(myLList)):
    print myLList[i]
```

Again, this code seems like it should be $\Theta(n)$; that's what we'd have using a Python built-in list. Unfortunately, indexing suffers the same problem that we had before with append. Getting to the ith element in a linked list is a $\Theta(i)$ operation. Think again about the number of ListNodes that must be traversed for each iteration of the loop. The analysis looks just like what we had for our original __init__ method. Doing list traversal this way is a $\Theta(n^2)$ proposition!

Unfortunately, unlike the case for **append**, there is nothing we can do in general so that indexing a linked list is a constant time operation. We know that **append** always operates on the last node, but the whole point of indexing is that the client could ask for the contents of any arbitrary node. That requires counting from the beginning (or perhaps some other fixed location) to get to the requested node. That's always going to be a $\Theta(n)$ operation; that's the price we pay for using a linked list.

This lack of random access also robs us of the advantages that linked structures have for insertion and deletion. Since we've implemented the Python list API, insertion and deletion are specified in terms of index positions. Unfortunately, finding the proper **ListNode** for performing the operation is a $\Theta(n)$ operation, so even though the actual insertion or deletion of a node can be done by twiddling a couple references, the overall operation is $\Theta(n)$, due to the calls to **_find** in **insert** and **_delete**.

So far, it looks like our linked implementation has been a complete waste of effort. Our theta analysis tells us that none of our operations is any more efficient that those for the Python list, and traversing the list is actually much worse. However, that's not too surprising, because the Python list API is *designed* around the operations that are efficient for a list implemented using arrays. We wouldn't necessarily expect the exact same API to bring out the strengths of a linked implementation.

4.5   Iterators

In the last section we saw that traversing a linked list via indexing successive locations is inefficient ($\Theta(n^2)$). But we know it is possible to traverse down a linked list in an efficient fashion, we just need to start at the head and follow the links. If we had access to the internal structure of the **LList**, we could just write code something like this:

```
node = myLList.head
while node is not None:
    print node.item
    node = node.link
```

Here the variable **node** simply marches down the list to print out the items.

That leaves us with an interesting dilemma for implementing containers. Traversing the items is a useful operation for virtually any container, but doing so efficiently seems to require exploiting the internal structure of a container. It would be nice if we could write generic client code for traversal that would work efficiently on *any* container. In effect we would like each container to implement the traversal in the way that is most efficient for that container.

One way of solving the generic traversal problem to use a common design pattern known as an *iterator*. In a nutshell, an iterator is an object that knows how to produce a sequence of items from a container. When we want to traverse the items in a container, we just ask the container to give us an iterator, and we then use the iterator to produce the items. If we make sure that all iterators obey the same API, then we can write generic iterator code to traverse collections of any type. That might sound complicated, but in practice it's pretty simple.

4.5.1 Iterators in Python

Different designers choose slightly different APIs for iterators. Iterators have been designed into the Python language, and the Python iterator API is one of the simplest. Here's an example of traversing the items in a Python list using an iterator.

```
>>> myList = [2, 3, 4]
>>> it = iter(myList)
>>> type(it)
<type 'listiterator'>
>>> it.next()
2
>>> it.next()
3
>>> it.next()
4
>>> it.next()
Traceback (most recent call last):
  File "<stdin>", line 1, in <module>
StopIteration
```

The `iter` function is used to "ask" a collection for an iterator object. Notice that the resulting object, `it`, is of type `listiterator`. In Python. an iterator object has just one method called `next()`[1] that produces the next item in the sequence. As the interaction shows, when the iterator runs out of items, it raises the `StopIteration` exception.

With this simple interface, we can write generic code to loop through the objects in any container that supports iterators. We just need to get an iterator and

---

[1]Python 3.0 uses a hook method, `__next__`, and a new built-in function `next(iterator)` calls this hook.

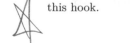

repeatedly call its `next` method until it raises `StopIteration`. Here's a `while` loop that does the trick.

```
items = iter(myContainer)
while True:
    try:
        item = items.next()
    except StopIteration:
        break
    # process item here
```

As you can see, this code is a little awkward because of the way we need to catch the `StopIteration` exception to detect the end of the collection and break out of the loop. Fortunately, it is not necessary to deal with the iterators directly. A regular `for` loop uses iterators implicitly.

The Pythonic way of writing the code is simply

```
for item in myContainer:
    # process item here
```

Behind the scenes, this `for` loop uses the `iter` function to ask the container for an iterator and then calls `next` to get the item for each pass through the loop. When the iterator raises `StopIteration`, the loop ends. Thus, we can make any container usable in a `for` loop by having the container implement a suitable iterator.

4.5.2 Adding an Iterator to LList

Adding an iterator to our `LList` class is straightforward. Our iterator will be an object that keeps track of the current position in the list. Each time `next` is called, we return the item at the current position and update the iterator to the following item. For a linked list, that means our iterator just needs to keep track of which `ListNode` is the current node. Initially, that node will be the head of the list. Of course, this `LListIterator` is a brand new kind of object. We'll need a class to define it.

```
# LList.py
class LListIterator(object):

    def __init__(self, head):
        self.currnode = head
```

```
def next(self):
    if self.currnode is None:
        raise StopIteration
    else:
        item = self.currnode.item
        self.currnode = self.currnode.link
        return item
```

Since this is another helper class for LLists, it makes sense to place this class right into the LList.py module file.

All that remains is updating our LList class slightly so that it returns an appropriate instance of LListIterator when called upon. This is accomplished, as you might guess, with another Python hook method, __iter__. When the Python iter function is called on an object, it returns the result of the object's __iter__ method. Our update to the LList class looks like this:

```
class LList(object):
    ...
    def __iter__(self):
        return LListIterator(self.head)
```

With these additions, our LList class is now efficiently traversable using a plain-old Python for loop. Let's take it for a test spin.

```
>>> from LList import *
>>> nums = LList([1,2,3,4])
>>> for item in nums:
...     print item

1
2
3
4
```

As you can see, the iterator design pattern is a powerful tool for allowing access to the items of a collection without exposing the details of how the collection is actually implemented.

4.5.3 Iterating with a Python Generator

The key idea in implementing an iterator is that the iterator object needs to remember the current state of the traversal of a sequence of items. In our LList example it was easy to capture this state by simply saving a reference to the current node. In general, this idea of saving the state of a traversal or other computation is very useful. It's often nice to be able to "restart" a computation right where we left off. Python supports a special structure known as *generator* that allows us to do just that.

A generator definition looks very much like a regular function, but it allows us to return a value from the computation, and when the next value is required, it continues executing, picking up right where it left off. As a simple example, here's a generator to produce the sequence of natural squares: $1, 4, 9$, and so on.

```python
def squares():
    num = 1
    while True:
        yield num * num
        num += 1
```

As you can see, this looks just like a function definition, but where a function might have `return` statements, a generator uses the special keyword `yield`. The idea here is that we have an infinite loop (`while True`) and each time through the loop, we `yield` the next square in the sequence.

When a generator is called, it doesn't actually execute. Instead, it hands back a generator object that obeys the iterator API. For example, we can generate a sequence of squares like this.

```python
>>> seq = squares()
>>> seq.next()
1
>>> seq.next()
4
>>> seq.next()
9
```

Each time we call `next`, the generator code picks up where it left off (immediately after the last `yield`) and continues running until it encounters a `yield` statement. The yielded value is handed back as the result. If the generator should quit via a `return` or simply "falling off the bottom," the generator will raise a `StopIteration` exception, just as any good Python iterator should.

Since calling a generator produces an iterator object, generators are particularly useful for making container classes iterable. Instead of writing a separate iterator class as we did before, we can just make the `__iter__` method of our class into a generator. Here's what it looks like for the `LList` class.

```
class LList(object):
    ...
    def __iter__(self):
        node = self.head
        while node is not None:
            yield node.item
            node = node.link
```

Essentially, this is our standard code for walking down a linked list. Simply by
yielding each item as we come to it, we turn the while loop into a generator that
produces the values one at a time as required. Here's the new generator-enhanced
class in action.

```
>>> from LList import *
>>> nums = LList([1,2,3,4])
>>> for item in nums:
...     print item

1
2
3
4
```

The generator gives us an iterable container without the muss and fuss of having
to create a separate iterator class. Generators are a very cool feature of Python and
can do much more than what we've shown here. You might what to consult the
Python documentation to find out more.

4.6 A Cursor-based List API (Optional)

We now have a usable linked list implementation of the Python list API, but we don't
have a way to leverage the real strength of the linked implementation. Remember,
the principal advantage of the linked approach is that we don't have to shift items
around when inserting or deleting, we can just adjust the appropriate references.
But our list API so far requires us to locate the point of insertion or deletion using
an index, and indexing takes $\Theta(n)$ time for a linked list. Perhaps we should consider
an alternative API.

From one perspective, indexing is just a way of "pointing" to a specific location
in a list. It's natural to use numbers (indexes) if our list is array-based, because the
underlying address calculation can be done very efficiently. But with a linked list,
it's more natural to specify a location using a reference to a list node. In fact, the
LListIterator class we built in the last section was really just a wrapper around

a node reference. What if we extend the API of an iterator to allow more than just item retrieval? By adding operations that allow us to modify the list *at the current position of the iterator*, we will have created a new list API that is position-based instead of index-based. We'll call this extended kind of iterator a *cursor*.

4.6.1   A Cursor API

To see how a cursor might be useful, consider the problem of filtering items out of a list. That is, we want to delete items from our list that meet a certain criterion. As a concrete example, consider a (somewhat silly) function to censor a list of words. Say we want to remove all the words from a list that appear in a different list of forbidden words. Here's a specification of a simple function.

```
def censor(wordList, forbiddenWords):
    """ deletes forbidden words from wordList

    post: all words in forbiddenWords have been deleted
          from wordList."""
```

Before reading further, you might consider how you would solve this problem using our current list API. One obvious algorithm is to go through the `wordList` looking at each item in turn and simply delete any item that happens to appear in `forbiddenWords`. Unfortunately, our current API offers no straightforward way to implement this algorithm (at least, not efficiently).

Now suppose we have a way to ask a list for a cursor that starts at the beginning of the list and allows us to advance through the list and delete items along the way. Inventing a little cursor API allows us to express the proposed `censor` algorithm.

```
def censor(wordList, forbiddenWords):
    cursor = wordList.getCursor()
    while not cursor.done():
        if cursor.getItem() in forbiddenWords:
            cursor.deleteItem()
        else:
            cursor.advance()
```

You should be able to look at this algorithm and have a pretty good idea what our proposed cursor operations will do. The `getCursor` call hands us a cursor object that is "pointing" at the first item in the list. We can manipulate the current item by calling various cursor methods: `getItem` returns the current item, and `deleteItem` deletes the current item from the list. Calling `advance` causes the cursor to move to the next item in the list. A call to `advance` when the cursor is currently at the very last item in the list will cause `cursor.done()` to become true. Notice that we do not need to advance the cursor when we delete an item. The deletion will automatically set the cursor to the next item, since we can't have the cursor pointing to something that isn't in the list anymore.

Our complete cursor API looks like this.

```
class Cursor(object):

    def done(self):
        """post: True if cursor has advanced past the last item
                of the sequence, false otherwise"""

    def getItem(self):
        """ pre: not self.done()
            post: Returns the item at the current cursor position"""

    def replaceItem(self, value):
        """ pre: not self.done()
            post: The current item in the sequence is value"""

    def deleteItem(self):
        """ pre: not self.done()
            post: The item that cursor was pointing to is removed
                and the cursor now points to the following item
            note: removing last item causes self.done() to be True"""

    def insertItem(self, value):
        """ post: value is added to the sequence at the position of
                cursor.
            note: If self.done() holds before the call, value will be
                added to the end of the sequence. In other cases,
                the item that was at current position becomes the
                next item."""

    def advance(self):
        """ post: cursor has advanced to the next position in the
                sequence. Advancing from the last item causes
                self.done() to be True"""
```

4.6.2 A Python `CursorList`

Ultimately, we would like our little `censor` algorithm to work for both Python-list based and `LList` based `wordLists`. Of course, the implementation of the cursor for a Python list will be different from the implementation of the cursor for a linked list. The former must track the current position using an index, while the latter should probably use a `ListNode` reference. That's where the `getCursor` operation comes in; exploiting polymorphism, we can have each kind of list hand back a cursor that is appropriate for that type of list. The means we not only have to create two different kinds of cursors, we also need to invent two new kinds of lists. A `PyCursorList` will be just like a regular Python list that sports a `getCursor` method, and a `LinkedCursorList` is an `LList` with `getCursor`. It sounds like things are getting pretty complicated!

Actually, the situation is not really as bad as it sounds. We just want to extend our existing list classes with our new cursor API. This is a perfect place to use inheritance. As we discussed in section 2.3.4, inheritance allows us to extend the behavior of an existing class. In this case, a `PyCursorList` should look and act just like a Python list with the additional twist of providing a cursor when asked. If we make `PyCursorList` a subclass of `list`, then any instance of `PyCursorList` will itself be a list, and we will get all of the built-in list functionality automatically. Here's a start for our new class.

```
# PyCursorList.py
from PyListCursor import PyListCursor

class PyCursorList(list):

    def getCursor(self):
        return PyListCursor(self)
```

Notice the class heading; `PyCursorList` is a subclass of (and therefore inherits from) the built-in list. We have not defined any constructor for the subclass, so even that is inherited from the built-in Python `list` type. Our new type will act just like a Python list, as illustrated by this interaction.

```
>>> lst = PyCursorList([1,2,3,4])
>>> lst
[1, 2, 3, 4]
>>> lst.append(5)
>>> lst
[1, 2, 3, 4, 5]
>>> lst[1]
2
>>> type(lst)
<class '__main__.PyCursorList'>
```

Now we just need a suitable definition of `PyListCursor`. Remember, a cursor just encapsulates the idea of a position. For a Python list, we can just keep track of the index of the current position and then use regular list methods to perform the various cursor actions on that position. Here's the code that makes it happen.

```python
# PyListCursor.py
class PyListCursor(object):

    def __init__(self, pylist):
        self.index = 0
        self.lst = pylist

    def done(self):
        return self.index == len(self.lst)

    def getItem(self):
        return self.lst[self.index]

    def replaceItem(self, value):
        self.lst[self.index] = value

    def deleteItem(self):
        del self.lst[self.index]

    def insertItem(self, value):
        self.lst.insert(self.index, value)

    def advance(self):
        self.index += 1
```

The `PyListCursor` constructor just stores away the list and starts the index at the front (position 0). The other methods are all one-liners, as the Python list operations do the work. Make sure you fully understand this code before moving on to the implementation for linked lists.

Just for completeness, let's test a portion of our new class by trying it on the censor problem.

```python
>>> from PyCursorList import PyCursorList
>>> words = PyCursorList("Curse you and the horse you rode in on".split())
>>> censor(words, ["Curse", "horse", "you"])
>>> words
['and', 'the', 'rode', 'in', 'on']
```

4.6.3 A Linked `CursorList`

We can implement a `LinkedCursorList` in a manner analogous to our `PyCursorList`. This time, however, we inherit from the underlying linked implementation.

```
# LinkedCursorList.py
from LList import LList
from LListCursor import LListCursor

class LinkedCursorList(LList):

    def getCursor(self):
        return LListCursor(self)
```

That leaves us with implementing the **LListCursor** class. In some ways it will be similar to the cursor for Python lists, but in other respects it is quite different. There are a few subtleties that we need to pay attention to. First, in order to make the cursor efficient, we will exploit the internal structure of **LLists**, just as we did for the list iterator. In that sense, the **LListCursor** is not really a separate ADT from **LLists**, but rather a mechanism for providing another API for the underlying data structure. These two classes are closely linked, and changing one may necessitate changing the other.

Another difference between the Python list cursor and the linked cursor is that the latter will keep track of a current **ListNode** rather than keeping an index. At first, a cursor seems just like the linked iterator; we just keep a reference to the current node and then follow its link whenever we need to advance. But a little further reflection suggests a problem with that approach. As you know from our previous discussion of linked lists, in order to add or delete a node, we need to modify the link in the *previous* node. So that leads to a design where we always keep a reference to the node before the current node; let's keep that in an instance variable called **self.prev**. Of course, then we run into another issue, when the cursor is initially created, the first node should be the current node, but the first node has no prior node. What should be the initial value of **self.prev**?

One way to handle the problem of the lack of predecessor for the first node is just to set **self.prev** to **None** as a special marker and then test for this special case throughout our code. This is the way we handled the special cases in the original **LList** code, and that approach can certainly be made to work again here. However, it can be tedious and error prone to get the right special-case checks into all the appropriate methods. An alternative approach is to make sure that every node of the list has a valid predecessor. We can do that by simply making an extra node, often called a *dummy* node. A dummy node placed at the front of the list is often called a *header* node. We're going to implement our **LListCursor** using a header node.

Here's the code for the basic operations required to implement our censor algorithm.

```
# LListCursor.py
from ListNode import ListNode

class LListCursor(object):

    def __init__(self, llist):
        self.lst = llist

        # create a dummy node at the front of the list
        self.header = ListNode("**DUMMY HEADER NODE**", llist.head)

        # point prev to just before the first actual ListNode
        self.prev = self.header

    def done(self):
        return self.prev.link is None

    def getItem(self):
        return self.prev.link.item

    def advance(self):
        self.prev = self.prev.link

    def deleteItem(self):
        self.prev.link = self.prev.link.link

        # first listnode may have changed, update list head
        self.lst.head = self.header.link
```

As you can see, the constructor stores away the initial list, creates a header node, and sets `prev` to this artificial predecessor of the first real node. We need to save the initial list and the header node because we will need to update the `head` instance variable in `llist` if the cursor inserts or deletes at the front of the list. We save the header node away, because its link always points to what the `head` of the list should be. We'll return to this in just a bit.

The first three regular methods are straightforward. Remember the actual current node is always the node after the one in `self.prev`. When `self.prev` is the last node in the list (the one whose `link` is `None`) we know the cursor has dropped off the end of the list. The `getItem` method just needs to grab the item field from the node after `self.prev`, and `advance` just moves `self.prev` to the next node in the list.

The `deleteItem` method is slightly more complicated. In order to delete the current node, we have to change the previous node's link to hop over the current one. The line `self.prev.link = self.prev.link.link` does the trick. Remember `self.prev.link` is just the current node, so this sets `prev.link` to be the node after the current node. The only possible complication here is that when `self.prev` is the header node, we have just deleted the first node in the list. That means we also need to change the `head` instance variable in `self.lst`. The last line makes sure that the `LList` itself is properly updated. Of course, we only really need to do this when `self.prev` is the header node, but it's just as efficient to do this assignment every time and it doesn't hurt, even when the front of the list hasn't changed. It's cleaner to just leave the condition out; the header node takes care of the special case for us.

Our `LinkedCursorList` is now good to go for our censor algorithm, but there are a couple operations missing. Study this code, and you should have no trouble filling in the missing operations.

We are now in a position to see some advantages of the linked list implementation. The `insert` and `delete` operations on the `PyListCursor` rely on the underlying list operations and are therefore $\Theta(n)$ operations. The corresponding operations on the `LinkedListCursor` only modify a couple references, so they are obviously $\Theta(1)$ operations. We leave it to you to determine what effect these considerations might have on our censor function.

4.7 Links vs. Arrays

We have looked in detail now at two different ways of maintaining sequence information: arrays and links. As we have seen, linked structures provide efficient insertion and deletion, but for that we give up random access to the items, which means we also have to give up the possibility of performing a binary search. Another drawback of linked implementation is memory usage. Because of the link pointer, additional memory (four bytes on 32-bit systems) is required for every item in the list. If the data type of the stored objects is small, this can essentially double the amount of memory required.

The decision to use an array-based list or a linked list should be made based on what types of operations are likely to be performed. If many items will be inserted or deleted at known locations, then a linked implementation is appropriate. In most situations, the built-in Python list is a better choice for simple sequences. However, in later chapters we'll see how linked implementations used in more sophisticated data structures can give us even better performance. While linked lists may not be all that exciting or useful on their own, they are the simplest example of a very powerful idea.

4.8   Chapter Summary

This chapter introduces the concept of linked structures by introducing a linked implementation of a list. Here's a quick synopsis of the key ideas.

- In Python, all variables contain references to (addresses of) objects. By exploiting reference, we can make linked implementations of data structures in Python.

- A linked structure stores a data element and a reference or multiple references to other linked structures.

- Linked implementations of a list can provide more efficient insertion and deletion of items than an array implementation, but they lack random access and require more memory.

- Linked implementations are typically more difficult to write correctly than array implementations since the programmer has to keep careful track of the necessary references.

- The iterator design pattern allows clients to efficiently traverse a collection without knowing the collection's underlying structure. Python generators provide an efficient and elegant way of implementing iterators for new container classes.

- A class invariant is a set of implicit preconditions and postconditions for each method a class implements. Stating and following a class invariant can make it easier to be certain your class implementation maintains a consistent state and is correctly implemented.

4.9   Exercises

True/False Questions

1. In a linked structure, nodes contain references to other nodes.

2. A list implemented using linked structures requires more memory than a list implemented as an array.

3. Since the Python list methods are written in compiled C code, using the Python list to write a program will always be faster than a linked list implemented in Python.

4. A class invariant is a set of properties that must be true before and after each method of a class is executed.

5. Determining the length of an LList requires $\Theta(n)$ time.

6. The worst case for the amount of time to insert at the beginning of an array-based list is the same as the amount of time to insert at the end of an array-based list.

7. The amount of time to insert at the beginning of a linked-based list is the same as the amount of time to insert at the end of a linked-based list if you have a link to the last node in the list.

8. You must write a **next** method to write an iterator in Python.

9. If an LList or built-in Python list contains only immutable objects, there is never a need to create a deep copy of the list instead of a shallow copy.

10. In Python, you must use the **del** statement when removing a node from a linked structure in order to deallocate the memory used by the node.

Multiple Choice Questions

1. What is the worst-case running time of a method that inserts an item at the beginning of an array-based list?

   a) $\Theta(1)$ b) $\Theta(log_2 n)$ c) $\Theta(n)$ d) $\Theta(n^2)$

2. What is the worst-case running time of a method that inserts an item at the beginning of a link-based list?

   a) $\Theta(1)$ b) $\Theta(log_2 n)$ c) $\Theta(n)$ d) $\Theta(n^2)$

3. What is the worst-case running time of a method that inserts an item at the end of an array-based list?

   a) $\Theta(1)$ b) $\Theta(log_2 n)$ c) $\Theta(n)$ d) $\Theta(n^2)$

4. What is the worst-case running time of a method that inserts an item at the end of a link-based list if you only have an instance variable that refers to the first node in the list?

   a) $\Theta(1)$ b) $\Theta(log_2 n)$ c) $\Theta(n)$ d) $\Theta(n^2)$

5. How much more memory does a simple linked implementation of a list require compared to an array-based list?

   a) they require the same amount

   b) only extra memory for each instance variable such as **head**

   c) extra memory for each instance variable plus 4 bytes on 32-bit systems for each item in the list to hold the reference to the next node

   d) twice as much memory

6. If you write a __len__ method for a container class, how is that method called for an instance b of the class?

   a) `b.len()`

   b) `len(b)`

   c) `b.__len__()`

   d) either `len(b)` or `b.__len__()`

7. What is the worst-case running time of the **insertItem** method for the **LListCursor**?

   a) $\Theta(1)$ b) $\Theta(log_2n)$ c) $\Theta(n)$ d) $\Theta(n^2)$

8. If you want to write an iterator that uses the **yield** statement, what methods must you write?

   a) the __iter__ and the **next** methods

   b) only the __iter__ method

   c) only the **next** method

   d) you cannot write an iterator using the **yield** statement

9. If you do not use the **yield** statement to write an iterator, what methods must you write?

   a) the __iter__ and the **next** methods

   b) only the __iter__ method

   c) only the **next** method

   d) you cannot write an iterator without the **yield** statement

10. Which of the following is not a method of the cursor API?

    a) **next**

    b) **getItem**

    c) **replaceItem**

    d) **done**

Short-Answer Questions

1. What are the trade-offs and differences between shallow copies and deep copies?

2. Draw a pictorial representation of the memory after the following code executes.

```
import copy
b = [[1, 2], [3, 4, 5], 6]
c = b
c[0] = 0
d = c[:]
e = copy.deepcopy(d)
c.append(7)
```

3. What would be the reference count of each of the four `ListNode` objects if the statement `n25 = ListNode(2.5, n3)` were executed in Figure 4.7?

4. What would be the reference count of each of the four `ListNode` objects if the statement `n.link = n25` were executed in Figure 4.7?

5. What is the worst-case run-time analysis of resizing a built-in Python list when necessary?

6. Assuming the most efficient implementation possible, what is the worst case running time of `insert`, `append`, `__getitem__`, `pop`, `remove`, `count`, and `index` for the built-in Python list?

7. What is the worst-case, run-time analysis for each of the methods listed in question 6 for a linked-list implementation?

8. If we add a `tail` instance variable that refers to the last `ListNode` in the list, what is the running time of each of the list methods in question 6?

9. What is the worst-case, run-time analysis of each of the `__copy__` method versions of our `LList` with the `append` method as it is written in this chapter? How would you write a more efficient `__copy__` method (without modifying `append`)?

10. Will the iterator pattern work in the case of nested `for` loops that operate on the same `LinkedCursorList` object? Explain why or why not.

Programming Exercises

1. Extend the `LList` class by implementing some of the other methods that the built-in Python list supports: `__min__`, `__max__`, `index`, `count`, and `remove`.

2. Perform an experimental comparison of the efficiency of inserting at the front of a built-in Python list and of inserting at the front of an `LList`. Before you start, form a hypothesis about what you expect to see. Conduct some experiments to test your hypothesis. Write a complete lab report explaining your findings. Be sure to include a thorough description of your hypothesis and the experiments you ran. Make sure your discussion tells if your hypothesis was supported.

3. Add a `last` instance variable to the `LList` class along the lines suggested in the chapter, so that the `append` method can be implemented in $\Theta(1)$ time. This will require you to update a number of the methods to ensure `self.last` is always a reference to the last `ListNode` in the linked structure.

4. Finish the implementation of the `LListCursor` class and provide a complete set of unit tests for the `LinkedCursorList` class using the list cursor API.

5. Suppose we want our list cursors to be able to move both directions. That is, in addition to the `advance` operation, we'd also like a `backup` operation. Add this ability to the `PyListCursor`. Make sure to write complete unit tests for your updated cursor.

6. Add the capability of the previous exercise to the `LListCursor` class. To do this your cursor will have to keep track of a "trail" of previous nodes. You can use a Python list for this purpose. The predecessor of each node is appended to the list as the cursor advances and then is popped back off the end of the list when the cursor backs up.

7. Modify the linked implementation of the Python list API so that it is a *doubly-linked list*, that is, each `ListNode` has a reference to the `ListNode` before it and the `ListNode` after it. Also add a method named `reverse_iter` that iterates over the list in reverse order using the `yield` keyword. Modify your unit testing code so it also checks the reverse links. Using your doubly-linked list, modify the cursor for this new list to that it solves the previous problem without having to mantain an internal list of predecessor nodes.

8. The Sieve of Eratosthenes is a famous algorithm for finding all the prime numbers up to a certain value. Here is an outline of the algorithm to find all primes $\leq n$ using cursors:

```
place the numbers 2 through n in a list
start primecursor at the front of the list
while primecursor is not done
    prime = value at primecursor
    create checkcursor as a copy of primecursor
    advance checkcursor
    while checkcursor is not done:
        if item at checkcursor is divisible by prime:
            delete the item from the list
        else:
            advance checkcursor
    advance primecursor
output values left in the list, they are prime
```

Write a program that implements this algorithm. Notice that you will need a way to make a copy of a cursor. You will have to figure out how to accomplish this task.

Chapter 5   Stacks and Queues

████████████████████████████

Objectives

- To understand the stack ADT and be familiar with various strategies for building an efficient stack implementation.

- To gain familiarity with the behavior of a stack and understand and anlayze basic stack-based algorithms.

- To understand the queue ADT and be familiar with various strategies for building an efficient queue implementation.

- To gain familiarity with the behavior of a queue and understand and analyze basic queue-based algorithms.

5.1   Overview

In the past two chapters, we have looked in detail at the list data structure. As you know, a list is a sequential structure. We have also looked at sorted lists, where the ordering of the items in the list is dictated by the "value" of the item. Sometimes it is useful for a sequential collection to be ordered according to the time at which items are added, rather than what the particular item is. In this chapter, we'll take a look at two simple examples of such structures, called stacks and queues.

5.2   Stacks

A stack is one of the simplest container classes. As you'll see however, despite its simplicy, a stack can be amazingly useful.

5.2.1 The Stack ADT

Imagine a list (a sequential data structure) where you have access to the data only at one end. That is, you can insert and remove items from one end of the list. Also, you can look at the contents of only the single item at the end of the list (called the top). The rather restrictive data structure just described is called a *stack*. You can think of it as modeling a real-world stack of items: you can only (safely) add or remove an item at the top of a stack. And if things are stacked neatly, only the top item is visible.

   If you are into sweet confections, you might also think of a stack as the computer science equivalent of a Pez candy dispenser. By convention our stacks are "spring loaded," and so adding an item to a stack is called **pushing** the item onto the stack. Removing the top item from a stack is called **popping** it. Notice that the last item pushed on a stack must always be the first item to be popped back off again. Because of this, a stack is also referred to as a last in, first out (LIFO) data structure. You could also call it a FILO structure, and of course a stack of filo dough makes a delicious pastry. The specification for a typical stack ADT looks like this.

```python
class Stack(object):

    def __init__(self):

        """post: creates an empty LIFO stack"""

    def push(self, x):

        """post: places x on top of the stack"""

    def pop(self):

        """pre: self.size() > 0
           post: removes and returns the top element of
                 the stack"""

    def top(self):

        """pre: self.size() > 0
           post: returns the top element of the stack without
                 removing it"""

    def size(self):

        """post: returns the number of elements in the stack"""
```

5.2.2 Simple Stack Applications

Even though they are very simple, stacks can be very handy. You have, no doubt, already come across many uses of stacks in computing, but you may not have recognized them. For example, you have probably used some applications that include an "undo" feature. For example, you might be editing a document in a word processing program and accidently delete a bunch of text; no problem, you quickly go to the Edit menu and select the undo command and your text is "magically" restored. Need to go back even further? Many applications allow you to keep undoing commands to rollback to virtually any previous state. Internally, this is accomplished using a stack. Each time an action is performed, the information about that action is saved on a stack. When "undo" is selected, the last action is popped off the stack and reversed. The size of the stack determines how many levels you can undo.

Another example of the use of stacks is inside the computer itself. You know that functions are an important aspect of programming languages, and modern systems provide hardware features to support programs that make extensive use of functions. When a function is called, the information about the function such as the values of local variables and the return address (where the program left off before calling the function) is pushed on a so-called run-time stack. The last function called is always the first to return, so when a function ends, its information is popped off the run-time stack and the return address is used to tell the CPU the location of the next instruction to execute. As functions are called, the stack grows; each time a function returns, the stack shrinks back. You may notice when you get an errror message in Python, the interpreter prints out a traceback that shows how the error message arose. This traceback shows the contents of the run-time stack at the time the exception was raised.

A stack is also important for the syntactic analysis of computer programs. Programming language structures must always be properly nested. For example, you can have an `if` completely inside of a loop or you can have it outside (before or after) the loop, but it is not correct for an `if` to "straddle" a loop boundary. A stack is the proper data structure for handling nested structures. We can illustrate this using a simpler nesting example, namely parentheses. In mathematics, expressions are often grouped using parentheses. Here's a simple example: $((x + y) * x)/(3 * z)$. In a correct expression, the parentheses are always properly nested, or *balanced*. Looking just at the parentheses, the structure of the previous expression is $(())()$. Every opening parenthesis has a matching closing one, and none of the opening-closing pairs "interleave" with other pairs.

Suppose you were writing an algorithm to check that a sequence of parentheses is properly balanced. How could that be done? Basically, we must guarantee that every time we see a closing parenthesis, there has already been an opening parenthesis that matches it. We can do this by checking that there is an equal number of opening and closing parentheses and that we never have a sequence where more closings have been seen than openings. One simple approach is to keep a "balance" of opening parentheses and make sure that it is always non-zero as we scan the string from left to right. Here's a simple Python function that scans a string to determine whether the parentheses are balanced.

```
# parensBalance1.py
def parensBalance1(s):
    open = 0
    for ch in s:
        if ch == '(':
            open += 1
        elif ch == ')':
            open -= 1
            if open < 0:
                # there is no matching opener, so check fails
                return False
    return open == 0  # everything balances if no unmatched opens
```

So far, this doesn't look very stack-like. However, things get much more interesting if we introduce different types of parenthesis. For example, mathematicians (and programming language designers) often use multiple types of grouping markers, such as parenthesis, (); square brackets, []; and curly braces, {}. Suppose these are mixed in a string such as $[(x + y) * x]/(3 * z)/[sin(x) + cos(y)]$. Now our simple counting approach doesn't work, as we have to ensure that each closing marker is matched to the proper type of opening marker. Even though they have the same number of opening and closing markers, an expression with the structure [()]() is OK, but [()]() is not. Here is where a stack comes to the rescue.

In order to assure proper balancing and nesting with multiple grouping symbols, we have to check that when a closing marker is found, it matches the most recent unmatched opening marker. This is a LIFO problem that is easily solved with a stack. We just need to scan the string from left to right. When an opening marker is found, it is pushed onto a stack. Each time a closing marker is found, the top item of the stack must be the matching opening marker, which is then popped. When we get all done, the stack should be empty. Here's some code to do it:

```
# parensBalance2.py

from Stack import Stack

def parensBalance2(s):
    stack = Stack()
    for ch in s:
        if ch in "([{":       # push an opening marker
            stack.push(ch)
        elif ch in ")]}":     # match closing with top of stack
            if stack.size() < 1: # no pending open to match it
                return False
            else:
                opener = stack.pop()
                if opener+ch not in ["()", "[]", "{}"]:
                    # not a matching pair
                    return False
    return stack.size() == 0 # empty stack means everything matched up
```

Figure 5.1 shows the intermediate steps of tracing the execution of the algorithm using the expression {[2 * (7 - 4) + 2] + 3} * 4. It shows five "snapshots" with the characters processed so far and the current stack contents below them. You should trace through the algorithm by hand to convince yourself that it works.

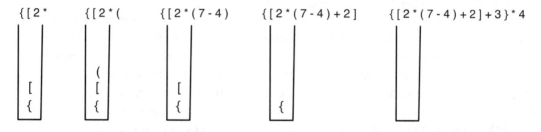

Figure 5.1: Example of tracing through parentheses matching

5.2.3 Implementing Stacks

In a language like Python, the simplest way to implement a stack is to use the built-in list. Given the flexibility of the Python list, each stack operation translates to a single line of code.

```
# Stack.py
class Stack(object):

    def __init__(self):
        self.items = []

    def push(self, item):
        self.items.append(item)

    def pop(self):
        return self.items.pop()

    def top(self):
        return self.items[-1]

    def size(self):
        return len(self.items)
```

Recalling our discussion of Python lists, each of these operations is performed in constant time, so a stack is very efficient. Of course, insertion at the end of a list can occasionally require extra work to create a new array and copy all the values into the new array, but Python does this automatically. As discussed in subsection 3.5.1, the average amount of time to append onto the end of a list remains constant since the array size is increased proportionally as necessary.

If a list type were not readily available, it would also be easy to implement a stack using an array. A stack with a fixed maximum size can be handled by allocating an array of the required maximum size and using an instance variable to keep track of how many "slots" in the array are actually being used. If the maximum stack size is unknown, then the push operation will have to handle allocating a larger array and copying items over when the stack exceeds the current array size.

Another reasonable implementation strategy for a stack is to use a singly linked list of nodes containing the stack data. A stack object would just need an instance variable with a reference to the first node of the linked list, which would be the top of the stack. Again, both pushing and popping are easily accomplished in constant time using a linked structure. As with the pure array implementation, keeping track of the size of the stack in an instance variable is advisable so that the size operation does not have to traverse the list to count items.

5.2.4 An Application: Expression Manipulation

In this section, we will examine some algorithms to manipulate numerical expressions using stacks. The most common way of representing a numerical expression uses a notation known as *infix notation*. The expression (2 + 3) * 4 is an example of an infix expression. The operators are between the numbers. Other possible representations of the expression are * + 2 3 4 and 2 3 + 4 *. The first representation is known as *prefix notation* or *Polish prefix notation* since it was developed by a Polish mathematician. The second representation is commonly known as *reverse Polish notation* or *postfix notation*.

The advantage of the prefix and postfix notation is that parentheses are not necessary to modify the order of operations. The infix expression 3 * (4 + 5) − 2 + (3 * 6) is equivalent to the postfix expression 3 4 5 + * 2 − 3 6 * +. The expression itself indicates the order in which operations are applied. Postfix expressions can also be evaluated very easily using a stack. Each time a number is encountered, it is pushed onto the stack. When an operator is encountered, two numbers are popped off the stack, the operator is applied to those two numbers, and the result is pushed on the stack.

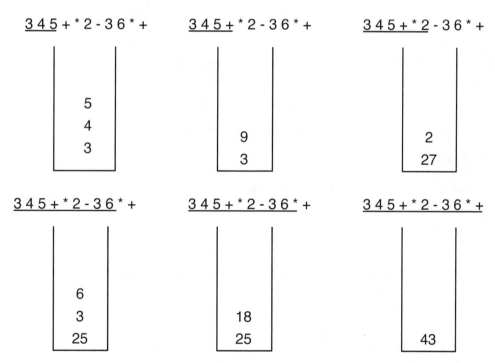

Figure 5.2: Processing a postfix expression

In our example, after processing the three numbers, the stack contains <3, 4, 5> (the top is on the right). When the first plus operator is encountered, we pop off the 5 and 4, add them, and push the answer onto the stack, giving us <3, 9> on the stack. To process the multiplication operator, we pop the 9 and 3, multiply them, and push 27 onto the stack. After processing the 2, the stack is <27, 2>. We process the subtraction operator by popping the 2 and 27 and pushing the resulting 25 onto the stack. After processing the next two numbers, the stack is <25, 3, 6>. We process the multiplication operator and the stack now contains <25, 18>. Finally, after processing the last plus operator, the stack contains the final result which is 43. Figure 5.2 shows these steps pictorially. The underlined portion of the expression is the input that has been processed, and the stack at that point is shown below it.

The algorithm to evaluate a postfix expression is quite simple, but what do we do with the more typical infix expression? One way to handle it is to first convert it to postfix. This is also accomplished with a simple stack algorithm. To explain the algorithm, we will assume that we have already split the expression into a sequence of "tokens" where each token is either a number, an operator, or a parenthesis. For simplicity, our algorithm also assumes that the expression is syntactically correct. Here's the pseudocode for an infix-to-postfix converter:

```
create an empty stack
create an empty list to represent the postfix expression

for each token in the expression:
    if token is a number:
        append it onto the postfix expression

    elif token is a left parenthesis:
        push it onto the stack

    elif token is an operator:
        while (stack is not empty and the top stack item is an operator
            with precedence greater than or equal to token):
            pop and append the operator onto the postfix expression
        push the token onto the stack

    else token must be a right parenthesis
        while the top item on the stack is not a left parenthesis:
            pop item from the stack and append it onto the postfix expression
        pop the left parenthesis

while the stack is not empty
    pop an item from the stack and append it onto the postfix expression
```

Figure 5.3 demonstrates the algorithm on the expression 3 * (4 + 5) - 2 + (3 * 6). Each step shows the state of the process as one more token is read from the infix expression. It is probably not obvious to the reader that the algorithm works in all cases. A couple general observations help clarify things. First, notice that the operands (numbers) in the prefix and postfix expression always occur in the same order. Second, the left-to-right order of the operators in the postfix expression corresponds to the evaluation order of the operations in the infix expression. Armed with these observations, it's pretty easy to decipher the algorithm.

As the numbers are processed, they are immediately appended to the postfix expression, so we know the numbers will remain in the same order. As for the order of operations, notice that the handling of an operator token is delayed by pushing the operator onto the stack so that the following number can first be appended to the output expression. So the expression 3 * 4 becomes 3 4 *. When there are multiple operators, the ordering in the output is determined by their relative precedence. Higher precedence operations are performed first, so they must be appended to the output before lower precedence operators. Consider processing 3 * 4 + 5. When we get to the + token, the output contains 3 4 and the stack contains <*>. Because * has a higher precedence, it is now popped and appended before processing continues, so that the final result is 3 4 * 5 +. A sequence of operators of equal precedence will get appended in a left-to-right order.

That just leaves handling parentheses. When a left parenthesis is processed, it is pushed onto the stack. When the matching right parenthesis is reached, all of the operands inside the parenthesized portion that have not yet been appended to the output are popped and appended. This ensures that these operations appear in the postfix expression before any operations that are evaluated later in the infix expression.

That should give you a basic idea of how and why the algorithm works, but even if you do not completely understand it, you can still implement the pseudocode listed earlier. In general, designing the algorithms and data structures for software systems is more difficult than implementing them.

5.2.5 An Application: Grammar Processing (Optional)

As the expression manipulation examples show, stacks are very useful in manipulating formal languages such as computer programming languages. One of the most common tools for expressing syntactic rules of both computer and natural languages is a *context-free grammar* (*CFG*). A grammar is just what you'd expect, a set of rules that describe the legal sentences of a language. A CFG defines a language in terms of a set of rewriting rules.

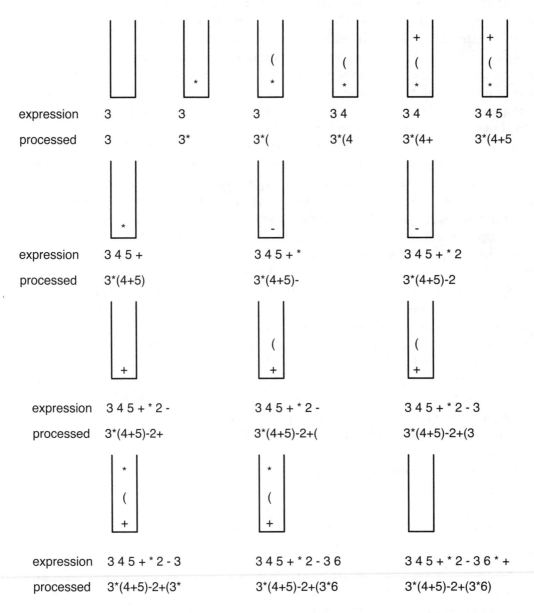

Figure 5.3: Converting the infix expression 3 * (4 + 5) - 2 + (3 * 6) to postfix

Let's consider a simple example. Here's a set of rules that describe a (very) small set of English sentences.

```
1: S -> NP VP
2: NP -> ART N
3: NP -> PN
4: VP -> V NP
5: V -> chased
6: ART -> the
7: N -> dog
8: N -> cat
9: PN -> Emily
```

Notice that each rule has a left-hand side and a right-hand side separated by an arrow. The left-hand side is always a single symbol and the right-hand side is a sequence of symbols. The first rule can be taken as stating that a sentence (S) consists of a noun phrase (NP) followed by a verb phrase (VP). Noun phrases and verb phrases are defined by subsequent rules. Rule 2 states that one way of forming a noun phrase is as an article (ART) followed by a noun (N). Rule 3 provides an alternative way to form a noun phrase; it can consist of a single proper noun (PN).

We can use these rules to form simple sentences. We start with the symbol S and rewrite it using rule 1 to produce the sequence NP VP. We keep applying rules to the sequence of symbols until there are no more rules that apply. The final sequence is our generated sentence. Here is a sample derivation of the sentence "the dog chased the cat." The numbers indicate which rule is being applied at each step.

```
      S
=1=> NP VP
=2=> ART N VP
=6=> the N VP
=7=> the dog VP
=4=> the dog V NP
=5=> the dog chased NP
=2=> the dog chased ART N
=6=> the dog chased the
=8=> the dog chased the cat
```

Since none of the words in the final sequence appears as the left-hand side of a rule in our sample grammar, there is no more rewriting to do, and the final sequence "the dog chased the cat" is a sentence that is produced (or accepted) by this grammar.

In more technical terms, the symbols that appear on the left-hand sides of grammar rules are called *non-terminal* symbols, and those that appear only on the right-hand side are *terminal* symbols. The rewriting continues until we get a sequence composed entirely of terminal symbols. Thus the set of terminal symbols (words in this case) are the tokens that can appear in sentences of the language described by the grammar. The non-terminal symbols are not part of the language being described, but are internal components of the grammar itself. You can think of the non-terminals as describing phrase categories for the language. While a natural language has categories such as noun phrase and verb phrase, a programming language would have categories such as expression and statement.

CFGs are very closely related to the stack data structure. In fact, an interesting result in theoretical computer science demonstrates that the set of languages that can be described by such grammars is exactly the same set of languages that can be recognized by a certain very simple kind of stack-based computer called a *pushdown automaton*. In practice, this means that many language processing tasks such as analyzing the syntax of computer programs or understanding natural language utterances often employ stack-based algorithms.

To illustrate the point, we'll walk through the design for a simple grammar ADT that will allow us to generate sentences using simple CFGs. Our grammar class will manage a set of grammar rules using a very simple API. To create a grammar, we'll add rules to an initially empty **Grammar** object. For example, here's an interactive session that begins creating the sample grammar we looked at above:

```
>>> gram = Grammar()
>>> gram.addRule("S -> NP VP")
>>> gram.addRule("NP -> ART N")
>>> gram.addRule("NP -> PN")
```

Once we've created a grammar, we want to be able to generate random phrases and sentences from the grammar.

```
>>> gram.generate("ART")
'the'
>>> gram.generate("N")
'dog'
>>> gram.generate("VP")
'chased the cat'
>>> gram.generate("S")
'the cat chased the dog'
```

Notice that the **generate** method takes a non-terminal symbol from the grammar as a parameter and then produces a phrase starting from that non-terminal. To generate a complete sentence, we start with S.

Let's try our hand at designing this class. As a first cut, we can use a Python list to store our grammar rules. While the rules are presented as strings, structurally, they really consist of a single non-terminal on the left and a sequence of non-terminal and terminal symbols on the right. We can represent each rule as an ordered pair (non-terminal, expansion) where the expansion is just a list of the symbols on the right-hand side. We can save these pairs in a list to represent all the rules of the grammar. Here's the contructor for our class:

```
# Grammar.py
from Stack import Stack

class Grammar(object):

    def __init__(self):
        self.rules = []
        self.nonterms = []
```

The `nonterms` list will keep track of the non-terminals in the grammar (symbols that appear on the left-hand side of any rule) so that we can distinguish terminals from non-terminals later on.

To add a rule to the grammar, we just need to split it into its constituent parts, add them to `rules`, and if necessary, update the `nonterms` list.

```
    def addRule(self, rule):
        # split the rule at the arrow
        lhs, rhs = rule.split("->")

        # extract the non-terminal, ignoring spaces
        nt = lhs.strip()

        # split the rhs into a list of symbols and reverse it
        symbols = rhs.split()
        symbols.reverse()

        # pair the non-terminal with the symbol sequence and store it
        self.rules.append((nt,symbols))

        # update the non-terminal list
        if nt not in self.nonterms:
            self.nonterms.append(nt)
```

The only quirk in this code is that the right-hand side of the rule is reversed before being stored in the rules list. This is done to facilitate the stack-based processing that will occur later. The sequence on the right-hand side will be pushed onto a stack, and we want the left-most symbol to be the top of the stack, so the order to push is right to left from the original rule. Doing the reversal here saves us from having to do the reversal every time the rule is used.

Now we are ready to generate sentences. If you go back to the sample derivation of the sentence "the dog chased the cat," you'll notice that we always chose to expand the left-most non-terminal in the developing sequence. That means we were always dealing with a (possibly empty) sequence of words that starts the sentence followed by a sequence of non-terminals that still needed to be expanded to complete the sentence. We can use a stack to model the remaining non-terminals, where the left-most one is at the top of the stack. From there, we just perform a loop that pops the top thing off the stack; if it's a terminal (a word) then we append it to the output. In the case of a non-terminal, we choose a rule to expand it and push the expansion (the symbols on the right-hand side of the rule) onto the stack. When the stack is empty, we've run out of things to expand and the derivation is complete.

Here's Python code to implement this algorithm:

```python
def generate(self, start):
    s = Stack()
    s.push(start)
    output = []
    while s.size() > 0:
        top = s.pop()
        if self.isTerminal(top):
            # doesn't expand, it's part of the output
            output.append(top)
        else:
            # choose one expansion from all that might be used
            cands = self.getExpansions(top)
            expansion = random.choice(cands)
            # push the chosen expansion onto the stack
            for symbol in expansion:
                s.push(symbol)
    return " ".join(output)

def isTerminal(self, term):
    return term not in self.nonterms

def getExpansions(self, nt):
    expansions = []
    for (nt1, expansion) in self.rules:
        if nt1 == nt:    # this rule matches
            copy = list(expansion)
            expansions.append(copy)
    return expansions
```

Notice that the output is built up using a list. The words in this list are then joined into a string to be returned as the function's result. Notice also that a couple helper methods have been used to simplify the coding. The `getExpansions` method simply looks through the set of rules to find all whose left-hand side match the current non-terminal. It returns a list containing all the corresponding right-hand sides. There we have it: a complete class for generating random sentences based on a context-free grammar. You might try your hand at writing some simple grammars and seeing what kind of sentences you come up with.

5.3   Queues

Another common data structure that orders items according to when they arrive is called a *queue*. Whereas a stack is a last in, first out structure, the ordering of a queue is first in, first out (FIFO). You are undoubtedly familiar with the concept since you often spend time in a queue yourself. When you are standing in line at a restaurant or store, you are in a queue. In fact, British English speakers don't stand in line, they "wait on queue."

5.3.1   A Queue ADT

Conceptually, a queue is a sequential structure that allows restricted access at both ends. Items are added at one end and removed from the other. As usual, computer scientists have their own terminology for these operations. Adding an item to the back of a queue is called an *enqueue*, and the operation to remove an item from the front is called *dequeue*. As with stacks, it is also handy to be able to peek at the item on the front of the queue without having to remove it. This is usually called *front*, but other terms are sometimes used like *head* or *first*.

Here is a specification of the `Queue` ADT:

```
class Queue(object):

    def __init__(self):

        """post: creates an empty FIFO queue"""

    def enqueue(self, x):

        """post: adds x at back of queue"""
```

```
    def dequeue(self):

        """pre: self.size() > 0
           post: removes and returns the front item"""

    def front(self):

        """pre: self.size() > 0
           postcondition: returns first item in queue"""

    def size(self):

        """postcondition: return number of items in queue"""
```

5.3.2　Simple Queue Applications

Queues are commonly used in computer programming as a sort of buffer between different phases of a computing process. For example, when you print out a document, your "job request" is placed on a queue in the computer operating system, and these jobs are generally printed in a first come, first served order. In this case, the queue is used to coordinate action across separate processes (the application that requests the printing and the computer operating system that actually sends information to the printer). Queues are also frequently used as intermediate, data way stations within a single computer program. For example, a compiler or interpreter might need to make a series of "passes" over a program to translate it into machine code. Often the first pass is a so-called *lexical analysis* that splits the program into its meaningful pieces, the tokens. A queue is the perfect data structure to store the sequence of tokens for subsequent processing by the next phase, which is typically some sort of grammar-based syntactic analysis.

As an example of using a queue for an intermediate data structure, consider the problem of determining whether or not a phrase is a palindrome. A palindrome is a sentence or phrase that has the same sequence of letters when read either forward or backward. Some famous examples are "Madam, I'm Adam" or "I prefer PI." Some words like "racecar" are palindromes all by themselves. Let's write a program to analyze user input and validate it as a palindrome. The heart of the program will be an isPalindrome function:

```
def isPalindrome(phrase):

    """pre:  phrase is a string
       post: returns True if the alphabetic characters in phrase
             form the same sequence reading either left-to-right
             or right-to-left.
    """
```

The tricky part of the `isPalindrome` function is that the palindromeness of a phrase is determined only by the letters; spaces, punctuation, and capitalization don't matter. We need to see if the sequence of letters is the same in both directions. One way to approach this issue is to break the problem down into phases. In the first phase we strip away the extraneous portions and boil the expression down to its constituent letters. Then a second pass can compare the letter sequence in both the forward and backward directions to see whether they match up. Conveniently, a queue data structure can be used to store the characters so they can be accessed again in the original order, and a stack can be used to store them for access in a reversed order (remember, a stack reverses its data).

Recasting this two-phase algorithm as a Python program, we get the following:

```
# palindrome.py
from MyQueue import Queue
from Stack import Stack

def isPalindrome(phrase):
    forward = Queue()
    reverse = Stack()
    extractLetters(phrase, forward, reverse)
    return sameSequence(forward, reverse)
```

Now we just need to define the functions that implement the two phases: `extractLetters` and `sameSequence`. The former must go through the phrase and add each letter to both the intermediate stack and queue. Here's one way to do that.

```
import string
def extractLetters(phrase, q, s):
    for ch in phrase:
        if ch.isalpha():
            ch = ch.lower()
            q.enqueue(ch)
            s.push(ch)
```

The `sameSequence` function needs to compare the letters on the stack and queue. If all the letters match up, we have a palindrome. As soon as two letters fail to match, we know that our phrase has failed the test.

```
def sameSequence(q, s):
    while q.size() > 0:
        ch1 = q.dequeue()
        ch2 = s.pop()
        if ch1 != ch2:
            return False
    return True
```

With the `isPalindrome` function in hand you should be able to easily complete our palindrome checking program. Try it out on these two examples: "Able was I, ere I saw Elba" and "Evil was I, ere I saw Elvis" Obviously, only one of these is really a palindrome. A quick search on the Internet will yield lots of interesting test data. Of course, you'll need an implementation of queues to get your program up and running; read ahead for some hints.

5.4 Queue Implementations

Implementing a queue with Python's built-in list is straightforward. We just need to insert at one end of the list and remove from the other end. Since the Python list is implemented as an array, inserting at the beginning is an inefficient operation if the list is very long. Removing an element from the beginning of the list is also inefficient; so neither option is ideal.

An alternative would be to use a linked implementation. The sequence of items can be maintained as a singly linked list. The queue object itself then maintains instance variables that point to the first and last nodes of the queue. As long as we do insertions at the end of the linked list and removals from the front, both of these operations can easily be done in constant ($\Theta(1)$) time. Of course, the linked implementation would be a lot trickier to code. Before pursuing this or other options, it might be wise to consider the words of Tony Hoare, a very famous computer scientist: "Premature optimization is the root of all evil." There are a number of justifications for this statement. It does not make sense to worry about optimizing code until you are certain what the bottlenecks are (i.e., where most of the time is being spent). If you double the speed of code that is 5% of the execution time of your program, your program will execute only about 3% faster. But if you double the speed of code that is 50% of the execution time, your program will execute about 33% faster. As we have already seen with the binary search algorithm, more efficient code is often more complex and more difficult to get correct. Before you worry about making a specific section of code more efficient, you should make certain that it will have a significant effect on the speed of your overall program.

In the case of implementing a queue in Python, there is the additional consideration that the underlying Python list operations are coded in very efficient C code and can take advantage of system-level calls that move blocks of memory around very quickly. In theory, we may be able to write linked code with better asymptotic (theta) behavior, but the queue sizes will have to be very large indeed before our linked code overtakes the optimized Python list code. Coding a linked implementation of a queue is a great exercise in using linked structures, but we have yet to encounter a situation in practice when such a queue actually out-performed one based on the built-in list.

In languages such as C/C++ and Java that support fixed-size arrays, an array is often the appropriate structure to use to implement a queue, particularly if the maximum queue size is known ahead of time. Instead of performing the `enqueue` and `dequeue` operations by shifting elements in the array, we can keep track of the indices that represent both the front/head and back/tail of the queue. As long as the maximum number of elements in the queue at any point in time does not exceed the size of the array, this is an excellent method for implementing queues. Each time an item is added to the queue, the tail index is increased by one. If we add one and use the modulus operator we can easily make the index wrap around to the beginning of the array, simulating a circular array representation. For an array of size 10, we'd increment the tail like this:

```
tail = (tail + 1) % 10
```

Since the index positions start at 0, the last position is index 9. When we add 1 to 9 we get 10 and 10 modulus (remainder) 10 is 0. This is a common technique used in many computer algorithms to wrap around back to 0 after some maximum value is reached. The same technique is used for incrementing `head` when an item is dequeued. The effect is that the `head` index chases the `tail` index around and around the array. As long as items remain in the queue, `head` never quite catches `tail`.

In Python, the circular array technique could also be used by simply starting with a list of the appropriate size. List repetition provides an easy way to do this.

```
...
self.items = [None] * 10
```

There is one subtlety in the circular array/list approach to queues. We need to think carefully about the values for `head` and `tail` that indicate when the queue is full or empty. Writing an invariant for the class that relates these values is an excellent technique to make certain we get it right. We would like the **head** index to indicate where the front item in the queue is located in the array. It makes sense for the **tail** index to indicate either the position of the last item in the queue or the following location where the next item inserted into the queue would be placed. When the queue is empty, it is not clear what the values should be for **head** and **tail**. Since we are using a circular array it is possible that the value for **tail** is less than **head**. And after inserting a few items and then removing those items, **head** and **tail** are in the middle of the array/list so we cannot use any fixed values of **head** and **tail** to indicate an empty queue. Instead, we must rely on their relative values.

Suppose we start with a empty queue having both **head** and **tail** set to index 0. Then clearly when **head == tail** the queue is empty. Suppose the size of the circular array is n. Now consider what happens if we enqueue n items without any dequeues. As the tail pointer is incremented n times, it will wrap around and land back at 0. Thus, for a full queue, we once again have the condition **head == tail**. That's a problem. Since both a full queue and an empty queue "look" exactly the same, we can't tell which we have by looking at the values of **head** and **tail**. We could rescue the situation by simply agreeing that a "full" queue contains only $n - 1$ items, in effect wasting one cell. However, a simpler approach is just to use a separate instance variable that keeps track of the number of items in the queue. This approach leads us to the following invariant:

1. The instance variable **size** indicates the number of items in the queue and 0 **<= size <= capacity** where **capacity** is the fixed size of the array/list.

2. If size > 0, the queue items are found at locations **items[(head+i)%capacity]**, for i in **range(size)**, where **items[head]** is the front of the queue and **tail == (head+size-1)%capacity**.

3. If **size == 0, head == (tail+1)%capacity**.

Using this invariant, you should be able to complete a circular list implementation of a queue without too much effort.

$\boxed{5.5}$ An Example Application: Queueing Simulations (Optional)

One common use of queues is modeling the behavior of real-world queues. You can find queues all over in the world from banks and theaters to car washes, assembly lines, and restaurants. For our example, let's look at a mom-and-pop retail store that has only a single check-out register. The store has been getting busier lately, and customers are starting to complain about the amount of time they spend waiting in line. The owner is in a quandry over whether to upgrade the register so that a single checker can work faster or whether she should remodel the store so that it can have more check-out lines. Obviously, the latter approach would be much more costly, and she doesn't know if it's worth the money.

We can write a simulation that models the check-out line at the store in order to try out various options and answer questions such as how long customers wait in line on average, what is the maximum wait, and how long does the line get? We can also parameterize our simulation so that we can experiment with different check-out rates to see the effect that a faster register might bring. Our simulation will illustrate a small part of an important field of applied mathematics known as operations research.

Our simulation will be a simple model of the check-out process. Customers arrive in the check-out line with a certain number of items and are served in the order that they arrive. Of course, customers don't arrive at a constant rate. There is a certain amount of randomness to their comings and goings. Similarly, the time it takes to check customers out varies randomly according to the number and type of items that they are purchasing. As with any simulation, we'll have to abstract away most of the specific details so that we can model the heart of the problem.

To start with, we need some way to keep track of the passage of time. Abstractly, it does not matter what units of times we use, we just need to choose a scale suitable for the simulation at hand. Measuring times to process customers in terms of seconds seems convenient, but we can keep our model more general by just talking in terms of "clock ticks." For our simulation a tick might be one second; for a simulation of a computer system, a tick might be one millisecond. For a climate simulation, a tick might be a year. Our simulation will start at time 0, and we'll increment a counter to represent the passage of time tick by tick.

Now we need to think about how to represent the customers. Ultimately, we are interested in how much time they spend in line. If we have a `time` variable that keeps track of the current time, we can look at this "clock" to see what time it is when we process the customer's items. If we know what time they arrived in line, then a simple subtraction will tell us how long they waited. We also need to know how long it takes to check them out, because that much time has to pass before we process the next customer. We can model this simply by associating a number of items with each customer and then multiplying that by the average time to process a single item. Ultimately then, we've decided that we need to know two

pieces of information about each customer: the time at which they arrive in line
(`arrivalTime`) and the number of items they have (`itemCount`).

The raw data for our simulation will be a sequence of customers that have
randomly generated arrival times and item counts. To make simulations as realistic
as possible, operations researchers rely on statisical models to produce events in a
way that models the real world. For example, if we were to look at a simple variable
like `itemCount`, we could analyze a sample of actual customers to find the "average"
number of items purchased on a given trip to the store. But this average does not
tell the whole story; obviously, not every customer gets exactly the average. The
actual number or items in various people's carts would be distributed around this
average. The problem is further complicated in that the distribution is probably not
symmetric, since the fewest items a customer can get is one, but there is (virtually)
no upper limit on the number of items they can have. Similar considerations apply
to the arrival times of customers. There is a certain average rate at which they
arrive, but they will not come at a constant fixed rate. Sometimes they will arrive
in bunches and other times there will be lulls.

Since this is not intended to be a book on operations research, we'll stick to some
fairly simple approaches to generate our sequence of customers. We will assume that
the number of items that customers buy is uniformly distributed between 1 and
some settable parameter `MAX_ITEMS`. We can just use Python's `randrange` function
to generate a random `itemCount` for each customer. We'll set the arrival time
for customers by setting an average arrival rate and then using a uniform random
generator to determine the times when customers actually arrive to satisfy that rate.
Armed with this much analysis, we're ready to write some code that can generate the
sequence of events (customer arrivals) that will serve as the input to our simulation.

We could just generate arrival events "on the fly" as we run our simulation,
just like it happens in the real world. However, there our advantages to generating
the sequence of events first and saving the information to a file. For one thing,
it allows us to try out different simulations on the exact same sequence of events.
For example, with a pregenerated sequence of events, we can run a simulation at
two different checker speeds to get a head-to-head comparison of the difference.
Another advantage is that it separates the simulation itself into two phases so that
we could later modify the way the input is generated, perhaps substituting different
probability distributions without having to make any changes to the simulation code.

Let's make this more concrete by writing some code to generate our customers.
Remember, we just need to generate `arrivalTime` and `itemCount` for each customer.
We'll save this information in a file where each line of the file corresponds to one

event. Each line contains an `arrivalTime` followed by an `itemCount`. Here are the first few lines of a sample file:

```
49 39
143 20
205 26
237 44
```

In this data, the first customer arrived at time 49 with 39 items, then the second customer arrived in line at time 143 with 20 items, and so on. Notice that the `arrivalTimes` are listed in increasing order.

Here's a function to generate our simulation data.

```
# simulation.py
from random import random, randrange

def genTestData(filename, totalTicks, maxItems, arrivalInterval):
    outfile = open(filename, "w")
    # step through the ticks
    for t in range(1,totalTicks):
        if random() < 1./arrivalInterval:
            # a customer arrives this tick
            # with a random number of items
            items = randrange(1, maxItems+1)
            outfile.write("%d %d\n" % (t, items))
    outfile.close()
```

In the parameter list, `filename` gives the name of the output file, `totalTicks` is the length of time over which the simulation will be run, `maxItems` is an upper limit on the number of items a customer will have, and `arrivalInterval` indicates, on average, the number of ticks between arrivals. Suppose the store normally averages about 30 customers an hour. That's a customer every two minutes. If a tick represents one second, then we expect about 120 ticks between customers. Notice how arrival times are handled in the code. If we expect one customer every 120 ticks, then for each tick, there's a 1 in 120 chance that a customer is arriving. The expression `random() < 1./arrivalInterval` succeeds (evaluates to True) with $1/$`arrivalInterval` probability. This gives us random arrivals that, over the long haul, occur at the desired rate. To generate a three-hour simulation with customers purchasing up to 50 items at an average of two-minute intervals, we would call the function like this:

```
genTestData("checkerData.txt", 3*60*60, 50, 120)
```

Our simulation program will deal with customers as they arrive in line. From the program's point of view, it doesn't matter if the customers are being read from a file or being provided in real time by another program or some other process. In fact, this is a perfect place to use a queue as an intermediary between whatever process is creating the data and our simulation. First, let's create a `Customer` class to encapsulate the details about each customer.

```python
class Customer(object):

    def __init__(self, arrivalTime, itemCount):
        self.arrivalTime = int(arrivalTime)
        self.itemCount = int(itemCount)

    def __repr__(self):
        return ("Customer(arrivalTime=%d, itemCount=%d)" %
                (self.arrivalTime, self.itemCount))
```

Since our customer information is just a "record" containing the `arrivalTime` and `itemCount` data, we'll just access this information directly later on when necessary (e.g., `customer.itemCount`). The `__repr__` method provides a nice, printable representation for customers. This is handy so that we can inspect our data structure during testing and debugging. Now it's a simple matter to write a function that will input a data file and create a queue of customer events.

```python
def createArrivalQueue(fname):
    q = Queue()
    infile = open(fname)
    for line in infile:
        time, items = line.split()
        q.enqueue(Customer(time,items))
    infile.close()
    return q
```

The actual simulation will be carried out in a `CheckerSim` object. The constructor accepts a queue of events and an average item-processing time as parameters. Here's one way of coding the `CheckerSim` class.

```python
# CheckerSim.py
from MyQueue import Queue

class CheckerSim(object):
```

```
    def __init__(self, arrivalQueue, avgTime):
        self.time = 0                      # ticks so far in simulation
        self.arrivals = arrivalQueue # queue of arrival events to process
        self.line = Queue()                # customers waiting in line
        self.serviceTime = 0               # time left for current customer
        self.totalWait = 0                 # sum of wait time for all customers
        self.maxWait = 0                   # longest wait of any customer
        self.customerCount = 0             # number of customers processed
        self.maxLength = 0                 # maximum line length
        self.ticksPerItem = avgTime  # time to process an item

    def run(self):
        while (self.arrivals.size() > 0 or
                self.line.size() > 0 or
                self.serviceTime > 0):
            self.clockTick()

    def averageWait(self):
        return float(self.totalWait) / self.customerCount

    def  maximumWait(self):
        return self.maxWait

    def maximumLineLength(self):
        return self.maxLength

    def clockTick(self):
        # one tick of time elapses
        self.time += 1
        # customer(s) arriving at current time enter the line
        while (self.arrivals.size() > 0 and
                self.arrivals.front().arrivalTime == self.time):
            self.line.enqueue(self.arrivals.dequeue())
            self.customerCount += 1
        # if line has reached a new maximum, remember that
        self.maxLength = max(self.maxLength, self.line.size())
        # process items
        if self.serviceTime > 0:
            # a customer is currently being helped
            self.serviceTime -= 1
        elif self.line.size() > 0:
            # help the next customer in line
            customer = self.line.dequeue()
            #print self.time, customer       # nice tracing point
            # compute and update statistics on this customer
            self.serviceTime = customer.itemCount * self.ticksPerItem
            waitTime = self.time - customer.arrivalTime
            self.totalWait += waitTime
            self.maxWait = max(self.maxWait, waitTime)
```

A simulation is executed by calling its `run` method. This method executes a loop that calls `clockTick` until the simulation is complete. This particular approach is an example of a *time-driven simulation*. We simply increment the clock one tick at a time and do whatever has to be done in that tick. Any events in the `arrivalQueue` that occur at the given tick are moved into the `line`. If the checker is currently helping a customer, the amount of time still needed to process the customer's items is stored in `serviceTime`. We simply need to decrement this variable. If service time is 0, then the checker can begin helping the next customer in line. If the line is empty, the checker doesn't do anything. You should study this code carefully to make sure you understand how it works.

For this particular problem, a time-driven solution is not necessarily the best approach. Many of our cycles around the tick-loop will essentially be idle time. An alternative approach is to use an *event-driven simulation*. The idea behind an event-driven approach is that we don't model each tick of the clock, but simply "jump ahead" to the next event that will have to be processed. For example, if the next customer in line will take 50 ticks to process, we don't really need to tick the clock 50 times, we can advance it 50 ticks in one step. Of course, that also means we will have to add to the line all of the arrival events that occur during that 50 tick window. A time-driven version is easy to understand, but the event-driven approach has the advantage that we need to go around the loop only once per customer, rather than once per clock tick. A three- hour simluation involves 10,800 ticks, but probably fewer than 100 customers, so that could be quite a savings. Completing an event-driven version of our simulation is left as an exercise.

5.6 Chapter Summary

This chapter has discussed two simple, but very common data structures: stack and queue. Key ideas of these structures are

- A stack is a sequential container that only allows access to one item, called the "top" of the stack. Items are added and removed in a last-in, first-out (LIFO) manner. Stacks naturally reverse a sequence and support the standard operations: `push`, `pop`, `top`, and `size`.

- Among the applications of stacks are maintaining "undo" lists, tracking function calls in a running program, and checking proper nesting of grouping symbols.

- A stack is easily implemented using list-based, array-based, or linked-list techniques.

- Expressions can be represented using prefix, infix, or postfix syntax. Stack-based algorithms are useful for converting between different expression types and evaluating expressions.

- Context-free grammars (CFGs) are a simple formalism for expressing the syntax of a wide class of languages. CFGs are closely related to stack-based computations.

- A queue is a sequential container object that allows restricted access to the front and back of the sequence. Items can only be added to the back and removed from the front. A queue is a first in, first out (FIFO) structure. Queues support the standard operations: `enqueue`, `dequeue`, `front`, and `size`.

- Queues are widely used as a "buffer" between different computational processes or phases of a single process.

- A queue implemented with a Python list will have $\Theta(n)$ behavior for either enqueue or dequeue, but is probably efficient enough for most applications. A circular array implementation or a linked implementation can be used to provide $\Theta(1)$ behavior for all operations.

- One use of queueing is in operations research simulations. Such simulations can be either time driven or event driven. A time-driven simulation increments a simulated clock one tick at a time and checks what events happen at each tick. An event-driven simulation processes one event at a time and adjusts the clock by the amount of time passed before the next event.

5.7 Exercises

True/False Questions

1. Items come out of a stack in the same order they go in.

2. The operation for adding an item to a stack is called `push`.

3. The `top` operation does not modify the contents of a stack.

4. An expression has balanced parentheses if it contains an equal number of opening and closing parentheses.

5. A Python list is not a very good choice for implementing a stack.

6. Items come out of a queue in the same order that they go in.

7. A queue allows for the inspection of items at either end.

8. The operation to remove an item from the front of a queue is called `front`.

9. "Racecar" is a palindrome.

10. A queue implemented using the `insert` and `pop` operations on a Python list will have $\Theta(1)$ efficiency for all operations.

Multiple Choice Questions

1. By definition, a stack must be a(n)

   a) FIFO structure
   b) LIFO structure
   c) linked structure
   d) array-based structure

2. Which of the following is not a stack operation?

   a) `push`   b) `unstack`   c) `pop`   d) `top`

3. Which of the following is not an application of a stack?

   a) Keeping track of command history for an "undo" feature.
   b) Keeping track of function calls in a running program.
   c) Checking for proper nesting of parentheses.
   d) All of the above are stack applications.

4. What is the result of evaluating the postfix expression `5 4 3 + 2 * -`?

   a) `-2`   b) `3`   c) `15`   d) None of these

5. What is the correct postfix form for `3 + 4 * 5`?

   a) `3 4 + 5 *`   b) `3 4 * 5 +`   c) `3 4 5 + *`   d) `3 4 5 * +`

6. By definition, a queue must be a(n)

   a) FIFO structure
   b) LIFO structure
   c) linked structure
   d) array-based structure

7. Which of the following is not an operation of the queue ADT?

   a) `enqueue`   b) `dequeue`   c) `requeue`   d) `front`

8. Which implementation of a queue cannot guarantee $\Theta(1)$ behavior for all operations:

   a) a circular list/array implementation
   b) a linked implementation with front and back references
   c) a Python list implementation using `insert` and `pop`
   d) All of the above yield $\Theta(1)$ operations.

9. The process of splitting a string up into its meaningful pieces is called

   a) splitation.
   b) semantic chopping.
   c) syntactic chopping.
   d) lexical analysis.

10. When using a linked implementation of a queue, where should insertions be done?

   a) at the front (head) of the linked list
   b) at the end (tail) of the linked list
   c) in the middle of the list
   d) either a) or b) will work

Short-Answer Questions

1. What is the running-time analysis of each stack method using

   a) a linked list implementation?
   b) a Python list implementation?

2. What is the running-time analysis of the infix-to-postfix converter in terms of the number of tokens in the expression?

3. What is the running-time analysis of each queue method using

   a) a Python list (non-circular) implementation?
   b) a circular list/array implementation?
   c) a linked implementation with only a head reference?
   d) a linked implementation with head and tail references?

4. Suppose you had a programming language with the only built-in container type being a stack. Explain how each of the following ADTs could be implemented, and give the running time for the basic operations. Try to come up with the most efficient implementation you can. Hint: you might use more than one stack to implement a given ADT.

   a) queue
   b) cursor-based List
   c) index-based list (random access)

5. Experiment with different scenarios using the checker simulation. What do you think the maximum line length will be as the average rate of arrivals approaches the average rate of check-out? Run some simulations to test your hypothesis.

Programming Exercises

1. Write a `Stack` and a `Queue` class with unit test code for each class. Test out the palindrome program from the chapter using your stack and queue.

2. Implement the infix-to-postfix algorithm described in this chapter.

3. Write a function that accepts a valid postfix expression and evaluates it.

4. Suppose a queue is being used to store numbers, and we want to see if the numbers currently in the queue are in order. Write and test a function `queueInOrder(someQueue)` that returns a Boolean indicating whether `someQueue` is in sorted order. After calling the function, the queue should look exactly like it did before the function call. Your function should only make use of the available queue ADT operations; accessing the underlying representation is not allowed.

5. Hypertext markup language (HTML) is a notation used to describe the contents of web pages. The latest HTML standard is XHTML. Web browsers read HTML/XHTML to determine how web pages should be displayed. HTML tags are enclosed in angle brackets ($<$ and $>$). In XHTML, tags generally appear in start tag, end tag combinations. A start tag has the form `<name attributes>`. The matching end tag contains just the name preceeded by a /. For example, a paragraph of text might be formatted like this:

```
<p align="center"> This is a centered paragraph </p>
```

XHTML also allows self-closing tags of the form `<name attributes />`. In a proper XHTML file, the tags will occur in properly nested pairs. Each start tag is matched by a corresponding end tag, and one structure may be embedded inside another, but they cannot overlap. For example `<p>...<ol>...</ol>...</p>` is OK, but `<p>...<ol>...</p>...</ol>` is not. A self-closing tag acts as a self-contained start-end pair.

Write a program that checks XHTML files (web pages) to see if the embedded XHTML tags balance properly. The program will read XHTML input from a file and print out an analysis of the file. The sequence of tags in the file should be echoed to the output; any other text in the XHTML file is ignored. If there is a tag balancing error or the program reaches the end of the file while in the middle of a tag, the program should quit and print an error message. If the end of the file is reached without any errors, a message to that effect should be printed.

6. A marble clock is a novelty timepiece that shows the current time via the configuration of marbles in its trays. Typically, such a clock has a reservoir of marbles at the bottom that acts like a queue. That is, marbles enter the reservoir and one end and are removed from the other. The clock keeps time via an arm that circulates once a minute lifting a marble from the front of the reservoir and dropping it into the top of the clock. The clock has a series of three trays for showing the time. Marbles enter and leave the trays from one end only (i.e., they function as stacks).

The top tray is the minute tray and is labeled with the numbers 1-4. The first marble rolls into position 1, the next into 2, and so on. The fifth marble entering the tray overbalances it, causing it to dump out. The last marble in then falls to the next tray, and the remaining four return to the reservoir. The second tray in the clock has 11 positions, labeled 5, 10, 15, 20, ... 55. When a twelfth marble enters this tray, it dumps its contents, with the last marble again dropping to the next tray, and the other 11 returning to the reservoir. The third and final tray shows hours. It has one marble permanently affixed at position 1, and then has 11 spaces for hours labeled 2, 3, 4, ..., 12. When a twelfth marble drops in this tray, it tips and all 12 marbles return to the reservoir. At that point, the clock has completed a 12-hour cycle, and there are no (free) marbles left in any of the trays.

You are to write a program that simulates the behavior of the marble clock to answer some questions about its behavior. As the clock runs, the marbles in the reservoir get shuffled up. We want to know how many 12-hour cycles it takes to put the marbles back in order. Your program should allow the user to enter a number, N ($>= 27$) that represents the number of marbles in the reservoir at the start. Your program should simulate the behavior of the clock and count how many 12-hour cycles pass before the marbles are all back in the reservoir in the original order. It should print this result.

Hints: you can use `ints` $0\ldots(N-1)$ to represent the marbles. You will need to write a function (see exercise 4) that determines when the resevior is back in order. For N = 27, the answer is 25.

7. The previous exercise, involves simulating the marble clock until the reservoir is back in order. Another approach to this problem is to consider a single cycle of the clock as defining a permutation. That is, we can extract the order of the marbles from the reservoir, and it tells us exactly how the marbles are shuffled. For example, if the first number in the queue is 8, that means that the number that was in position 8 moved to position 0.

   Design a permutation class to represent a rearrangement. You need a constructor and a method that applies the permutation to a list. Then redo the clock problem by running the clock for just one cycle, extracting the permutation, and then repeatedly applying the permutation until you get a list that is back in order.

8. The number of times a permutation must be applied before it restores a sequence to its original order is called the "order of the permutation." The order of a permutation can be determined by partitioning the permutation into its cycles and then finding the least common multiple of the cycle lengths. For example, the permutation that turns [0, 1, 2, 3, 4] into [4, 3, 0, 1, 2] contains two cyles: (0, 2, 4) and (1, 3). The first cycle shows that the item in position 0 moves to position 2, the item in position 2 moves to position 4 and the item in position 4 moves to position 0. The second cycle shows that positions 1 and 3 just swap places. This permutation has the order $3(2) = 6$. So applying the rearrangement six times puts a sequence back in order.

   Extend your permutation class from the previous exercise with a method that calculates the order of the permutation. Use your new method to solve the marble clock problem again. Experimentally compare the efficiency of this approach to the previous versions.

9. Write an event-driven version of the checker simulation. Make sure it produces the same results as the time-driven simulation in the chapter.

10. Suppose our retail store is going to upgrade from one to two checkers. Either we can have a single line with the person at the front of the line going to whichever checker is free (similar to airline check-in and some banks) or we can have two separate lines where we assume that arriving customers will queue up in the shortest line. Write a simulation to determine if there is any significant advantage to one approach over the other in terms of the average waiting time for the customers.

Chapter 6 — Recursion

_____

Objectives

- To understand the basic principles of recursion as a problem solving technqiue.

- To be able to write well-formed recursive functions.

- To be able to analyze the behavior of simple recursive functions and predict their run-time efficiency.

- To be able to analyze the benefits and drawbacks of recursion vis-à-vis iteration and employ each where appropriate.

6.1 Introduction

As you surely know by now, one of the best techniques to use when designing programs is to break a problem down into smaller subproblems. In some situations, you may end up with smaller versions of the same problem. For example, think back to the basic binary search algorithm for finding an item in a sorted list; we covered it way back in subsection 1.3.2. To jog your memory, here's the code that we developed:

```
def search(items, target):
    low = 0
    high = len(items) - 1
    while low <= high:          # There is still a range to search
        mid = (low + high) // 2 # position of middle item
        item = items[mid]
        if target == item :     # Found it! Return the index
            return mid
        elif target < item:     # x is in lower half of range
            high = mid - 1      #    move top marker down
        else:                   # x is in upper half
            low = mid + 1       #    move bottom marker up
    return -1                   # no range left to search,
                                # x is not there
```

We determined that the time complexity of this algorithm is $\Theta(\log n)$ where n is the size of the list, because each iteration through the main loop cuts the number of items to consider in half. If you've forgotten this important algorithm, this would be a perfect time to go back and review it.

The binary search uses a so-called "divide and conquer" approach, which often leads to very efficient algorithms. This class of algorithms also has the interesting feature that the original problem divides into subproblems that are actually smaller versions of the original. In the case of binary search, the first step is to look at the middle element of the list; if it is not the target, we continue *by performing binary search on either the top half or the bottom half of the list.* Using this insight, we might express the binary search algorithm in a slightly different form:

```
Algorithm: binarySearch -- search for x in nums[low]...nums[high]

mid = (low + high) / 2
if low > high
    x is not in nums
elif x < nums[mid]
    perform binary search for x in nums[low]...nums[mid-1]
else
    perform binary search for x in nums[mid+1]...nums[high]
```

Rather than using a loop as in the original algorithm, this definition of the binary search seems to refer to itself. What is going on here? Can we actually make sense of such a thing?

6.2 Recursive Definitions

A description of something that refers to itself is called a *recursive definition*. In our last formulation, the binary search algorithm makes use of its own description. That is, a "call" to binary search "recurs" inside of the definition—hence, the label "recursive definition."

At first glance, you might think recursive definitions are just nonsense. Surely you have had a teacher who insisted that you can't use a word inside its own definition? That's called a circular definition and is usually not worth much credit on an exam.

In mathematics, however, certain recursive definitions are used all the time. As long as we exercise some care in the formulation and use of recursive definitions, they can be quite handy and surprisingly powerful. The classic recursive example in mathematics is the definition of factorial.

The factorial function is often denoted with an exclamation point (!), and n factorial is computed as

$$n! = n(n-1)(n-2)\ldots(1)$$

For example, we can compute

$$5! = 5(4)(3)(2)(1)$$

Using this definition, it is fairly easy to write a function `fact(n)` that returns the factorial of its parameter. You just need a `for` loop that accumulates the product of all the factors from 2 up to `n`. We leave coding that up to you, as that's not the solution of interest to us here.

Looking at the calculation of 5!, you will notice something interesting. If we remove the 5 from the front, what remains is a calculation of 4!. In general, $n! = n(n-1)!$. In fact, this relation gives us another way of expressing what is meant by factorial in general. Here is a recursive definition:

$$n! = \begin{cases} 1 & \text{if } n = 0 \\ n(n-1)! & \text{otherwise} \end{cases}$$

This definition says that the factorial of 0 is, by definition, 1, while the factorial of any other number is defined to be that number times the factorial of one less than that number.

Even though this definition is recursive, it is not circular. In fact, it provides a very simple method of calculating the factorial of any natural number. Consider the value of 4!. By definition we have

$$4! = 4(4 - 1)! = 4(3!)$$

But what is 3!? To find out, we apply the definition again.

$$4! = 4(3!) = 4[(3)(3 - 1)!] = 4(3)(2!)$$

Now, of course, we have to expand 2!, which requires 1!, which requires 0!. Since 0! is simply 1, that's the end of it.

$$4! = 4(3!) = 4(3)(2!) = 4(3)(2)(1!) = 4(3)(2)(1)(0!) = 4(3)(2)(1)(1) = 24$$

You can see that the recursive definition is not circular because each application causes us to request the factorial of a smaller number. Eventually we get down to 0, which doesn't require another application of the definition. This is called a *base case* for the recursion. When the recursion bottoms out, we get a closed expression that can be directly computed. All good recursive definitions have these key characteristics:

1. There are one or more base cases for which no recursion is required.

2. All chains of recursion eventually end up at one of the base cases.

The simplest way to guarantee that these two conditions are met is to make sure that each recursion always occurs on a *smaller* version of the original problem. A very small version of the problem that can be solved without recursion then becomes the base case. This is exactly how the factorial definition works.

As we mentioned above, the factorial can be computed using a loop with an accumulator. That implementation has a natural correspondence to the original definition of factorial that we presented. Can we also implement a version of factorial that follows the recursive definition?

If we write factorial as a function, the recursive definition translates directly into code.

```
# fact.py
def fact(n):
    if n == 0:
        return 1
    else:
        return n * fact(n-1)
```

Do you see how the definition that refers to itself turns into a function that calls itself? This is called a *recursive function*. The function first checks to see if we are at the base case `n == 0` and, if so, returns 1. If we are not yet at the base case, the function returns the result of multiplying `n` by the factorial of `n-1`. The latter is calculated by a recursive call to `fact(n-1)`.

This is a reasonable translation of the recursive definition. The really cool part is that it actually works! We can use this recursive function to compute factorial values.

```
>>> from fact import fact
>>> fact(4)
24
>>> fact(10)
3628800
```

Some programmers new to recursion are surprised by this result, but it follows naturally from the standard semantics of function calls. Remember that each call to a function starts that function anew. Thanks to the run-time stack, each invocation of the function gets its very own references to any local values, including the values of the parameters. Figure 6.1 shows the sequence of recursive calls that computes 5!. Note especially how each return value is multiplied by the value of `n` that is remembered for each function invocation. The values of `n` are automatically stored on the stack on the way down the chain and then popped off and used on the way back up as the function calls return.

6.3 Simple Recursive Examples

There are many problems for which recursion can yield an elegant and efficient solution. In this section we'll try our hand at some simple recursive problem solving.

6.3.1 Example: String Reversal

Python lists have a built-in method that can be used to reverse the list. Suppose that you want to compute the reverse of a string. One way to handle this problem effectively would be to convert the string into a list of characters, reverse the list, and turn the list back into a string. Using recursion, however, we can easily write a function that computes the reverse directly, without having to detour through a list representation.

The basic idea is to think of a string as a recursive object; a large string is composed of smaller objects, which are also strings. In fact, one very handy way

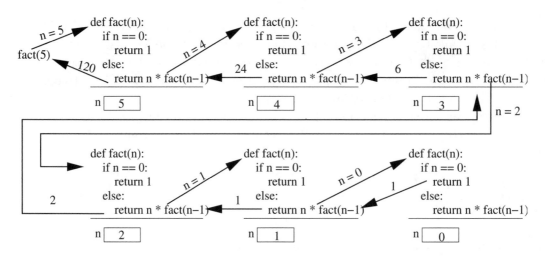

Figure 6.1: Recursive computation of 5!

to divide up virtually any sequence is to think of it as a single first item that just happens to be followed by another sequence. In the case of a string, we can divide it up into its first character and "all the rest." If we reverse the rest of the string and then put the first character on the end of that, we'll have the reverse of the whole string.

Let's code that algorithm and see what happens.

```
def reverse(s):
    return reverse(s[1:]) + s[0]
```

Notice how this function works. The slice `s[1:]` gives all but the first character of the string. We reverse the slice (recursively) and then concatenate the first character (`s[0]`) onto the end of the result. It might be helpful to think in terms of a specific example. If `s` is the string `"abc"`, then `s[1:]` is the string `"bc"`. Reversing this yields `"cb"` and tacking on `s[0]` yields `"cba"`. That's just what we want.

Unfortunately, this function doesn't quite work. Here's what happens when we try it out:

```
>>> reverse("Hello")
Traceback (most recent call last):
  File "<stdin>", line 1, in ?
  File "<stdin>", line 2, in reverse
  File "<stdin>", line 2, in reverse
...
  File "<stdin>", line 2, in reverse
RuntimeError: maximum recursion depth exceeded
```

We've shown only a portion of the output; it actually consisted of 1,000 lines! What's happened here?

Remember, to build a correct recursive function we need a base case for which no recursion is required, otherwise the recursion is circular. In our haste to code the function, we forgot to include a base case. What we have written is actually an *infinite recursion*. Every call to `reverse` contains another call to `reverse`, so none of them ever returns. Of course, each time a function is called it takes up some memory (to store the parameters and local variables on the run-time stack), so this process can't go on forever. Python puts a stop to it after 1,000 calls, the default "maximum recursion depth."

Let's go back and put in a suitable base case. When performing recursion on sequences, the base case is often an empty sequence or a sequence containing just one item. For our reversing problem we can use an empty string as the base case, since an empty string is its own reverse. The recursive calls to `reverse` are always on a string that is one character shorter than the original, so we'll eventually end up at an empty string. Here's a correct version of `reverse`:

```
# reverse.py
def reverse(s):
    if s == "":
        return s
    else:
        return reverse(s[1:]) + s[0]
```

This version works as advertised.

```
>>> reverse("Hello")
'olleH'
```

6.3.2   Example: Anagrams

An anagram is formed by rearranging the letters of a word. Anagrams are often used in word games, and forming anagrams is a special case of generating the possible permutations (rearrangements) of a sequence, a problem that pops up frequently in many areas of computing and mathematics.

Let's try our hand at writing a function that generates a list of all the possible anagrams of a string. We'll apply the same approach that we used in the previous example by slicing the first character off of the string. Suppose the original string is "abc", then the tail of the string is "bc". Generating the list of all the anagrams of the tail gives us ["bc", "cb"], as there are only two possible arrangements of two characters. To add back the first letter, we need to place it in all possible positions in each of these two smaller anagrams: ["abc", "bac", "bca", "acb", "cab", "cba"]. The first three anagrams come from placing "a" in every possible place in "bc", and the second three come from inserting "a" into "cb".

Just as in our previous example, we can use an empty string as the base case for the recursion. The only possible arrangement of characters in an empty string is the empty string itself. Here is the completed recursive function:

```
# anagrams.py
def anagrams(s):
    if s == "":
        return [s]
    else:
        ans = []
        for w in anagrams(s[1:]):
            for pos in range(len(w)+1):
                ans.append(w[:pos]+s[0]+w[pos:])
        return ans
```

Notice in the `else` we have used a list to accumulate the final results. In the nested `for` loops, the outer loop iterates through each anagram of the tail of `s`, and the inner loop goes through each position in the anagram and creates a new string with the original first character inserted into that position. The expression `w[:pos]+s[0]+w[pos:]` looks a bit tricky, but it's not too hard to decipher. Taking `w[:pos]` gives the portion of `w` up to (but not including) `pos`, and `w[pos:]` yields everything from `pos` through the end. Sticking `s[0]` between these two effectively inserts it into `w` at `pos`. The inner loop goes up to `len(w)+1` so that the new character is also added to the very end of the anagram.

Here is our function in action:

```
>>> anagrams("abc")
['abc', 'bac', 'bca', 'acb', 'cab', 'cba']
```

We didn't use "Hello" for this example because that generates more anagrams than we wanted to print. The number of anagrams of a word is the factorial of the length of the word.

6.3.3 Example: Fast Exponentiation

Another good example of recursion is a clever algorithm for raising values to an integer power. The naive way to compute a^n for an integer n is simply to multiply a by itself n times, $a^n = a * a * a * \ldots * a$. We can easily implement this using a simple accumulator loop.

```
# power.py
def loopPower(a, n):
    ans = 1
    for i in range(n):
        ans = ans * a
    return ans
```

The strategy of divide and conquer suggests another way to perform this calculation. Suppose we want to calculate 2^8. By the laws of exponents, we know that $2^8 = 2^4(2^4)$. So if we first calculate 2^4, we can just do one more multiplication to get 2^8. To compute 2^4, we can use the fact that $2^4 = 2^2(2^2)$. And, of course, $2^2 = 2(2)$. Putting the calculation together we start with $2(2) = 4$ and $4(4) = 16$ and $16(16) = 256$. We have calculated the value of 2^8 using just three multiplications. The basic insight is to use the relationship $a^n = a^{n//2}(a^{n//2})$.

In the example we gave, the exponents were all even. In order to turn this idea into a general algorithm, we also have to handle odd values of n. This can be done with one more multiplication. For example, $2^9 = 2^4(2^4)(2)$. Here is the general relationship:

$$a^n = \begin{cases} a^{n//2}(a^{n//2}) & \text{if } n \text{ is even} \\ a^{n//2}(a^{n//2})(a) & \text{if } n \text{ is odd} \end{cases}$$

In this formula we are exploiting integer division; if n is 9 then $n//2$ is 4.

We can use this relationship as the basis of a recursive function, we just need to find a suitable base case. Notice that computing the nth power requires computing two smaller powers $(n//2)$. If we keep using smaller and smaller values of n, it will eventually get to 0 $(1//2 = 0)$. As you know from math class, $a^0 = 1$ for any value of a (except 0). There's our base case.

If you've followed all the math, the implementation of the function is straightforward.

```
# power.py
def recPower(a, n):
    # raises a to the int power n
    if n == 0:
        return 1
    else:
        factor = recPower(a, n // 2)
        if n % 2 == 0:                      # n is even
            return factor * factor
        else:                               # n is odd
            return factor * factor * a
```

One thing to notice is the use of an intermediate variable **factor** so that $a^{n//2}$ needs to be calculated only once. This makes the function more efficient.

6.3.4   Example: Binary Search

Now that you know how to implement recursive functions, we are ready to go back and look again at binary search recursively. Remember, the basic idea was to look at the middle value and then recursively search either the lower half or the upper half of the list.

The base cases for the recursion are the conditions when we can stop, namely, when the target value is found or we run out of places to look. The recursive calls will cut the size of the problem in half each time. In order to do this, we need to specify the range of locations in the list that are still "in play" for each recursive call. We can do this by passing the values of **low** and **high** as parameters along with the list. Each invocation will search the list between the low and high indexes.

Here is a direct implementation of the recursive algorithm using these ideas:

```
# bsearch.py
def recBinSearch(x, nums, low, high):
    if low > high:                      # No place left to look, return -1
        return -1
    mid = (low + high) // 2
    item = nums[mid]
    if item == x:                       # Found it! Return the index
        return mid
    elif x < item:                      # Look in lower half
        return recBinSearch(x, nums, low, mid-1)
    else:                               # Look in upper half
        return recBinSearch(x, nums, mid+1, high)
```

We can then implement our original search function using a suitable call to the recursive binary search, telling it to start the search between 0 and **len(nums)-1**.

```
def search(items, target):
    return recBinSearch(target, items, 0, len(items)-1)
```

Of course, our original looping version is probably a bit faster than this recursive version because calling functions is generally slower than iterating a loop. The recursive version, however, makes the divide-and-conquer structure of binary search much more obvious. Below we will see examples where recursive, divide-and-conquer approaches provide a natural solution to some problems where loops are awkward.

6.4   Analyzing Recursion

By now you've certainly noticed that there are some similarities between iteration (looping) and recursion. Recursive functions are a generalization of loops. Anything that can be done with a loop can also be done by a simple kind of recursive function. In fact, there are programming languages that use recursion exclusively. On the other hand, some things that can be done very simply using recursion are quite difficult to do with loops.

For a number of the problems we've looked at so far, we have had both iterative and recursive solutions. In the case of factorial and binary search, the loop version and the recursive version do basically the same calculations, and they will have roughly the same efficiency. The looping versions are probably a bit faster because of the function call overhead of recursion, but in a modern language the recursive algorithms are probably fast enough.

In the case of the exponentiation algorithm, the recursive version and the looping version actually implement very different algorithms. The `loopPower` function has a simple counted loop that spins n times. Clearly this is a linear time ($\Theta(n)$) algorithm. In `recPower`, the number of "iterations" is determined by the number of recursions. We have to figure out how deep the stack of nested function calls will get. Since each successive call is made on a number that is half as large, it will only take $\log_2 n$ recursive calls to get to 0. Each call does at most two multiplications, so we have a log time ($\Theta(\log n)$) algorithm. The difference between these two is similar to the difference between linear search and binary search, so the recursive algorithm is clearly superior. In the next section, you'll be introduced to a recursive sorting algorithm that is also very efficient.

As you have seen, recursion can be a very useful problem-solving technique that can lead to efficient and effective algorithms. But you have to be careful; it's also possible to write some very inefficient recursive algorithms. One classic example is calculating the nth Fibonacci number.

The Fibonacci sequence is the sequence of numbers $1, 1, 2, 3, 5, 8, \ldots$. It starts with two 1s, and successive numbers are the sum of the previous two. One way to compute the nth Fibonacci value is to use a loop that produces successive terms of the sequence.

In order to compute the next Fibonacci number, we always need to keep track of the previous two. We can use two variables, `curr` and `prev`, to keep track of these values. Then we just need a loop that adds these together to get the next value. At that point, the old value of `curr` becomes the new value of `prev`. Here is one way to do it in Python:

```python
# fib.py
def loopFib(n):
    # pre: n > 0
    # returns the nth Fibonacci number

    curr = 1
    prev = 1
    for i in range(n-2):
        curr, prev = curr+prev, curr
    return curr
```

Here simultaneous assignment is used to compute the next values of `curr` and `prev` in a single step. Notice that the loop goes around only $n-2$ times, because the first two values have already been assigned and do not require an addition. Clearly this is a $\Theta(n)$ algorithm, where n is the input parameter.

The Fibonacci sequence also has an elegant recursive definition.

$$fib(n) = \begin{cases} 1 & \text{if } n < 3 \\ fib(n-1) + fib(n-2) & \text{otherwise} \end{cases}$$

We can turn this recursive definition directly into a recursive function.

```python
# fib.py
def recFib(n):
    if n < 3:
        return 1
    else:
        return recFib(n-1) + recFib(n-2)
```

This function obeys the rules that we've set out. The recursion is always on smaller values, and we have identified some non-recursive base cases. Therefore, this function will work, sort of. It turns out that this is a horribly inefficient algorithm. While our looping version can easily compute results for very large values of `n` (`loopFib(50000)` is almost instantaneous on a relatively new microcomputer), the recursive version is useful only up to around $n = 30$ or so. After that, the wait gets too long.

The problem with this recursive formulation of the Fibonacci function is that it performs lots of duplicate computations. Figure 6.2 shows a diagram of the computations that are performed to compute `fib(6)`. Notice that `fib(4)` is calculated twice, `fib(3)` is calculated three times, `fib(2)` four times, etc. If you start with a larger number, you can see how this redundancy really piles up. Notice, at the bottom of the diagram, that each recursive chain bottoms out at a 1. If you work your way up the chain from a 1, you get to the calling function that adds that 1 into the total result. As this diagram shows, computing `fib(6)` with this algorithm requires $fib(6) - 1$ additions! In general, this algorithm requires $fib(n) - 1$ steps to compute `fib(n)`. That means it's a $\Theta(fib(n))$ algorithm. Try out some numbers, and you'll see that this function grows very rapidly. If you're curious where this fits into our hierarchy of common run-time analyses, you should do a little research on the Fibonacci sequence. Suffice it to say, the run-time of this function is exponential in the value of n.

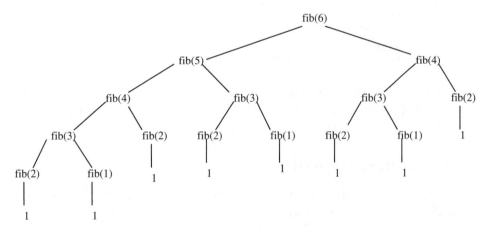

Figure 6.2: Computations performed for `fib(6)`

So what does this tell us? Recursion is just one more tool in your problem-solving arsenal. Sometimes a recursive solution is a good one, either because it is more elegant or more efficient than a looping version; in that case use recursion. Often, the looping and recursive versions are quite similar; in that case, the edge probably goes to the loop, as it will be slightly faster. Sometimes the recursive version is terribly inefficient. In that case, avoid it, unless of course, you can't come up with an iterative algorithm. As you'll see later in the chapter, sometimes there just isn't an efficient solution.

6.5 Sorting

Back in Chapter 3 we discussed the selection sort algorithm for putting a list in order. Recall that the basic selection sort algorithm puts a list in order by searching through the list to find the smallest (or largest) element and swapping it to the front. Then we search through the remaining items to find the next smallest and swap it into the next spot. The process continues until every item has been placed in the proper spot. As a refresher, here's a version of the selection sort in Python.

```
# selectionSort.py
def selectionSort(lst):
    n = len(lst)
    for i in range(n-1):
        min_pos = i
        for j in range(i+1,n):
            if lst[j] < lst[min_pos]:
                min_pos = j
        lst[i], lst[min_pos] = lst[min_pos], lst[i]
```

As we discussed when this algorithm was first presented, selection sort executes in $\Theta(n^2)$ time, where n is the size of the list. This is fine for small lists, but not very efficient for large collections.

6.5.1 Recursive Design: Mergesort

As discussed earlier, one technique that often works for developing efficient algorithms is the divide-and-conquer approach. Suppose you and a friend are working together trying to put a deck of cards in order. You could divide the problem up by splitting the deck of cards in half with one of you sorting each of the halves. Then you just need to figure out a way of combining the two sorted stacks.

The process of combining two sorted lists into a single sorted result is called *merging*. The basic outline of our divide-and-conquer algorithm, called *mergesort* looks like this:

```
Algorithm: mergeSort nums

split nums into two halves
sort the first half
sort the second half
merge the two sorted halves back into nums
```

The first step in the algorithm is simple, we can just use list slicing to handle that. The last step is to merge the lists together. If you think about it, merging is not hard. Let's go back to our card stack example to flesh out the details. Since our two stacks are sorted, each has its smallest value on top. Whichever of the top values is the smaller will be the first item in the merged list. Once the smaller value is removed, we can look at the tops of the card stacks again, and whichever top card is smaller will be the next item in the list. We just continue this process of placing the smaller of the two top values into the big list until one of the stacks runs out. At that point, we finish out the list with the cards from the remaining stack.

Here is a Python implementation of the merging process. In this code, `lst1` and `lst2` are the smaller lists and `lst3` is the larger list where the results are placed. In order for the merging process to work, the length of `lst3` must be equal to the sum of the lengths of `lst1` and `lst2`. You should be able to follow this code by studying the accompanying comments:

```python
# mergeSort.py
def merge(lst1, lst2, lst3): # merge sorted lists lst1 and lst2 into lst3

    i1, i2, i3 = 0, 0, 0     # track current position in each list
    n1, n2 = len(lst1), len(lst2)
    while i1 < n1 and i2 < n2:  # while both lst1 and lst2 have more items
        if lst1[i1] < lst2[i2]:  # top of lst1 is smaller
            lst3[i3] = lst1[i1]  #  copy it into current spot in lst3
            i1 = i1 + 1
        else:                    # top of lst2 is smaller
            lst3[i3] = lst2[i2]  #  copy it into current spot in lst3
            i2 = i2 + 1
        i3 = i3 + 1              # item added to lst3, update position

    while i1 < n1:    # Copy remaining items (if any) from lst1
        lst3[i3] = lst1[i1]
        i1 = i1 + 1
        i3 = i3 + 1

    while i2 < n2:    # Copy remaining items (if any) from lst2
        lst3[i3] = lst2[i2]
        i2 = i2 + 1
        i3 = i3 + 1
```

OK, now we can slice a list into two, and if those lists are sorted, we know how to merge them back into a single list. But how are we going to sort the smaller lists? Well, let's think about it. We are trying to sort a list, and our algorithm requires us to sort two smaller lists. This sounds like a perfect place to use recursion. Maybe we can use `mergeSort` itself to sort the two lists. Let's go back to our recursion guidelines to develop a proper recursive algorithm.

In order for recursion to work, we need to find at least one base case that does not require a recursive call, and we also have to make sure that recursive calls are always made on smaller versions of the original problem. The recursion in our `mergeSort` will always occur on a list that is about half as large as the original, so the latter property is automatically met. Eventually, our lists will be very small, containing only a single item. Fortunately, a list with just one item is already sorted! Voilà, we have a base case. When the length of the list is less than 2, we do nothing, leaving the list unchanged.

Given our analysis, we can update the `mergeSort` algorithm to make it properly recursive.

```
if len(nums) > 1:
    split nums into two halves
    mergeSort the first half
    mergeSort the second half
    merge the two sorted halves back into nums
```

We can translate this algorithm directly into Python code.

```python
# mergeSort.py
def mergeSort(nums):
    # Put items of nums in ascending order
    n = len(nums)
    # Do nothing if nums contains 0 or 1 items
    if n > 1:
        # split into two sublists
        m = n // 2
        nums1, nums2 = nums[:m], nums[m:]
        # recursively sort each piece
        mergeSort(nums1)
        mergeSort(nums2)
        # merge the sorted pieces back into original list
        merge(nums1, nums2, nums)
```

You might try tracing this algorithm with a small list (say eight elements), just to convince yourself that it really works. In general, though, tracing through recursive algorithms can be tedious and often not very enlightening.

Recursion is closely related to mathematical induction, and it requires practice before it becomes comfortable. As long as you follow the rules and make sure that every recursive chain of calls eventually reaches a base case, your algorithms *will* work. You just have to trust and let go of the grungy details. Let Python worry about that for you!

6.5.2 Analyzing Mergesort

A good way get a handle on the mergesort algorithm is to run the code on a small list and print out some of the intermediate results so you can see the code in action. Figure 6.3 shows a pictorial representation of calling `mergeSort` with a list of seven items. The lists are split in half by the recursive calls until each sublist contains one item. As noted before, a list of one item is sorted. As the recursive calls return, the `merge` function is called and two sublists are merged together. After returns from all the recursive calls, we have a list of seven items that is sorted.

The running time of the `merge` function is $\Theta(n)$, where n is the length of `lst3`. The three loops eventually move each item from the two sublists of size $n//2$ to the correct position in the list of size n. At most two items (one from each sublist) are examined each time to determine which item to place in the new list. To calculate the work done by the `mergeSort` function, we need to determine the number of steps required to reach the base case. We have seen this pattern before with the binary search algorithm. Since we are dividing the list in half each time, there are $\log_2 n$ steps to get to the base case. At each level, the sum of all the work done is $\Theta(n)$, where n is the length of the original list. After the first split, we are merging two lists of length $n/2$. After the second split, we need two merges of sublists that are length $n/4$. You can verify this by looking at the diagram; for each level, up to n items must be copied back. Thus we have $\log_2 n$ levels, each of which requires $\Theta(n)$ work, resulting in the run-time of the overall algorithm being $\Theta(n \log n)$. This is a much more efficient algorithm than selection sort, and mergesort is a very good algorithm. In fact, it's possible to prove that no algorithm that relies on comparing elements to each other can sort a list in time less than $\Theta(n \log n)$. But that doesn't mean mergesort is *the* best sorting algorithm.

One drawback of mergesort is the amount of memory that it requires. If you examine our Python implementation carefully, you may be concerned that we are creating separate sublists rather than just keeping track of the indices of the two sublists, since creating these sublists requires $\Theta(n)$ work and memory. The mergesort algorithm does require separate lists/arrays for the sublists and the list/array used during the merging step. The merging code cannot swap items, so it must have a separate list/array to put the items in rather than use the same memory as the

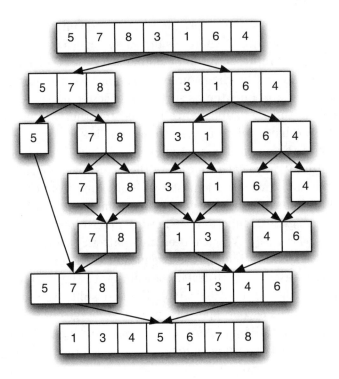

Figure 6.3: Graphical representation of mergesort

sublists. It does not matter whether we split the list by tracking the starting and ending indices for the list and use a separate list for the merging step or if we create separate sublists and then use the original list during the merging step; in either case, mergesort requires twice as much memory as the original list/array requiring $\Theta(n)$ work at some point during the algorithm. This does not change our analysis since that step is performed $\Theta(\log n)$ times. However, there are other recursive algorithms that can sort in $\Theta(n \log n)$ time and also perform the sort in place. Since they do not require a copying step, the constant that the theta notation hides is smaller and the algorithms are generally faster and less memory-intensive than mergesort. One such algorithm is known as *quicksort* and is discussed in subsection 15.2.2.

6.6 A "Hard" Problem: The Tower of Hanoi

Using our divide-and-conquer approach we were able to design efficient algorithms for the searching, sorting, and exponentiation problems. Divide and conquer and recursion are very powerful techniques for algorithm design. However, not all problems have efficient solutions. One very elegant application of recursive problem solving is the solution to a mathematical puzzle usually called the Tower of Hanoi or Tower of Brahma. This puzzle is generally attributed to the French mathematician Édouard Lucas, who published an article about it in 1883. The legend surrounding the puzzle goes something like this:

Somewhere in a remote region of the world is a monastery of a very devout religious order. The monks have been charged with a sacred task that keeps time for the universe. At the beginning of all things, the monks were given a table that supports three vertical posts. On one of the posts was a stack of 64 concentric, golden disks. The disks are of varying radii and stacked in the shape of a beautiful pyramid. The monks were charged with the task of moving the disks from the first post to the third post. When the monks complete their task, all things will crumble to dust and the universe will end.

Of course, if that's all there were to the problem, the universe would have ended long ago. To maintain divine order, the monks must abide by certain rules.

1. Only one disk may be moved at a time.

2. A disk may not be "set aside." It may only be stacked on one of the three posts.

3. A larger disk may never be placed on top of a smaller one.

Versions of this puzzle were quite popular at one time, and you can still find variations on this theme in toy and puzzle stores. Figure 6.4 depicts a small version containing only eight disks. The task is to move the tower from the first post to the third post using the center post as sort of a temporary resting place during the process. Of course, you have to follow the three sacred rules given above.

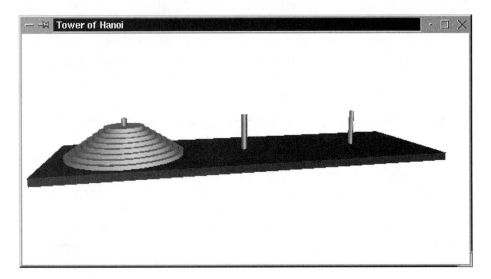

Figure 6.4: Tower of Hanoi puzzle with eight disks

We want to develop an algorithm for this puzzle. You can think of our algorithm either as a set of steps that the monks need to carry out or as a program that generates a set of instructions. For example, if we label the three posts A, B, and C, the instructions might start out like this:

```
Move disk from A to C.
Move disk from A to B.
Move disk from C to B.
...
```

This is a difficult puzzle for most people to solve. Of course, that is not surprising, since most people are not trained in algorithm design. The solution process is actually quite simple—*if* you know about recursion.

Let's start by considering some really easy cases. Suppose we have a version of the puzzle with only one disk. Moving a tower consisting of a single disk is simple enough; we just remove it from A and put it on C. Problem solved. OK, what if there are two disks? Then we need to get the larger of the two disks over to post C, but the smaller one is sitting on top of it. The solution is to move the smaller disk out of the way, and we can do this by moving it to post B. Now the large disk on A is clear; we can move it to C and then move the smaller disk from post B onto post C.

Now let's think about a tower of size three. In order to move the largest disk to post C, we first have to move the two smaller disks out of the way. The two smaller disks form a tower of size two. Using the process outlined above, we could move this tower of two onto post B, and that would free up the largest disk so that it can move to post C. Then we just have to move the tower of two disks from post B onto post C. Solving the three disk case boils down to three steps:

1. Move a tower of two from A to B.

2. Move one disk from A to C.

3. Move a tower of two from B to C.

The first and third steps involve moving a tower of size two. Fortunately, we have already figured out how to do this. It's just like solving the puzzle with two disks, except that we move the tower from A to B using C as the temporary resting place, and then from B to C using A as the temporary place.

We have just developed the outline of a simple recursive algorithm for the general process of moving a tower of any size from one post to another.

```
Algorithm: move n-disk tower from source to destination via resting place

move n-1 disk tower from source to resting place
move 1 disk tower from source to destination
move n-1 disk tower from resting place to destination
```

What is the base case for this recursive process? Notice how a move of n disks results in two recursive moves of $n - 1$ disks. Since we are reducing n by one each time, the size of the tower will eventually be 1. A tower of size 1 can be moved directly by just moving a single disk; we don't need any recursive calls to remove disks above it.

Fixing up our general algorithm to include the base case gives us a working `moveTower` algorithm. Let's code it in Python. Our `moveTower` function will need parameters to represent the size of the tower, `n`; the source post, `source`; the destination post, `dest`; and the temporary resting post, `temp`. We can use an `int`

for n and the strings "A", "B", and "C" to represent the posts. Here is the code for
moveTower:

```
# hanoi.py
def moveTower(n, source, dest, temp):
    if n == 1:
        print "Move disk from", source, "to", dest+"."
    else:
        moveTower(n-1, source, temp, dest)
        moveTower(1, source, dest, temp)
        moveTower(n-1, temp, dest, source)
```

See how easy that was? Sometimes using recursion can make otherwise difficult
problems almost trivial.

To get things started, we just need to supply values for our four parameters.
Let's write a little function that prints out instructions for moving a tower of size n
from post A to post C.

```
# hanoi.py
def hanoi(n):
    moveTower(n, "A", "C", "B")
```

Now we're ready to try it out. Here are solutions to the three- and four-disk
puzzles. You might want to trace through these solutions to convince yourself that
they work.

```
>>> hanoi(3)
Move disk from A to C.
Move disk from A to B.
Move disk from C to B.
Move disk from A to C.
Move disk from B to A.
Move disk from B to C.
Move disk from A to C.

>>> hanoi(4)
Move disk from A to B.
Move disk from A to C.
Move disk from B to C.
Move disk from A to B.
Move disk from C to A.
Move disk from C to B.
Move disk from A to B.
Move disk from A to C.
Move disk from B to C.
Move disk from B to A.
```

```
Move disk from C to A.
Move disk from B to C.
Move disk from A to B.
Move disk from A to C.
Move disk from B to C.
```

So, our solution to the Tower of Hanoi is a "trivial" algorithm requiring only nine lines of code. What is this problem doing in a section labeled "A Hard Problem"? To answer that question, we have to look at the efficiency of our solution. In this case, the difficulty of the problem is determined by the number of disks in the tower. The question we want to answer is *how many steps does it take to move a tower of size* n?

Just looking at the structure of our algorithm, you can see that moving a tower of size n requires us to move a tower of size $n - 1$ twice, once to move it off the largest disk, and again to put it back on top. If we add another disk to the tower, we essentially double the number of steps required to solve it. The relationship becomes clear if you simply try out the program on increasing puzzle sizes.

Number of Disks	Steps in Solution
1	1
2	3
3	7
4	15
5	31

In general, solving a puzzle of size n will require $2^n - 1$ steps.

This is clearly a $\Theta(2^n)$ algorithm, meaning that it requires *exponential time*, since the measure of the size of the problem, n, appears in the exponent of this formula. Exponential algorithms blow up very quickly and can be practically solved only for relatively small sizes, even on the fastest computers. Just to illustrate the point, if our monks really started with a tower of just 64 disks and moved one disk every second, 24 hours a day, every day, without making a mistake, it would still take them over 580 *billion* years to complete their task. Considering that the universe is roughly 15 billion years old now, we don't need to worry about turning to dust just yet.

Even though the algorithm for Towers of Hanoi is easy to express, it belongs to a class known as *intractable* problems. These are problems that require too much computing power (either time or memory) to be solved in practice, except for the simplest cases. And in this sense, our toy-store puzzle does indeed represent a hard problem.

6.7   Chapter Summary

This chapter has introduced you to some important concepts in algorithm design. Here are the key ideas:

- Binary search is an example of a divide-and-conquer approach to algorithm development. Divide and conquer often yields efficient solutions.

- A definition or function is recursive if it refers to itself. To be well founded, a recursive definition must meet two properties:

  1. There must be one or more base cases that require no recursion.
  2. All chains of recursion must eventually reach a base case.

  A simple way to guarantee these conditions is for recursive calls to always be made on smaller versions of the problem. The base cases are then simple versions that can be solved directly.

- Sequences can be considered recursive structures containing a first item followed by a sequence. Recursive functions can be written following this approach.

- Mergesort is a recursive divide-and-conquer algorithm that can sort a collection in $n \log n$ time.

- Recursion is more general than iteration. Choosing between recursion and looping involves the considerations of efficiency and elegance.

- Problems that are solvable in theory but not in practice are called "intractable." The solution to the famous Tower of Hanoi can be expressed as a simple recursive algorithm, but the algorithm is intractable.

6.8   Exercises

True/False Questions

1. Any definition that refers to itself is circular, and therefore not useful.

2. Recursion is a more general form of iteration than looping.

3. All proper recursive functions must have exactly one base case.

4. An infinite recursion in Python will "hang" the computer.

5. A sequence can be viewed as a recursive data collection.

6. A string of length n has $n!$ anagrams.

7. Mergesort is an example of a $\Theta(n^2)$ algorithm.

8. A looping implementation of an algorithm is generally a bit faster than a recursive version.

9. Recursive algorithms tend to be slow in practice.

10. The Tower of Hanoi is an example of an intractable problem.

Multiple Choice Questions

1. The non-recursive part of a recursive function is called a(n)
   a) bottom case.
   b) terminating case.
   c) end case.
   d) base case.

2. An algorithm design technique involving breaking a problem into smaller versions of the original is called

   a) top-down design.
   b) test-driven development.
   c) divide and conquer.
   d) search and destroy.

3. Which of the following is a correct coding of the recursive expression for reversing a string?
   a) `reverse(s[1:]) + s[0]`
   b) `s[0] + reverse(s[1:])`
   c) `s[-1] + reverse(s[:-1])`
   d) both a and c

4. How many anagrams are there for a four-letter word?

   a) 4   b) 8   c) 16   d) 24

$$x^n = \begin{cases} 1 & \text{if } n=0 \\ x \cdot x^{n-1} & \text{if } n > 0 \end{cases}$$

5. The `loopPower` function shown in the chapter has what time analysis?

   a) $\Theta(\log n)$ b) $\Theta(n \log n)$ c) $\Theta(n)$ d) $\Theta(2^n)$

6. The `recPower` function shown in the chapter has what time analysis?

   a) $\Theta(\log n)$ b) $\Theta(n \log n)$ c) $\Theta(n)$ d) $\Theta(2^n)$

7. The mergesort algorithm has what time analysis?

   a) $\Theta(\log n)$ b) $\Theta(n \log n)$ c) $\Theta(n)$ d) $\Theta(2^n)$

8. The Tower of Hanoi algorithm has what time analysis?

   a) $\Theta(\log n)$ b) $\Theta(n \log n)$ c) $\Theta(n)$ d) $\Theta(2^n)$

9. An infinite recursion will result in

   a) a program that "hangs."
   b) a broken computer.
   c) a reboot.
   d) a run-time exception.

10. The recursive Fibonacci function is inefficient because

    a) recursion is inherently inefficient compared to iteration.
    b) calculating Fibonacci numbers is an intractable problem.
    c) it performs many repeated calculations.
    d) all of the above

Short-Answer Questions

1. Must a proper recursive function always have some sort of decision structure in it? Explain your answer.

2. In your own words, explain the two rules that a proper recursive definition must obey.

3. What list is returned by `anagram("foo")`?

4. Trace `recPower(3,6)` and figure out exactly how many multiplications it does.

5. Write pre and postconditions for `loopPower` and `recPower`.

Programming Exercises

1. Modify the recursive Fibonacci program given in the chapter so that it prints
   tracing information. Specifically, have the function print a message when it is
   called and when it returns. For example, the output should contain lines like
   these:

   ```
   Computing fib(4)
   ...
   Leaving fib(4) returning 3
   ```

   Use your modified version of fib to compute fib(10) and count how many
   times fib(3) is computed in the process.

2. This exercise is another variation on "instrumenting" the recursive Fibonacci
   program to better understand its behavior. Write a program that counts how
   many times the fib function is called to compute fib(n) where n is a user
   input.

   Hint: to solve this problem, you need an accumulator variable whose value
   "persists" between calls to fib. You can do this by making the count an
   instance variable of an object. Create a FibCounter class with the following
   methods:

   __init__(self) Creates a new FibCounter setting its count instance vari-
       able to 0.

   getCount(self) Returns the value of the count.

   fib(self,n) Recursive function to compute the nth Fibonacci number. It
       increments the count each time it is called.

   resetCount(self) Set the count back to 0.

3. Write a recursive function that implements the same algorithm as the looping
   version of the nth Fibonacci function. Hint: in changing the for loop into a
   recursion, you will need to pass all of the variables whose values change during
   the loop as parameters to the recursive function.

4. The previous problem shows that a recursive function can compute the nth
   Fibonacci number as efficiently as a looping version. But with a little ingenuity,
   we can do better. Another way to find the nth Fibonacci number is through
   matrix operations. In order to compute the Fibonacci sequence, we have to

keep track of the last two values computed (`curr` and `prev`). The next "state" of these two values can be computed through a simple matrix multiplication:

$$\begin{bmatrix} 1 & 1 \\ 1 & 0 \end{bmatrix} \begin{bmatrix} \text{curr} \\ \text{prev} \end{bmatrix} = \begin{bmatrix} \text{curr} + \text{prev} \\ \text{curr} \end{bmatrix}$$

We can compose an entire sequence of iterations by taking advantage of matrix exponentiation. It is then possible to replace the loop in the Fibonacci program with this computation:

$$\begin{bmatrix} 1 & 1 \\ 1 & 0 \end{bmatrix}^{n-2} \begin{bmatrix} 1 \\ 1 \end{bmatrix} = \begin{bmatrix} \text{fib}(n) \\ \text{fib}(n-1) \end{bmatrix}$$

Create an appropriate matrix data type using operator overloading so that matrices can be multiplied just like numbers. Then use the fast exponentiation algorithm presented in this chapter in a program that computes the nth Fibonacci number. Once you have it working, do a time analysis of your program.

5. Write a recursive function that detects whether a string is a palindrome. The basic idea is to check that the first and last letters of the string are the same letter; if they are, then the entire string is a palindrome if everything between those letters is a palindrome. There are a couple of special cases to check for. If either the first or last character of the string is not a letter, you can check to see if the rest of the string is a palindrome with that character removed. Also, when you compare letters, make sure that you do it in a case-insensitive way.

    Use your function in a program that prompts a user for a phrase and then tells whether or not it is a palindrome. Here's a classic for palindrome testing: "A man, a plan, a canal, Panama!"

6. Write and test a recursive function `max` to find the largest number in a list. The maximum is the larger of the first item and the maximum of all the other items.

7. Computer scientists and mathematicians often use numbering systems other than base 10. Write a program that allows a user to enter a number and a base and then prints out the digits of the number in the new base. Use a recursive function `printDigits(num, base)` to print the digits.

Hint: consider base 10. To get the right-most digit of a base 10 number, simply look at the remainder after dividing by 10. For example, 153%10 is 3. To get the remaining digits, you repeat the process on 15, which is just 153/10. This same process works for any base. The only problem is that we get the digits in reverse order (from right to left).

Write a recursive function that first prints the digits of $num/base$ and then prints the last digit, namely $num\%base$. You should put a space between successive digits, since bases greater than 10 will print out with multi-character digits. For example, `printDigits(245, 16)` should print 15 5.

8. Write a recursive function to print out the digits of a number in English. For example, if the number is 153, the output should be "One Five Three." See the hint from the previous problem for help on how this might be done.

9. In mathematics, C_k^n denotes the number of different ways that k things can be selected from among n different choices. For example, if you are choosing among six desserts and are allowed to take two, the number of different combinations you could choose is C_2^6. Here's one formula to compute this value:

$$C_k^n = \frac{n!}{k!(n-k)!}$$

This value also gives rise to an interesting recursion:

$$C_k^n = C_{k-1}^{n-1} + C_k^{n-1}$$

Write both an iterative and a recursive function to compute combinations and compare the efficiency of your two solutions. Hint: when $k = 1$, $C_k^n = n$, and when $n < k$, $C_k^n = 0$.

10. Some interesting geometric curves can be described recursively. One famous example is the Koch curve. It is a curve that can be infinitely long in a finite amount of space. It can also be used to generate pretty pictures.

The Koch curve is described in terms of "levels" or "degrees." The Koch curve of degree 0 is just a straight line segment. A first degree curve is formed by placing a "bump" in the middle of the line segment (see Figure 6.5). The original segment has been divided into four, each of which is one third of the length of the original. The bump rises at 60 degrees, so it forms two sides of an equilateral triangle. To get a second degree curve, you put a bump in each of the line segments of the first degree curve. Successive curves are constructed by placing bumps on each segment of the previous curve.

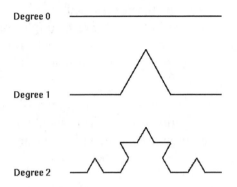

Figure 6.5: Koch curves of degrees 0 to 2

You can draw interesting pictures by "Kochizing" the sides of a polygon. Figure 6.6 shows the result of applying a fourth degree curve to the sides of an equilateral triangle. This is often called a "Koch snowflake." You are to write a program to draw a snowflake.

Hint: Think of drawing a Koch curve as if you were giving instructions to a turtle. The turtle always knows where it currently sits and what direction it is facing. To draw a Koch curve of a given length and degree, you might use an algorithm like this:

```
Algorithm Koch(Turtle, length, degree):
    if degree == 0:
        Tell the turtle to draw length steps in the current direction
    else:
        length1 = length/3
        degree1 = degree-1
        Koch(Turtle, length1, degree1)
        Tell the turtle to turn left 60 degrees
        Koch(Turtle, length1, degree1)
        Tell the turtle to turn right 120 degrees
        Koch(Turtle, length1, degree1)
        Tell the turtle to turn left 60 degrees
        Koch(Turtle, length1, degree1)
```

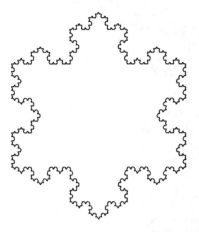

Figure 6.6: Koch snowflake

Implement this algorithm using a suitable graphics package. You can use the `Turtle` module from the Python standard library or implement your own turtle in another graphics package. Write a program that allows a user to enter the degree of snowflake desired and then proceeds to draw it.

11. Another interesting recursive curve (see the previous problem) is the C-curve. It is formed similarly to the Koch curve except whereas the Koch curve breaks a segment into four pieces of $length/3$, the C-curve replaces each segment with just two segments of $length/\sqrt{2}$ that form a 90-degree elbow. Figure 6.7 shows a degree-12 C-curve.

   Using an approach similar to the previous exercise, write a program that draws a C-curve. Hint: your turtle will do the following:

   ```
   turn left 45 degrees
   draw a c-curve of size length/sqrt(2)
   turn right 90 degrees
   draw a c-curve of size length/sqrt(2)
   turn left 45 degrees
   ```

12. Write a program that solves word jumble problems. You will need a large file of English words. If you have a Unix or Linux system available, you can

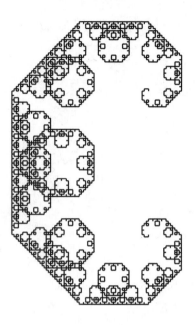

Figure 6.7: C-curve of degree 12

probably find a spelling dictionary in a system directory (e.g., **/usr/dict** or
/usr/share/dict). Otherwise, a quick search on the Internet should turn
up something useful. The program proceeds by having the user type in a
scrambled word. It then generates all anagrams of the word and then checks
which (if any) are in the dictionary. The anagrams appearing in the dictionary
are printed as solutions to the puzzle.

13. Write a maze solving program. The problem of finding a path through a
maze can be cast as a recursive searching process. Suppose locations in a two-
dimensional maze are specified using (x, y) coordinates. Here is an algorithm
to find and mark a path from an arbitrary starting point to an exit. It returns
True if it is able to mark a path to an exit and False if not.

```
algorithm pathToExit((x,y)):

    if (x,y) is an exit:
        return True
```

```
if (x,y) is not an open unvisited cell:
    return False

Mark (x,y) as visited

# Try 4 possible directions from (x,y)
if pathToExit((x+1,y)):
    return True
if pathToExit((x,y+1)):
    return True
if pathToExit((x-1,y)):
    return True
if pathToExit((x,y-1)):
    return True

# Cannot reach an exit from this cell
unMark (x,y)  # it's not on a path to the exit
return False
```

You will have to design a suitable representation for mazes. One simple approach is just to use ASCII text to represent a rectangular maze. For example, you might use * to indicate a wall and . to indicate an open cell. The letters S and E could be used for the start and exit. Here's a simple example:

```
S **......
..*...***.
*.***.*.*.
........*.
.*******.
.***....*.
.**..**...
.**...****
..**.**...
*..*....*E
```

Even if you want to build a nice graphical maze program, a simple text-based representation like this is very handy for specifying mazes, since they can be created with a basic text editor.

Chapter 7   Trees

![black bar]

Objectives

- To learn the terminology of tree data structures.

- To learn about different applications where a tree data structure is appropriate.

- To be able to implement tree structures using link-based and array-based techniques and be familiar with basic, tree-based algorithms.

- To understand the binary search tree structure and the efficiency of its various operations.

- To get more practice and develop greater comfort with recursive algorithms.

7.1 | Overview

So far we have dealt mostly with linear data structures, such as lists, stacks, and queues, that represent items in a sequence. In this chapter, we are going to "branch out" a bit and consider a non-linear data structure known as a *tree*. Trees represent data in a hierarchical fashion, which makes them very handy for modeling real-world hierarchies. You are certainly familiar with the idea of a family tree for representing kinship information; other examples include things like taxonomies and corporate reporting structures.

For example, we can use a tree to represent animals in the taxonomic groups that biologists use. Animals can be subdivided into vertebrates and invertebrates; vertebrates can be subdivided into reptiles, fish, mammals, and so on. The tree for this would look something like Figure 7.1. Hierarchical relationships turn up everywhere, and trees arise as a natural representation for the data in many applications.

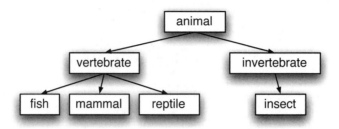

Figure 7.1: Portion of biologists' taxonomic groups

Perhaps surprisingly, it also turns out that trees are very useful in implementing plain old sequential data. In this chapter, we'll see that certain kinds of trees called *binary search trees* can be used to provide collections that allow for efficient insertion and deletion (similar to linked lists) but also allow for efficient search (similar to an ordered array). Tree-based data structures and algorithms are essential for handling large collections of data such as databases and file systems efficiently.

7.2   Tree Terminology

Computer scientists represent trees as a collection of nodes (similar to the nodes in a linked list) that are connected with *edges*. Figure 7.2 shows a tree with seven nodes, each containing an integer. The node at the very top of the diagram is called the *root*. In this tree the root contains the data value 2. A tree has exactly one root; notice that you can follow edges (the arrows) from the root to get to any other node in the tree.

Each node in a tree can have *children* connected to it via an edge. In a general tree, a node can have any number of children, but we'll only concern ourselves here with *binary trees*. In a binary tree, each node has at most two children. As you can see, the tree depicted in Figure 7.2 is a binary tree. Relationships inside the tree are described using a mixture of family and tree-like terminology. The root node has two children: the node containing 7 is its *left child*, and the one containing 6 is its *right child*. These two nodes are also said to be *siblings*. The nodes containing 8 and 4 are also siblings. The *parent* of node 5 is node 7. Node 3 is a *descendant* of node 7 and node 7 is an *ancestor* of node 3. A node that does not have any children is a *leaf* node. The *depth* of a node indicates how many edges are between it and the root node. The root node has a depth of zero. Nodes 7 and 6 have a depth of one and node 3 has a depth of three. The *height* or *depth* of a *tree* is the maximum depth of any node.

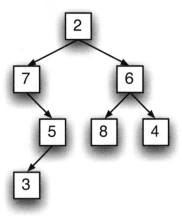

Figure 7.2: Sample binary tree

In a *full binary tree* each depth level has a node at every possible position. At the bottom level, all the nodes are leaves (i.e., all the leaves are at the same depth and every non-leaf node has two children). A *complete binary tree* has a node at every possible position except at the deepest level, and at that level, positions are filled from left to right. A complete binary tree can be created by starting with a full binary tree and adding nodes at the next level from left to right or by removing nodes at the previous level from right to left. See Figure 7.3 for examples of both.

Each node of a tree along with its descendants can be considered a *subtree*. For example, in Figure 7.2 the nodes 7, 5, and 3 can be considered a subtree of the entire tree, where node 7 is the root of the subtree. Seen in this way, a tree is naturally viewed as a recursive structure. A binary tree is either an empty tree or it consists of a root node and (possibly empty) left and right subtrees.

Just as with lists, one very useful operation on trees is traversal. Given a tree, we need a way to "walk" through the tree visiting every node in a systematic fashion. Unlike the situation with lists, there is no single, obvious way of traversing the tree. Notice that each node in the tree consists of three parts: data, left subtree, and right subtree. We have three different choices of traversal order depending on when we decide to deal with the data. If we process the data at the root and then do the left and right subtrees, we are performing a so-called *preorder traversal* because the

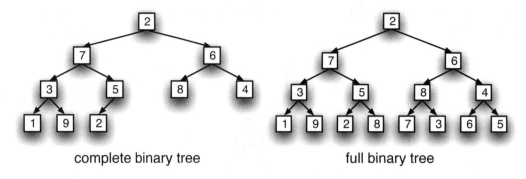

complete binary tree   full binary tree

Figure 7.3: A complete binary tree on the left and a full binary tree on the right

data at the root is considered first. A pre-order traversal is easily expressed as a recursive algorithm:

```
def traverse(tree):
    if tree is not empty:
        process data at tree's root    # preorder traversal
        traverse(tree's left subtree)
        traverse(tree's right subtree)
```

Applying this algorithm to our tree from Figure 7.2 processes the nodes in the order 2, 7, 5, 3, 6, 8, 4.

Of course we can easily modify the traversal algorithm by moving where we actually process the data. An *inorder traversal* considers the root data between processing the subtrees. An in-order traversal of our sample tree yields the sequence of nodes 7, 3, 5, 2, 8, 6, 4. As you have probably guessed by now, a *postorder traversal* processes the root after the two subtrees, which gives us the ordering: 3, 5, 7, 8, 4, 6, 2.

7.3 An Example Application: Expression Trees

One important application of trees in computer science is representing the internal structure of programs. When an interpreter or compiler analyzes a program, it constructs a *parse tree* that captures the structure of the program. For example, consider a simple expression: $(2 + 3) * 4 + 5 * 6$. The form of this expression can be represented by the tree in Figure 7.4. Notice how the hierarchical structure of the tree eliminates the need for the parentheses. The basic operands of the expression end up as leaves of the tree, and the operators become internal nodes of the tree. Lower level operations in the tree have to be performed before their results are available for higher level expressions. It is clear that the addition of $2 + 3$ must be the first operation because it appears at the lowest level of the tree.

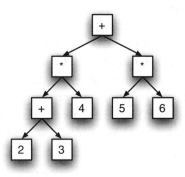

Figure 7.4: Tree representation of a mathematical expression

Given the tree structure for an expression, we can do a number of interesting things. A compiler would traverse this structure to produce a sequence of machine instructions that carry out the computation. An interpreter might use this structure to evaluate the expression. Each node is evaluated by taking the values of the two children and applying the operation. If one or both of the children is itself an operator, it will have to be evaluated first. A simple postorder traversal of the tree suffices to evaluate the expression.

```
def evaluateTree(tree):
    if tree's root is an operand:
        return root data
    else:   # root contains an operator
        leftValue = evaluateTree(tree's left subtree)
        rightValue = evaluateTree(tree's right subtree)
        result = apply operator at root to leftValue and rightValue
        return result
```

If you think about it carefully, you'll see that this is basically a recursive algorithm for evaluating the postfix version of an expression. Simply walking the expression tree in a postorder fashion yields the expression 2 3 + 4 * 5 6 * +, which is just the postfix form of our original expression. In Chapter 5, we used a

stack algorithm to evaluate postfix expressions. Here, we are implicitly using the
computer's run-time stack via recursion to accomplish the same task. By the way,
you can get the prefix and infix versions of the expression by doing the appropriate
traversal. Isn't it fascinating how this all weaves together?

7.4   Tree Representations

Now that you've gotten a taste of what trees can do, it's time to consider some
possible concrete representations for our trees. One straightforward and obvious
way to build trees is to use a linked representation. Just as we did for linked lists,
we can create a class to represent the nodes of our trees. Each node will have an
instance variable to hold a reference to the data of the node and also variables for
references to the left and right children. We'll use the **None** object for representing
empty subtrees. Here's a Python class:

```
# TreeNode.py
class TreeNode(object):

    def __init__(self, data = None, left=None, right=None):

        """creates a tree node with specified data and references to left
        and right children"""

        self.item = data
        self.left = left
        self.right = right
```

Using our **TreeNode** we can easily create linked structures that directly mirror
the binary tree diagrams that you've seen so far. For example, here's some code
that builds a simple tree with three nodes:

```
left = TreeNode(1)
right = TreeNode(3)
root = TreeNode(2, left, right)
```

We could do the same thing with a single line of code by simply composing the calls
to the **TreeNode** constructor.

```
root = TreeNode(2, TreeNode(1), TreeNode(3))
```

We can follow this approach even farther to create arbitrarily complex tree structures
from our nodes. Here's some code that creates a structure similar to that of
Figure 7.2.

```
root = TreeNode(2,
          TreeNode(7,
              None,
              TreeNode(5,
                  TreeNode(3),
                  None
              )
          )
          TreeNode(6,
              TreeNode(8),
              TreeNode(4)
          )
      )
```

We have used indentation to help make the layout of the expression match the structure of the tree. Notice, for example, that the root (2) has two subtrees indented under it (7 and 6). If you don't see it as a tree, try turning your head sideways.

Of course, we will not generally want to directly manipulate TreeNodes to build complicated structures like this. Instead, we will create a higher level container class that encapsulates the details of tree building and provides a convenient API for manipulating the tree. The exact design of the container class will depend on what we are trying to accomplish with the tree. We'll see an example of this in the next section.

We should mention that the linked representation, while obvious, is not the only possible implementation of a binary tree. In some cases, it is convenient to use an array/list-based approach. Instead of storing explicit links to children, we can maintain the relationships implicitly through positions in the array.

In the array approach, we assume that we always have a complete tree and pack the nodes into the array level by level. So, the first cell in the array stores the root, the next two positions store the root's children, the next four store the grandchildren, and so on. Following this approach, the node at position i always has its left child located at position 2*i+1 and its right child at position 2*i+2. The parent of node i is in position (i-1)//2. Notice that it's crucial for these formulas that every node always has two children. You will need some special marker value (e.g., None) to indicate empty nodes. The array representation for the sample binary tree in Figure 7.2 is: [2, 7, 6, None, 5, 8, 4, None, None, 3]. If you want to simplify the calculations a bit, you can leave the first position in the array (index 0) empty and put the root at index 1. With this implementation, the left child is in position 2*i and the right child is in position 2*i+1, while the parent is found in position i//2.

The array-based tree implementation has the advantage that it does not use memory to store explicit child links. However, it does require us to waste cells for empty nodes. If the tree is sparsely filled, there will be a large number of None entries and the array/list implementation does not make efficient use of memory. In these cases, the linked implementation is more appropriate.

7.5 An Application: A Binary Search Tree

In this section, we're going to exercise our tree implementation techniques by building another container class for ordered sequences. Back in section 4.7 we discussed the trade-offs between linked and array-based implementations of sequences. While linked lists offer efficient insertions and deletions (since items don't have to be shifted around), they don't allow for efficient searching. A sorted array allows for efficient searching (via the binary search algorithm) but requires $\Theta(n)$ time for insertions and deletions. Using a special kind of tree, a binary search tree, we can combine the best of both worlds.

7.5.1 The Binary Search Property

A *binary search tree* is just a binary tree with an extra property that holds for every node in the tree: the values in the left subtree are less than the value at the node and the values in the right subtree are greater than the value at the node. Figure 7.5 shows a sample binary search tree.

It is usually very efficient to search for an item in a binary search tree. We start at the root of the tree and examine the data value of that node. If the root value is the one we are searching for, then we're done. If the value we are searching for is less than the value at the root, we know that if the value is in the tree, it must be in the left subtree. Similarly, if the value we are searching for is larger than the value at the root, it is in the right subtree. We can continue the search process to the appropriate subtree and apply the same rules until we find the item or reach a node that has an empty subtree where the value would be located. If the tree is reasonably well "balanced," then at each node we are essentially cutting the number of items that we have to compare against in half. That is, we are performing a binary search, which is why this is called a binary search tree.

7.5.2 Implementing A Binary Search Tree

Following good design principles, we will write a BST class that encapsulates all the details of the binary search tree and provides an easy-to-use interface. Our tree

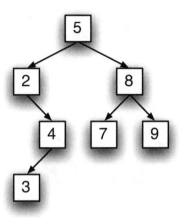

Figure 7.5: Sample binary search tree

will maintain a set of items and allow us to add, remove, and search for specific values. We're going to use a linked representation for practice with references, but you could easily convert this to the array-based implementation discussed above. A BST object will contain a reference to a `TreeNode` that is the root node of a binary search tree. Initially, the tree will be empty, so the reference will be to None. Here's our class constructor.

```
# BST.py
from TreeNode import TreeNode

class BST(object):

    def __init__(self):

        """create empty binary search tree
        post: empty tree created"""

        self.root = None
```

Now let's tackle adding items to our binary search tree. It's pretty easy to grow a tree one leaf at a time. A key point to realize is that given an existing binary search tree, there is only one location where a newly inserted item can go. Let's consider an example. Suppose we want to insert 5 into the binary search tree shown in Figure 7.6. Starting at the root node 6, we see that 5 must go in the left subtree.

The root of that tree has the value 2 so we proceed to its right subtree. The root of that subtree has the value 4 so we would proceed to its right subtree, but the right subtree is empty. The 5 is then inserted as a new leaf at that point.

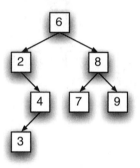

Figure 7.6: Example for inserting into a binary search tree

We can implement this basic insertion algorithm using either an iterative or a recursive approach. Either way, we start at the top of the tree and work our way down going left or right as needed until we find the spot where the new item will go. As is typical with algorithms on linked structures, we need to take some care with the special case when the structure is empty, since that requires us to change the `root` instance variable. Here's a version of the algorithm that uses a loop to march down the tree.

```
def insert(self, item):

    """insert item into binary search tree
    pre: item is not in self
    post: item has been added to self"""

    if self.root is None:   # handle empty tree case
        self.root = TreeNode(item)
```

```
        else:
            # start at root
            node = self.root
            # loop to find the correct spot (break to exit)
            while True:
                if item == node.item:
                    raise ValueError("Inserting duplicate item")

                if item < node.item:          # item goes in left subtree
                    if node.left is not None: # follow existing subtree
                        node = node.left
                    else:                      # empty subtree, insert here
                        node.left = TreeNode(item)
                        break
                else:                          # item goes in right subtree
                    if node.right is not None: # follow existing subtree
                        node = node.right
                    else:                      # empty subtree, insert here
                        node.right = TreeNode(item)
                        break
```

This code looks rather complicated with its nested decision structures, but you should not have too much trouble following it. Notice the precondition that the item is not already in the tree. A plain binary search tree does not allow multiple copies of a value, so we check for this condition and raise an exception if an equivalent item is already in the tree. This design could easily be extended to allow multiple values by keeping a count in each node of the number of times that value has been added.

With the algorithm fresh in your mind, let's also consider how we might tackle this problem recursively. We said above that trees are a naturally recursive data structure, but our BST class is not really recursively structured. It is the interlinked structure of tree nodes themselves that is recursive. We can think of any node in the tree as being the root of a subtree that itself contains two smaller subtrees. A value of None, of course, indicates a subtree that is empty. With this insight, it's very easy to cast our insertion algorithm as a recursive method that operates on subtrees. We'll write this as a recursive helper method that is called to perform the insertion. Using this design, the insert method itself is trivial.

```
def insert_rec(self, item):

    """insert item into binary search tree
    pre: item is not in self
    post: item has been added to self"""

    self.root = self._subtreeInsert(self.root, item)
```

It's important to clearly understand what `_subtreeInsert` is up to. Notice that it takes a node as the root of a subtree into which `item` must be inserted. Initially, this is the entire tree structure (`self.root`). The `_subtreeInsert` both performs the insertion and returns the node that is the root of the resulting (sub)tree. This approach makes sure that our `insert` will work even for an initially empty tree. For that case, `self.root` will start out as `None` (indicating an empty tree) and `_subtreeInsert` will return a proper `TreeNode` containing `item` that becomes the new root of the tree.

Now let's write the recursive helper function `_subtreeInsert`. The parameter to the function gives us the root of a tree structure that the item is being inserted into, and it must return the root of the resulting tree. The algorithm is very simple. If this (sub)tree is empty, we just hand back a `TreeNode` for the item, and we're done. If the tree is not empty, we modify it by recursively adding the item to either the left or right subtree, as appropriate, and return the original root of the tree as the root of the new tree (since that didn't change). Here's the code that gets the job done.

```
def _subtreeInsert(self, root, item):

    if root is None:            # inserting into empty tree
        return TreeNode(item)   # the item becomes the new tree root

    if item == root.item:
        raise ValueError("Inserting duplicate item")

    if item < root.item:                        # modify left subtree
        root.left = self._subtreeInsert(root.left, item)
    else:                                       # modify right subtree
        root.right = self._subtreeInsert(root.right, item)

    return root # original root is root of modified tree
```

So far we can create and add items to our `BST` objects, now let's work on a method to find items in the tree. We've already discussed the basic searching algorithm. It is easily implemented with a loop that walks down the tree from the root until either the item is found or we reach the bottom of the tree.

```
    def find(self, item):

        """ Search for item in BST
            post: Returns item from BST if found, None otherwise"""

        node = self.root
        while node is not None and not(node.item == item):
            if item < node.item:
                node = node.left
            else:
                node = node.right

        if node is None:
            return None
        else:
            return node.item
```

You might wonder why this method returns the item from the tree instead of just returning a Boolean value to indicate the item was found. For simplicity, our illustrations so far have used numbers, but we could store arbitrary objects in a binary search tree. The only requirement is that the objects be comparable. In general two objects might be == but not necessarily identical. Later on we'll see how we can exploit this property to turn our BST into a dictionary-like object.

For completeness, we should also add a method to our BST class for removing items. Removing a specific item from a binary search tree is a bit tricky. There are a number of cases that we need to consider. Let's start with the easy one. If the node to be deleted is a leaf, we can simply drop it off the tree by setting the reference in its parent node to None. But what if the node to delete has children? If the victim node has only a single child, our job is still straightforward. We can simply set the parent reference that used to point to the victim to point to its child instead. Figure 7.7 illustrates the situation where the left child of the victim is promoted to be the left child of the victim's parent. You might want to look at other single-child cases (there are three more) to convince yourself that this always works.

That leaves us with the problem of what to do when the victim node has two children. We can't just promote either child to take the victim's place, because that would leave the other one hanging unconnected. The solution to this dilemma is to simply leave the node in place, as we need it to maintain the structure of the tree. Instead of removing the node, we can replace its contents. We just need to find an easily deletable node whose value can be transferred into the target node while maintaining the tree's binary search property.

Consider the tree on the left side of Figure 7.8. Suppose we want to delete the 6 from this tree. What value in the tree could take its place? We could place

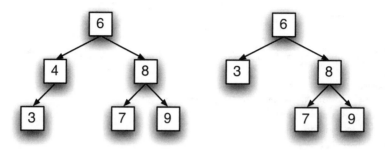

Figure 7.7: Deleting 4 from the binary search tree

either 5 or 7 in this node and the search property would be maintained. In general, it's correct to replace the victim's item with either its immediate predecessor or its immediate successor, since those values are guaranteed to stand in the same relation to the rest of the nodes in the tree. Let's say we decide to use the predecessor. We just place this value into the victim node and delete the predecessor node from the tree. Doing this gives us the tree pictured on the right side of Figure 7.8.

You might be a little concerned at this point about how we are going to delete the predecessor node. Couldn't this be just as hard as deleting the original victim? Thankfully, this is not the case. The predecessor value will always be the largest value in the victim's left subtree. Of course, to find the largest node in a binary search tree, we just march down the tree always choosing to follow links on the right. We stop when we run out of right links to follow. That means the predecessor node must have an empty right subtree, and we can always delete it by simply promoting its left subtree.

We'll again implement this algorithm using recursion on subtrees. Our top-level method just consists of a call to the recursive helper.

```
def delete(self, item):

    """remove item from binary search tree
    post: item is removed from the tree"""

    self.root = self._subtreeDelete(self.root, item)
```

The _subtreeDelete method implements the heart of the deletion algorithm. It must return the root node of the subtree from which the item is removed.

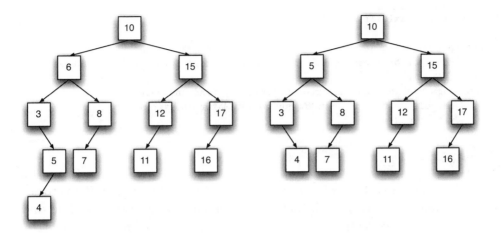

Figure 7.8: Deleting 6 from the binary search tree

```
def _subtreeDelete(self, root, item):
    if root is None:    # Empty tree, nothing to do
        return None
    if item < root.item:                            # modify left
        root.left = self._subtreeDelete(root.left, item)
    elif item > root.item:                          # modify right
        root.right = self._subtreeDelete(root.right, item)
    else:                                           # delete root
        if root.left is None:                       # promote right subtree
            root =  root.right
        elif root.right is None:                    # promote left subtree
            root = root.left
        else:
            # overwrite root with max of left subtree
            root.item, root.left = self._subtreeDelMax(root.left)
    return root
```

As you get the hang of trees as recursive structures, this code should not be too hard to follow. If the item to delete is in the left or right subtrees, we call `_subtreeDelete` recursively to produce the modified subtree. When the root is the node to be deleted, we handle the three possible cases: promoting the right subtree, promoting the left subtree, or replacing the item with its predecessor. That last case is actually handled by another recursive method `_subtreeDelMax`. This method finds the maximum value of a tree and also deletes the node containing that value. It looks like this.

```
def _subtreeDelMax(self, root):

    if root.right is None:          # root is the max
        return root.item, root.left  # return max and promote left subtree
    else:
        # max is in right subtree, recursively find and delete it
        maxVal, root.right = self._subtreeDelMax(root.right)
        return maxVal, root
```

7.5.3 | Traversing a BST

At this point we have a useful abstraction of a set of items. We can add items to the set, find them, and delete them. All that's really missing at this point is some easy way to iterate over the collection. Given the organization of the binary search tree, an in-order traversal is particularly nice, as it produces the items in sorted order. But users of our BST class should not have to know the internal details of the data structure in order to write their own traversal algorithms. There are a number of possible ways to accomplish this.

One approach would be to simply write a traversal algorithm that assembles the items from the tree into some sequential form, say a list or a queue. We can easily write a recursive in-order traversal algorithm to produce a Python list. Here's the code to add an asList method to our BST class.

```
def asList(self):

    """gets item in in-order traversal order
    post: returns list of items in tree in orders"""

    items = []
    self._subtreeAddItems(self.root, items)
    return items
```

```
def _subtreeAddItems(self, root, itemList):

    if root is not None:
        self._subtreeAddItems(root.left, itemList)
        itemList.append(root.item)
        self._subtreeAddItems(root.right, itemList)
```

Here the helper function _subtreeAddItems does a basic in-order traversal of the tree where the processing of an item just requires appending it to itemList. You should compare this code with the generic traversal algorithm from section 7.2. Our asList method just creates an initial list and calls _subtreeAddItems to populate the list. With the addition of this method, we can easily convert a BST into a sorted list. Of course that also means we could loop over all the items in the collection. For example, we could print out the contents of our BST in order like this:

```
for item in myBST.asList():
    print item
```

The only real problem with this approach is that it produces a list that is just as large as the original collection. If the collection is huge and we are just looking for a way to loop over all of the items, producing another collection of the same size is not necessarily a good idea.

Another idea is to use a design pattern sometimes called the *visitor pattern*. The idea of this pattern is that the container provides a method that traverses the data structure and performs some client-requested function on each node. In Python, we can implement this pattern via a method that takes an arbitrary function as a parameter and applies that function to every node in the tree. We again use a recursive helper method to actually perform the traversal.

```
    def visit(self, f):

        """perform an in-order traversal of the tree
        post: calls f with each TreeNode item in an in-order traversal
        order"""

        self._inorderVisit(self.root, f)

    def _inorderVisit(self, root, f):
        if root is not None:
            self._inorderVisit(root.left, f)
            f(root.item)
            self._inorderVisit(root.right, f)
```

Notice that throughout this code, f represents some arbitrary function that the client wants applied to each item in the BST. The function is applied via the line f(root.item). Again, this is just a variation on our generic recursive-traversal algorithm.

In order to use the visit method, we just need to construct a suitable function to apply to each item. For example, if we want to print out the contents of the BST in order again, we can now do it by visiting.

```
def prnt(item):
    print item

...
myBST.visit(prnt)
```

The main thing to note here is that in the call to `visit` there are no parentheses on `prnt`. We put the parentheses on when we call a function. Here we are not actually calling the function, but rather passing the function object itself along to the `visit` method that will actually do the calling.

The visitor pattern provides a nice way for clients to perform a traversal of a container without looking through the abstraction barrier. But it is sometimes cumbersome to code an appropriate function to do the processing, and the resulting code is not very Pythonic. As with our other containers, the ideal solution in Python is to define an iterator for our `BST` using the Python generator mechanism. The basic idea is that we will just code a generic in-order traversal that `yields` the items in the tree one at a time. By now, you should have a pretty good idea what the code will look like.

```
def __iter__(self):

    """in-order iterator for binary search tree"""

    return self._inorderGen(self.root)

def _inorderGen(self, root):

    if root is not None:
        # yield all the items in the left subtree
        for item in self._inorderGen(root.left):
            yield item
        yield root.item
        # yield all the items from the right subtree
        for item in self._inorderGen(root.right):
            yield item
```

The only new wrinkle in this code is the form of the recursive generator function. Remember, when you call a generator you do not get an item, rather you get an iterator object that provides items on demand. In order to actually produce the items from the left subtree, for example, we have to loop through the iterator provided by `self._inorderGen(root.left)` and yield each item.

Now we have a very convenient way of iterating through our `BST` container. Our code for printing the items in sorted order couldn't be simpler:

```
for item in myBST:
    print item
```

By the way, now that we have an iterator for the BST class, we really don't need a separate asList method. Python can produce a list of the items from a BST using the iterator via list(myBST). Being able to create a list of the items in a BST is particularly handy in writing unit tests for the BST class, as it provides an easy way to check the contents of a tree in assertions. Of course, getting a sorted list out of the BST does not guarantee that the tree has the correct form. For that, it might be helpful to have another traversal method (either pre- or postorder) as well. It's possible to deduce the true structure of a binary tree by examining two different traversals, so if both traversals come out right, you know the tree is structured the way you expect it to be.

7.5.4 A Run-time Analysis of BST Algorithms

In the introduction to this section, we suggested that a binary search tree can maintain an ordered collection quite efficiently. We've shown how a binary search tree gives us an ordered collection, but we haven't yet examined the run-time efficiency of the operations in any detail. Since many of the tree algorithms are written recursively, the analysis might seem daunting, but it's actually pretty easy if we just consider what's going on in the underlying structure.

Let's start by considering the operations that traverse the tree. Since the work we have to do at each node is constant, the time to do a traversal is just proportional to the number of nodes in the tree, which is just the number of items in the collection. That makes those operations $\Theta(n)$ where n is the size of the collection.

For the algorithms that examine only part of the tree (e.g., searching, inserting, and deleting) our analysis depends on the shape of the tree. The worst case for all of these methods requires walking a path from the root of the tree down to its "bottom." Clearly the number of steps required to do this will be proportional to the height of the tree. So the interesting question becomes how high is the tree? Of course that depends on the exact shape of the tree. Consider the tree that results from inserting a set of numbers in sorted order. The tree will end up being a linked list as each node is added as a right child of the previous number. For this tree with n elements, an insertion takes n steps to get to the bottom of the tree.

However, if the data in a tree is well distributed, then we expect that about half the items in any given subtree lie to the left and about half lie to the right. We call this a "balanced" tree. A relatively well-balanced tree will have an approximate height of $\log_2 n$. In this case, operations that have to find a particular spot in the tree will have $\Theta(\log n)$ behavior. Fortunately, if data is inserted into the tree in a random fashion, then at each node an item is equally likely to go into the left or right subtree as we work our way down from the root. On average, the result will be a nicely balanced tree.

In practice then, a binary search tree will offer very good performance, provided some care is taken in how the data is inserted and deleted. For the paranoid, there are well-known techniques (covered in section 13.3) for implementing insertion and deletion operations that guarantee the preservation of (approximately) balanced trees.

7.6 Implementing a Mapping with BST (Optional)

The BST object outlined in the previous section implements something akin to an ordered set. We can insert items, delete items, check membership, and get the items out in sorted order. Often trees are used in more database-like applications where we don't want to just ask if a particular item is in a set, but where we want to look up an item that has some particular characteristic. As a simple example, we might be maintaining a club membership list. Of course we need to be able to add and delete members from the club, but we also need something more. We need a way to bring up the record for a particular member of the club, for example to get their telephone number.

In this section we're going to take a look at how we might extend the usefulness of our binary search tree by using it to implement a general mapping similar to that provided by Python dictionaries. In our membership list example, we might use a special "key" value constructed from a member's name as a way to look up his data record. Assuming we have an appropriate `membershipList` object, we might get a phone number by doing something along these lines:

```
...
info = membershipList["VanRossum, Guido"]
print info.home_phone
```

Here our `membershipList` is an object that maps from a member's name to the corresponding record of his information. We could just use a Python dictionary for this task, but a dictionary is an unordered mapping, and we'd also like to be able to efficiently output our (huge!) membership list in sorted order.

One way to approach this problem would be rework the BST class so that all the methods take an extra parameter for the key and maintain a tree of key-value pairs. However, that's a lot more work than we really need to do. We can get a similar effect simply by using the existing BST implementation and building a wrapper around it to implement a general mapping interface. That way, we can get the advantages of a tree-based mapping object without having to modify or duplicate the BST class. Whenever possible, it's better to extend existing code than to duplicate or modify.

So how do we turn our BST from a set into a mapping? The key is to exploit the existing ordering and lookup functions of the BST class. Our existing class can be used to store any objects that are comparable. We will store items as key-value combinations, but the trick is that these items will be ordered according to just their keys. The first step is to create a new class to represent these key-value items. Let's call this combination item a KeyPair. In order to make our KeyPairs comparable, we just implement some comparison operations.

```
# KeyPair.py
class KeyPair(object):

    def __init__(self, key, value=None):
        self.key = key
        self.value = value

    def __eq__(self, other):
        return self.key == other.key

    def __lt__(self, other):
        return self.key < other.key

    def __gt__(self, other):
        return self.key > other.key
```

We have implemented only three of the six comparison operators, because all of the routines in BST use only these. For safety sake, we probably should implement the other three comparisons, just in case the BST code changes in the future. We leave this as an exercise.

Armed with this KeyPair class, we can now define a dictionary-like mapping based on BST. Here's the constructor for our class.

```
# TreeMap.py
from BST import BST
from KeyPair import KeyPair

class TreeMap(object):

    def __init__(self, items=()):
        self.items = BST()
        for key,value in items:
            self.items.insert(KeyPair(key,value))
```

We use the instance variable `items` to keep track of a BST that will store our `KeyPair` items. Just as a Python dictionary can be initialized with a sequence of pairs, we allow our `TreeMap` constructor to accept a sequence of pairs. We just need to loop through the pairs and call the BST `insert` operation to populate our tree. Of course, `insert` will keep the underlying binary search tree ordered according to the key values, since that's how `KeyPairs` compare to each other.

Once a `KeyPair` is in our BST we need to be able to retrieve it again by its key value. We can do this using the `find` operation from BST. The parameter we supply to the `find` operation will be a new `KeyPair` that is equivalent to (has the same key as) the one we are looking up. A line of code like this does the trick.

```
result = self.items.find(KeyPair(key))
```

Remember that the `find` operation searches the binary search tree for an item that is `==` to the target. In this case `KeyPair(key)` "matches" the pair in the BST that has the same key, and it returns this matching `KeyPair`. Our partial record with just the key filled in is sufficient to retrieve the actual record for that key.

To make our `TreeMap` class work like a Python dictionary, we implement the usual Python hooks for indexing: `__getitem__` and `__setitem__`.

```
def __getitem__(self, key):
    result = self.items.find(KeyPair(key))
    if result is None:
        raise KeyError()
    else:
        return result.value
```

```
def __setitem__(self, key, item):
    partial = KeyPair(key)
    actual = self.items.find(partial)
    if actual is None:
        # no pair yet for this key, add one
        actual = partial
        self.items.insert(actual)

    actual.value = item
```

Each of these methods does just a little bit of extra work to handle cases when the given key is not yet in the dictionary. The `__getitem__` method just raises a `KeyError` exception in this case. When `__setitem__` is passed a new key, it needs to insert a `KeyPair` for it into the BST. Since we already created the new `KeyPair` `partial` to do the initial search, it's a simple matter to use it for the new entry.

That's enough to get our `TreeMap` class up and running. It's still missing an iterator that allows us to access the items in order (to print out a membership list, for example). We leave it as an exercise to add the additional functionality.

7.7 Chapter Summary

We have covered some basic algorithms and data structures for implementing trees. Here is a quick rundown of important highlights:

- A tree is a non-linear container class for storing hierarchical data or for organizing linear data so it can be accessed efficiently.

- Trees are commonly stored using a linked structure but can also be stored as an array.

- Many tree applications use binary trees, which means that each node has zero, one, or two children, but it is also possible to implement trees with an arbitrary number of children.

- The binary search tree property is that for every node, the value of each node in its left subtree is less than or equal to the node's value and the value of each node in its right subtree is greater than the node's value.

- A binary search tree can support a $\Theta(\log n)$ implementation of the search, insertion, and deletion operations while maintaining the binary search tree property.

- Tree algorithms are often written using recursion since the tree itself is a recursive data structure.

- The three common binary tree traversal orders are: preorder, in-order, and postorder. An in-order traversal of a binary search tree produces the items in sorted order.

7.8 Exercises

True/False Questions

1. Every node in a tree has at most two children.

2. The depth of a tree node is the number of nodes between it and the root of the tree.

3. A tree has exactly one root node.

4. A complete binary tree is necessarily a full binary tree.

5. A full binary tree is necessarily a complete binary tree.

6. An in-order traversal of any binary tree produces the items in sorted order.

7. A postorder traversal of an expression tree yields the postfix (reverse Polish) form of an expression.

8. The worst-case search time for a binary search tree is $\Theta(n)$.

9. Every subtree of a binary search tree is also a binary search tree.

10. Since binary trees are non-linear, they cannot be easily implemented using an array.

Multiple Choice Questions

1. A tree is a natural representation of

   a) arbitrarily interconnected data.
   b) linear data.
   c) hierarchical data.
   d) sappy data.

2. Which of the following is not necessarily true of a non-empty tree?

   a) it has height of at least 0
   b) it has at least one leaf
   c) it has at least one root
   d) all of the above are true of a non-empty tree

3. In an expression tree, non-leaf nodes represent:

   a) operands.
   b) operators.
   c) parentheses.
   d) tokens.

4. In what order should an expression tree be traversed to evaluate the expression?

   a) preorder
   b) in-order
   c) postorder
   d) precedence order

5. Which of these design patterns allows clients to traverse a data structure without knowing its internal structure?

   a) visitor pattern
   b) iterator pattern
   c) both a and b
   d) none of the above

6. Which of the following orders will produce a binary search tree with the best search times?

   a) inserting the items in a random order
   b) inserting the items in order
   c) inserting the items in reverse order
   d) all will result in the same search times

7. What is the running time of the recursive tree traversals?

   a) $\Theta(1)$ b) $\Theta(\log n)$ c) $\Theta(n)$ d) $\Theta(n \log n)$

8. What is the maximum number of items in a binary tree with a height of 5?

   a) 5   b) 31   c) 32   d) 63

9. What is the minimum height of a tree with 64 nodes?

   a) 5   b) 6   c) 7   d) 32

10. What is the maximum height of a tree with 64 nodes?

   a) 6   b) 7   c) 63   d) 64

Short-Answer Questions

1. What is the drawback of the array/list representation of a general binary tree? What types of binary trees would be particularly well suited to the array/list representation?

2. Consider the binary search tree from the left side of Figure 7.8 (before the 6 is deleted). List the order that the nodes would be visited for each traversal order (preorder, in-order, and postorder).

3. Write an invariant for the BST class.

4. Write pre- and postconditions for the `delete` operation of the BST class.

5. A tree sort algorithm proceeds by inserting items into a binary search tree and then reading them back out with an in-order traversal. What is the asymptotic running time of sorting n items using a tree sort. Discuss both worst case and expected case results.

6. Consider the mathematical expression $3 + 4 * 5$. Draw two different expression trees whose in-order traversals produce this expression. Evaluate both of your trees using the evaluation algorithm given in section 7.3. Which tree corresponds to the "usual" interpretation of this expression?

7. Using the `TreeNode` class, write an expression that would produce the tree structure shown in Figure 7.5.

8. In the chapter, we saw that a value in a binary search tree can be deleted by replacing the item in its node with its in-order predecessor. As was noted, it would also work to use the in-order successor. Suppose that instead of always doing one or the other we implement a strategy that chooses between these two "on the fly." Suggest a suitable criterion for selecting which one to use and write pseudocode for an algorithm that performs the criterion test.

Programming Exercises

1. Write unit tests for the BST class.

2. Write and test a recursive version of the `find` function in the BST class.

3. Write `preorder` and `postorder` traversal generators for the BST class. For example, to generate a list for a pre-order traversal, we could write code like this `list(myBST.preorder())`.

4. Write a `__copy__` method for the BST class.

5. Add a `__len__` operation to the BST class. Calling `len(myBST)` should return the number of items in `myBST`.

6. Implement an improved `delete` operation for BST along the lines suggested in the last short-answer question above.

7. Implement and test an ordered multi-set class based on a BST. A multi-set is a set that allows multiple occurrences of any given value. The basic idea is that each item in the tree will consist of both a value and a count of the number of occurrences of that value. Your `MultiSet` class should include operations for insertion, deletion, counting, length, and traversal. The `count(x)` operation returns the number of times x occurs in the set. Here's a short interactive session showing its use:

```
>>> s = MultiSet()
>>> for x in [3,1,4,1,5,9,2,6,5,3,5]:
...     s.insert(x)

>>> len(s)
11
>>> s.delete(5)
>>> len(s)
10
>>> s.count(5)
2
>>> s.count(8)
0
>>> list(s)
[1,1,2,3,3,4,5,5,6,9]
```

Note: you can either write a new class similar to the BST class or use the technique of section 7.6 to leverage the existing BST class.

8. Write a simplified version of a decompression program. The following is a sample input file and the tree representation for its code. The first set of lines contains the letter and its code (separated by a space). There is a blank line before the actual coded message. Note that the first line contains the code for a space and that the last line is actually one long line, but it is wrapped for display purposes on this page. This file decodes into:
the magic word is abracadabra

```
   011
a 00
b 1001
c 1000
d 1010
e 11000
g 11001
h 11010
i 1011
m 11011
o 11100
r 010
s 11101
t 11110
w 11111

1111011010110000111101100110011011100001111111111000101010011101111110101
10010010100010000010100010010100101000
```

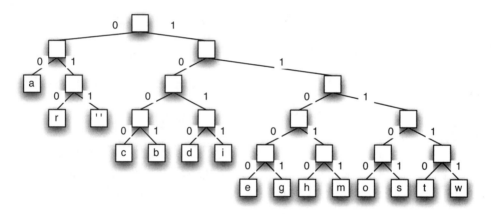

Copy the TreeNode.py file from the book. Create a class named PrefixCodeTree in a file named PrefixCodeTree.py. The class must have a constructor and the following two methods:

```
    def add_code(self, letter, code):

        """add the letter and its code to the tree

        pre: letter is a string, code is a string of 0s and 1s
        corresponding to the code for the letter; code does not
        contain a prefix that has already been added
        post: the tree is updated to store the code and its
        corresponding letter"""

    def decipher_code(self, coded_msg):

        """using the tree created by the add_code calls, decipher the
        coded_msg

        pre: add_code has been called to create the tree
        coded_msg contains valid codesfor the calls to add_code
        post: returns the decode string"""
```

Prefix codes are codes such that no code is a prefix for another code. In our tree representation, this corresponds to the letters at leaf nodes. To decode a message, start at the root of the tree and move down the tree based on the 0s (go left) or 1s (go right) until you reach a leaf and add that letter. Once you reach a letter, start at the root of the tree with the next code. Normally the codes would be stored in binary format, allowing us to represent eight 0s or 1s in a single byte, making the compressed file smaller if the common letters take less than eight 0s or 1s. To make the exercise simpler, the codes in the file are all plain text.

9. Think about a different way to solve exercise 8 using one of Python's built-in data types instead of a binary tree. Solve the problem using that data type.

10. Write a program to play the animal guessing game. Here's a sample output showing how the game works. User input is shown in bold.

```
Welcome to the Animal Game!
You pick an animal, and I will try to guess what it is.  You can help
me get better at the game by giving me more information when I make
a mistake.

The more you play, the better I get.

Think of an animal, and I'll try to guess what it is.
Is it green?  no
```

Does it purr? **n**
Does it have black and white stripes? **y**
Does it have hooves? **yes**
Is your animal a(n) zebra? **yes**
I'm soooo smart!

Do you want to play again? **y**

Think of an animal, and I'll try to guess what it is.
Is it green? **yes**
Does it hop? **yes**
Is your animal a(n) frog? **no**
Rats! I didn't get it. Please help me improve.

What is your animal? **grasshopper**
Please enter a yes/no question that would select between
a(n) grasshopper and a(n) frog:
» **Does it eat leaves**
What would the answer be for a(n) grasshopper? **yes**

Do you want to play again? **yes**

Think of an animal, and I'll try to guess what it is.
Is it green? **y**
Does it hop? **y**
Does it eat leaves? **y**
Is your animal a(n) grasshopper? **yes**
I'm soooo smart!

Do you want to play again? **n**

Thanks for playing!

As you can see, this program demonstrates a simple form of machine learning. When it fails to guess the user's animal, it asks for more information so that it can get the animal right the next time.

You can implement this program using a kind of binary tree known as a *decision tree*. The leaf nodes of the tree represent categories (animals, in this case), and the non-leaf nodes contain yes/no questions. A round of the game consists of starting at the root of the tree and navigating down by asking the question and then going left or right depending on whether the answer is yes or no. When arriving at a leaf, the program guesses the animal at the leaf. When the guess is incorrect, the leaf becomes an interior node with the category that was there demoted to one child and the correct answer to the other child.

Your initial tree can just consist of a single node that contains your favorite animal; the tree can grow from there by playing the game. Of course, you will need a way to store the tree to a file between playings so that the program can accumulate experience rather than starting from scratch each time. The easiest way to write the tree to a file is to use Python's serialization capabilities. Take a look at the documentation for the `pickle` module to see how to do this.

Chapter 8

A C++ Introduction for Python Programmers

Objectives

- To understand the C++ compilations process.

- To learn the syntax and semantics of a major subset of C++ including built-in data types, input/output, decision statements, and looping statements.

- To learn the syntax and usage of C++ arrays.

- To learn the details of C++ functions and parameter passing mechanisms.

- To understand the scope and lifetime of C++ variables.

8.1 Introduction

The earlier chapters in this book focused on developing algorithms and data structures using the Python language. Python is a great language for beginners because of its relatively simple syntax and powerful, built-in data structures and library of functions. Python's usage in industry is fairly small but is continuing to grow. However, even if Python were to become the most commonly used language, all computer scientists should know more than one computer language. Different languages provide different capabilities, making no single language the best choice for every problem. Learning new languages will help expand your problem solving skills as their different capabilities will encourage you to think about more ways to solve a problem.

The Python language's data structures and many of its built-in functions hide many of the underlying implementation details from programmers. As we discussed earlier, when using Python you do not need to worry about deallocating memory as you do in some languages. Obviously the people developing higher level languages and writing interpreters and run-time environments for them need to understand all the low-level details necessary to implement them. It should be clear that Python is generally not the best language for applications that process very large amounts of data or require extensive computation since it uses extra memory to store a reference count and data type for every object and its interpreter must convert the byte codes for each Python statement to machine code each time it executes the statement.

This chapter and the next four chapters will introduce a large subset of the C++ programming language. C++ is an excellent complementary language for Python programmers as it is a lower level language that requires you to understand many low-level implementation details, including memory management. C++ can make much more efficient use of the computer's memory and CPU. Having programming abilities in both Python and C++ will allow you to choose the appropriate language for a given problem. In fact, it is very common for a Python program to make use of compiled C or C++ code when speed and memory usage are important.

8.2 C++ History and Background

The C programming language was developed in the early 1970s as a cross-platform systems language. In the 1960s when new computers were built, new operating systems were written in the assembly language for each machine. Brian Kernigan and Dennis Ritchie at AT&T Bell Labs decided to develop a high-level, cross-platform language for systems code. They, along with Ken Thompson, developed the Unix operating system in C, and this allowed them to easily port it to new computer hardware. The C programming language is still widely used for applications in which speed is crucial such as operating systems and scientific computing. In fact, the Python interpreter is written in C.

In the late 1970s and early 1980s, computer scientists began to realize that object-oriented design and programming allowed them to write more maintainable and reusable code. There were a couple existing object-oriented languages at the time, but the C programming language was extremely popular. In the early 1980s, Bjarne Stroustrup at AT&T decided to develop an object-oriented language that would be relatively easy for C programmers to learn. He added explicit object-oriented programming support to the C programming language and called the new language C++. The C++ language is mostly backward compatible with the C programming language other than the new keywords that C++ uses, making it fairly easy for C programmers to get started with C++. The complete C++ language is much larger and more complex than the C language and many programmers use only a subset of C++ when writing C++ code.

C and C++ are lower level languages than Python. C does not provide built-in list or dictionary types. C++ does support some higher level data structures using a collection of classes and methods known as the Standard Template Library. C and C++ are terser and use more special characters (e.g., **&&** is used for **and** and **||** is used for **or**). Newer versions of C++ do allow **and** and **or** to be used in addition to the special symbols.

This book covers the C++ language although most of what is included in this chapter also applies to the C language. Some of the topics in later chapters also apply to the C language, but we will generally not point out what does and what does not. In general, any discussion that involves classes does not apply to the C language.

As you read the previous paragraphs, you may be asking yourself why would you want to learn C++ since it seems it is more difficult to write code using it. While you will likely find it more difficult to write C++ code and your C++ source code will almost always be longer than the corresponding Python source code that does the same thing, Python is not the best language for all applications. Writing code in a compiled language such as C or C++ allows you to write code that typically executes an order of magnitude faster and uses less memory than the corresponding interpreted Python code. There are still a number of application areas where you want to maximize execution speed and use memory efficiently so your code can handle large amounts of data. For example, you would not want to write an operating system or a server such as a web server or database server in Python. Learning C++ will also help you gain a better understanding of what is going on inside the Python interpreter.

C and C++ source code is compiled into machine language code while Python uses a hybrid process of compiling into byte code and then interpreting the byte code. There are advantages and disadvantages to both methods. Compiled code executes much faster than interpreted code, but is less flexible than interpreted code. We will discuss some of these differences in later sections. A pictorial representation of the process of compiling C++ code is shown in Figure 8.1. We will use the following simple C++ program to describe how that compilation process works.

```
// hello.cpp
#include <iostream>
using namespace std;

int main()
{
  cout << "hello world\n";
  return 0;
}
```

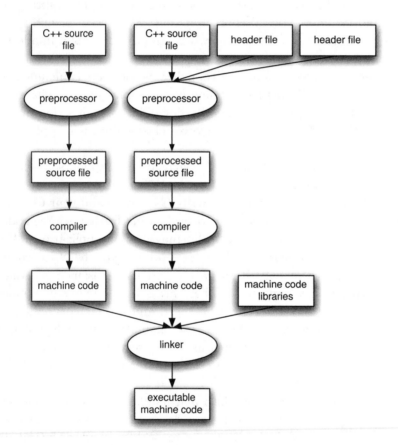

Figure 8.1: Compile-and-link process for C++ code

If we tell you that cout is used to produce output, you can probably guess that
the program does the same as the Python program print "hello world". The

preprocessor (commonly known as the *C preprocessor*), takes the source code and processes all the lines that start with a pound sign (#). The #include preprocessor directive in the sample program tells the preprocessor to copy all the code from the iostream file into our source file. This has the same effect as if we had copied and pasted that file into our program where the #include statement is. The iostream file is known as a *header file*. Each C++ source file can include any number of header files. We will discuss header files in more detail later in this chapter and again in later chapters; for now what you need to know is that header files contain information about source code that is written in other files.

The output of the preprocessor is still C++ source code that is then sent to a C++ compiler. The compiler's job is to convert the C++ source code into machine language code (the 0s and 1s that the computer's CPU can execute) for a specific chip and a specific operating system. The first step the compiler does is check the code for any syntax errors. Since a syntax error means the program is not correct, the compiler cannot determine what you mean and complete its process. If your code has syntax errors, the compiler stops and gives you an error message indicating what it could not understand. This means you cannot try to run your program until you fix all your syntax errors. Once your source code is syntactically correct, the compiler will produce machine language code corresponding to your code in the C++ source file. This machine language code is also commonly known as *object code*.

Just as we split Python programs into multiple files, all but the simplest C++ programs are typically split into multiple source files. As Figure 8.1 shows, each source file is compiled independently. One source file may call a function defined in another source file. This is the main reason for header files: by including information about the function defined in another file, the compiler can make certain that you correctly called the function. The job of the *linker* is to combine the various machine code object files into one executable program, making certain that each function that is called exists in exactly one of the object files. Most operating systems also support machine code libraries. In this context, a library is the object/machine code for commonly used classes or functions. In C++, the input and output statements are part of a library declared in the iostream header file. As Figure 8.1 shows, the linker also copies the code from the libraries your program uses into the final executable code.

Since the resulting executable program is in machine language, it can be executed only on computers that support that machine language and that operating system. For example, a program compiled for an Intel chip running a version of the Windows operating system will generally run on any Intel-compatible computer (of the same generation or a newer version of the Intel chip) and that version or newer compatible versions of the Windows operating system. A program compiled on an Intel computer for the Linux operating system will not run on a Windows system and vice versa. Simple C/C++ programs can be recompiled for another operating sytem or computer chip. *Porting* a program refers to the process of getting it to execute on a different chip or operating system. The real difficulty in porting code to another operating system is that different operating systems support different libraries of functions for input/output and graphical user interfaces (GUIs). Many operating systems also provide additional libraries of code. Any program that uses these operating system–specific libraries of code is more difficult to port to other operating systems. These libraries would also need to be ported to the other operating system or the code rewritten to avoid using the libraries.

Python code is machine independent and can be executed on any machine containing the Python interpreter. This means that the Python interpreter itself must be ported and compiled for that machine and operating system. If your program uses extra Python modules that are specific to that operating system such as a GUI toolkit that exists only on that operating system, then your Python code will not be portable. Python programs that use only the standard Python modules can be executed on any machine or operating system containing the interpreter without any changes to the code. Just as the Python interpreter can be compiled on many different systems, many of the extra modules can also be ported to other operating systems; this of course requires more work.

The process of executing Python code is significantly different from the process of compiling and linking C++ code. Figure 8.2 shows a pictorial representation of the process. You directly execute only one Python file, but by importing other Python files, you are effectively combining the code from multiple source files. Python source code is first compiled into a machine-independent set of instructions known as *byte code*; this process happens automatically when you run a Python program or import a Python module. You may have noticed files with a .pyc extension on your computer. These are the byte code files created when you import a Python module. A single byte code instruction corresponds to code such as a function call or adding two operands.

The Python interpreter then starts processing the byte code corresponding to the first statement in your program. Each time a byte code statement is processed, it is converted to machine language and executed. It is this process of interpreting each byte code statement and converting it to machine language every time the byte code is executed that results in Python code executing slower than compiled C++ code. The byte code can be converted to machine language faster than pure Python

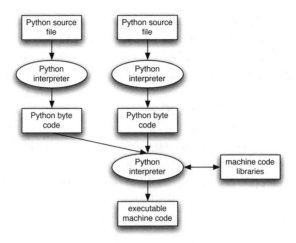

Figure 8.2: Python hybrid compilation and interpretation process

source code; that is the reason the Python source code is converted once to the byte code instead of converting each Python statement to machine language every time that Python statement is executed.

As the figure shows, your Python code can call compiled C or C++ code in machine code libraries. This allows you to mix Python, C, and C++ code in your program. Writing C or C++ code that can be called from the Python interpreter requires following certain conventions; we will not cover the details of this in this book. Any C or C++ code that you want to call from Python must be compiled on the specific version of the operating system and for the chip that you will be executing your Python program on.

The execution speed difference between Python and C/C++ becomes more noticeable when loops are explicitly written in Python. Instead of writing a loop that executes a large number of iterations, it is better to call a built-in Python method or function that does the same thing (if one exists) since the Python method or function is implemented in compiled C code. You should have noticed this in the use of the `index` method compared to our hand-coded linear search function in subsection 1.3.1. In summary, the main trade-off between Python and C/C++ is the speed of execution vs. the amount of code and development time required.

The basic statements of Python and C++ are similar; because of this, it is relatively easy for Python programmers to learn to read C++ code. Learning to write C++ code is more difficult because you need to learn the exact syntax details of C++. It is easier for Python programmers to learn C++ than for someone with no programming experience. This is because programmers who know one language already understand the common concepts such as decision statements, loops, functions, etc. Many programming languages, including C, C++, Python, Java, C#, and Perl, use similar statements and syntax making it fairly easy to learn additional languages. We think that Python is an ideal language for beginners because of its simple syntax and that C++ is a good second language because it is similar to Python, but allows students to gain experience with the low-level details of programming that the Python interpreter hides.

Many of the C++ concepts presented in this chapter and the next few chapters also apply to the C language, but not all of them. Specifically, the input/ouput mechanisms are different in C and C++, and C does not completely support classes. This book does not cover the C language mechanisms for input/ouput or C structs, which are a simplified version of classes. These chapters on C++ are not intended to provide all the details of the C++ language, but rather to quickly get Python programmers started with C++ and to help them learn about explicit memory management. To become a C++ expert, we suggest you read a C++ reference book such as the one authored by Bjarne Stroustrup. Since C++ is a fairly complex language, there are a number of topics that must be covered before we can write a complete C++ program. We will begin covering these concepts assuming a knowledge of Python.

$\boxed{8.3}$ Comments, Blocks of Code, Identifiers, and Keywords

C++ supports two types of comments. The equivalent to Python's # comment marker is two forward slashes (//). Anything on a line, from the two forward slashes to the end of the line, is considered a comment and ignored by the compiler. The C++ compiler also supports multi-line comments. This type of comment begins with /* and ends with */.

```
// this is a one-line C++ comment

/* this is a
multi-line
C++ comment */
```

Python denotes blocks of code using indentation. C++ uses braces ({}) to mark the beginning and ending of blocks. Indentation in C++ has no effect, but for readability, programmers generally follow the same indentation rules that Python requires. Whitespace (spaces, tabs, and new lines) have no effect on C++ code except within strings. Since spaces, tabs, and new lines have no effect in C++, each C++ statement must be terminated with a semicolon. Forgetting the semicolon at the end of a statement is a common mistake, especially for programmers familiar with Python. Unfortunately, when you forget a semicolon, many C++ compilers indicate there is a problem with the next line of code. When tracking down compilation errors, it is often necessary to look at the line or lines of code just above the line on which the compiler indicates there is an error.

The rules for legal C++ identifiers are the same as Python's rules. Identifiers must start with a letter or an underscore. After the initial letter or underscore, the additional characters may be letters, numbers, or underscores. Also, identifiers may not be a C++ keyword. Figure 8.3 lists all the C++ keywords.[1] This book does not cover the details of all the C++ keywords.

and	and_eq	asm	auto	bitand	bitor
bool	break	case	catch	char	class
compl	const	const_cast	continue	default	delete
do	double	dynamic_cast	else	enum	explicit
export	extern	false	float	for	friend
goto	if	inline	int	long	mutable
namespace	new	not	not_eq	operator	or
or_eq	private	protected	public	register	reinterpret_cast
return	short	signed	sizeof	static	static_cast
struct	switch	template	this	throw	true
try	typedef	typeid	typename	union	unsigned
using	virtual	void	volatile	wchar_t	while

Figure 8.3: C++ Keywords

8.4 Data Types and Variable Declarations

C++ requires that all variables be explicitly declared before they are used and supports the following built-in data types: `int`, `char`, `float`, `double`, and `bool`. Variables are declared with a specified data type and a variable can hold data values of only that type. The `int` type corresponds to integers in Python and supports the

---

[1]The list of keywords is from Bjarne Stroustrup, *The C++ Programming Language*, (Reading, Massachusetts: Addison-Wesley, 1997), 3rd ed. 794.

same operations including the modulus operator (%). Unlike Python, where integers are automatically converted to long integers as necessary, C++ `int` types silently overflow if a value is too large to store. A C++ `int` type must use at least 16 bits, which allows values in the approximate range of +/- 32,000; however, most systems use at least 32 bits, allowing numbers in the +/- 2 billion range. The `char` type holds a single character. Internally it is stored as the ASCII value for the character, so a `char` variable can store a value between -128 and 127.

C++ also supports the modifiers `short` and `long` for `int` types. On most 32-bit systems, a `short int` is 16 bits, an `int` is 32 bits, and a `long int` is also 32 bits. The `long int` type is guaranteed to be at least 32 bits whereas the `int` is only guaranteed to be at least 16 bits. The `int` and `char` types support the `unsigned` modifier indicating that only non-negative numbers are supported and allow larger values. A 32-bit `unsigned int` supports values from 0 to approximately 4 billion instead of +/- 2 billion. An `unsigned char` can store a value between 0 and 255.

The `float` and `double` data types correspond to what mathematicians call *real* numbers but on the computer they are not represented exactly. Because of how they are represented internally using bits of 0s and 1s, they are more appropriately referred to as *floating point* numbers. The `float` type uses 32 bits to represent the number and provides 6 or 7 significant decimal digits. The `double` type uses 64 bits and provides 15 or 16 significant digits. Python uses the C `double` type to implement floating point numbers. Because modern computers have plenty of memory and most implement floating point arithmetic in hardware, you should use the `double` type instead of the `float` type in almost every situation. Figure 8.4 summarizes the details of the C++ data types.

In C++, variables can be defined anywhere and are accessible from that point to the end of the block of code in which they are declared. For style and readability purposes, many C++ programmers declare all variables they will need in a block of code at the top of that block. A variable is declared by specifying the type followed by the variable name. Multiple variables of the same type may be declared on one line by separating the variable names by commas. The following shows a simple program with a few variable declarations. Based on our earlier discussion that `cout` is used to produce output and your knowledge of Python, you can probably guess what this C++ program outputs.

Data type	Typical range of values	Typical # of bytes	Comments
int	-2,147,483,648 to 2,147,483,647	4	integer values only
unsigned int	0 to 4,294,967,295	4	integer values only
short int	-32,768 to 32,767	2	integer values only
unsigned short int	0 to 65,535	2	integer values only
char	-128 to 127	1	integer values only
unsigned char	0 to 255	1	integer values only
float	approximately $+/-10^{38}$	4	real numbers with 6 or 7 significant digits
double	approximately $+/-10^{308}$	8	real numbers with 15 or 16 significant digits
bool	true or false	1	true and false are constants

Figure 8.4: C++ built-in data types

```
// output.cpp
#include <iostream>
using namespace std;
int main()
{
  int i, j;
  double x, y;

  i = 2;
  j = i + i;
  x = 3.5;
  y = x + x;
  cout << j << "\n" << y << "\n";
  return 0;
}
```

You may be wondering why C++ requires you to declare variables while Python does not. Remember that C++ code is compiled directly to machine language. Machine language instructions are performed on specific data types. All CPUs have instructions for adding two integers, and most modern CPUs have instructions for adding two floating point numbers. Some older CPUs did not have direct floating point instructions, but implemented floating point calculations in software using a number of integer instructions, making them much slower. In our preceding example, the compiler needs to know to generate the machine instruction to add two integers for the statement j = i + i; and to generate the machine instruction to add two floating point numbers for the statement y = x + x;. The variable declarations indicating the data types allow the compiler to determine the correct machine instruction.

The Python interpreter converts the corresponding two Python addition statements to the same byte code such as add i, i and add x, x. The same byte code is used in both cases for the add statement. When the Python interpreter is then executing the byte code, it determines the data type for the two operands and in the first case generates an integer add instruction and in the second case it generates a floating point add instruction. If the two operands were strings, it would generate the machine instructions to concatenate two strings. Since Python does not create the machine instructions until it is ready to execute the statement, it does not need to know the data type when the code is written as the C++ compiler does. This allows the code to work properly even if the data type for variables changes between multiple executions of the statement. The following silly Python program shows an example of this. The first time through the loop, the statement x + x is adding two integers and the second time it is concatenating two strings. This type of code is not possible in C++ without using separate variables for each different type.

```
for i in range(2):
    if i == 0:
        x = 1
    else:
        x = 'hi'
    print x + x
```

The terminology for these issues is *dynamic typing* and *static typing*. Python uses dynamic typing which means the data types for a variable or name can change, whereas C++ uses static typing which means the data type of a specific variable is fixed at compile time and cannot change. Another significant difference in how Python and C++ handle variables is that C++ variables have their memory allocated when a function is called and the same memory location is used for that variable through the execution of the function. Technically, it is incorrect to use the term *variables* in Python. The term *name* is correct; a Python name refers to an object in memory. During the execution of a Python function, the memory location that a name refers to can change. We discussed this in section 4.2. In the following simple program, the name x refers to two different objects at two different addresses.

```
x = 3
x = 4
```

A Python name is not assigned to an address until it is used in your code and changes each time you assign a new object to it. Again, C++ variables are allocated a specific memory location that does not change during the execution; the same memory location is used to store the 3 and then the 4. We will examine these issues in more detail in section 8.7 and again in Chapter 10.

C++ also supports constants and a compile time check to make certain a program does not attempt to change a value. A sample constant definition is `const double PI = 3.141592654;`. If a program defines a constant and contains another statement that assigns a value to the defined constant (e.g., `PI = 5`), that is a syntax error and the program will not compile. Many programmers use the convention of all capital letters for constants.

C++ does not provide built-in, high-level data structures such as lists, tuples, and dictionaries as Python does. C++ supports arrays (covered in section 8.11) that can be used to build similar data structures. As you would expect since C++ is an object-oriented language, it provides classes that allow you to encapsulate data members and functions so you can build your own list, tuple, and dictionary classes that provide methods for manipulating the data. We will learn about C++ classes in section 9.1.

8.5 Include Statements, Namespaces, and Input/Output

Python uses the `import` statement to access code written in another file. C++ uses a `#include` statement to copy the class and function declarations defined in a different file into your current file so the compiler can check if you are using the function or class correctly. The files containing these declarations are known as *header files*. Header files can contain items other than class and function declarations but we will not worry about those items now. The details of function prototypes are discussed in section 8.12, but the basic idea is that a function prototype specifies the number of parameters, the data type for each parameter, and the return type for the function. The prototype allows the compiler to create a list of functions and classes that exist. Thus, when you attempt to call a function not defined in your file, the compiler can determine if a function with that name has been declared elsewhere and if you are calling the function with appropriate parameters. The same concept applies to including the definitions of classes so that the compiler can determine if you use a class correctly (i.e., a class exists with that name and contains the methods you use). A header file typically does not contain the code for the function or class methods, just the declaration. Usually, a separate implementation file includes the definition of the function (i.e., the body of the function). There are exceptions to this that we will discuss later. The actual machine code for the functions and classes are combined together by the *linker* to create the executable code (as we showed in Figure 8.1). We will cover additional details of compiling and linking later in this chapter.

C++ supports namespaces that are similar to the namespaces created by Python modules. Each Python file is its own module and effectively has its own namespace. C++ does not require the use of namespaces, but some of the built-in C++ classes and functions are defined within namespaces. We will cover the details of writing your own namespace in the optional subsection 8.17.2; we just cover the basics of using an existing namespace in this section. The most commonly used namespace is the standard namespace that is abbreviated `std` and is part of the definition of the C++ programming language. Since a number of C++ built-in functions and classes are declared in the `std` namespace, we need to know how to use a namespace in order to write almost every C++ program.

C++ uses a library of functions for input and output and requires a file to be included to access this library. The simplest way to access this library is to place the following statements at the top of your file:

```
#include <iostream>
using namespace std;
```

As we discussed earlier, the `#include` statement causes the C++ compiler to effectively copy the contents of the `iostream` header file into your file and then to compile the complete file. This header file defines the various input/output functions and classes. The input/output functions and classes are in the namespace `std`. The C++ output statement uses the `cout` instance of the `ostream` class defined in the `iostream` file. The `using namespace std` statement tells the compiler to allow direct access to all the elements defined in the `std` namespace. This is similar to the Python version of the import statement, `from math import *`, that allows access to all the items defined in the `math` module. Without a `using` statement, it must be referred to using the full name `std::cout`. Another option is to write the statement `using std::cout` after the include statement. This allows us to specify the `cout` instance without the `std::` prefix, but does not allow us to access any other members of the `std` namespace directly. This is similar to the Python statement `from math import sqrt` which allows us to access the `sqrt` function defined in the `math` module, but not any of the other items defined in the `math` module. The main difference between C++ and Python namespaces (each Python file is a separate namespace) is that items defined in a C++ namespace can always be accessed with the full name (`namespace::item`) without a `using` statement while you must use an `import` statement to access items in a Python namespace.

The C++ `cout` instance works similarly to the Python `print` statement to output variables, expressions, and constants. Python uses commas to separate multiple items being output in one statement. C++ uses the symbols « to separate multiple items to be output with one statement. C++ does not automatically insert a space as Python does with each comma-separated item, and C++ does not automatically output an end-of-line character as the Python `print` statement does. As with Python, any items not inside of quotation marks are evaluated. C++ strings must be denoted using the double quotation mark. In C++, a single quotation mark is used only to denote a single character (i.e., the built-in `char` data type).

All C++ programs must have one function named `main` that is called when the program is executed. The `main` function must return an `int` value. Putting together all the concepts we have learned so far, you should now understand most of the syntax of our "hello world" example.

```
// hello.cpp
#include <iostream>
using namespace std;

int main()
{
  cout << "hello world\n";
  return 0;
}
```

The backslash escape characters in C++ are the same as they are in Python. The above program uses \n to output a new line character after printing `hello world`. C++ also allows the use of `endl`, which is declared in the `std` namespace (if the `using namespace std` line is not specified, it must be referred to as `std::endl`). The above `cout` statement could also be written as `cout « "hello world" « endl`. A common style is to use \n when the output statement ends in quotation marks and to use `endl` when the last item in the `cout` statement is not a string constant. One difference between using "\n" and `endl` is that `endl` forces the output buffer to be flushed. With buffered output, the operating system may wait and send the outputted data to the screen (or a file, if you are writing to a file) at a later time for efficiency purposes. The output buffer is flushed when your program exits normally, but if your program crashes, you may not see some of the output that your program actually generated. This can lead you to think that your program crashed earlier than it actually did. Because of this, you may want to use **endl** if you use **cout** statements to help you track down where a program is crashing.

Similar to the **cout** instance, C++ has a **cin** instance of the **istream** class that is part of the standard namespace and is used for input. The symbols » are used to separate multiple input values. The **cin** statement uses whitespace to separate multiple values and will skip past any whitespace (space, tab, or new line) to find the next number, character, string, etc. The following program and sample execution of it show a program similar to what you studied in your first programming course. We have used the symbol ␣ to indicate where spaces are in the source code and in the output since **cout** does not automatically output spaces or new lines as the Python **print** statement does.

```
//␣ctof.cpp
#include␣<iostream>
using␣namespace␣std;

int␣main()
{
␣␣double␣celsius,␣fahrenheit;

␣␣cout␣<<␣"Enter␣Celsius␣temperature:␣";
␣␣cin␣>>␣celsius;
␣␣fahrenheit␣=␣9.0␣/␣5.0␣*␣celsius␣+␣32.0;
␣␣cout␣<<␣celsius␣<<␣"␣degrees␣Celsius␣is␣";
␣␣cout␣<<␣fahrenheit␣<<␣"␣degrees␣Fahrenheit\n";
␣␣return␣0;
}
```

```
Enter␣Celsius␣temperature:␣22.5
22.5␣degrees␣Celsius␣is␣72.5␣degrees␣Fahrenheit
```

If we had declared the **celsius** variable as an **int**, then the user could type in only integer values. This would make the program less general so when declaring variables you should ask yourself what are the possible values for this variable. If it could possibly be a floating point value, use the **double** type, but if it will always be an integer, use the **int** type.

When using **cin** to input multiple values, the user can type in any amount of whitespace to separate the values. The input may be entered by typing two values separated by one or more spaces or a tab, or by pressing the **Return** key after each number is entered. As with Python, the input is not processed until the **Return** key is pressed. The following is a complete example showing two values being input with the same **cin** statement. We leave it as an exercise to show the output for this program for a specific input.

```
// input1.cpp
#include <iostream>
using namespace std;
int main()
{
  double x, y;
  cout << "enter x and y: ";
  cin >> x >> y;
  cout << "x = " << x << " and y = " << y << endl;
  cout << "x + y = " << x + y << endl;
  return 0;
}
```

The fact that inputing values using `cin` in C++ skips whitespace can lead to some confusion when using it to input characters. It is certainly useful that it skips spaces when reading numbers, but since it also does this with the `char` data type, there is no way for a user to enter a space that will be stored in a `char` when reading the `char` data type using `cin`. For example, if the user enters x␣y␣z when the following program is executed, the program outputs `xyz`, not x␣y as you might expect.

```
// input2.cpp
#include <iostream>
using namespace std;

int main()
{
  char a, b, c;

  cin >> a >> b >> c;
  cout << a << b << c;
  return 0;
}
```

8.6 Compiling

We have covered enough background material that you are now ready to start writing your own simple C++ programs. We will now briefly discuss how to compile programs on your computer. The three major operating systems in use today are Microsoft's Windows, Unix/Linux, and Mac OS X. Each of these operating systems provides its own applications for editing and compiling programs. Microsoft sells a full-featured version of their development environment currently known as Visual Studio. It also provides a free, but limited, version known as Visual Studio Express.

If you are using Microsoft Windows, you can download it from Microsoft's web site. Even though it does not have all the capabilities of the full system, it should work fine for all the C++ examples and exercises in this book. Apple provides its full featured development environment, named Xcode, for free to anyone. It may have come preinstalled on your Mac computer or you can download it from Apple's web site (registration is required at the time of this writing, but it is free). Unix refers to a number of different operating systems. We will not go into the history of Unix in this book, but realize that different companies sell slightly different versions of Unix. In fact, Apple's Mac OS X is built on top of a Unix operating system. The Linux operating system is a free clone of Unix. We will use the term Unix in this book to refer to all Unix systems including Linux.

The graphical development environments for Visual Studio and Xcode change over time so we will not go into the details of using these applications for writing and compiling C++ code in this book. You may be able to figure out how to use them on your own fairly easily or with a little help from your instructor. On most Unix systems, the GNU g++ compiler is used for compiling C++ programs. There are also commercial C++ compilers available for various Unix systems. The Mac Xcode application is just a graphical front for the g++ compiler so you can use g++ from the Terminal application on a Mac. Since the command line usage of g++ has not changed in years for simple programs, we will cover the basic usage of g++ for compiling C++ programs on Unix systems.

The file extensions .cpp, .C, and .cc are commonly used for C++ programs. We will use the .cpp extension in our examples in this book since it can be used easily on all three major operating systems. For a single file named program.cpp that does not use any additional libraries, the command `g++ program.cpp -o program` creates the executable file named program from the C++ source file program.cpp assuming your program is syntactically correct. You may recall from our discussion of compilation at the beginning of the chapter that there are multiple steps: preprocessing, compiling, and linking. The `g++` command we specified performs all three of these steps.

Depending on the version of `make` on your Unix system, the command `make program` might produce the same result. Remember that the program.cpp file must contain a `main` function, and that is where the execution of the `program` file will start. To execute your code, type `./program` and press the `Return` key. The `./` preceding the name of the executable program is the safest way to ensure that the operating systems executes the program in your current directory. Depending on how your Unix account is set up, you may be able to type in just `program` to execute it, but we recommend you get in the habit of typing in `./program` since this will always work.

Just as with Python, it is good practice to split larger programs into a number of smaller source files that are appropriately organized. As we discussed at the beginning of this chapter, each file is compiled separately producing the machine language code for the C++ code in that file. Using **g++**, each source file ending with a .cpp extension can be compiled into an object file with a .o extension by using the `-c` flag for the **g++** command; this corresponds to the preprocessing and compilation step. If you leave off the `-c` flag, the **g++** command attempts to perform the preprocessing, compilation, and linking phases which is not what you want if you have multiple source files.

Figure 8.5 shows an example of compiling two source files with the **main** function in the test_sort.cpp file. The last line is the linking step which checks that the test_sort.o file contains one function named **main** and that each function called by all the files appears exactly once in one of the .o files. In this example, we have also added the `-g` flag to the **g++** command so it includes the symbol names; this allows debuggers to provide information about the actual names of variables and functions instead of just the address where they are stored.

```
g++ -g -c test_sort.cpp
g++ -g -c sort.cpp
g++ -g test_sort.o sort.o -o test_sort
```

Figure 8.5: Compiling multiple source files

As with most repetitive tasks this process can be automated. The Unix operating system provides the **make** command for recompiling the source files that have been modified since the corresponding object file was last created and linking all the object files. The **make** command checks for a file named **Makefile** or **makefile** that describes how to create the executable from the source files. Figure 8.6 shows the contents of a **Makefile** for use with the sort example in Figure 8.5.

This book does not cover all the details of makefiles, but the basic idea is that the lines with colons have the name of a file before the colon and the file names after the colon indicate the files on which that file depends (i.e., if one of the files after the colon changes, the file before the colon needs to be regenerated). The line following the line with the colon specifies how to generate the file before the colon on the above line and must start with a tab character (i.e., you cannot just use spaces to indent the line). When you enter just **make** and press the **Return** key, it builds the first item listed in the makefile (in this case, it builds the executable

```
test_sort: test_sort.o sort.o
        g++ -g test_sort.o sort.o -o test_sort

test_sort.o: test_sort.cpp
        g++ -g -c test_sort.cpp

sort.o: sort.cpp
        g++ -g -c sort.cpp

clean:
        /bin/rm -rf test_sort *.o
```

Figure 8.6: Makefile for test_sort

test_sort). You can also tell it to build other items by using the name of the item with the **make** command (i.e., you can enter **make linear_sort.o** and it will execute the command to create the file named linear_sort.o). A **clean** target that deletes all the object and executable files is commonly added so you can type the **make clean** command to delete all of them and then rebuild the entire executable using all the source files. You can find additional details on makefiles in most introductory Unix books or on the Internet. If you are using a non-Unix system, your integrated development environment (IDE) most likely has a build system to automate compiling your programs.

8.7 Expressions and Operator Precedence

Expressions in C++ are similar to those in Python, but C++ does not support assignment of all data types and uses different Boolean operators. The C++ assignment statement's syntax is the same as the Python assignment statement except that the tuple assignment syntax is not supported (and the data type for the expression on the right-hand side must be compatible with the data type of the variable it is assigned to on the left-hand side). The C++ language requires that only one variable appear on the left-hand side of the assignment operator. To accomplish the C++ equivalent of the Python statement x, y = y, x, it is necessary to use a temporary variable. The following C++ program demonstrates this.

```
// swap.cpp
#include <iostream>
using namespace std;
```

```
int main()
{
  int x = 3, y = 5, temp;
  cout << x << " " << y << endl;
  temp = x;
  x = y;
  y = temp;
  cout << x << " " << y << endl;
  return 0;
}
```

The output of this program is

```
3 5
5 3
```

In the preceding example, note that all variables must be declared and that variables may be assigned an initial value in the declaration statement. C++ does support assignments such as x = y = z. As with Python, it is right associative; y is assigned the value of z and then x is assigned the value of y.

Forgetting to assign a variable before it is used in an expression usually produces strange results. The following program compiles and executes without error but produces undefined results. One time it might output 134514708 and another time it might output -3456782.

```
// uninit.cpp
#include <iostream>
using namespace std;

int main()
{
  int x, y;

  y = x;
  cout << y << endl;
  return 0;
}
```

Standard locally declared variables inside a function are known as *automatic variables*. Automatic variables are assigned a memory location when the function starts but are not initialized with a value. Until you assign a value to them, they hold the value corresponding to whatever bits are in the memory location when the function starts. This is why you can, but may not, get different results each time you run the program in the preceding example. This programming error does not go undetected in Python, but does in C++. In Python, a `NameError` exception will be generated if the first line of code is `y = x` since the name `x` does not exist.

The supported operators in C++ are essentially the same as Python's operators with some minor syntax differences as mentioned previously (e.g., `&&` for `and`, `||` for `or`, and `!` for `not`). The operator precedence rules are also the same although C++ has additional operators that Python does not have. Two of the additional operators that C++ provides are the increment and decrement operators. There are both prefix and postfix versions of these operators. The operators can be used to add one to or subtract one from an integer variable. The increment operator that adds one is the `++` operator and the decrement operator is the `--` operator. These operators can be used with or without an assignment statement. The following example demonstrates the increment operator. The decrement operator works exactly the same except that it subtracts one. Notice that the difference betwen the prefix version and the postfix version matters when it is used as a part of an assignment statement. Many C++ programmers avoid using the increment and decrement operators as part of an assignment statement to make the code clearer.

```cpp
// increment.cpp
#include <iostream>
using namespace std;
int main()
{
  int a, b, c, d;
  a = 2;
  b = 5;
  a++; // increments a to 3
  ++a; // increments a to 4
  c = ++b; // increments b to 6 and then assigns 6 to c
  d = c++; // assigns 6 to d and then increments c to 7
  cout << a << " " << b << " " << c << " " << d << endl;
  return 0;
}
```

All names in Python are actually references to memory locations. Every C++ variable is associated with a memory location that holds the actual value. Unlike Python where the assignment of one variable to another ends up with both referring to the same location, the assignment operator in C++ copies the data from the memory location(s) for the variable on the right side of the assignment statement to the memory location(s) for the variable on the left side. This difference between C++ and Python is not noticeable when only Python immutable types are used. The corresponding C++ functionality to Python references are C++ pointer variables; references are essentially pointers without the pointer notation. The details of the memory usage and allocation for automatic variables, references, and pointers are covered in Chapter 10.

8.8 Decision Statements

C++ supports the same basic decision statement, namely the `if` statement, as Python. There are some syntax differences but the semantics are the same. C++ uses the two words `else if` instead of the Python version `elif`. C++ also requires that parentheses be placed around the Boolean expression whereas Python does not. Remember that the braces `{}` are used to mark blocks of code and are thus used to indicate which code should be executed when the Boolean expression of the `if` statement is true. One exception in C++ is that if only one statement is to be executed when the `if` statement is true, then the braces are unnecessary. This can lead to confusing errors if a second statement is later added; many programmers always use braces to avoid this problem. The following example demonstrates this problem.

```
// if1.cpp
#include <iostream>
using namespace std;

int main()
{
  int x = 5, y = 3;

  // incorrect example: misleading indentation
  if (x < y)
    cout << "x is less ";
    cout << "than y\n";
  cout << "the end\n";
  return 0;
}
```

The output of this program is

```
than y
the end
```

In this case, the indentation is misleading and the line `cout << "than y\n";` is executed even if the Boolean expression is false. Remember that in C++, the indentation does not matter. To write the above program correctly requires the use of braces and is as follows:

```
// if2.cpp
#include <iostream>
using namespace std;

int main()
{
  int x = 5, y = 3;

  if (x < y) {
    cout << "x is less ";
    cout << "than y\n";
  }
  cout << "the end\n";
  return 0;
}
```

The output of this program is

```
the end
```

The location of the beginning brace is not standardized. Some programmers prefer to put it on the same line as the `if` statement and others prefer to put it on the line below. Just about everyone agrees that the ending brace should be on its own line and should line up with the `if` statement or the `{` if the brace is on its own line. Even when the beginning brace for an `if` statement and other C++ statements is placed on the same line as the statement, many programmers place the beginning brace for a function on its own line as we did with the beginning brace for the **main** function. Most employers pick one technique and require that their programmers follow the style for consistency and ease of readability. Below is the same example with the brace on its own line.

```
// if3.cpp
#include <iostream>
using namespace std;

int main()
{
  int x = 5, y = 3;

  if (x < y)
  {
    cout << "x is less ";
    cout << "than y\n";
  }
  cout << "the end";
  return 0;
}
```

Even though indentation does not matter, C++ programmers generally follow the same indentation rules as Python programmers for readability. Python allows any amount of indentation to indicate a new block of code, but most Python programmers use exactly four spaces per indentation level. C++ seems to be less standardized and programmers use two, three, four, or eight spaces, although eight spaces is often entered as a tab. The examples in this text use two spaces since the braces provide additional visual cues to denote the blocks of code. Fewer spaces also means that nested blocks can have longer lines without going past the 80th column (most programmers limit the length of their lines to the 80th column).

If the same indentation rules as Python are not followed in C++, the indentation may be misleading with regard to the semantics of nested if/else statements. In Python, the indentation clearly indicates which `if` statement an `elif` or `else` statement matches up with. The rule for matching `if` and `else` statements in C++ is essentially the same; you just need to remember that the braces mark blocks of code and that a single statement after an `if` or `else` statement can be its own block of code even if there are not braces. One way to state the rule is that the `else` statement goes with the closest `if` statement above it that is at the same level of braces. The following example is a code fragment; it is not a complete program and will not compile since it does not contain a `main` function and all the necessary statements for a complete program, but it demonstrates a programming concept without all the extra code. Which `if` statement does each `else` statement match up with?

```
if (x < y)
  if (y < z)
    cout << "a";
else
    cout << "b";

if (x < y) {
  if (y < z)
    cout << "a";
}
else
    cout << "b";
```

The first `else` statement goes with the `if (y < z)` statement two lines above; note that it is the closest `if` statement above it at the same level of braces. The second `else` statement goes with the `if (x < y)` statement four lines above it for the same reason. The `if (y < z)` statement two lines above is at a different level of braces. This example demonstrates another reason to always use braces: it makes it easier to match the `else` and `if` statements.

The following example shows nested **if** statements along with **else if** statements. Based on your knowledge of Python and the material presented here, the semantics of the code should be clear (and the program does what the output indicates it does). Note that in C++, it must be written as **else if**, not **elif** as it is in Python.

```cpp
// grades.cpp
#include <iostream>
using namespace std;

int main()
{
  double grade;

  cout << "Enter your grade average (i.e., 93.2): ";
  cin >> grade;

  if (grade >= 90.0) {
    if (grade > 92.0) {
      cout << "Your grade is an A\n";
    }
    else {
      cout << "Your grade is an A-\n";
    }
  }
  else if (grade >= 80.0) {
    if (grade > 87.0) {
      cout << "Your grade is a B+\n";
    }
    else if (grade > 82.0) {
      cout << "Your grade is a B\n";
    }
    else {
      cout << "Your grade is a B-";
    }
  }
  return 0;
}
```

The previous example used nested **if** statements although an equivalent version could be written with an **if** statement followed by four **else if** statements that are not nested. We chose the nested version to demonstrate both the **else if** statement and nested statements.

Python uses the keywords **and**, **or**, and **not** as Boolean operators. C++ uses the symbols **&&**, **||**, and **!** for **and**, **or**, and **not**, respectively. The C++ equivalent of the

Python statement if (x < 3) and not (y > 4) is if ((x < 3) && !(y > 4)). More recent C++ compilers also support the use of and, or, and not in addition to using &&, ||, and !.

Unlike Python, C++ allows assignment statements in the test expression for the if statement and for looping statements. This means the C++ compiler will not mark if (x = 0) as an error even though it is probably not what you meant. This if statement creates the side effect of assigning zero to x and then that result is used as the Boolean expression. The result of an assignment statement is the value that is assigned so it is equivalent to x = 0; if (0). That is why assignment statements can be chained (for example, x = y = 0). Because of this, the test if (x = 0) will always result in x being assigned the value of zero and the Boolean expression evaluating to false. As Python does, C++ considers any non-zero value to be true and zero to be false. The statement if (x = 10) will assign 10 to x and the test will always evaluate to true. This type of mistake can be extremely difficult to debug. When using a constant, some programmers write if (0 == x). When writing it this way, forgetting one of the equal signs will result in an error. This does not help when you want to write a statement such as if (x == y) and mistakenly write if (x = y).

C++ also supports the switch decision statement but we do not cover it in this section since anything that can be written with a switch statement can also be written as if/else if statements. The switch statement is discussed in the optional subsection 8.17.1.

8.9 Type Conversions

In Python, many type conversions are implicit. In the following Python code, during the evaluation of b + c, the 3 obtained from b is implicitly converted to the floating point value 3.0 since the operand c is a floating point value. The value of b remains the integer 3. In the statement d = float(b), the 3 stored in b is explicitly converted to 3.0 and stored in d as a floating point value. Again, b remains the integer 3. In the statement e = int(c), the value of c (5.5) is explicitly converted to 5 and stored in e as an integer. When a value is converted to an integer, its decimal portion is chopped off instead of being rounded.

```
b = 3
c = 2.5
c = b + c
d = float(b)
e = int(c)
```

C++ also supports implicit type conversion within expressions and explicit conversions. The following C++ example corresponds to the preceding Python example. If you remove the explicit conversion for the assignment to d and write it as d = b;, most compilers will not produce an error, but will produce a warning indicating the line contains a type conversion. C++ uses the same rules as Python in that the decimal portion is chopped off when a value is converted from a floating point type to an integer type.

```
int b, e;
double c, d;
b = 3;
c = 2.5;
c = b + c; // c holds 5.5
d = double(b); // d holds 3.0
e = int(c); // e holds 5; this could also be written as e = (int) c;
```

Although the syntax of specifying the data type name and putting the variable/expression in parentheses works for type conversions in Python and C++, newer compilers support a different syntax that is preferred for new C++ code. The following example demonstrates this syntax with the keyword **static_cast**:

```
int b, e;
double c, d;
b = 3;
c = 2.5;
c = b + c; // c holds 5.5
d = static_cast <double> (b); // d holds 3.0
e = static_cast <int> (c); // e holds 5
```

8.10 Looping Statements

C++ supports three looping statements: **for**, **while**, and **do while**. The **while** loop is basically the same as the Python **while** statement. The **while** loop is classified as a *pretest loop* since the Boolean expression is tested before the loop body. The syntax differences match the differences between the Python and C++ if statements. In a C++ **while** statement, parentheses must be placed around the Boolean expression, the C++ Boolean operators **&&**, **||**, and **!** are used (again, new compilers also support **and**, **or**, and **not**), and the braces, **{}**, are used to denote the block of code that is to be repeated instead of indentation. As is the case with the C++ if statement, if the loop body is only one line of code, the braces are not necessary, but many programmers still use the braces. The following is a code fragment containing a sampe C++ `while` statement. All the loop examples in this section output 0 through 9.

```
int i = 0;
while (i < 10) {
  cout << i << endl;
  i += 1;
}
```

C++ supports a `do while` statement that does not have a Python equivalent. Unlike the `while` loop, the body of a `do while` statement is always executed at least once. As the syntax indicates, the loop test is not done until the loop body executes and thus the `do while` loop is classified as a *posttest loop*. The syntax for it is

```
do {
    // loop body
} while (<Boolean-expression>);
```

The `do while` statement does not require the braces to mark the beginning and ending of the loop body if there is only one statement in the loop body, but does if there is more than one statement. The semantics of the statement are that the loop body is executed and then the Boolean expression is tested. If it is true, the loop body is executed again, the Boolean expression tested again, and so on. The equivalent `do while` statement to the above `while` example is

```
int i = 0;
do {
  cout << i << endl;
  i += 1;
} while (i < 10);
```

The C++ `for` looping statement is significantly different from the Python `for` statement. The Python `for` statement performs iteration over a sequence of items, but the C++ `for` statement is a more generic loop statement that is effectively equivalent to a `while` loop. The C++ `for` statement is best explained by looking at an example that also outputs 0 through 9. Figure 8.7 shows a flowchart diagram for it.

```
int i;
for (i=0; i<10; ++i) {
  cout << i << endl;
}
```

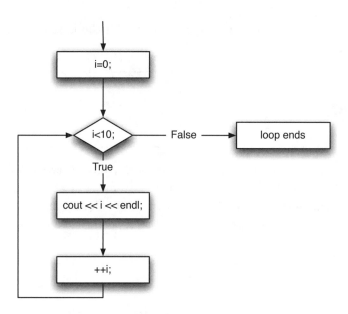

Figure 8.7: Flowchart of C++ `for` statement example

Inside the parentheses of the `for` statement are three statements separated by two semicolons. The first statement, `i=0;` in this case, is typically used as an initialization statement and is only executed once by the `for` statement. After the initialization statement is executed, the second statement, which is treated as a Boolean expression, is executed. If it is true, the loop body is executed and then the third statement, typically known as the *increment* or *update action*, is executed. In our example, the increment statement can be either the postfix version `i++` or the prefix version `++i`; we will use the prefix version as some uses of the C++ Standard Template Library use the prefix version. After the increment statement is executed, the second statement is executed again. If it is true, the loop body is executed again, followed by the increment statement, Boolean expression, and so on.

As you should be able to tell, any `for` loop can be rewritten as a `while` loop. Look at the flowchart diagram again and compare the `while` loop and `for` loop code fragments in this section if you have trouble seeing the correspondence between the location of the statements in the `for` loop and the `while` loop. C++ `for` statements can be more complicated with multiple initialization statements separated by commas and multiple increment statements although we will not demonstrate these in this book; some programmers think that `while` statements should be used for these more complicated versions.

The C++ `for` loop also supports declaring the loop iteration variable inside the statement. If you do this, the variable can be accessed only inside the loop body. After the loop body, the variable no longer exists. The following example demonstrates this.

```
for (int i=0; i<10; ++i) {
  cout << i << endl;
}
// you cannot access the variable i here
```

If you already have a variable declared with the same name as the variable you define as the loop iteration variable inside a for loop, the previously declared variable is not accessible inside the loop body, but is accessible after the loop body and retains the value it had before the loop started execution. Because this can lead to confusion, we do not recommend you use the syntax of declaring a variable inside the `for` statement. This issue is part of topics known as *scope* and *lifetime*; the details of the scope and lifetime of variables in C++ are covered in section 8.15.

As with the C++ `if`, `while`, and `do while` statements, the braces are not necessary if the loop body consists of only one statement, but many programmers always use the braces. As Python does, C++ also supports the `break` statement that causes a loop to terminate. Just as is suggested with Python, the `break` statement should only be used when it increases readability over a loop written without a `break` statement.

8.11   Arrays

Python has lists and tuples that allow indexed access to groups of data. Python lists also support methods for sorting, finding elements, and many other useful algorithms. C++ arrays support indexed operation but are much lower level and do not have all the flexibility of Python lists. C++ arrays must hold items that are all the same type and do not support slices or using negative indices to access items from the end of the array.

8.11.1   Single-Dimension Arrays

C++ arrays are declared with brackets and accessed using brackets. As with Python, the first index is 0 and the last index is one less than the size. The code fragment below declares an array and sets a value for each element in the array. The array is declared with a fixed size of 10, is indexed using 0 through 9, and can store only integers.

```
int i, a[10];

for (i=0; i<10; ++i) {
  a[i] = i;
}
```

Most recent C and C++ compilers support the use of a variable to specify the size when defining arrays known as *variable length automatic arrays* (this is part of the update to the C language made in the late 1990s known as C99). The other technique to delay specifying the size of an array until the program is run uses pointers and dynamic memory; it is covered in section 10.3. The following code fragment demonstrates variable length automatic arrays.

```
int i, n;

cout << "Enter size: ";
cin >> n;

int a[n];
for (i=0; i<n; ++i) {
  a[i] = i;
}
```

Unlike Python, no index range checking is done for any C++ array. If a program attempts to access beyond the boundaries of an array, you can get undefined results, the program may crash, or it may appear to work correctly. We will discuss these memory errors in more detail in Chapter 10. On many operating systems when a C++ program crashes, it does not show you the stack trace (the line at which the program crashed and the sequence of function calls the program executed to reach that point) as Python does. Most Unix systems create a **core** file containing information about the execution and crash location. On Unix systems, the gdb debugger program can display the stack trace information stored in the core file. The command is `gdb <executable-filename> core` and then enter **bt** (short for "backtrace") and press the Return key. Most integrated development environments (IDEs) provide a compiler and debugging environment that provides a stack trace when a program crashes.

C++ does support initialization of arrays in the declaration statement using the following syntax: `int a[5] = {0, 0, 0, 0, 0};`. C++ does not support direct assignment of array variables. To accomplish this, each individual element of the array must be assigned as the code fragment below shows:

```
int i, a[5], b[5];

a[0] = 0; a[1] = 1; a[2] = 2; a[3] = 3; a[4] = 4;
// b = a; cannot be used
for (i=0; i<5; ++i) {
  b[i] = a[i];
}
```

8.11.2 Multi-Dimensional Arrays

C++ supports multi-dimensional arrays with no limit on the number of dimensions other than the amount of memory the system supports. The syntax for declaring multi-dimensional arrays is similar to single-dimensional arrays except that additional brackets are used for each dimension. The code fragment that follows declares a three-dimensional array that contains a total of 120 elements and initializes each element to zero.

```
double a[4][10][3];
int i, j, k;

for (i=0; i<4; ++i) {
  for (j=0; j<10; ++j) {
    for (k=0; k<3; ++k) {
      a[i][j][k] = 0.0;
    }
  }
}
```

8.11.3 Arrays of Characters

Arrays of characters (the **char** type) can be used in C++ as they are used in the C language to represent strings, but when programming in C++ you usually want to use the built-in C++ **string** class covered in section 9.2. When using raw arrays of characters to represent a string, a trailing byte of zero is used to indicate the end of the string, so the array size needs to be one larger than the maximum number of characters you are storing. The byte zero is indicated by the single character '\0'. Note that the single quotation mark is used to denote a single character (which is of the **char** type) while the double quotation mark is used to denote a **string**. Since a few of the C++ library functions use C-style strings (arrays of characters) instead of the C++ string class, we will cover the very basics of C-style strings. The following shows the use of a C-style string, but it is an extremely bad example because it allows a buffer overflow exploit. It allows you to type in your name and then says "hello" to you.

```cpp
// buffer.cpp
#include <iostream>
using namespace std;

int main()
{
  char c[20];

  cout << "enter your first name: ";
  // this code is a security risk
  // a buffer overflow occurs if the user enters
  // more than 19 characters
  cin >> c;
  cout << "Hello " << c << endl;
}
```

If you enter Dave, the program stores the characters D, a, v, e, and \0 in positions zero through four of the array. When the code outputs the variable c, it starts at the beginning of the array and outputs characters until it reaches the \0 that indicates the end of the string. If the user types in more than 19 characters, the data will go past the end of the array, allowing the user to write data to memory that your program has not allocated for data. Clever computer crackers can in some cases use this situation to enter executable code, allowing them to steal private data that you may have entered in the program such as passwords or financial information. This is another reason to use the C++ string class instead of C-style strings. The remaining details and the C functions for manipulating strings are not covered in this text since the C++ string class is recommended.

8.12   Function Details

Functions are used in Python to split code into smaller subproblems and to avoid rewriting the same code multiple times. Functions are used for the same reasons in C++, but there are more issues to be concerned with regarding functions in C++ than there are in Python. As we have already seen, all C++ executable statements must occur inside a function and each C++ executable program must contain exactly one function named main. We will start our discussion of functions in C++ with the terminology that you do not have to concern yourself with in Python.

8.12.1 Declarations, Definitions, and Prototypes

Unlike Python, all C++ code, with the exception of definitions of non-local variables and classes and declarations of variables or functions, must occur inside a function. To understand what this means, we need to understand the difference between a *declaration* and a *definition*. A simple way to distinguish between the two is to remember that a definition causes memory storage to be allocated while a declaration tells the compiler that a name exists and what it is (a variable of a specific type, a class, or a function with parameters). Variables, classes, and functions can be *declared* multiple times, but they must be *defined* exactly once. What is commonly referred to as a *variable declaration* is technically a *variable definition*. Listing the variables and their types at the beginning of a function is correctly called a variable definition even though programmers commonly refer to this as variable declarations. Definitions also serve as declarations since they tell the compiler about a name, but declarations are not definitions.

Now that we have stated the difference between a declaration and a definition, let's look at a simple example of a function declaration and a function definition.

```cpp
#include <iostream>
using namespace std;

// this is a function declaration
int main();

// this is a function definition
int main()
{
  // this is a variable definition which is also a declaration
  int x;

  x = 42;
  cout << "x = " << x << endl;
  return 0;
}
```

All C++ functions must have a return type (it is an `int` for the `main` function). A function declaration indicates the return type, the name, and any parameters inside the parentheses after the name. A function declaration ends with a semicolon and does not contain the body of the function. Function declarations are also referred to as *function prototypes*. A function declaration/prototype tells the compiler enough information about the function so the compiler knows it exists and can determine if you use it correctly if you call it. A function definition contains the same information as the declaration, but instead of the terminating semicolon, the braces are used to state the body of the function. In our earlier examples, we did not use a separate declaration of the `main` function as we did in the most recent example. In those cases, the definition of the `main` function also served as a declaration of it. Unless other code calls a function, we generally do not write a separate declaration.

In addition to the data types listed in section 8.4 and the user-defined data types covered in section 9.1, C++ supports a `void` return type. This is used when a function does not return a value. Functions with a `void` return type do not require a `return` statement, but may include a `return` statement. Most C++ compilers will produce a warning if a non-void function does not return a value, unlike Python which returns `None` if your function does not explicitly return a value. As with Python, C++ functions can have more than one `return` statement, and as soon as a `return` statement is executed, no other code in the function is executed and control transfers back to the statement after the point of call. Unlike with Python, only one value can be returned by a C++ function. This is not a significant limitation of C++ and can be solved by encapsulating the multiple values in a single class and returning an instance of that class or by using pass by reference (covered in subsection 8.12.3).

It is often necessary to write a function prototype so that your code will compile. Most compilers require a prototype if you want to call a function before it is declared. The reason a prototype is required when a function that has not been declared yet is called is that the compiler must be able to determine that the function is called with the correct number of parameters and that the types of those parameters are correct. Recall from your Python studies that the parameters in the function declaration or definition are known as *formal parameters* and the expressions or variables used when you call the function are known as *actual parameters*. The following example shows the problem of calling a function before it has been declared or defined.

```
// this example will not compile
int main()
{
  double a=2.5, b=3.0, c;
  // the compiler has not yet seen the f function
  // so it cannot determine if f is called correctly
  c = f(a, b);
}

double f(double x, double y)
{
  return x * x + 2 * x * y;
}
```

Most compilers will give an error for the line `c = f(a, b)` stating that `f` was not declared. There are two ways to solve this problem. In this case, the simplest method is to write the `f` function above the `main` function. In this case, the definition of `f` also serves as its declaration. Another option is to write a prototype for the `f` function above the `main` function as the following example shows.

```
double f(double x, double y);

// you do not need to list the formal parameter names in the prototype
// this example also shows you that you can declare a function multiple
// times even though you generally do not do this
double f(double, double);

int main()
{
  double a=2.5, b=3.0, c;

  // the prototype allows the compiler to determine
  // that f is called correctly
  c = f(a, b);
}

double f(double x, double y)
{
  return x * x + 2 * x * y;
}
```

The prototype for the function `f` specifies that its return type is a **double** value and that it takes two parameters each of which is a **double** value. As the commented lines in the example show, you do not have to specify the name of the formal parameters but you may if you wish. Most programmers do specify the names of the formal parameters since the names of the parameters often indicate what the parameters represent. It is important to note that a semicolon is required after a prototype, but when defining the function you do not put a semicolon after the right parenthesis. Also note that the data type name must be placed in front of each formal parameter; it is not correct to write **double f(double x, y)** in either the prototype or the actual implementation of the function.

A common mistake beginning C++ programmers make is to also declare the formal parameters as local variables as the following code fragment does. This is incorrect since the local variables prevent the formal parameters from being accessible. Your C++ compiler will likely generate a warning indicating the variables *shadow* a parameter. Some compilers may compile the program while others will indicate this is an error and refuse to compile the program.

```
#include <iostream>
using namespace std;

void f(int a, int b)
{
  int a, b; // incorrect - compiler error/warning: variables shadow parameter
  cout << a << " " << b << endl;
}

int main()
{
  int x = 2, y = 3;
  f(x, y);
  return 0;
}
```

You have probably realized by now that the header files you include contain the declarations of items your code is using. The **iostream** header file contains the declarations of **cout** and **cin**. The definitions of these items are not included in header files. In these cases, their definitions are in a library of machine code that the linker automatically links with as it creates your executable code. We discuss how to write your own header files in section 8.13.

8.12.2   Pass by Value

The default mechanism for parameter passing in C++ is pass by value. Pass-by-value causes a separate copy of the data value for each parameter to be made. Since a completely separate copy is used, any changes to the formal parameters in the function are not reflected in the actual parameters. This allows you to effectively treat the formal parameters as additional local variables since changes made to them do not directly affect other parts of the program. As with Python, it does not matter whether the names of the formal and actual parameters match. The next example demonstrates this.

```
// value.cpp
#include <iostream>
using namespace std;

void f(int a, int b) // a and b are the formal parameters
{
  cout << a << " " << b << endl;
  a += 3;
  b += 5;
  cout << a << " " << b << endl;
}
```

```
int main()
{
  int x = 1, y = 2;

  f(x, y); // x and y are the actual parameters
  cout << x << " " << y << endl;
}
```

The output of this program is

```
1 2
4 7
1 2
```

8.12.3 Pass by Reference

C++ also supports a second parameter passing mechanism known as *pass by reference*. Instead of making a copy of the data value, a reference (the address in memory) to the data is passed. Because of this, any changes made to the formal parameters are reflected in the actual parameters. In Python if you pass a mutable data type (a list, dictionary, or class instance) to a function and modify it inside the function, the change is reflected in the actual parameter, but if you assign a new instance to the formal parameter, the change is not reflected in the actual parameter. With pass by reference in C++, any change, including assigning a new value, to the formal parameter is reflected in the actual parameter. Pass by reference is indicated by putting an ampersand (&) in front of the formal parameter (but not the actual parameter). Placing an ampersand in front of the actual parameter has a different effect (see section 10.2). The example below is similar to the previous example but one parameter is passed by reference and results in different output.

```
// reference.cpp
#include <iostream>
using namespace std;

void f(int a, int &b) // a and b are the formal parameters
{
  cout << a << " " << b << endl;
  a += 3;
  b += 5;
  cout << a << " " << b << endl;
}
```

```
int main()
{
  int x = 1, y = 2;

  f(x, y); // x and y are the actual parameters
  cout << x << " " << y << endl;
}
```

The output of this program is

```
1 2
4 7
1 7
```

The corresponding actual parameter for any formal parameter that uses pass by reference must be a variable, not an expression. In the example, we could not write `f(2, 4);`. Making a copy of the 2 and storing it in the location for the formal parameter a is fine, but the problem is that if we change the formal parameter b, we do not have a corresponding actual parameter to make the change to (since it is a constant).

8.12.4   Passing Arrays as Parameters

C++ automatically passes arrays by reference for efficiency reasons; you do not use the & to designate that the array contents are passed by reference. Instead of making a copy of the array, a copy of the starting memory address of the array is passed. Because of this, any changes made to the contents of the array by the function will be reflected in the array passed to the function. This is effectively the same as passing a Python mutable type (e.g., a Python list) to a function. You can change only the contents of the array, not the memory location that the array uses. When we cover pointers and dynamic memory in Chapter 10 the details and ramifications of this will be clearer.

You do not need to specify the exact size of the array in the formal parameter for the array, but the function does need to be careful not to access beyond the array size. A common technique is to pass an additional parameter that specifies the size of the array. The following code example demonstrates this with an implementation of selection sort. The square brackets after the formal parameter (`int a[]`) indicate a single-dimensional array without a specified size is being passed to it. You can also specify the size if you wish but it will be ignored. The second parameter specifies the size of that array. Since arrays are not passed by value, the modification to the array inside the `selection_sort` function affects the actual parameter passed. The output of the program (not shown) is the array in sorted order.

```cpp
// selection.cpp
#include <iostream>
using namespace std;

void selection_sort(int a[], int size)
{
  int i, j, min_pos, temp;

  for (i=0; i<size-1; ++i) {
    min_pos = i;
    for (j=i+1; j<size; ++j) {
      if (a[j] < a[min_pos]) {
        min_pos = j;
      }
    }
    temp = a[i];
    a[i] = a[min_pos];
    a[min_pos] = temp;
  }
}
```

```cpp
int main()
{
  int i;
  int a[5] = {7, 6, 4, 2, 3};
  int b[10] = {3, 0, 5, 7, 4, 6, 8, 1, 9, 2};

  selection_sort(a, 5);
  selection_sort(b, 10);
  for (i=0; i<5; ++i) {
    cout << a[i] << " ";
  }
  cout << endl;
  for (i=0; i<10; ++i) {
    cout << b[i] << " ";
  }
  cout << endl;
  return 0;
}
```

Multi-dimensional arrays can also be passed to functions. The size of all the dimensions except the first must be specified. In C++, multi-dimensionsal arrays are stored in *row major* order. For an array declared as `int b[2][3]`, the order the values are stored in memory is `b[0][0]`, `b[0][1]`, `b[0][2]`, `b[1][0]`, `b[1][1]`, `b[1][2]`. In order to calculate the address of a specified position in the array, we must know all the dimensions except the first. In the previous example, b[i][j] is at offset i*3*4+j*4 from the start of the array. Remember that we are assuming that integers take four bytes. To move to row i we must move past i*3*4 bytes, and then to the corresponding spot j in that row we must move past j*4 bytes. The following function prototype accepts a three-dimensional array in which the size of the last two dimensions are 10 and 20, respectively: void f(int b[][10][20], int size);. Since the first dimension is not needed to calculate the address of a position in the array, it does not need to be specified in the formal parameter array declaration; the size parameter is used to indicate the size of the first dimension so the code in the function knows how large the array passed as the actual parameter is.

8.12.5 const Parameters

C++ supports marking parameters const which means that the function cannot change the parameter. This is useful for having the compiler check if you accidently try to change a parameter when there is no reason your code should try to change it. If your code does change a parameter marked const, the code will not compile and will generate an error indicating the reason. The following example demonstrates the syntax:

```
void f(const int a, int b)
{
  a = 2; // this will generate a compiler error
  b = 2; // this is fine
}
```

The const designation can also be used with parameters passed by reference. At first this might seem to be a contradiction since pass by reference is used when we want to modify a parameter. Recall that pass by value makes a copy of the data being passed. Making a copy of values that do not require much memory such as an int or a double is not a problem, but copying a variable that is hundreds or thousands of bytes takes time and requires a significant amount of extra memory. Pass by reference passes the starting address of the variable as a reference to the existing data without making a copy of the data; this requires only four bytes on 32-bit systems no matter what the actual size of the data value is. When you want to pass a large data structure, but do not want a function to change it, you can pass it by reference with the const designation. The following example assumes we have a class named LargeType defined:

```
void f(const LargeType &big)
{
  // any changes to parameter big will generate a compiler error
}
```

This is one reason Python treats everything as a reference. Assigning, passing, or returning any object only requires the reference (and possibly the reference count) to be changed instead of copying the potentially large amounts of data in an object such as a list or dictionary.

8.12.6   Default Parameters

C++ supports default parameters to functions similarly to the way Python does. Default parameters allow a function or method to be called with fewer actual parameters than formal parameters; default values defined in the function/method declaration are substituted for the missing actual parameters. The following example shows the use of default parameters.

```
void f(int a, int b, int c=2, int d=3)
{
    // do something with the parameters
}

int main()
{
  f(0, 1); // equivalent to f(0, 1, 2, 3);
  f(4, 5, 6); // equivalent to f(4, 5, 6, 3);
  f(4, 5, 6, 7); // no default values used
}
```

The example has two parameters that must always be specified and two default parameters. This allows the function to be called with two, three, or four parameters. As the comments state, the default values for the parameters are used when necessary. As with Python, the default parameters must be the last parameters so the compiler can match up the actual and formal parameters based on the order. Default values are specified only in the declaration of the function, not the definition of the function. The exception is that if the definition is also the declaration, then you need to list them as the previous example shows. The following example shows the use of default parameters when there is both a declaration and a definition. We will show another example of default parameters with header files in section 8.13.

```
double f(double x=0, double y=0);

double f(double x, double y)
{
  return x * x + 2 * x * y;
}

int main()
{
  double x=2.5, y=3.0, z;

  z = f(x, y);
}
```

Passing an arbitrary number of parameters as you can do in Python with ***args** is possible, but is more complicated in C++ and beyond the scope of this book.

8.13   Header Files and Inline Functions

The purpose of header files is to declare functions, classes (classes are covered in section 9.1), and non-local variables so that they can be used in other C++ source files. We have included the **iostream** header file in our examples and now we will see how to write our own header files. We will use our sorting example to demonstrate them. We will start with a header file declaring two different sorting functions.

```
// sort.h
#ifndef __SORT__H
#define __SORT__H

void selection_sort(int a[], int size);
void merge_sort(int a[], int size);

#endif
```

The first thing to notice is that we have added some new preprocessor commands; recall that preprocessor commands start with a pound sign (#). The **ifndef** line checks if the symbol **__SORT__H** has been defined. If it has not, the next line defines the symbol **__SORT__H** and then we have the function declarations. If the symbol was already defined, none of the code between the **#ifndef** and **#endif** line is copied when we include this file. Using these preprocessor commands is the standard way to prevent your header file from being included twice. Including a header file that contains only declarations does not produce errors, but will slow down the compilation since the compiler has more lines of code to process. Including a header file that contains definitions (as header files for classes do) will cause a problem since we can have only one definition of a name.

While it is unlikely one file would directly include the file twice, a header file often includes other header files. So if your header file included the file `<cmath>` and an implementation file included both your header file and `<cmath>` then the `<cmath>` file would effectively be included twice. The use of the name `__SORTS__H` as the defined symbol does not have to follow that pattern exactly. Typically, some combination of underscores along with the name of the file are used so that each header file has a unique symbol associated with it.

The `sort.cpp` file would usually include the `sort.h` file although in this case it does not need to since neither function calls the other. It would look like

```
// sort.cpp

#include "sort.h"

void selection_sort(int a[], int size)
{
  // code for selection_sort function
}

void merge(int a[], int low, int mid, int high)
{
  // code for merge function
}

void merge_sort(int a[], int size)
{
  // code for merge_sort function
}
```

A file that wants to call one or both of our sort functions needs to include the header file `sort.h` and link with the `sort.o` file that the compiler generates. Note that we did not put the `merge` function in the header file since it is only called by the `merge_sort` function. A simple example using our sorting code is the following; these three files could be compiled and linked on Unix systems using our **g++** commands listed in section 8.6.

```
// test_sort.cpp
#include <iostream>
using namespace std;
#include "sort.h"
```

```
int main()
{
  int i;
  int a[10] = {9, 8, 7, 6, 5, 4, 3, 2, 1, 0};
  int b[10] = {9, 8, 7, 6, 5, 4, 3, 2, 1, 0};

  selection_sort(a, 10);
  merge_sort(b, 10);
  for (i=0; i<10; ++i) {
    cout << a[i] << " " << b[i] << endl;
  }
  return 0;
}
```

We will look at another example of header files so that we can point out a common mistake made when using default parameter values. We will write a couple functions to perform temperature conversions and put them in a separate file so many different programs can easily use them. Our header file and implementation file are the following:

```
// conversions.h
#ifndef __CONVERSIONS_H
#define __CONVERSIONS_H

double f_to_c(double f=0.0);
double c_to_f(double c=0.0);

#endif
```

```
// conversions.cpp
#include "conversions.h"

// the next line is commented out since it is incorrect
// double f_to_c(double f=0.0)
double f_to_c(double f)
{
  return (f - 32.0) * (5.0 / 9.0);
}
double c_to_f(double c)
{
  return (9.0 / 5.0) * c + 32.0;
}
```

The common mistake is to cut and paste the function declarations from the header file into the implementation file. This results in the default parameter values being specified in the implementation file also. We have shown this in our example, but commented out the incorrect lines and added the correct lines without the default values. The C++ compiler will give an error message if you forget to remove the default values from the implementation file when you cut and paste the function prototypes from the header file.

Since the code for these functions is short, the overhead of making the function call can take more execution time than the execution of the actual function code. C++ provides a mechanism known as *inline functions* to allow for more efficient execution. An inline function is generally written in a header file and is written exactly the same as the function would be in the implementation file except the keyword `inline` is placed before the function definition. In this case, the definition is also a declaration. For our conversion example, the header file with inline functions is

```
// conversions2.h

#ifndef __CONVERSIONS_H
#define __CONVERSIONS_H

inline double f_to_c(double f=0.0)
{
  return (f - 32.0) * (5.0 / 9.0);
}

inline double c_to_f(double c=0.0)
{
  return (9.0 / 5.0) * c + 32.0;
}

#endif
```

When writing all the functions inline in a header file, you do not need an implementation (`conversion.cpp`) file since all the information is contained in the header file. The `inline` keyword prevents multiple definitions of the file from being created when you link a number of different files that all include the `conversion.h` header file.

If your inline function is relatively short, the compiler will generate the machine code for the function body and place it right in the code instead of creating the code to call a function. If your function is relatively long, the compiler will ignore your inline directive; instead it will create a normal function call since copying the machine code corresponding to a long function will make the program much larger if that function is called from a number of different places. A general rule is to declare functions that are less than five lines long as inline functions.

The original C programming language did not include inline functions and instead used preprocessor macros to accomplish the same result of not creating a function call for short functions. C++ also supports *macros* since they are part of the C language, but it is recommended that you use inline functions since they enforce type checking and are safer. A sample source file that defines and uses a macro for `c_to_f` is the following.

```cpp
// macro.cpp
#include <iostream>
using namespace std;

#define c_to_f(c) (9.0 / 5.0) * c + 32.0

int main()
{
  int x = 10;
  cout << c_to_f(x) << " ";
  cout << c_to_f(x + 10) << endl;
}
```

The `#define` preprocessor command is used to define macros. The preprocessor performs a search and replace for the item(s) inside the parentheses. Based on that, what do you think the output of this program is?

The two lines that use the macro are expanded by the preprocessor to

```cpp
cout << (9.0 / 5.0) * x + 32.0 << " ";
cout << (9.0 / 5.0) * x + 10 + 32.0 << endl;
```

Given those expansions, you should now realize why the output of the program is 50 60. The correct value for 20 degrees Celsius is 68 degrees Fahrenheit. You could fix this by using more parentheses in the macro, but there are still other potential problems with macros. So when writing C++ code, you should use the inline keyword instead of a macro to avoid the overhead of a function call.

There is an important issue regarding namespaces and header files. You should not use the version using namespace ... for any namespace in header files. The reason for this is that any file that includes your header file effectively would have that using namespace statement in it. This could cause problems if the source file defines a name that is also defined in the specified namespace. If you need to refer to a name defined within a namespace in a header file, always refer to it using the namespace::name syntax rather than including a using statement in your header file. We will see an example of this in section 9.4.

As Python contains a number of modules with useful functions, C++ has a standard library of functions. We have already seen the `iostream` header that the C++ language uses for input and output libraries. Many of the functions available in C++ are part of the original C standard library, but the header files have been updated for C++. The name of some of the C library header files are stdio.h, stdlib.h, and math.h. To use these header files in a C++ program, the .h extension is removed and the letter "c" is prepended, resulting in the names: cstdio, cstdlib, and cmath. For example, to use the `sqrt` function that is defined in the C math header file, you need the following statement at the top of your C++ file: `#include <cmath>`. There are other standard C++ header files, some of which will be covered later, but these along with `iostream` are the common ones beginning C++ programmers need.

The standard convention is to use less-than and greater-than signs around the names of header files that are part of the C++ library or libraries that are common and located in standard directories. Your C++ compiler also provides a method for specifying additional directories to search. On most systems the compiler first searches the additional directories you specify and then a set of standard directories containing header files. The first header file that matches the name is used. Double quotation marks must be used around header files that are in the same directory as the C++ source files you are compiling. For header files specified with double quotation marks, the compiler first searches the current directory. If the compiler cannot find the header file in the current directory, the compiler searches the additional user-specified include directories and the standard directories. You cannot use the less-than and greater-than signs around header files that are in the current directory since it is not searched by default, but you can use double quotation marks around standard header files since both the current directory and standard directories are searched. Even though it is possible to always use double quotation marks, C++ programmers follow the convention of using the less-than and greater-than signs for standard header files.

8.14 Assert Statements and Testing

Unlike Python which includes a unit testing framework, the C++ standard does not include a unit testing framework. There are a number of third-party, C++ unit testing frameworks that you can download and install. Most, if not all, of these frameworks are similar to Python's unit testing framework as both the C++ and Python unit testing frameworks are based on Java's unit testing framework. Instead of covering one of the C++ unit testing frameworks, we will discuss the C++ `assert` statement since it allows you to easily write unit tests.

The Python unit testing framework provides a number of methods that verify if something is true and include "assert" as part of their name (e.g., `assertEquals` and `assertRaises`). These methods are based on the C++ `assert` statement (technically, it is a macro that the preprocessor expands) which takes a Boolean expression. If the Boolean expression is true, the program continues, but if it is false, the program exits immediately and indicates the line of code at which the `assert` statement fails. Unlike the Python unit testing framework which runs additional tests even after one of the tests fails, using the C++ `assert` statement causes your program to exit immediately if the assertion is not true. This means the tests following an `assert` statement that fails are not executed.

We will modify our `test_sort.cpp` file from section 8.13 to use the `assert` macro. The `assert` macro takes an expression and evaluates it. If the expression evaluates to true, execution continues. If the expression evaluates to false, the program immediately exits and prints an error message indicating the line of source code containing the assertion that failed.

```cpp
// test_sort2.cpp
#include <iostream>
using namespace std;
#include <cassert>
#include "sort.h"
int main()
{
  int i;
  int a[10] = {9, 8, 7, 6, 5, 4, 3, 2, 1, 0};
  int b[10] = {9, 8, 7, 6, 5, 4, 3, 2, 1, 0};

  cout << "test selection sort" << endl;
  selection_sort(a, 10);
  for (i=0; i<9; ++i) {
    assert(a[i] <= a[i+1]);
  }
  cout << "selection sort passed" << endl;
  cout << "test merge sort" << endl;
  merge_sort(b, 10);
  for (i=0; i<9; ++i) {
    assert(b[i] <= b[i+1]);
  }
  cout << "merge sort passed" << endl;
  return 0;
}
```

In order to use the C++ `assert` macro, you must include the `cassert` header file. Unlike Python's unit testing framework which indicates that tests pass, using this simple strategy will not produce any output if all the tests pass. If you want output, you can place output statements after each `assert` statement or after a group of `assert` statements to indicate that tests pass as we did in our example. Remember that output is buffered by the operating system and may not appear if the program crashes before the operating system sends the buffered output to the screen. Outputting a new line using `endl` forces the buffer to be flushed, so always use an `endl` at the end of output statements when testing code.

For files that test a number of functions or class methods, you may want to create a separate test function that tests each method and then have the `main` function call each of the test functions. This would be similar to the Python unit testing framework calling all the methods that start with the four characters `test`.

8.15 The Scope and Lifetime of Variables

The *scope* of a variable is the section of source code where it can be accessed and the *lifetime* of a variable is the execution time period starting when the memory for the variable is allocated and ending when it is deallocated. The scope and lifetime of variables in C++ is similar to Python. The scope of a variable in C++ is the block of code in which it is declared. If an inner block declares a variable with the same name as one declared in the outer block, the variable declared in the outer block is not accessible inside that inner block. The following example (that outputs 2 1) demonstrates this, but for readability reasons, it is not recommended that you declare two different variables with the same name in different blocks of the same function.

```cpp
// scope.cpp
#include <iostream>
using namespace std;

int main()
{
  int x = 1;

  {
    int x = 2;
    cout << x << " ";
  }
  cout << x << endl;
  return 0;
}
```

Many programmers prefer to only declare variables at the top of a function and the scope of these variables is the function body. As mentioned in section 8.10, you can also declare the loop variable inside the **for** statement and that variable is accessible only inside the body of the loop.

The lifetime of automatic C++ variables starts when the function declaring the variable begins execution and ends when the function completes. Each time a function is called, memory for its automatic variables is allocated on a stack and when the function ends, the memory is deallocated from the stack. This means that the local automatic variables of a function are usually bound to a different memory location each time the function is called and thus, do not remember the value they had the previous time the function was called. If you need a function's local variable to have a "history" and remember its value from the previous call, declare it with the **static** prefix. The following example uses the local static variable **count** to keep track of how many times the function is called. The lifetime of static variables is the lifetime of the program. When the program is started, memory for the variable **count** is allocated and initialized to zero based on the statement inside the function. That same memory location is used for the variable **count** until the program ends; the initialization to zero is executed only once when the memory is first allocated for the variable, not each time the function is called. The scope of the variable **count** is inside the function **f**, but its lifetime is from the start of program execution until the program ends.

```
void f()
{
  static int count = 0;

  count++;
}
```

8.16 Common C++ Mistakes by Python Programmers

Some common mistakes that Python programmers make when learning C++ are

- forgetting the semicolon after each statement

- putting a semicolon at the end of a **for** statement or after the Boolean expression for an **if** or **while** statement

- putting a colon at the end of a **for** statement or after the Boolean expression for an **if** or **while** statement

- forgetting the braces to mark blocks or putting a semicolon after a brace that marks a block of code

- forgetting the parentheses around Boolean expressions in `if`, `while`, and `do while` statements

- forgetting to put the data type in front of each formal parameter in a function/method; for example, writing `void f(int a, b)` instead of the correct `void f(int a, int b)`

- putting the semicolon after the right parenthesis marking the end of a function's parameters when you are writing the code or forgetting that a semicolon is required after the right parenthesis when defining the function prototype but not writing the code

- attempting to directly assign one array variable to another; you must assign each element individually, typically with a loop or nested loops in the case of multi-dimensional arrays

8.17 Additional C++ Topics (Optional)

The topics covered in this section are included to provide a more detailed, but still not complete, introduction to C++ for the interested reader. An understanding of the topics covered in this section is not required to understand the other chapters in this book.

8.17.1 The C++ Switch Statement

C++ supports another decision statement that Python does not have. The C++ `switch` statement is less general than the `if` statement. Any statement written with a `switch` statement can be written using `if` and `else if` statements, but not all `if` statements can be written as `switch` statements. The following C++ code shows an example of a `switch` statement.

```
// switch.cpp
#include <iostream>
using namespace std;

int main()
{
  int choice;
```

```
    cout << "enter your choice of 1, 2, 3, 4: ";
    cin >> choice;

    switch(choice) {
    case 1:
      cout << "you chose 1\n";
      break;
    case 2:
      cout << "you chose 2\n";
      break;
    case 3:
      cout << "you chose 3\n";
      break;
    case 4:
      cout << "you chose 4\n";
      break;
    default:
      cout << "you made an invalid choice";
    }
    return 0;
}
```

As the example demonstrates, the keyword **switch** is used followed by an expression inside parentheses. The expression must be an *ordinal* value which for our purposes means its type must be **int**, **char**, or **bool**. The expression cannot be a floating point value or a string. The keyword **case** is used to list one of the possible values for the expression. If the value of the expression (**choice** in our example) matches the **case** value then the code under that **case** statement is executed. The execution continues until a **break** statement is encountered or the end of the **switch** statement is reached. When a **break** statement is reached, execution continues with the statement after the ending brace for the **switch** statement (**return 0** in our example). The keyword **default** is used to indicate the code that is to be executed if the expression does not match any of the **case** statements.

Since the **break** statement is required to indicate the end of the code to be executed when a **case** statement matches, you can use this fact to write code such as the following:

```
// switch2.cpp
#include <iostream>
using namespace std;

int main()
{
  int choice;
```

```
  cout << "enter your choice of 1, 2, 3, 4: ";
  cin >> choice;

  switch(choice) {
  case 1:
  case 2:
    cout << "you chose 1 or 2\n";
    break;
  case 3:
  case 4:
    cout << "you chose 3 or 4\n";
    break;
  default:
    cout << "you made an invalid choice";
  }
  return 0;
}
```

Since the **break** statement is required to change the flow of execution, forgetting the **break** statement does not create a syntax error but can be a semantic error as the following example shows:

```
// switch3.cpp
#include <iostream>
using namespace std;

int main()
{
  int choice;
  cout << "enter your choice of 1, 2, 3, 4: ";
  cin >> choice;
  switch(choice) {
  case 1:
    cout << "you chose 1\n";
    break;
  case 2:
    cout << "you chose 2\n";
  case 3:
    cout << "you chose 3\n";
    break;
  case 4:
    cout << "you chose 4\n";
    break;
  default:
    cout << "you made an invalid choice";
  }
  return 0;
}
```

If you enter 2 when running this program it outputs both `you chose 2` and `you chose 3`. You should be able to convert each of these `switch` statements to an `if` statement with the same semantics. As we mentioned earlier, one specific value must follow a `case` statement. You cannot write: `case (choice > 0 && choice < 3):`. The `switch` statement is not commonly used because of these restrictions, although it can be used for menu choices as our examples showed. Another important point to notice is that braces are not used to mark the blocks of code under a `case` statement. This is an inconsistency with how C++ marks blocks of code.

8.17.2 Creating C++ Namespaces

You can create your own namespace using the `namespace` keyword. The following example demonstrates a namespace.

```
namespace searches
{
  // function/class definitions
  void binary_search()
  {
    // code here
  }
}
```

To access the function `binary_search` outside of the namespace block, you have three choices. You can refer to it using the full name `searches::binary_search` each time you want to access it. Another option is to place the statement `using namespace searches` at the top of your file. This allows you to refer to all the functions, classes, etc. defined in the `searches` namespace without prefixing them with `searches::`. This corresponds to the Python statement `from searches import *`. The third option is to put the statement `using searches::binary_search` at the top of your file. This is similar to the Python statement `from searches import binary_search`. This C++ version of the `using` statement allows you to access the `binary_search` function without the need for the `searches` prefix in your code, but any other names defined in the `searches` namespace that you want to access would need to be specified with the `searches::` prefix.

8.17.3 Global Variables

C++ also supports global variables although the use of global variables is generally bad design. One exception to this is that constants are commonly defined as global variables. The lifetime of any global variable is the entire execution time of the program. To create a global variable, define it at the top of the file outside of any function blocks. A global variable is accessible in any functions in that file and can be accessed in other files if those files declare the variable with an **extern** prefix. If you wish to make a variable accessible only inside the current file, define it with the **static** prefix. In formal terms, the scope of global variables defined with the **static** prefix is the file it is declared within. The memory for global and static variables is allocated when the program is loaded into memory just before its execution starts, and the same memory location is used for global and static variables throughout the entire execution of the program. As you may have noticed, the keyword **static** has multiple meanings depending on the context in which it is used.

Only one file that is part of a program may define a global variable with a specific name (just as there can be only one function with a specific name defined per program), but any number of files may declare that variable **extern** and access the global variable. This is the issue that there can be many declarations, but only one definition. The following example with three files demonstrates a global and a static variable. It also demonstrates another use of **extern** to indicate that the functions f and g with the specified prototypes exist in another file; this is not recommended and instead you should use header files as discussed in subsection 8.12.1. In either case, you will get an error during the linking phase of building the executable code if the functions cannot be found in one of the compiled object files or the global variables are defined non-**extern** in more than one file.

```
// file1.cpp
int x; // this global variable is potentially accessible
       // in any file linked with file1.o
const double PI=3.141592654; // global constant
static int y; // this variable is only accessible in file1.cpp

extern void f();
extern void g();

int main()
{
  x = 2;
  y = 3;
  f(); // calls f defined in another file
  g(); // calls g defined in another file
  return 0;
}
```

```
// file2.cpp
extern int x; // this allows access to the global variable x defined
              // in another file
void f()
{
  x = 3; // sets x declared in another file (file1.cpp in this case)
}
```

```
// file3.cpp
extern int x;

void g()
{
  x = 4; // sets x declared in another file
}
```

8.18   Chapter Summary

This chapter covers the basic syntax and semantics of much of the C++ language assuming you understand Python. Here is a summary of some of the important concepts.

- C++ code is compiled while Python uses a hybrid technique of compiling to byte code and interpreting the byte code.

- C++ requires you to declare all variable names with a specified type; the built-in types are int, char, float, double, and bool.

- C++ uses braces, {}, to mark blocks of code.

- C++ requires parentheses to be placed around the Boolean expression for the if, while, and do while statements.

- C++ uses the two words else if instead of the elif keyword that Python uses.

- C++ supports a basic array type for storing groups of data of the same type. C++ arrays are similar to Python lists, but C++ arrays are not a class and thus only support the use of brackets to access individual elements; you cannot slice, concatenate, or assign entire arrays with one statement.

- A declaration indicates the type for an identifier name, while a definition allocates memory (for a variable or the code for a function or method).

- C++ supports two parameter passing methods: pass by value which copies the parameters and pass by reference which causes the formal parameters to refer to the same memory locations as the actual parameters.

- C++ arrays are automatically passed by reference.

- Header files are used to declare functions and global variables; we will learn how header files are used with classes in the next chapter.

- The scope of a variable refers to the section of code in which a variable can be accessed; the lifetime of a variable is the time during the execution of the program in which a specific memory location is associated (bound) to the variable.

8.19   Exercises

True/False Questions

1. All C++ programs must have a function named `main`.

2. Any variable used in a C++ program must be declared with a type before it can be used.

3. A C++ function must return a value.

4. A C++ program that compiles will output the results that you intend it to.

5. A C++ program that does not compile can be executed.

6. If the C++ compiler outputs a warning, it will never compile the program.

7. C++ compiler warnings should be ignored.

8. If you compile a C++ program using the Linux operating system on an Intel chip, you can execute the generated program on a computer running the Windows operating system on the same Intel chip.

9. For simple text-based programs you can usually recompile a C++ program on different architectures and operating systems without changing your code.

10. In general, a compiled C++ program will execute faster than a similar Python program on the same computer.

11. A C++ program that solves a specific problem such as sorting numbers will always execute faster on the same computer than a Python program that solves the same problem.

12. Passing an `int` type by reference is faster and more efficient than passing an `int` type by value.

Multiple Choice Questions

1. Which of the following programs would you expect to be significantly faster when written in C++ than when written in Python?

   a) a program to convert miles to kilometers
   b) a program with a loop that runs a million times
   c) a program with a loop that runs 10 times
   d) all of the above

2. If a C++ function uses a variable that has not been declared, what happens?

   a) The code will not compile.
   b) When executing that function, an error message will be generated similar to Python's `NameError` message.
   c) The program crashes.
   d) none of the above

3. Compiling a C++ file that does not contain a `main` function produces

   a) an executable program.
   b) an object file containing the machine code for that C++ file.
   c) another C++ file.
   d) none of the above

4. The linker

   a) copies header files into a C++ file.
   b) compiles a C++ file into machine code.
   c) combines machine code from multiple files to produce an executable program.
   d) loads a program into memory and executes it.

5. C++ functions can return

   a) at most one variable or expression.
   b) multiple variables or expressions.

c) arrays.

d) C++ functions do not return a value.

6. Which of the following statements is the most similar in Python and C++?

a) the `for` statement

b) a function definition

c) the `if/else` statement

d) the `while` statement

7. Which of the following is not true about the C++ pass by reference mechanism?

a) All changes to the formal parameter that are made in the function affect the actual parameter.

b) A copy of the actual parameter is made.

c) It allows you to effectively return multiple values calculated by the function.

d) It is slower than pass by value.

8. Which of following is true about C++ arrays?

a) Arrays can be passed by value.

b) Arrays include a method to sort the values in the array.

c) The values in the array must be the same type.

d) Arrays can be returned by a function.

9. What is the main purpose of a header file?

a) to comment the code in a source file

b) to declare items so they can be used in C++ source files

c) to define items so they can be used in C++ source files

d) none of the above

10. The *scope* of a variable refers to

a) the different values it can hold.

b) where the variable can be accessed.

c) the time during which memory is allocated for the variable.

d) the name of the variable.

Short-Answer Questions

1. What is the exact output (indicate where there are spaces) of the program `input1.cpp` if the user enters 3.5 4?

2. What is the output of the following C++ program?

```
#include <iostream>
using namespace std;
void f(int a, int &b)
{
  cout << a << " " << b << endl;
  a = a + 2;
  b = b + 3;
  cout << a << " " << b << endl;
}
int main()
{
  int x = 4, y = 5;
  cout << x << " " << y << endl;
  f(x, y);
  cout << x << " " << y << endl;
  return 0;
}
```

3. What are the five basic built-in C++ data types?

4. What are the differences between the Python conditional statement and the corresponding C++ conditional statement?

5. What are the differences between the Python and C++ **while** loop statements?

6. What are the differences between the Python **list** type and C++ arrays?

7. What is the purpose of a C++ header file?

8. What do the terms *scope* and *lifetime* mean with respect to variables?

Programming Exercises

1. Write a C++ program that prints the multiplication table for all possible products of the numbers 0 through 9.

2. Write a C++ program that inputs the number of cents (an integer between 0 and 99) and outputs the number of quarters, dimes, nickels, and pennies that add up to that amount and minimizes the number of coins needed.

3. Write a C++ program that allows the user to enter non-negative numbers (pressing the **Return** key after each number is entered). A negative number entered by the user indicates the end of the list of numbers. Output the total and average of the numbers the user entered excluding the negative number.

4. Write a C++ program that asks a user to enter the coefficients a, b, and c of a quadratic equation $a * x^2 + b * x + c = 0$ and outputs the solution(s). The program should indicate if there are no real solutions.

5. Write a C++ function that determines if the **int** parameter it is passed is a prime number. Use this function to write a program that outputs all the prime numbers less than or equal to a number the user inputs.

6. Write a C++ program that inputs an annual investment amount, the interest rate earned every year, and the number of years. The program outputs the final value of the investment assuming the same amount is invested at the beginning of each year and the interest is compounded annually.

7. Modify the **selection_sort** code in this chapter to use an inline **swap** function that accepts two parameters passed by reference.

8. Write a C++ function named **linear_search** that accepts an integer value to search for, an array of integers, and the number of integers in the array. Using the linear search algorithm, the function must return the position of the first parameter in the array. If the first parameter is not in the array, the function returns -1.

9. Write a C++ **binary_search** function with the same parameters as the **linear_search** function described in the previous exercise. Search the list using the binary search algorithm and return the location of the first parameter in the array (returning -1 if the value is not found). The array that is passed to the binary search algorithm must be sorted.

10. Place the **linear_search** and **binary_search** functions in a file named **searches.cpp** with a corresponding header file named **searches.h**. Create a file named **test_searches.cpp** that initializes an array of one million integers in order and tests the searches with inputs that result in both the best and worst running time of each algorithm.

Chapter 9

C++ Classes

Objectives

- To write non-dynamic memory C++ classes.

- To learn how to use the built-in C++ string class.

- To learn how to read and write ASCII files in C++.

- To learn how to overload operators in C++ as methods and as functions.

- To learn how to write class variables and methods in C++.

9.1 Basic Syntax and Semantics

The reasons for and benefits of using classes in C++ are the same as they are in Python. Classes allows us to encapsulate the data and methods for interacting with the data into one syntactic unit. Data hiding allows programmers to use the class without worrying about or understanding the internal implementation details. If the programmer using the class only calls the methods for interacting with the data and does not directly change the instance variables, we are assured that the data integrity of our class is maintained (i.e., assuming the class implementation is correct, manipulating the class through the methods will not result in inconsistent data in the class instance). Classes also make it easier to reuse the code in more than one application. This section covers the basic syntax and semantics of C++ classes. We will examine some of the more advanced class topics in later sections and later chapters.

Before we start examining the syntax for C++ classes, we will discuss some of the terminology differences between Python and C++. Python officially calls members

319

of a class *attributes*; attributes can be either variables or functions. Python has a built-in function named `getattr` that stands for "get attribute" and is used to access the attributes of a class. If we have an instance `r` of the `Rational` class defined in section 2.5, the following two statements are equivalent:

```
print r.num
print getattr(r, 'num')
```

Note that the `getattr` function takes an object and a string and returns the attribute specified by the string for the object. The returned attribute can be either data or a function or method. Python has a built-in function named `hasattr` that also takes the same two parameter types and returns `True` or `False` indicating whether or not the object has an attribute with that name. Python also has a built-in function named `setattr` that takes three parameters: an object, a string, and an object to assign for the attribute. An example of this is `setattr(r, 'num', 4)`; this is equivalent to `r.num = 4`.

We have also used the terms *instance variables* and *instance methods* or just *methods* to discuss attributes of a Python class since they are the more commonly used object-oriented terminology. C++ uses the terms *instance variables* or *data members* for data and the terms *instance methods* or simply *methods* for function members. The term *members* is typically used to refer to both data members and data methods, corresponding to the Python term *attributes*.

C++ allows the interface of the class and the implementation of the class to be separated to a greater degree than Python, but does not require that they be separated. Typically the declaration of the methods and the instance variables is placed in the header file with a `.h` extension and the implementation is placed in a file with the same name except it uses a .C, .cpp, or .cc extension. We are using the .cpp extension in our examples throughout this book.

The header file defines the class name, the methods it provides, the instance variables, and sometimes the implementation of some of the short methods. The implementation file uses the `#include` preprocessor command to include the header file and provides the implementation for each of the methods (except the methods whose implementations are written in the header file). We will now examine a simplified C++ `Rational` class and cover the additional details of C++ classes starting with the header file followed by the corresponding implementation file.

```
#ifndef _RATIONAL_H
#define _RATIONAL_H

class Rational {
```

```
public:
  // constructor
  Rational(int n = 0, int d = 1);

  // sets to n / d
  bool set(int n, int d);

  // access functions
  int num() const;
  int den() const;

  // returns decimal equivalent
  double decimal() const;

private:
  int num_, den_; // numerator and denominator
};

#endif
```

After the `#ifndef` and `#define` preprocesser directives, the class definition starts. Note that even though this header file contains only prototypes for the methods, this is a *class definition*, not a *class declaration*. A declaration of the `Rational` class is just the code `class Rational;`. A class declaration only tells the compiler a class name exists, while a class definition specifies the name along with the instance variables and methods. Because a header file contains a class definition, the use of the `#ifndef` and `#define` processors is even more important than in a header file that just contains a number of function declarations or prototypes. Without the preprocessor directives, if the header file is included twice, you will have two definitions of the class and that is not allowed.

As in Python, the `class` keyword followed by the name of the class is used to start the class definition. C++ uses the beginning and ending braces (`{` and `}`) to mark the beginning and ending of the class definition. A semicolon is used after the ending brace for a class definition. The only places a semicolon is used after an ending brace in C++ are after class definitions, struct definitions (structs are not covered in this book), and statically initializing arrays. Forgetting the semicolon after the ending brace often leads to confusing compiler errors. Most compilers will indicate there is an error at the first line after the include statement in the file that included this header file. Many programmers immediately type the ending brace and semicolon after typing the beginning brace so they do not forget it and then enter the code between the two braces to help avoid this error. In Python, you typically specify the instance variables by initializing them in the constructor (e.g., `self.num = 0`) although other methods can create additional instance variables using the same syntax. In C++, all the instance variables must be defined with their name and type inside the class definition; you cannot add new instance variables in the implementation file as you can in any Python method.

C++ supports enforced data and method protection. The keywords `public`, `private`, and `protected` are used to specify the level of protection. As you can see in the sample `Rational` class definition, the protection keyword is followed by a colon and specifies the level of protection until another protection keyword is specified. In our `Rational` example, all the methods are public and all the instance variables are private. You may specify each protection level multiple times inside a class definition if you wish, although in most cases you will only want to list each protection level once.

Any data members or methods that are `public` can be accessed by any other code; this corresponds to Python's lack of enforced protection. We discussed that the convention when writing Python code is that only the methods should be accessed by other code and that with a few exceptions such as our `ListNode` and `TreeNode` classes that are used to help implement another class, the instance variables should be accessed only by the methods of the class. Instance variables and methods that are declared `private` may be accessed only by methods of the class; the compiler will generate an error if code outside the class attempts to access a private member. Thus, in most cases instance variables should be declared `private`. There are also cases where we want some methods to be called only by other methods of the class; we saw an example of this with our `_find` method in our linked implementation of a list. The convention in Python is to name these private methods starting with one or two underscores. C++ allows you to explicitly declare methods private by listing them in a `private` or `protected` section of the class definition. This is where you declare instance variables and methods that you want to be accessed only by the methods of this class. The compiler will generate an error if code outside of the class attempts to access a private method.

The `protected` designation is similar to the `private` designation except that subclasses may also access the protected members of a class. The compiler will generate an error if any code other than the code in the class itself or a subclass attempts to access a protected method. For now, we will use only the `public` and `private` designations.

The purpose of the *constructor* in C++ is to initialize the instance variables just as it is in Python. A C++ constructor has the same name as the class and does not have a return type. As with Python, you may define a constructor that takes additional parameters, but it is a good idea to define a constructor that does not require any parameters. A constructor that does not take any parameters is known as a *default constructor* whether you write it or the compiler automatically generates it. We used default parameters to allow the `Rational` constructor to be called with zero, one, or two parameters; because this constructor can be called without any parameters, it is a default constructor. A C++ constructor is called automatically when a variable of that type is defined (i.e., `Rational r1, r2;` would cause the constructor to be called for `r1` and for `r2`). You do not need to and cannot call a constructor directly (i.e., after declaring `r1` as a `Rational` type, you cannot write `r1.Rational()` or `r1.Rational(2, 3)`); instead you specify the parameters when you define the variable (e.g., `Rational r1(2, 3);`). Unlike in Python, you do not write code such as `r1 = Rational()` to call the constructor (you do write something similar when using dynamic memory, covered in Chapter 10); instead, you declare variables with the specified type as you do for the built-in types (e.g., `int i;` and `Rational r;`).

If you do not write any constructors, the C++ compiler implicitly creates a default constructor (it does not appear in your implementation file) with an empty body; this means the compiler does not initialize any of the instance variables. Since the compiler defined default constructor has no code, you typically want to write one to ensure that your instance variables are initialized. The default constructor is also called when you declare arrays of objects. The following variable definition causes the `Rational` constructor to be called 10 times, once for each item in the array: `Rational r[10]`.

Some of the `Rational` methods (e.g., `num()`, `den()`, and `decimal()`) have the keyword `const` after the method declaration. This use of `const` indicates the method does not change any of the instance variables of the class. It should be clear that a method marked `const` can call only other `const` methods (since if it called a non-`const` method, that method could modify the instance variables). You may recall that we can also mark formal parameters with a `const` designation. For example we can write a standalone function `void f(const Rational r)`. This means the function `f` is not allowed to modify the parameter so it can only call `Rational` methods that are designated as `const` methods.

Next, we will examine the syntax details of class implementation files using the `Rational` class as an example. To reduce space, we have left out comments, preconditions, and postconditions.

```
#include "Rational.h"

Rational::Rational(int n, int d)
{
  set(n, d);
}
```

```
bool Rational::set(int n, int d)
{
  if (d != 0) {
    num_ = n;
    den_ = d;
    return true;
  }
  else
    return false;
}

int Rational::num() const
{
  return num_;
}

int Rational::den() const
{
  return den_;
}

double Rational::decimal() const
{
  return num_ / double(den_);
}
```

The Rational implementation file includes the header file Rational.h so it has access to the prototypes for each method and the compiler can check that the proper type and number of parameters are used in the implementation. The syntax for writing methods is the return type for the method, a space, the class name, two colons, and then the method with its parameters. If the method was declared const in the class definition, that also must be indicated in the implementation file. Again, note that the constructor does not have a return type. The method prototypes must exactly match the return type, parameter types, and constant designations in the header file. If they do not, you will get a compiler error. Recall that we do not put the default parameter values (for the constructor in this example) in the implementation file; they appear only in the method prototype in the header file.

The two colons separating the class name and method name are known as the *scope resolution operator*. With Python, the methods are defined inside the class and the indentation indicates that the methods are part of the class. In C++ the implementation of the methods is written separately from the class definition so the class name and two colons are used to indicate that a method is part of the specified class. You may also write standalone functions that are not part of a class in a C++ class implementation file by not using the class name and the two colons. Writing a standalone function in a C++ class implementation file is typically only done if the function is used by the class methods and not by any other code.

C++ does not use an explicit `self` parameter as Python does. Since the class definition specifies the names of all the instance variables, the compiler knows the names of the instance variables and does not need something similar to `self` to indicate items that are members of the class. The same is true when calling a method of the class. The methods can be called without a prefix as we called the `set` method from the constructor. C++ does contain a pointer named `this` that corresponds to Python's `self`; we will discuss it in Chapter 10 after we have discussed what a C++ pointer is.

Since an explicit indication that you are referring to instance members is not required in C++, many programmers prefix or suffix an underscore onto the names of instance variables. Use of the underscore makes it clear that you are referring to an instance variable and also allows you to use a similar name for parameters and instance variables. If a method has a formal parameter with the same name as an instance variable, the parameter makes the instance variable inaccessible unless you use the `this` pointer. If you accidently use the same name, all uses of the identifier are the parameter instead of the instance variable inside that method so your instance variables are not set or changed. The compiler does not generate an error when you name a formal parameter the same as an instance variable. This can be a difficult error to track down and is one reason many programmers add the underscore to instance variables. The explicit use of `self` in Python avoids this error. Python programmers often rely on the explicit use of `self` and name parameters and instance variables the same. Because of this, Python programmers learning C++ often make this mistake. In C++, make certain you use names for the formal parameters that are different than the class instance variables. The following example shows the problem. This example also demonstrates that you can place both the class definition and implementation code in one file; however, you do not want to do this unless your entire program is in one file. If you want to allow your program to be split among multiple files or your class to be reused in other programs, you must create a separate header and implementation file for the class.

```
#include <iostream>
using namespace std;

class Rational {

public:
  Rational(int num_=0, int den_=1);
```

```
   int num() const { return num_; }
   int den() const { return den_; }

private:
  int num_, den_;
};

// this is incorrect
// do not use the same name for formal parameters and instance variables
Rational::Rational(int num_, int den_)
{
  num_ = num_;
  den_ = den_;
  cout << num_ << " / " << den_ << endl;
}

int Rational::num() const
{
  return num_;
}

int Rational::den() const
{
  return den_;
}

int main()
{
  Rational r(2, 3);

  cout << r.num() << " / " << r.den() << endl;
}
```

The output of this program on our computer is

```
2 / 3
-1881115708 / 0
```

The same problem occurs if you redeclare a local variable with the same name as an instance variable as the following example shows:

```
#include <iostream>
using namespace std;
class Rational {

public:
  Rational(int num=0, int den=1);

  int num() const;
  int den() const;

private:
  int num_, den_;
};

Rational::Rational(int num, int den)
{
  // this is incorrect
  // do not declare local variables with the same name as
  // instance variables
  int num_, den_;

  num_ = num;
  den_ = den;
  cout << num_ << " / " << den_ << endl;
}
int Rational::num() const
{
  return num_;
}
int Rational::den() const
{
  return den_;
}

int main()
{
  Rational r(2, 3);

  cout << r.num() << " / " << r.den() << endl;
}
```

The output for this example on our computer is the same as in the previous example. The instance variables are never initialized in either case so their value is whatever is in the memory location used for them before the program starts. In both cases, the actual instance variables are hidden from use in the constructor. In the first example, the formal parameters with the same name as the instance variables are the variables accessed inside the constructor. In the second example the local variables are accessed in the constructor instead of the instance variables. Never use the same name for instance variables and local variables or formal parameters. The use of an underscore for instance variables (but never local variables or formal parameters) is a common technique to avoid this problem.

Another common beginner's mistake is to write code such as `r.num() = 3;` where `r` is an instance of the `Rational` class. This is not correct in Python or C++. The return value of `r.num()` is a number, not a variable in which a value can be stored. This is the same issue as incorrect code such as `4 = 3;` or `sqrt(5) = x;`. What appears on the left-hand side of the assignment statement must be a variable. The term for this is appropriately named an *l-value* since it appears on the left-hand side of the assignment statement. C++ does support a reference return type that allows a return value of a class method to be assigned a value. The details of this are covered in Chapter 10.

For functions and methods that are very short (typically less than five lines of C++ code), the overhead of making the function call takes more time than executing the actual code in the function. In these cases, it usually makes sense to avoid the overhead of a function call. C++ provides a mechanism known as *inlining* that allows you to write the code as if it is a function or method, but avoids the overhead of a function call. In effect, the compiler replaces the function call with the actual body of the function. When copying the function or method, it also properly handles the effect of passing the parameters and returning a value. For methods of a class there are two different ways to write them as inline methods. The following rewrite of our `Rational` class demonstrates both techniques. The `num()` and `den()` methods demonstrate the one technique and the `decimal` method demonstrates the other technique.

```
class Rational {

public:
  // constructor
  Rational(int n = 0, int d = 1);

  // sets to n / d
  bool set(int n, int d);
  // access functions
  int num() const { return num_; }
  int den() const { return den_; }
  // returns decimal equivalent
  double decimal() const;
```

```
private:
  int num_, den_; // numerator and denominator
};


inline double Rational::decimal() const
{
  return num_ / double(den_);
}
```

The num() and den() methods are written inline when they are declared. Immediately after the method definition, a semicolon is not used and instead the code follows inside braces. This technique is commonly used when the code fits on the line with the method name. The decimal() method is written inline after the class declaration. This is the same technique used for writing standalone functions inline that we discussed in section 8.13. The keyword inline is used followed by the code just as if you were writing the method in the implementation file. This technique is typically used when the code is a few lines long. The inline keyword is used to prevent multiple definitions of the method when multiple files include this header file. If you forget the inline keyword, you get a linking error indicating multiple definitions of the function if more than one file includes the header file with the method code. Inline methods should be written in the header file, not the implementation file. The exception is if the inline method is called only from one implementation file, then you could write the inline method at the top of that implementation file.

Our Rational constructor calls the set method. Notice that the method call looks like a normal function call, unlike in Python where we need to use self to indicate a method is being called. The reason for adding the set method is to prevent having two copies of code that do the same thing. It does add the overhead of an additional function call in the constructor. To solve that problem, we could make the constructor or the set method an inline method. It is generally a good idea to avoid duplicate code since if you change it in one place, you need to remember to change it in the other place(s) also.

With both techniques for writing a method inline in the header file, the compiler can just copy the code for the method into the function or method that called it, avoiding the overhead of a function call. Most compilers will create a normal function or method if the inline function or method is too long since copying the code for large functions will increase the size of your executable program. Whether or not the compiler actually creates an inline function is transparent to the programmer. In both cases, the return type and parameter types are checked and the parameters are effectively passed using the specified mechanism (either by value or by reference).

The only reason for writing inline functions is to avoid the overhead of a function call.

9.2   Strings

Now that we have learned the basics of C++ classes, we will examine the **string** class that is part of the standard C++ library. C++ strings correspond to Python's **string** data type and are used to represent sequences of characters that are usually (but not always) treated as a unit. Since C++ is for the most part backward compatible with C, it supports C-style strings and some C++ library functions require that a C string be passed as the actual parameter, so we will briefly discuss C-style strings. The C language uses an array of **char** to store string data and uses a special character \0 to indicate the end of the string; this requires that the array size be at least one unit larger than the string of characters you want to store. Since C does not directly support classes, a C library provides separate functions that are used to manipulate the arrays of characters.

C++ strings are implemented as a class that has an array of **char** as an instance variable. As you should expect, the C++ string methods allow you to access and manipulate a string without concerning yourself with the internal implementation. The C++ **string** class provides a number of methods for manipulating the string data, but does not include all the capabilities that Python strings have. In addition to the methods the C++ **string** class supports, it also overloads many of the operators so you are able to assign and compare strings. You can read and write C++ **string** variables using the instances **cin** and **cout** and file classes defined in the **<iostream>** header file. We will not cover all the string methods, but will introduce the basics of the C++ **string** class in this section.

To use the C++ **string** class, you must **#include <string>** at the top of your file along with any other header files you are including. The **string** class is also defined within the standard namespace so you must have the statement **using namespace std** at the top of your file or refer to the class as **std::string**. When a C++ executable program reads strings using the » operator, it stops processing characters at the first whitespace (space, tab, or new line). For example, to read in a person's first and last name entered with a space between them, you would need to use two strings:

```
string first, last;
cout << "Enter your first and last name (separated by a space): ";
cin >> first >> last;
```

You may create and output strings that contain whitespace, but when using the » operator, you need to remember that it stops reading each time a whitespace character is encountered. The code `string name; name = "Dave Reed"; cout «` `name « endl;` works as you would expect, outputting `Dave Reed` followed by a new line. C++ provides a `getline` function that reads from the current input pointer to a delimiter; the default delimiter is the `\n` end-of-line character. The `getline` function requires two parameters: the input stream from which to read and a string that is passed by reference and will contain the string that is read. The input stream can be the `cin` instance or a file handle for reading data from a disk file. The optional third parameter for the `getline` function is the character to use as a delimiter. The `getline` function reads all the characters up to and including the delimiter and returns a string containing all the characters read except the delimiter. Using the `getline` function, we can input a first and last name as one string:

```
string name;
cout << "Enter your first and last name: ";
getline(cin, name);
```

You can mix the use of the `getline` function and the » operator with `cin` or a file handle, but it requires that you carefully process the input. When you use `cin` to read a variable, it skips leading whitespace, but leaves the trailing whitespace, including the new line character in the input stream. The `getline` function reads everything up to the delimiter, including the delimiter, so if a `getline` follows a `cin` that reads everything on the line, it gets an empty string. You must make two calls to `getline` in this case, and the second one will get the data on the next line.

The C++ `string` class supports the standard comparison operators `<`, `<=`, `>`, `>=`, `==`, and `!=`. The rules for comparison are the same as in Python; dictionary order is used and lowercase letters are greater than uppercase letters since the ASCII codes for lowercase letters are larger. Unlike Python strings, C++ strings are mutable. You can both access individual characters and set individual characters using the brackets operator (`[]`). As you should expect, the indexing starts at zero and you cannot use negative values since internally the string is represented as a C++ array. There is no range checking, so you need to ensure that you do not access beyond the end of the string. C++ strings also support the assignment operator `=` for assigning a string variable or expression on the right-hand side of the assignment statement to the string variable on the left-hand side.

The C++ string assignment operator creates a separate copy of the data, unlike Python which would have two references to the same data. If after assigning one C++ string variable to another, you change one of the strings, it does not change the other. The + and += operators work the same as they do in Python. The following example demonstrates some of these concepts.

```cpp
// stringex.cpp
#include <iostream>
#include <string>
using namespace std;

int main()
{
  string first = "Dave";
  string last = "Reed";
  string name;

  name = first + " " + last;
  cout << name << endl;

  first[3] = 'i';
  first += "d";

  name = first + " " + last;
  cout << name << endl;
  cout << name.substr(6, 4) << endl;
  return 0;
}
```

The preceding example outputs Dave Reed, David Reed, and Reed on three separate lines. Notice that the single quotation mark is used with the bracket operator since first[3] is a single character. You cannot use Python's slicing syntax for accessing a substring; C++ does provide a substr method. Its prototype is string substr(int position, int length). It returns a string starting at the specified starting position with the specified length. This is different than Python slicing which takes the starting and ending positions. The string class also has a method named c_str() for returning a C array of characters. This is useful when you need to call a function that requires a C-style string instead of a C++ string. The find method takes a string to search for and optional starting position for the search. It returns the index of the first occurrence of the search string in the string. There are a number of additional string methods, but these are a few of the ones that are commonly used.

9.3 | File Input and Output

File input and output often involves the use of strings although you can input ASCII numeric data directly as numbers or read a file in a binary format corresponding directly to how the computer represents an internal data type. We will not cover the reading of binary files in this book. C++ uses instances of classes to perform file input and output as it does for keyboard and monitor input and output. The `fstream` header file contains the class declarations of `ifstream` and `ofstream` for file input and output, respectively. These are also in the namespace `std`. Similarly as in Python, you must associate the file variable with a filename using the `open` method. The following example demonstrates file input and output in C++ by prompting the user for a file name and writing the string `David Reed` to the file. It then opens the file for reading, reads the first line in the file using the `getline` function, and outputs it using the `cout` statement.

```cpp
// getline.cpp
#include <iostream>
#include <fstream>
using namespace std;

int main()
{
  string filename, name, first, last;
  ofstream outfile;
  ifstream infile;

  cout << "Enter file name: ";
  cin >> filename;
  outfile.open(filename.c_str());
  outfile << "David" << " " << "Reed" << endl;
  outfile.close();
  infile.open(filename.c_str());
  getline(infile, name);
  cout << name << endl;
  infile.close();
  return 0;
}
```

Notice that the **open** method requires the C version of a string which is an array of characters, so we need to use the `c_str()` method of the **string** class when opening the file. As with Python, you need to close the file to ensure that data written to the file is flushed to the disk. In this example we demonstrated the use of the **getline** function although we could have followed the same pattern as we did

when writing the file and read two separate strings and combine them using the **+**
operator. The code fragment for this method is

```
infile.open(filename.c_str());
infile >> first >> last;
infile.close()
name = first + " " + last;
cout << name << endl;
infile.close();
```

You can also read numeric data from an ASCII file using a similar technique.
You open the file and then specify a numeric data variable (**int**, **float**, or **double**).
Just as when reading numeric values using the keyboard, whitespace (space, tab,
or new line) is used to separate numeric values and the amount of whitespace does
not matter. Each time you attempt to read a value, it skips past any whitespace
to attempt to find a numeric value. If it encounters any non-numeric characters
immediately after any preceding whitespace while attempting to read a number, a
run-time error is generated. When reading a number with a non-numeric digit after
it, it reads the number, but not the other non-numeric digit, leaving the file pointer
at that location. The next input will start with that character. The following would
read a file named **in.txt** containing 10 integer values as ASCII text with each one
separated by any amount of whitespace and output each value on a line as it reads
it.

```
// readfile.cpp
#include <iostream>
#include <fstream>
using namespace std;
int main()
{
  ifstream ifs;
  int i, x;
  ifs.open("in.txt");
  for (i=0; i<10; i++) {
    ifs >> x;
    cout << x << endl;
  }
  return 0;
}
```

The **open** method of both the **ifstream** and **ofstream** classes has a second
parameter for specifying the mode for opening the file. It should be clear from the
preceding examples that the second parameter has a default value. This book does

not cover the details of the second parameter or how to read or write binary files with C++.

9.4 Operator Overloading

As you may have determined based on the discussion of strings, C++ supports user-defined operator overloading. As with Python, the purpose of operator overloading is to allow for more concise, readable code. Because C++ does not use references by default, it is also necessary to use operator overloading to override the assignment operator for classes that use dynamic memory; we will discuss this in Chapter 10.

With C++, you may choose to make the operators methods of the class or standalone functions (a few must be standalone functions). Some programmers prefer the standalone functions, since the binary operator functions take two parameters corresponding to the two instances of the class to which the operator is applied. If you implement the operator as a method of the class, only one parameter appears in the method prototype; the left parameter for the operator is the implicit parameter corresponding to the instance with which the method was called. In Python both parameters appear in the definition since the `self` parameter is explicit. The drawback of using standalone functions is they cannot access the private data of the class. Because of this, the class must provide methods to access and possibly modify the private data. C++ also provides a `friend` construct for allowing certain functions or methods from other classes to access the private data. We will examine this technique when we learn how to overload the input and output operators.

C++ names the methods for operator overloading using the word `operator` followed by the actual symbol for the operator that is being overloaded. We will first examine the technique where the operator is not a member of the class, so we will be writing standalone functions. The following is the complete `Rational` header and implementation file for the addition operator written as a standalone function.

```
// Rationalv1.h
class Rational {

public:
  // constructor
  Rational(int n = 0, int d = 1) { set(n, d); }
  // sets to n / d
  bool set(int n, int d);

  // access functions
  int num() const { return num_; }
  int den() const { return den_; }
```

```
  // returns decimal equivalent
  double decimal() const { return num_ / double(den_); }

private:
  int num_, den_; // numerator and denominator
};

// prototype for operator+ standalone function
Rational operator+(const Rational &r1, const Rational &r2);
```

```
// Rationalv1.cpp
#include "Rationalv1.h"

bool Rational::set(int n, int d)
{
  if (d != 0) {
    num_ = n;
    den_ = d;
    return true;
  }
  else
    return false;
}

Rational operator+(const Rational &r1, const Rational &r2)
{
  int num, den;

  num = r1.num() * r2.den() + r2.num() * r1.den();
  den = r1.den() * r2.den();
  return Rational(num, den);
}
```

Note that since the operator is a standalone function, the class name and two colons (`Rational::`) is not placed in front of the name of the function (`operator+`). A sample program that calls the operator is

```
// mainv1.cpp
#include "Rationalv1.h"
int main()
{
  Rational r1(2, 3), r2(3, 4), r3;

  r3 = r1 + r2; // common method of calling the operator function
  r3 = operator+(r1, r2); // direct method of calling the function
}
```

Since the function is not a member of the class, it cannot access the private data members directly and needs to use the public methods to access the numerator and denominator. The function prototypes for the standalone function version of many of the operators that can be written are summarized in the following table (this is not a complete list). For other classes, you obviously need to replace `Rational` with the name of that class type. We pass the parameters as `const` reference parameters; this means only `const` methods of the `Rational` class can be called inside these functions. This does not cause a problem since applying any of the operators should not change the parameter(s). Remember that the reason for passing class instances using the `const` designation and by reference is that when using pass by reference, only the address of the object is passed. This results in less data being copied than if we used pass by value so it is faster and uses less memory. The first column in the table shows the prototype for the function. The second column shows how the function/operator is called for two instances of the `Rational` class and what result it computes and returns.

Function	Computes
`Rational operator+(const Rational& r1, const Rational& r2)`	`r1 + r2`
`Rational operator-(const Rational& r1, const Rational& r2)`	`r1 - r2`
`Rational operator*(const Rational& r1, const Rational& r2)`	`r1 * r2`
`Rational operator/(const Rational& r1, const Rational& r2)`	`r1 / r2`
`Rational operator-(const Rational& r1)`	`-r1`
`bool operator<(const Rational& r1, const Rational& r2)`	`r1 < r2`
`bool operator<=(const Rational& r1, const Rational& r2)`	`r1 <= r2`
`bool operator>(const Rational& r1, const Rational& r2)`	`r1 > r2`
`bool operator>=(const Rational& r1, const Rational& r2)`	`r1 >= r2`
`bool operator==(const Rational& r1, const Rational& r2)`	`r1 == r2`
`bool operator!=(const Rational& r1, const Rational& r2)`	`r1 != r2`

The operator overloading code can also be written as a method (i.e., a member of the class). Usually the operator would be written in the .cpp file and the prototype for it would be written in the .h file. Since we are writing a member method, the prototype needs to be declared in the `public` section of the class declaration. The object the method is called with is the implicit first parameter `r1` that is visible in the function version, so it is not used in the method version. The following shows the header file and implementation file for the addition operator written as a method of the class.

```
// Rationalv2.h
class Rational {

public:
  // constructor
  Rational(int n = 0, int d = 1) { set(n, d); }

  // sets to n / d
  bool set(int n, int d);

  // access functions
  int num() const { return num_; }
  int den() const { return den_; }

  // returns decimal equivalent
  double decimal() const { return num_ / double(den_); }

  Rational operator+(const Rational &r2) const;

private:
  int num_, den_; // numerator and denominator
};
```

```
// Rationalv2.cpp
#include "Rationalv2.h"

// code for set method is also required
// see previous example for the code

Rational Rational::operator+(const Rational &r2) const
{
  Rational r;

  r.num_ = num_ * r2.den_ + den() * r2.num();
  r.den_ = den_ * r2.den_;
  return r;
}
```

Since the method is a member of the class, it can directly access the private data members of any instance of the class. Also note that the first parameter is implicit in the method prototype as it is in all C++ class methods. Because of this, that instance's data and methods are accessed by specifying the name of the data/method member without a variable name before it while the explicit second parameter's (**r2**) data is accessed by specifying the name of that parameter followed by a period and then the data/method member. The preceding example uses both **num_** and **den()** to demonstrate that instance variables and methods, respectively, can be accessed directly for the implicit parameter; normally you would pick one style and use it consistently. Some programmers prefer the non-member function so that the function prototype is symmetric and shows both parameters. Others prefer the class method so all the code is encapsulated within the class and the methods can access the private data.

The common way of calling the method is using the operator notation as we did when using the function technique for writing operators. The direct way of calling it is the standard syntax for calling a method (i.e., a class instance, followed by a period, followed by the method name).

```
// mainv2.cpp
#include "Rationalv2.h"
int main()
{
  Rational r1(2, 3), r2(3, 4), r3;

  r3 = r1 + r2; // common method of calling the operator method
  r3 = r1.operator+(r2); // direct method of calling the operator
}
```

The following table shows the prototypes for the operators when they are members of the class. The second column again shows how to call the methods and what value the operator computes and returns.

Method	Computes
`Rational operator+(const Rational& r2)`	`r1 + r2`
`Rational operator-(const Rational& r2)`	`r1 - r2`
`Rational operator*(const Rational& r2)`	`r1 * r2`
`Rational operator/(const Rational& r2)`	`r1 / r2`
`Rational operator-()`	`-r1`
`bool operator<(const Rational& r2)`	`r1 < r2`
`bool operator<=(const Rational& r2)`	`r1 <= r2`
`bool operator>(const Rational& r2)`	`r1 > r2`
`bool operator>=(const Rational& r2)`	`r1 >= r2`
`bool operator==(const Rational& r2)`	`r1 == r2`
`bool operator!=(const Rational& r2)`	`r1 != r2`

If you wish to override the input (») and output («) operators, they must be written as standalone functions. The reason for this is the first parameter of a method must be an instance of that class. Consider the code `cin » r1`. You might be tempted to write it as a member method, but recall that this would imply the method would be called as `cin.operator»(r1)`. Since `cin` is not an instance of the `Rational` class, the input operator cannot be a member of the `Rational` class and must be written as a standalone function. This is also the case when using the output operator « with an instance of the `ostream` class such as `cout`. A standalone function of the output operator for our `Rational` class is

```
std::ostream& operator<<(std::ostream &os, const Rational &r)
{
  os << r.num() << "/" << r.den();
  return os;
}
```

The operator needs to return the instance of the output stream variable `os` that is of type `ostream` so that it can be chained together (e.g., `cout` « `r1` « `r2`). In this example, the returned result of `cout` « `r1` needs to be the `ostream` instance `cout` so it is now the first parameter to the call for outputting `r2`. The `ostream` parameter `os` also needs to be passed by reference and returned as a reference since outputting the variable to the stream changes the stream. We will cover returning by reference in more detail in Chapter 10, but for now just learn the syntax for returning by reference which is appending an ampersand onto the return type (e.g., `ostream&` for the output operator).

Since the operator is a non-member function, it cannot access the private data of the `Rational` class. There are times where we want to allow certain other classes or certain functions to be able to access the private data of a class. C++ provides a mechanism for permitting this using the `friend` keyword. One common example where allowing a non-member function to access the private members directly makes sense is the input/output operator functions. Another example would be our `ListNode` class. We may want to allow the `LList` class to access the `ListNode` data members directly since those two classes are tightly coupled together. A function or class is specified as a `friend` inside the class that wants to make it a friend. The following code example demonstrates this for our `Rational` class. If we wanted to make an entire class a friend, an example of the syntax is `friend class LList`. If we placed that line inside our `ListNode` class then all the `LList` methods would have access to the private data of the `ListNode`. We will demonstrate a complete example of this when we examine linked structures using C++ in Chapter 11.

The following code is the header file for the complete, simplified `Rational` class demonstrating operator overloading and friends. For brevity, the pre- and postconditions and comments are not included for all the methods.

```
// Rationalv3.h
#ifndef _RATIONAL_H
#define _RATIONAL_H

// needed for definition of ostream and istream classes
#include <iostream>

class Rational {

// declare input and output operators functions as friends
// to the class so they can directly access the private data
friend std::istream& operator>>(std::istream& is, Rational &r);
friend std::ostream& operator<<(std::ostream& os, const Rational &r);

public:
  // constructor
  Rational(const int n = 0, const int d = 1) { set(n, d); }

  // sets to n / d
  bool set(const int n, const int d);

  // access functions
  int num() const { return num_; }
  int den() const { return den_; }

  // returns decimal equivalent
  double decimal() const;

private:
  int num_, den_; // numerator and denominator
};

// prototypes for operator overloading
Rational operator+(const Rational &r1, const Rational &r2);

// declare the non-member input output operator functions
std::istream& operator>>(std::istream &is, Rational &r);
std::ostream& operator<<(std::ostream &os, const Rational &r);

#endif
```

The corresponding .cpp implementation file is

```
// Rationalv3.cpp
using namespace std;
#include "Rationalv3.h"
```

```
bool Rational::set(const int n, const int d)
{
  if (d != 0) {
    num_ = n;
    den_ = d;
    return true;
  }
  else
    return false;
}

Rational operator+(const Rational &r1, const Rational &r2)
{
  int num, den;

  num = r1.num() * r2.den() + r2.num() * r1.den();
  den = r1.den() * r2.den();
  return Rational(num, den);
}

std::istream& operator>>(std::istream &is, Rational &r)
{
  char c;

  is >> r.num_ >> c >> r.den_;
  return is;
}

std::ostream& operator<<(std::ostream &os, const Rational &r)
{
  os << r.num() << "/" << r.den();
  return os;
}
```

The `Rational` object passed to the input operator function must be passed by reference since we want the value we read to be stored in the actual parameter sent (i.e., when we execute `cin >> r` we want the value the user enters to be stored in `r`). This is also why it cannot be passed as a `const` parameter. To allow us to type in a value such as 2/3, we need to read the forward slash in the input operator function. We declare the variable `c` as a `char` to store the slash but ignore the value after reading it since our `Rational` class encapsulates the number by storing two integers.

Also notice in our example that we did not put the **using namespace std** line in the header file. Instead we used the prefix syntax **std::** when referring to the names of the `ostream` and `istream` classes that are defined within the **std** namespace. Remember that the reason for this is that if we had put the **using namespace std** line in the header file, any file that included our Rational.h file would effectively have the `using namespace std` line in it. For this reason, you should never put a `using` statement in a header file. We did put the `using namespace std` line in our Rational.cpp file so that we did not need to write `std::` in front of all the names defined in the namespace; this is not a problem since you never include an implementation (.cpp) file.

9.5 Class Variables and Methods

C++ also supports a mechanism for creating class variables. You may recall that we discussed how to create class variables in Python in subsection 2.3.2. With instance variables, each instance of a class gets its own separate copy of the instance variables. With class variables, all instances of the class share the same variable (i.e., there is only one copy of the class variable no matter how many instances of the class exist). The `Card` class we discussed in subsection 2.3.2 is a good example in which using class variables makes sense. We will create a similar `Card` class in this section using C++ class variables.

```cpp
// Card.h
#ifndef __CARD_H__
#define __CARD_H__
#include <string>

class Card {
public:
  Card(int num=0) { number_ = num; }
  void set(int num) { number_ = num; }
  std::string suit() const;
  std::string face() const;
private:
  int number_;
  static const std::string suits_[4];
  static const std::string faces_[13];
};
inline std::string Card::suit() const
{
  return suits_[number_ / 13];
}
inline std::string Card::face() const
{
  return faces_[number_ % 13];
}
#endif // __CARD_H__
```

The mechanism for creating class variables is to declare them with the `static` prefix. In C++, there are a number of different uses for the keyword `static` and it is easy to confuse them. This use of `static` has a completely different meaning than the use of `static` we discussed in the previous chapter to create local variables that always use the same memory location. Declaring an instance variable `static` indicates it is a class variable and thus there is only one copy of that variable that all instances of the class share. Using a class variable in our example makes sense since we do not need a separate copy of the face and suit names for each instance of the class. Making these instance variables would be a huge waste of memory. With class variables, each instance of our class requires only four bytes of memory. If the face and suit name variables were not class variables, each instance of our `Card` class would require around 100 bytes to store the number and all the strings. The following is the implementation file for the `Card` class.

```
// Card.cpp
#include "Card.h"

const std::string Card::suits_[4] = {
  "Hearts", "Diamonds", "Clubs", "Spades" };

const std::string Card::faces_[13] = {
  "Ace", "Two", "Three", "Four", "Five", "Six", "Seven", "Eight", "Nine",
  "Ten", "Jack", "Queen", "King" };
```

Class variables are defined as if they were non-local variables (i.e., outside of any function) and the variables are initialized using the assignment statement once when the program is first executed. Since there is only one copy of the class variables, we do not want to assign the values inside the constructor. We declared the class variables with the `const` prefix in the header file so once we initialize the variables with these statements, we cannot change their values. Even if the class variables were not declared with the `const` prefix, we would still need to define them once in the implementation file (with or without providing initial values). A class definition does not actually cause any memory to be allocated; it is only when we create an instance of the class that memory is allocated. This is why we must define the class variables in an implementation file so that memory is allocated for them.

The following is a sample program that uses our `Card` class containing the class variables.

```
// test_Card.cpp
#include <iostream>
using namespace std;
#include "Card.h"
```

```
int main()
{
  Card c[52];
  int i;

  for (i=0; i<52; ++i) {
    c[i].set(i);
  }
  for (i=0; i<52; ++i) {
    cout << c[i].face() << " of " << c[i].suit() << endl;
  }
  return 0;
}
```

Even though there is no need to do this, what would happen if we tried to put the statement `cout << Card::faces_[0] << endl;` in our main function? This does demonstrate the correct usage of accessing a class variable using the class name followed by two colons followed by the name of the class variable. However, the class variables were declared `private` so they are not accessible outside of the class even though the variable definitions are not inside the class. If we declared the class variables in the `public` section this would work.

You may be wondering why we needed to create a separate implementation file since all the methods were defined inline in the header file. If we instead put the class variable definitions in the header file as the following code shows, we could end up with the same names being defined multiple times. Recall that each variable or function can have only one definition.

```
// this code should not be used

#ifndef __CARD_H__
#define __CARD_H__

#include <string>

class Card {
public:
  Card(int num=0) { number_ = num; }
  void set(int num) { number_ = num; }
  std::string suit() const;
  std::string face() const;
private:
  int number_;
  static const std::string suits_[4];
  static const std::string faces_[13];
};
```

```
const std::string Card::suits_[4] = {
  "Hearts", "Diamonds", "Clubs", "Spades" };

const std::string Card::faces_[13] = {
  "Ace", "Two", "Three", "Four", "Five", "Six", "Seven", "Eight", "Nine",
  "Ten", "Jack", "Queen", "King" };

//------------------------------------------------------------------

inline std::string Card::suit() const
{
  return suits_[number_ / 13];
}

inline std::string Card::face() const
{
  return faces_[number_ % 13];
}

//------------------------------------------------------------------

#endif // __CARD_H__
```

This header file works correctly if only one file includes it since that creates one definition of the class variables `suits_` and `faces_`. However, if multiple implementation files that are used to create one executable program include this header file, then we have multiple definitions of the class variables and we get a linker error indicating multiple definitions of the symbols. For this reason, class variables should always be defined in an implementation file as our original example did.

In our example the class variables were declared `const` since it does not make sense to change them. But in some cases you may want class variables that are not `const`. One possible use of a non-`const` class variable is to keep track of the number of instances of the class that are created. To do this, we create a class that has the constructor increment the class variable. The value of this class variable tells us the total number of instances of the class that have been created. To do this, we add a class variable to the class using the following line inside the class definition in the header file: `static int count_;`. We then add the line `int Card::count_ = 0;` to the implementation file. If we declare the class variable in the `public` section of the header file, then we can access it directly. This would allow us to put the following line in our `main` function: `cout << Card::count_ << endl;`. Of course, normally you do not want to declare data members of a class in the `public` section. Someone could put the line `Card::count_ = 100;` in their code and destroy the integrity of the value `count_` storing the number of instances of the `Card` class that have been created.

Classes can also have class methods that are called without an instance of the class. Using a class method to access the class variable `count_` is the proper way to ensure the integrity of the data. We need to add a class method that returns the value of the class variable. Class methods are also declared with the `static` prefix. The declaration and definition of the method is `static int count() { return count_; }`. We call the method using the code `cout << Card::count() << endl`. You should realize that class methods can access class variables, but they cannot access instance variables. The reason for this is that when calling a class method, you are not specifying an instance of the class as we do when we call an instance method (e.g., `Card::count()` vs. `c.face()`). A class method cannot know which instance data to use since an instance is not specified when the method is called.

You may have noticed that our sample code to count the number of cards never decreases the class variable storing the number. This means the class variable will store the number of instances that have been created even though some of them may not exist. To make the class variable indicate the number of instances of the class that currently exist as the program is executing, we need to decrease the value of the class variable when the lifetime of a `Card` instance ends. We will learn in Chapter refC++ dynamic memory about destructors; they could be used to accomplish this task.

9.6 Chapter Summary

This chapters covers the syntax and concepts for writing and using C++ classes. The following is a summary of some of the important concepts.

- C++ classes are usually written in two parts that are in separate files: the class definition in a header file and the code for the methods in an implementation file.

- A semicolon must be placed after the ending brace of a class definition.

- C++ constructors have the same name as the class and are called automatically when a variable of that type is defined.

- Programmers commonly prefix or suffix an underscore onto instance variables so they do not accidently use the same identifier name for instance variables as they do for formal parameters and local variables.

- C++ provides a built-in **string** class that can be used with the standard input/output techniques. The C++ **string** class also implements the common operators (**[]**, **+**, and **+=**) which work the same as the operators in Python.

- The built-in types and **string** class can also be read from and written to files using the same syntax for standard input and output.

- C++ allows programmers to overload operators for their own classes; most of the operators can be written as standalone functions or as members of the class. The names of these functions/methods is **operator** followed by the actual operator symbol(s).

- Class variables should be used when only one copy of the data is needed for all instances of the class. Class methods can only access class data. In C++, class variables and methods are designated using the **static** keyword.

9.7 Exercises

True/False Questions

1. C++ classes have a constructor that has the same name as the class.

2. C++ constructors are called automatically.

3. You must write code for the C++ constructor of every class you write.

4. Methods of a C++ class can create or add additional instance variables to the class.

5. Methods may be declared in the **private** section of the class definition.

6. Instance variables must be declared in the **private** section of the class definition.

7. A compiler error is generated if a method has a variable with the same name as an instance variable.

8. Methods may be written **inline** in the header file.

9. The **string** class is defined within the **std** namespace.

10. The default input operator for a string reads one line of text just as the Python **raw_input** function does.

11. The `string` class has a method named `getline`.

12. When using `getline`, the new line character is removed from the input stream.

13. C++ uses class instances to read from and write to both files and the keyboard or screen.

14. When overloading C++ operators, you can write most methods as either a function or a method.

15. A class method can access instance variables.

16. A method can access both class variables and instance variables.

Multiple Choice Questions

1. In C++, instance variables may be declared

   a) private only.
   b) public only.
   c) protected only.
   d) public, private, or protected.

2. In C++, instance methods may be declared

   a) private only.
   b) public only.
   c) protected only.
   d) public, private, or protected.

3. Members of a class that are declared private may be accessed

   a) only by methods of the class.
   b) only by methods of the class or friends of the class.
   c) only by methods of the class, subclasses of the class, or friends of the class.
   d) by any code.

4. Members of a class that are declared protected may be accessed

   a) only by methods of the class.
   b) only by methods of the class or friends of the class.
   c) only by methods of the class, subclasses of the class, or friends of the class.
   d) by any code.

5. Members of a class that are declared public may be accessed

    a) only by methods of the class.
    b) only by methods of the class or friends of the class.
    c) only by methods of the class, subclass, or friends of the class.
    d) by any code.

6. Methods that are declared `const`

    a) declare constants within the method.
    b) cannot modify any of the instance variables.
    c) must have parameters that are all `const`.
    d) must return a constant.

7. If you are examining a C++ class that someone else wrote, how do you determine if a variable is a local variable or an instance variable?

    a) The same variable name is used in more than one method.
    b) The variable is used in the constructor.
    c) Instance variables are always preceded by an underscore.
    d) Instance variables are declared within the class definition, not in one of the methods.

8. How can C++ operators be written?

    a) They can only be written as members of a class.
    b) They can only be written as functions.
    c) They can be written as either members of a class or functions.
    d) Some can only be written as functions while many can be written as functions or methods.

9. Where are C++ class variables accessible?

    a) Their access depends on whether they are declared private, protected, or public.
    b) They are accessible only by the methods in the class.
    c) They are accessible only by class methods.
    d) They are accessible anywhere.

10. C++ class variables are declared by

    a) using the keyword `class` before the variable type.
    b) using the keyword `static` before the variable type.
    c) putting them in the header file, but after the ending brace for the class.
    d) declaring them inside the constructor.

Short-Answer Questions

1. What is a common convention used to indicate instance variables so they are not confused with local variables in a method, since C++ does not require syntax similar to the use of `self` in Python?

2. What does the `const` specification for a method mean?

3. What can go wrong if you write a method in a header file but do not specify it as an `inline` method.

4. What is the exact output of the following program:

```cpp
#include <iostream>
#include <fstream>
#include <string>

using namespace std;

int main()
{
  ifstream ifs;
  string first, last, name1, name2, name3;

  ifs.open("getline.txt");
  ifs >> first >> last;
  getline(ifs, name1);
  getline(ifs, name2);
  getline(ifs, name3);

  cout << first << " " << last << endl;
  cout << name1 << endl;
  cout << name2 << endl;
  cout << name3 << endl;
}
```

if the input file `getline.txt` contains the following:

```
Dave Reed
John Zelle
Jane Doe
John Doe
```

5. What operators must be written as functions and cannot be written as members of a class and why is this?

6. Why can class methods not access instance variables of the class?

7. What is the difference between a class variable and an instance variable?

Programming Exercises

1. Write a class to represent a deck of playing cards and use the class to play a game of blackjack. You may also want to use another class to represent the blackjack game.

2. Write the Markov gibberish generator from Chapter 3 using a C++ class. Extend it to allow the size of prefix to be determined when the model is created. The constructor will take a parameter specifying the length of the prefix.

3. Add four basic mathematical operators +, -, *, and /, the six comparison operators <, <=, >, >=, ==, and !=, and the input and output operators to the Rational class. Write the mathematical and comparison operators as methods. Store the numerator and denominator in reduced form.

4. Add the operators listed in the previous exercise to the Rational class as functions.

5. Write a LongInt class that stores numbers as an array of single digits (i.e., each entry in the array is a number between 0 and 9). Your class should support numbers up to 100 digits. Using operator overloading have your class support addition, subtraction, and multiplication. Write a set method that allows you to pass a string of digits and sets the number based on the string. Each char element in the string can be treated as a number between 0 and 127; subtracting 48, which is the ASCII value for 0, will allow you to convert the char to a number between 0 and 9. Also, provide a method for outputting the number. Write a program that tests your LongInt class.

6. Write a class to represent a polynomial. The class should store an array of the coefficients and the degree of the polynomial. You may assume a maximum degree of 100 for the polynomial. Write the methods for the addition, subtraction, and multiplication operators and write the input and output operators for the class. Also provide a method for evaluating the polynomial at a specific value. Write a program that tests your Polynomial class.

7. Write a class to represent a Set. Include the methods addElement, removeElement, removeAll, union, intersect, and isSubset.

Chapter 10

C++ Dynamic Memory

Objectives

- To understand the similarities and differences between C++ pointers and Python references.

- To learn how to use the C++ operators that access memory addresses and dereference pointers.

- To understand how to dynamically allocate and deallocate memory in C++.

- To learn how to write classes in C++ that allocate and deallocate dynamic memory.

$\boxed{10.1}$ Introduction

As we briefly discussed in earlier chapters, the internal mechanisms that Python and C++ use for storing data in variables and names are different. In this chapter we will discuss these differences in detail. C++'s default mechanism for storing variables is different than Python's, but C++ does support pointer variables that are similar to Python references. C++ programmers can choose which mechanism to use depending on the efficiency and capabilities they need. C++ pointers give us the flexibility to delay memory allocation decisions until run-time. This makes it possible to change the size of arrays at run-time and create linked structures in C++. Using C++ pointers does require much more care than using Python references; it is easy to make mistakes with pointers and create a program that gives unexpected results or crashes. This chapter and the next chapter will cover the use of dynamic memory and pointers. We will begin by reviewing the basic memory models of Python and C++.

Python names are a reference to a memory location where the actual data is stored along with type information and a reference count; different names can refer to the same data object and assignment statements make the name refer to a different data object. C++ associates (binds) a memory location with each variable and the same memory location is used for that variable throughout the lifetime of the variable. Each assignment statement causes different data to be stored in the memory location bound to the variable. Here is a C++ example:

```
// memory.cpp
#include <iostream>
using namespace std;

int main()
{
  int x, y, z;
  x = 3;
  y = 4;
  z = x;
  x = y;
  cout << x << " " << y << " " << z << endl;
  return 0;
}
```

The following table shows a representation of memory while this program is executing. When the **main** function begins execution, four bytes are allocated for each of the three integers. We have started our table at the memory location 1000, but the specific memory address used is not important and can vary each time the program is run. The key point to notice is that the memory location used for each variable does not change; the data stored at the memory location does change as different values are assigned to the variable. As you would expect, the program outputs 4 4 3.

Memory address	Variable name	Data value
1000	x	3 then 4
1004	y	4
1008	z	3

The Python version of this program is the following:

```
# memory.py
x = 3
y = 4
z = x
x = y
print x, y, z
```

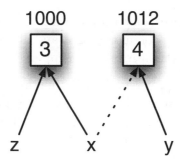

Figure 10.1: Picture of Python memory references

The end result of executing comparable code for C++ variables and Python references to immutable types is the same even though the internal representations are different. The Python program also outputs 4 4 3. Figure 10.1 shows a pictorial representation of the memory for this Python code. The key point to notice here is that there is one copy of the 3 object and one copy of the 4 object at fixed memory locations; the names refer to these objects and as the code executes, the memory location that x refers to changes from 1000 to 1012. At the end, we have multiple names referring to the same memory location. We have not shown the reference count and type information for the object, but each Python integer object requires 12 bytes on 32-bit systems.

The important differences between Python and C++ are

- Each C++ variable corresponds to a fixed memory location where data is stored; each time a value is assigned to that variable, the same memory location is used to store the data.

- A Python name refers to an object in memory. Python objects must also store information about their type and a reference count, so storing data in Python requires more space than storing the same data in C++.

- Assigning a Python name to an object changes the reference so that it refers to a different object (i.e., the memory address the name refers to changes).

- It is possible to have multiple names refer to the same object in Python. Modifying a mutable object via one name affects the other name. In C++, each variable gets its own fixed address so changing one variable does not affect other variables.

- C++ does support references, but they are not commonly used. C++ also supports pointers, which are commonly used and allow us to perform similar types of operations that Python references support.

The differences between using references in Python and storing the actual data in variables in C++ become apparent when you modify a mutable type instead of assigning a variable to a new or different object. We will use our `Rational` class presented in earlier chapters to demonstrate this. The corresponding Python and C++ code fragments we will examine are

```
# Python code
r1 = Rational()
r1.set(2, 3)
r2 = r1
r1.set(1, 3)
print r1
print r2
// C++ code
Rational r1, r2;
r1.set(2, 3);
r2 = r1;
r1.set(1, 3);
cout << r1 << endl;
cout << r2 << endl;
```

These assume we have defined the appropriate methods for our classes. The `set` method in Python and C++ is

```
# Python code
    def set(self, num, den):
        self.num = num
        self.den = den
// C++ code
void Rational::set(int n, int d)
{
  num_ = n;
  den_ = d;
}
```

In Python, both `r1` and `r2` refer to the same object that we will assume is stored at memory location 1000, as the following table shows. Additional memory is required in Python to store information about the data type for the object and the reference count for the object, but we will not include that here. Since we are creating a `Rational` object that has the instance variables `num` and `den`, we have named the variable name column based on the instance variable names of the `Rational` object.

Memory address	Variable name	Data value
1000	`.num`	reference to 2, then 1
1004	`.den`	reference to 3

If you recall our discussions from section 4.2, you will understand that the sample Python code will change the one `Rational` object to which both names refer.

The corresponding C++ declaration of `r1` and `r2` results in two `Rational` objects being created, requiring a total of 16 bytes of memory being allocated as the following table shows. Each `Rational` object requires eight bytes since it has two `int` instance variables that each require four bytes. No additional memory is needed in C++ since the C++ run-time environment does not need to keep track of the data type or the reference count.

Memory address	Variable name	Data value
1000	`r1.num`	?
1004	`r1.den`	?
1008	`r2.num`	?
1012	`r2.den`	?

After the statement `r1.set(2, 3)`, the memory now holds

Memory address	Variable name	Data value
1000	`r1.num`	2
1004	`r1.den`	3
1008	`r2.num`	?
1012	`r2.den`	?

Unless we have defined our own `operator=` (we will discuss this in subsection 10.4.3) for the C++ `Rational` class, the execution of `r2 = r1` effectively causes the two statements `r2.num = r1.num` and `r2.den = r1.den` to be executed. We cannot explicitly write those two statements ourselves since the instance variables are private, but the compiler generates the code that performs those two assignments. This causes the data stored at memory location 1000 to be copied to memory location 1008 and the data stored at memory location 1004 to be copied to memory location 1012. The following table shows the memory representation after the assignment statement.

Memory address	Variable name	Data value
1000	r1.num	2
1004	r1.den	3
1008	r2.num	2
1012	r2.den	3

After the statement `r1.set(1, 3)`, the memory now holds

Memory address	Variable name	Data value
1000	r1.num	1
1004	r1.den	3
1008	r2.num	2
1012	r2.den	3

Unlike in the Python version, `r1` and `r2` now hold different values so the output for `r1` is 1/3 and the output for `r2` is 2/3. If we had instead executed the statement `r2.set(1, 3)`, the output for `r1` would be 2/3 and the output for `r2` would be 1/3. The difference between Python and C++ is that each declared C++ variable gets its own memory location to store the instance variables and assigning one variable to another copies the data, but assigning one Python name to another results in both names referring to the same object.

These different mechanisms for managing memory have trade-offs. Python's mechanism allows dynamic typing and supports linked structures. However, overall Python uses more memory since we have to store the identifier name in a dictionary, the references, and the actual data with type information and a reference count. It also requires two memory accesses to get the data for a given Python name. C++'s mechanism uses less memory, and is almost always faster. One case where Python is faster is assignment of two names that are a class with a large amount of data. C++ effectively gives a deep copy while Python makes a reference to the same data. So assignment is faster in Python for class objects, but is not performing an equivalent operation. This is the reason variables that are instances of a class are typically passed by reference in C++ even when we do not want to change the data for the variable. As we discussed, the `const` designation is used when we do not want to change the data so the compiler will make certain our code does not change it. Computer scientists use the term *reference semantics* to describe how Python's assignment statement works, since it creates another reference, and use the term *value semantics* to describe how C++'s assignment statement works, since it copies the value of the variable.

Python's memory management mechanism is known as *implicit heap dynamic*. The Python interpreter automatically allocates and deallocates memory as needed. A section of memory known as a *dynamic memory heap* (sometimes referred to simply as a *heap*) is used for these allocations and deallocations. The default C++ memory management mechanism is known as *stack dynamic*. When a function is called, the amount of space needed for the variables is allocated on a stack. Since in most cases we can determine at compile time how much memory is needed for all the local variables, one machine language instruction can be used to allocate the space on the stack. When the function ends, the stack shrinks back to the space it was before the function call, effectively deallocating the memory for the local variables.

One drawback of the stack dynamic technique is that it does not directly support linked structures. Another issue is that we cannot change the amount of memory allocated for a variable after its first allocation. In most cases, the exact amount of memory that is allocated for a variable is determined at compile time; the one exception we saw was the variable length arrays discussed in section 8.11. In this case, the amount of memory to be allocated is not determined at compile time, but once it is allocated, we cannot make the array larger using the same variable. This makes it impossible to make a stack-dynamic-based data structure similar to Python's built-in list that can grow in size as needed.

As you might have figured out by now, C++ must support another mechanism for allocating memory for variables since the Python interpreter is written in C. C++'s other technique is known as *explicit heap dynamic*. Like Python, a section of memory known as the *dynamic memory heap* (or just *heap*) is used for these allocations and deallocations. However, as the term explicit heap dynamic implies, in C++ your program code must include instructions that directly allocate and deallocate the memory. C++ uses pointer variables to support this dynamic memory allocation and deallocation. With C++ pointers we can write code that allows us to determine and change the amount of memory allocated at run-time (rather than setting the amount at compile time). We can write data structures that can grow in size as needed and write linked structures using C++ pointers. This chapter will discuss how to use C++ pointers, how they are similar to Python references, and how to write C++ classes that use dynamic memory. We will learn how to write linked structures in C++ in Chapter 11.

10.2   C++ Pointers

In C++, a pointer variable stores a memory address. C++ requires that a pointer be defined with a specific type. The type indicates how the data at the memory address should be interpreted. Remember that internally, the computer's memory stores 1s and 0s and the type of a C++ variable tells the compiler how the code it generates should interpret those bits. Since pointer variables store an address, all pointer variables require the same amount of space (four bytes on 32-bit systems). This should remind you of Python references. A C++ pointer is a concept similar to a Python reference. The difference is that with a C++ pointer, you have access to both the address and the data that the pointer points to (i.e., the data at that address), while a Python reference gives you access only to the data that the reference points to.

C++ pointers are declared using the asterisk (*) as a prefix to the variable name. This indicates the variable will hold the address of a memory location where a data value of the specified type is stored. A common mistake is to forget the asterisk before each variable name when you want to declare multiple pointers in one definition statement. In the following example, b and c are declared as pointers to an int and d is declared as an int. The second line is also legal, although we recommend you do not use this style. Placing the asterisk immediately after the word int makes it appear that all variables in that statement are to be pointers to an int, but only e is a pointer and f is an int. This example allocates 20 bytes since both int types and pointer types require four bytes.

```
int *b, *c, d; // b and c are pointers to an int, d is an int
int* e, f; // only e is a pointer to an int, f is an int
```

The next question you should be asking yourself is how do we store an address in a pointer variable. We have no idea which memory addresses our program is allowed to use so we have to request a valid address. One way is to use the address of an existing variable. The following example demonstrates this and also shows us how to access the data that a pointer variable points to.

```
// p1.cpp
#include <iostream>
using namespace std;
```

```
int main()
{
  int *b, *c, x, y;
  x = 3;
  y = 5;
  b = &x;
  c = &y;
  *b = 4;
  *c = *b + *c;
  cout << x << " " << y << " " << *b << " " << *c << " ";
  c = b;
  *c = 2;
  cout << x << " " << y << " " << *b << " " << *c << endl;
  return 0;
}
```

The unary ampersand operator computes the address of its operand. Thus, the statement b = &x causes the program to store the memory address of x in the memory for the variable b. The following table indicates that the computer used memory addresses 1000 through 1015 to store our variables and shows the value of each variable after the statement c = &y is executed. The computer does not necessarily use the address starting at 1000, but we commonly use that address in our examples in this book.

Memory address	Variable name	Data value
1000	b	1008
1004	c	1012
1008	x	3
1012	y	5

The unary asterisk operator is used to *dereference* a pointer. Dereferencing a pointer means to access the data at the address the pointer holds. The statement *b = 4 causes the program to store the data value 4 at memory address 1008 (since b currently holds 1008). Based on this knowledge, see if you can determine the output of the sample program before reading the next paragraph.

The statement *c = *b + *c determines the integer values at memory address 1008 (the address b points to) and memory address 1012 (the address c points to) and adds the 4 and 5 together. The result, 9, is stored at memory address 1012 (the address that c points to). The statement c = b copies the data value for b, which is the address 1008, to the memory for c (i.e., 1008 is now stored at memory location 1004). You should note that assigning pointer variables is essentially the same as assigning two names in Python; both b and c now refer to the same data. Based on the information in the preceding paragraphs, you should be able to determine that the output of the program is 4 9 4 9 2 9 2 2. After the statement *c = 2, the memory representation is

Memory address	Variable name	Data value
1000	b	1008
1004	c	1008
1008	x	2
1012	y	9

You may have already realized this, but another important concept to understand is that a pointer to an int and an int are not the same type. Using the variable declarations in the previous example, the statements b = x and x = b are not legal. The variable b is a pointer so it must be assigned an address whereas x is an int so it must be assigned an integer. This is more obvious if we declare the pointer variables with another type such as double since on 32-bit systems they do not use the same amount of storage. No matter what the type, a pointer to that type and the actual type are not compatible data types.

We will now write a more practical example demonstrating the address and dereferencing operators. The C programming language does not support pass by reference as C++ does, so the only way to effectively change the actual parameters using the C language is to use pointers. The necessary technique is to pass the address of the actual parameter and then have the function or method dereference the pointer so it changes the value at the address corresponding to the formal parameter. You can do this in C++ also, but programmers typically use pass by reference to accomplish this. The following example shows a **swap** function that swaps two integer variables.

```
// swap.cpp
#include <iostream>
using namespace std;

void swap(int *b, int *c)
{
  int temp = *b;
  *b = *c;
  *c = temp;
}
```

```
int main()
{
  int x = 3, y = 5;
  swap(&x, &y);
  cout << x << " " << y << endl;
  return 0;
}
```

The formal parameters b and c are given the values of the addresses of x and y respectively. Thus, the assignment statement *b = *c is equivalent to writing x = y in the main function. You should note the similarity between this and pass by reference. What happens if we add the line b = &temp to the end of the swap function; does it change x? The statement would have no effect on x. The variable b changes to hold the address of temp, but this does not change x or the value at the memory address corresponding to x.

In our examples so far, we used the unary ampersand operator to assign a valid address to a pointer variable. The other way to set a pointer to a valid address is the new statement. The C++ new statement is used to allocate dynamic memory from the heap and it returns the starting address of the memory that was allocated. When you use the new statement, you must indicate the data type for the object that you want to allocate; the specified data type is used to determine how much memory to allocate. When you explicitly allocate memory in C++, you must also deallocate the memory when it is no longer needed. The delete statement is used to deallocate memory that was dynamically allocated. The following example shows the explicit heap dynamic version of our Python and C++ program written in section 10.1.

```
// p2.cpp
#include <iostream>
using namespace std;

int main()
{
  int *x, *y, *z;
  x = new int;
  *x = 3;
  y = new int;
  *y = 4;
  z = x;
  x = y;
  cout << *x << " " << *y << " " << *z << endl;
  delete z;
  delete y;
  return 0;
}
```

The pointer variables x, y, and z are stack dynamic variables and the 12 bytes required for them are automatically allocated when the function begins and deallocated when the function ends. In the following table, we have used the memory locations 1000–1011 for them. The **new** statement allocates memory from the dynamic memory heap that we have started at memory location 2000. Notice that we have two **new** statements so we must have two **delete** statements. We did not use the same variable names with the **new** and **delete** statements, but the memory allocated by the x = **new int** statement is deallocated by the **delete** z statement since z holds the address that was allocated by that **new** statement. The **delete** y statement deallocates the memory allocated by the y = **new int** statement. We could have used **delete** x instead of **delete** y since the statement x = y causes both x and y to hold the same address. The key point to remember is that each **new** statement that is executed must eventually have a corresponding **delete** statement that is executed to deallocate the memory that the **new** statement allocated. If you forget a **delete** statement, your program will have a *memory leak*. Even though a program with a memory leak may not crash, the code is not considered correct.

Memory address	Variable name	Data value
1000	x	2000 then 2004
1004	y	2004
1008	z	2000
2000		3
2004		4

Normally you would write this program as we did in section 10.1 since that is more efficient. This pointer version requires more memory, and dereferencing a pointer requires the computer to access two memory locations (**cout** « ***x** requires accessing memory location 1000 followed by memory location 2004). The C++ version in this section is similar to the Python version as far as how the memory is allocated. Compare the table for this version to the memory picture in Figure 10.1. This demonstrates how Python references and C++ pointers are essentially the same concept with different syntaxes.

Since Python only uses references, it does not need the extra syntax that C++ pointers do for dereferencing a pointer. When you assign one C++ pointer variable to another, the result is they both point to the same object or value. Using pointers, we can implement the same **Rational** example we did earlier in the chapter so that the C++ version allocates memory similarly to the Python version.

One issue when using pointers to access members of a class instance is that the dot operator (the period) has a higher precedence than the asterisk (the unary *) for dereferencing a pointer. This means that if we have a `Rational` instance `r`, we cannot write `*r1.set(2, 3)`; we need to write `(*r1).set(2, 3)`. C++ provides an additional operator so we can deference a pointer and access a member without the parentheses; the notation for this is `->` (the minus sign followed by a greater-than sign) so `(*r1).set(2, 3)` can be written as `r1->set(2, 3)`. The form using `->` is more commonly used than the parentheses version.

The C++ code using C++ pointers that corresponds to the same Python `Rational` example earlier in the chapter is the following

```
Rational *r1, *r2; // constructors not called

r1 = new Rational; // constructor is called
r1->set(2, 3);
r2 = r1;
r1->set(1, 3);

cout << *r1 << endl;
cout << *r2 << endl;
delete r1;
```

This example outputs 1/3 for `r1` and 1/3 for `r2` since `r1` and `r2` are pointers to the same memory locations. The memory table for this code fragment is:

Memory address	Variable name	Data value
1000	r1	? then 2000
1004	r2	? then 2000
2000		2 then 1
2004		3

The declarations of `r1` and `r2` result in four bytes being allocated for each one since pointers require four bytes. The `Rational` constructor is not called when you declare a pointer since we are creating a pointer, not a `Rational` object. The statement `r1 = new Rational` results in eight bytes being allocated since the two integer instance variables `num_` and `den_` require a total of eight bytes. The `r1 = new Rational` statement also causes 2000 to be stored in the memory location for variable `r1`. The constructor is called by `r1 = new Rational` since it creates a `Rational` object. The `r1->set(2, 3)` statement results in 2 being stored at memory location 2000 and 3 being stored at memory location 2004.

The statement `r2 = r1` results in 2000 being stored in memory location 1004 since the value of `r1` is 2000. We now effectively have the same memory structure as our Python example with both `r1` and `r2` referring to the same `Rational` object. When we execute `r1->set(1, 2)` statement we are not changing `r1` but are changing the object stored at the memory location that `r1` points to. Since `r2` points to the same object as `r1` we get the same results as we do in Python. When the function containing our C++ code fragment ends, the memory locations for the declared variables (1000–1007) is automatically deallocated as we discussed earlier, but we need the `delete r1` statement to deallocate the memory at locations 2000–2007 which we explicitly allocated with the `new Rational` statement. We could have written `delete r2` instead since both pointers refer to the same locations, but we cannot write `delete r1; delete r2` since each `new` statement must have one and only one corresponding `delete` statement. Trying to delete the same memory locations a second time may corrupt the dynamic memory heap, resulting in a crash.

Using pointers with dynamic memory in C++ gives you the flexibility of Python references, but because you are in charge of explicitly handling the allocation and deallocation, it is much more difficult to get correct than Python versions of the same code. If you are not careful when using dynamic memory, your program can produce different results each time you run it or may crash. We will discuss these issues for explicit heap dynamic memory throughout this chapter.

10.3 Dynamic Arrays

The built-in array data structure with a fixed size was discussed in section 8.11. In many cases, we do not know the size of the array at compile time or we want to change the size of the array as the program is running, so we need a mechanism for allocating an array of a specified size at run-time. As we saw in the previous section, C++ pointers can be used to *dynamically allocate* memory. This means that the memory is allocated as the program is running and the amount of memory allocated may be determined at run-time instead of being set at compile time. The following code fragment demonstrates dynamic memory allocation and deallocation for arrays:

```
int i, n;
double *d;

cout << "Enter array size: ";
cin >> n;
```

```
d = new double[n];
for (i=0; i<n; ++i) {
  cout << "Enter number " << i << ": "
  cin >> d[i];
}
delete [] d;
```

The example allows the user to specify the array size at run-time. The **new** command allocates the specified amount of memory and returns the starting address of the allocated memory. When the brackets (**[]**) are used after the data type in the **new** statement, the amount of memory necessary to store the number of items specified inside the brackets is allocated and the starting address is returned. In this case, n*8 consecutive bytes would be allocated on machines that use eight bytes to store a double value. The expression inside the brackets indicates how many values of the type double to allocate; an array of size **n** was allocated so the valid index values are 0 through n-1. After the dynamic memory has been allocated, it can be accessed using the array bracket notation. The same index array calculations discussed in section 8.11 can be used since the pointer variable holds the starting address of a contiguous section of memory.

Whenever you allocate memory dynamically, you must also deallocate the memory with a statement that executes later in your program. Since we allocated an array, we must tell the **delete** statement to deallocate an array instead of the memory that holds a single value. The square brackets are used with both the **new** statement and the **delete** statement when allocating and deallocating arrays. You do not indicate the size of the array when deallocating a dynamic array; the C++ run-time environment knows how much memory to deallocate. Repeatedly allocating memory and forgetting to deallocate memory in a C++ program will eventually result in your program using up a large percentage of the computer's memory, causing the computer to slow as it uses the hard disk for extra memory. This is why it is important to deallocate memory when it is no longer needed.

The main reason for using dynamic arrays is that you do not need to know the size of the array at compile time. In many cases, you still may not know the size needed when the array is first allocated. The Python built-in list allows you to append as many items as you want so there is no need to determine how much memory to allocate the first time you allocate memory; it would be impossible to anticipate how much memory to allocate ahead of time since different uses of the list will require different sizes. Once the array fills up, we may need to make the array larger. Because the memory immediately following the dynamic array may already be in use (remember that array elements must be in consecutive memory locations), we cannot make the array larger. The solution is to allocate a new larger array, copy the values from the original array to the new array, and then delete the original array. The following code fragment demonstrates this:

```cpp
int *data, *temp;
int i;

// create original array
data = new int[5];
for (i=0; i<5; ++i) {
  data[i] = i;
}
// create new larger array
temp = new int[10];
// copy from original array to larger array
for (i=0; i<5; ++i) {
  temp[i] = data[i];
}
// deallocate original array
delete [] data;
// make data point to new larger array
data = temp;
// now we can access positions 0-9
for (i=5; i<10; ++i) {
  data[i] = i;
}
// deallocate last allocation
delete [] data;
```

The memory table for this code after the first **new** statement and **for** loop are executed is below. We will assume the memory addresses used for the local variables start at memory location 1000 and that the dynamically allocated memory is the block of memory from 2000 through 2019 (four bytes for each of the five integers).

Memory address	Variable name	Data value
1000	data	? then 2000
1004	temp	?
1008	i	5
2000		0
2004		1
2008		2
2012		3
2016		4

After the memory is allocated for the `temp` pointer, the values are copied from the original array, and the values 5 through 9 are stored in the larger array, the memory table is the following assuming the memory starting at location 3000 is used for the `temp` pointer.

Memory address	Variable name	Data value
1000	data	2000
1004	temp	3000
1008	i	10
2000		0
2004		1
2008		2
2012		3
2016		4
3000		0
3004		1
3008		2
3012		3
3016		4
3020		5
3024		6
3028		7
3032		8
3036		9

After the first `delete [] data` statement, the memory at locations 2000–2019 is deallocated and returned to the dynamic memory heap so it can be used again. The statement `data = temp` stores 3000 at memory location 1000 (i.e., `data` now points to the second larger allocated array). At this point, both `data` and `temp` point to the same dynamically allocated array. This is the same concept as having two references to the same data in Python. After that assignment statement, the next loop fills in the values 5 through 9 in memory locations 3020 through 3039. The final `delete [] data` statement then deallocates the memory locations 3000–3039 so they can be used again.

Figure 10.2 shows a pictorial representation of this. The top part of the figure shows the representation after we have created the new larger array and copied the values from the first array. The middle part of the figure shows the state after the first `delete data` statement. The bottom part of the figure shows the state just before the final `delete [] data` statement.

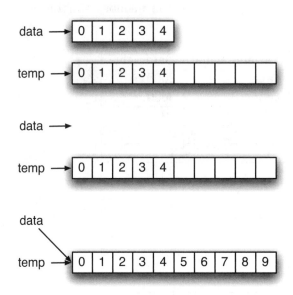

Figure 10.2: Pictorial representation of resizing a dynamic array

If we then fill up this new array and need a larger array, we allocate a larger array, copy the values from the previously allocated array, and then delete the previous array. Each resizing operation results in the previous array being deleted so that we do not have a memory leak if we perform this resizing operation multiple times. In our example, `data` points to the last array that was allocated (once we execute the `data = temp` statement). This pattern of allocating a new section of dynamic memory using a different pointer variable, copying the values from the old section to the new section, deallocating the old section, and setting the original pointer variable to the new section is a common pattern in C++ dynamic memory, so make certain you fully understand how it works and why the order of the steps is important. In the next section, we will examine this pattern using a class.

10.4 Dynamic Memory Classes

When you write a class that dynamically allocates memory for pointer instance variables, you need to make certain that the memory is properly deallocated. There are three additional C++ methods that dynamic memory classes must use to properly allocate and deallocate memory. These three methods are the destructor, copy constructor, and assignment operator (`operator=`). If your class does not use dynamic memory, you do not need to write any of these methods. Classes that use dynamic memory must write a destructor that deallocates the memory. The other two methods may be implemented or declared in the `private` section but not implemented. Declaring them in the `private` section but not implementing them prevents them from being called. We will discuss the details of when these methods are called and what they must do in this section. Implementing them correctly will prevent your class from having memory leaks or other memory errors.

10.4.1 Destructor

As discussed in the previous sections, in C++ you must explicitly deallocate any memory that you explicitly allocate with the `new` command. C++ classes have a special method known as a *destructor* that is used for deallocating memory. The destructor method has the same name as the class, with a tilde (~) in front of it. Just as constructors do not have a return type, the destructor also does not have a return type. The purpose of the destructor is to deallocate any dynamic memory the class has allocated that has not yet been deallocated. You never directly call the destructor using the name of the method; it is called automatically when an instance of the class goes out of scope or when you use the `delete` operator on a pointer to an instance of the class. If your class uses dynamic memory and does not have a destructor, your code will in most cases have a memory leak.

We will start with a simple dynamic array class that we will extend throughout this chapter to demonstrate how to correctly write dynamic memory classes. In this first version of the class, we will write all the methods inline in the header file. We have added a few output statements so you can see that the constructor and destructor are called. This `List` class uses three instance variables. The instance variable `data_` is used to hold the starting address of the dynamic array containing the list's values. The `size_` instance variable indicates how many items are currently in the list. The `capacity_` instance variable indicates how large the dynamic array is (i.e., how many items the list can hold before the dynamic array needs to be resized).

```
// List1.h
#ifndef __LIST_H__
#define __LIST_H__

#include <iostream>

class List {

public:
  List(int capacity=10);
  ~List() { delete [] data_; std::cout << "destructor\n";}

private:
  int size_;
  int capacity_;
  int *data_;
};

inline List::List(int capacity)
{
  std::cout << "constructor\n";
  data_ = new int[capacity];
  size_ = 0;
  capacity_ = capacity;
}

#endif __LIST_H__
```

We did not put the **using namespace std** statement in the header file since any file that included the header file would have this statement. Also note that we put the default value for the parameter **size** only in the declaration of the **List** constructor and not in the implementation of the constructor. Here is a simple program that uses our class:

```
// test_List1.cpp
#include <iostream>
using namespace std;

#include "List1.h"

int main()
{
  List b;
  return 0;
}
```

When this program is compiled and executed, it outputs

```
constructor
destructor
```

The declaration `List b` causes the constructor to be called and it allocates dynamic memory. At the end of the `main` function, the variable `b` goes out of scope so the destructor method is automatically called and it deallocates the dynamic memory. This is why the program outputs the two lines. The following program also causes the same output.

```cpp
// test_Listp.cpp
#include <iostream>
using namespace std;

#include "List1.h"

int main()
{
  List *b; // constructor is not called here

  b = new List(20); // constructor is called here
  delete b; // destructor is called here
}
```

The comments indicate when the constructor and destructor are called. Remember the declaration `List *b` causes four bytes that can store an address to be allocated. The `new` statement causes a `List` object to be created by calling the constructor with the specified size. The `delete` statement causes the `List`'s destructor to be called and the dynamic memory the constructor allocated is deallocated. When the variable `b` goes out of scope at the end of the `main` function, the four bytes for the pointer are automatically deallocated just as the memory for any variables are when they go out of scope. This is the reason you only need to write a destructor when your class allocates dynamic memory.

10.4.2 Copy Constructor

As the name implies, the purpose of a *copy constructor* is to create a new object by copying an existing object. In C++, the copy constructor for a class is called when you pass an instance of a class by value to a function or method. Remember that pass by value requires that a separate copy of the actual parameter be created. You can also call a copy constructor directly when declaring a variable as we will demonstrate later in this section.

Unless you write a copy constructor for a class, the C++ compiler generates a default copy constructor for you. The default copy constructor it creates effectively assigns each instance variable of the existing object to the corresponding instance variable in the newly created object. For a class that does not use dynamic memory and pointers, this is exactly what you want. Consider our `Rational` class we have been discussing. To create an exact copy of a `Rational` object, we want to assign its numerator and denominator instance variables and this is exactly what the default copy constructor does.

For classes that use dynamic memory, the default copy constructor will create a shallow copy of the dynamically allocated data; the pointer variable in both instances will refer to the same section of dynamically allocated memory. This will cause problems. When the destructor for one of the objects is called, it will deallocate the dynamic memory that is shared by both objects. The other object can no longer legally access that data and when the destructor is called for it, it will attempt to deallocate the same memory a second time. The second deallocation is illegal and will lead to memory corruption errors that can cause your program to give incorrect results or crash. As we discussed earlier, each memory section that is dynamically allocated must be deallocated exactly once.

We will continue extending our dynamic array example by adding the copy constructor to it. Since it is a constructor, it has the same name as the class and since it is to copy an instance of the class, we must pass that instance as a parameter. Remember that the copy constructor is called when we pass an instance of the class by value. If the copy constructor parameter was passed by value, it would need to call itself to make a copy, leading to an infinite number of calls. The copy constructor parameter must be passed by reference to avoid this. Remember that to pass an object by reference, all that needs to be done is pass the address of the object. We showed the equivalence of this with the **swap** function we wrote in section 10.2. Here is the updated header file for the dynamic array class with a copy constructor added.

```
// List2.h
#ifndef __LIST_H__
#define __LIST_H__

#include <iostream>

class List {

public:
  List(int capacity=10);
  List(const List &source);
  ~List() { delete [] data_; std::cout << "destructor\n";}
```

```
private:
  int size_;
  int capacity_;
  int *data_;
};

inline List::List(int capacity)
{
  std::cout << "constructor\n";
  data_ = new int[capacity];
  size_ = 0;
  capacity_ = capacity;
}

inline List::List(const List &source)
{
  int i;

  std::cout << "copy constructor\n";
  size_ = source.size_;
  capacity_ = source.capacity_;
  data_ = new int[capacity_];
  for (i=0; i<size_; ++i) {
    data_[i] = source.data_[i];
  }
}

#endif __LIST_H__
```

As the code shows, the copy constructor parameter is passed by reference and with the const designation so that the method does not need to call itself and does not change the existing data. You can use any name you want for the formal parameter, but one common convention is to name it source to indicate this is the source instance of the class that you are copying. When we refer to size_, that is the instance variable for the new object we are creating. When we refer to source.size_, that is referring to the instance variable of the object we are copying. You may be surprised that we can refer to the other object's instance variables using the code such as size_ = source.size_ since the instance variables are private; however, we are writing a method of the class so it is allowed to access the private data of any instance of the class, not just the instance with which it is called.

For the instance variables that are not pointers, we want to assign each one of them so the newly created object has the same values for the size and capacity. We then need to allocate a new array with the same capacity and copy the elements from the source object's array into it. This will create a deep copy. Notice that we only copied up to the value of `size_` since the values past that are not relevant to the object. At this point we do not have any way of putting elements in our simplified class to cause `size_` to be more than zero, but our final version will. The following example using this class allows us to see when the copy constructor is called.

```cpp
// test_List2.cpp
#include <iostream>
using namespace std;
#include "List2.h"

void f(List c)
{
  cout << "start f\n";
  cout << "end f\n";
}

void g(List &d)
{
  cout << "start g\n";
  cout << "end g\n";
}

int main()
{
  List b;
  f(b);
  g(b);

  List e(b);
  return 0;
}
```

The output of the program is the following. The comments in parentheses are obviously not part of the output, but explain what caused each of the methods to be called.

```
constructor (create b in main function)
copy constructor (create the copy c from b in f function)
start f
end f
destructor (destructor for c when function f completes)
start g
end g
copy constructor (create e in main function)
destructor (destructor for e or b)
destructor (destructor for e or b)
```

The first issue to note is the implicit call of the copy constructor when the function f is called. The copy constructor executes before the function begins execution to make a copy of the parameter. After the function completes, the destructor is automatically called to deallocate the memory dynamically allocated by the copy constructor. Since the function g passes the parameter by reference, the copy constructor is not called. Also, the destructor is not called for d when the function g completes; if it were, we would be deallocating the dynamic memory for the variable b in the main function. The statement List e(b) explicitly causes the copy constructor to be called to create e from the existing object b. When the main function completes, both e and b are destructed to deallocate their dynamic memory. You should not rely on the order that the destructor is called for e and b. All you need to care about is that both objects will be properly destructed when the main function completes. As this example demonstrates, if you correctly write each method, the rules for when the constructor, copy constructor, and destructor are called will correctly allocate and deallocate memory.

As we mentioned earlier, you can declare the copy constructor private and not implement it. This prevents code that uses your class from causing the copy constructor to be called; the code would not be able to pass an instance of your class by value to a function or method or explicitly call the copy constructor. Code that attempts to perform either of those actions will generate a compiler error. If your class uses a large amount of memory, you may want to do this to prevent a user of your class from making a copy of it. The following header file demonstrates this.

```
// List3.h
#ifndef __LIST_H__
#define __LIST_H__

#include <iostream>

class List {
public:
  List(int capacity=10);
  ~List() { delete [] data_; std::cout << "destructor\n";}
private:
  List(const List &source);
  int size_;
  int capacity_;
  int *data_;
};
```

```
inline List::List(int capacity)
{
  std::cout << "constructor\n";
  data_ = new int[capacity];
  size_ = 0;
  capacity_ = capacity;
}

#endif __LIST_H__
```

10.4.3   Assignment Operator

The other method you must write or declare private when using dynamic memory is the `operator=` method. This method is called when you assign an instance of your class to another instance of the class (e.g., `b = c`). This is a very similar operation to the copy constructor except that the instance on the left-hand side (`b` in the example) already exists so it already has dynamic memory allocated for it. When the copy constructor is called, the object has not yet been allocated, but for the assignment operator, the constructor was previously called with the object so it likely has dynamic memory already allocated for it.

Similarly to the copy constructor, the compiler will write a default assignment operator for your class if you do not write one. It will do what you expect and assign each instance variable individually. If your class does not use dynamic memory, this is exactly what you want. For the same reasons discussed for the copy constructor, you do not want this for classes that use dynamic memory; it will result in two instances of the object sharing the same dynamically allocated memory. The following header file demonstrates the three methods you need to write. We have written these examples with inline methods in the header file to keep the examples shorter, but we could have written them with a separate implementation file. We have removed the output statements now that we know when each method is called.

```
// List4.h
#ifndef __LIST_H__
#define __LIST_H__

class List {

public:
  List(int capacity=10);
  List(const List &source);
  ~List() { delete [] data_; }
  void operator=(const List &source);
```

```
private:
  int size_;
  int capacity_;
  int *data_;
};

inline List::List(int capacity)
{
  data_ = new int[capacity];
  size_ = 0;
  capacity_ = capacity;
}

inline List::List(const List &source)
{
  int i;

  size_ = source.size_;
  capacity_ = source.capacity_;
  data_ = new int[capacity_];
  for (i=0; i<size_; ++i) {
    data_[i] = source.data_[i];
  }
}

inline void List::operator=(const List &source)
{
  int i;

  if (this != &source) {
    delete [] data_;
    size_ = source.size_;
    capacity_ = source.capacity_;
    data_ = new int[capacity_];
    for (i=0; i<size_; ++i) {
      data_[i] = source.data_[i];
    }
  }
}

#endif __LIST_H__
```

Since the object has already been created, the assignment operator is a little more complicated than the copy constructor. We must properly deallocate memory that has already been allocated and ensure that the class is not accidently assigning the object to itself or we will deallocate the only copy of the data. In C++ classes, the identifier this is an implicit pointer to the object with which the method is explicitly called. For example, if we have two `List` objects `b` and `c` and write `b = c`, this is equivalent to writing `b.operator=(c)`; review section 9.4 if you need a refresher on operator overloading. The assignment operator must be written as a member of the class; it cannot be written as a standalone function as many of the other operators can. For the assignment statement `b = c`, the `this` pointer will hold the address of `b`. The `this` pointer is equivalent to the explicit `self` reference that all Python methods have. We could use the `this` pointer to explicitly refer to all instance variables and methods such as `this->size_` instead of just `size_` if we wanted to, but most C++ programmers do not use this style.

The `if` statement in the method checks if the method on the left-hand side of the assignment statement (`b` in our example) is the object at the same address as the object on the right-hand side of the assignment statement (`c` in our example). If they are the same object, we do not want to do anything. Deleting the dynamic memory would delete the one copy of dynamic memory. You may have noticed that the copy constructor and assignment operator share most of the code; because of this, it is common to write the shared code in a private method that both the copy constructor and assignment operator call. We will demonstrate this in our final version of the dynamic array class later in this section.

You might be wondering how a programmer could end up assigning an object to itself. Certainly, no programmer would write `b = b;` in their code and it would be possible to write a compiler to catch this mistake. You need to remember that since we can use pointers, we can end up with two pointers with different names referring to the same object. The following example is still contrived, but you can imagine a function that would return a pointer to a `List` object and the programmer would not have any idea what other `List` pointer variables also point to it.

```
#include "List3.h"

int main()
{
  List *b, *c, d;
  b = &d;
  c = b;

  *b = *c; // causes operator= to be called
  return 0;
}
```

In the example, both `b` and `c` refer to the `List` object that is the variable `d` so the statement `*b = *c` causes the `List::operator=` method to be called. Notice that the statement `b = c` does not call the `List::operator=` method to be called.

The variables b and c are pointers so this is the assignment of two pointers, causing them both to store the same address.

10.4.4 A Complete Dynamic Array Class

We will now write a realistic version of the List class, adding a few more new concepts to the ones we discussed earlier. Without the use of dynamic memory, we could not write a List class in C++ that could grow beyond the initial size of the array. The following example shows all the methods necessary to correctly implement a realistic use of dynamic memory (a copy constructor, assignment operator, and destructor). In the following example we use the data type size_t, which is a synonym for an unsigned int (i.e., a non-negative integer), for the instance variables and parameters that specify a position in the array since an array cannot have a negative size. There are some potential pitfalls with using an unsigned int that we will discuss later in the section.

```
// List.h
#ifndef _LIST_H_
#define _LIST_H_

#include <cstdlib>
class List {
public:
  List(size_t capacity=10); // constructor - allocates dynamic array
  List(const List &a); // copy constructor
  ~List(); // destructor

  int& operator[](size_t pos); // bracket operator
  List& operator=(const List &a); // assignment operator
  List& operator+=(const List &a); // += operator
  void append(int item);
  size_t size() const { return size_; }
private:
  void copy(const List &a);
  void resize(size_t new_size); // allocate new larger array
  int *data_; // dynamic array
  size_t size_; // size of dynamic array
  size_t capacity_; // capacity of dynamic array
};

inline int& List::operator[](size_t pos)
{
  return data_[pos];
}
#endif // _LIST_H_
```

The bracket operator (`operator[]`) provides the same functionality as the Python `__getitem__` and `__setitem__` methods. It is declared inline after the class definition and demonstrates a reference return type. The ampersand after the type name indicates that a reference to an integer is returned, meaning it effectively returns the address of the position in the array. This allows the operator to be used on the left-hand side of an assignment statement as `b[0] = 5` where `b` is an instance of our `List` class. It can also be used on the right-hand side of an assignment statement or as part of an expression just as a non-reference return type can. Without the reference return type, the operator could only be used on the right-hand side of an assignment statement (corresponding to only the Python `__getitem__` method). Returning a reference only makes sense if it is a reference to an instance variable or dynamically allocated memory. We will discuss this later in the chapter.

The `List` class provides an array of integers whose initial size is specified when the constructor is called. The constructor allocates a dynamic array with the specified capacity and initializes the `size_` instance variable to indicate the list is empty. If we did not allocate the memory in the constructor, but instead deferred it to another method (such as the first time the **append** method is called), we would initialize the pointer variables to `NULL`. The `NULL` constant is defined in the `cstdlib` header file. The value `NULL` is defined to be zero which is never a valid address for memory that has been dynamically allocated. The use of `NULL` in C++ to indicate an invalid pointer is similar to the use of `None` in Python to indicate a reference that is not initialized to an object of a specific type.

The class makes use of a private method named `copy` to implement the code that is needed in both the copy constructor and assignment operator. The assignment operator needs extra code to deallocate the existing dynamic array before allocating a new dynamic array of the appropriate size and copying the data. Remember that a copy constructor is creating a new object, so no memory has been previously allocated for the object when the copy constructor is called. However, the variable on the left-hand side of an assignment statement has already had its constructor called and memory allocated, so that needs to be deallocated. The code for the destructor follows the copy constructor. The destructor simply deallocates the dynamic array and is called automatically when a non-pointer instance of `List` goes out of scope. Note that it does not deallocate the non-pointer instance variables since the memory for those is automatically deallocated. In this example, we are using a separate implementation file unlike the earlier simplified examples in which the entire class was written in the header file.

```
// List.cpp
#include "List.h"

List::List(size_t capacity)
{
  data_ = new int[capacity];
  capacity_ = capacity;
  size_ = 0;
}

List::List(const List &list)
{
  copy(list);
}

List::~List()
{
  delete [] data_;
}
```

We have written the `operator=` method slightly differently so that we can use it in a chained assignment statement. The method returns a reference to a `List` object. By returning `*this`, we are returning the `List` object that we just assigned. This allows us to write the chained form of the assignment statement (e.g., `b = c = d`. Remember that the assignment operator is right to left so it is equivalent to `c = d; b = c`. By returning a reference to the left-hand parameter, the result of `c = d` is the object `c` that we then use as the right-hand parameter when assigning `b`.

The `copy` method that is used by both the `operator=` and the copy constructor allocates an array of the same size as the `List` object that is passed to it and copies all the data from the parameter object's array into the newly allocated array. We have also added the `operator+=` method so we can demonstrate another potential pitfall.

```
void List::copy(const List &list)
{
  size_t i;
  size_ = list.size_;
  capacity_ = list.capacity_;
  data_ = new int[list.capacity_];
  for (i=0; i<list.capacity_; ++i) {
    data_[i] = list.data_[i];
  }
}
```

```
List& List::operator=(const List &list)
{
  if (&list != this) {
    // deallocate existing dynamic array
    delete [] data_;
    // copy the data
    copy(list);
  }
  return *this;
}
List& List::operator+=(const List &list)
{
  size_t i;
  size_t pos = size_;
  if ((size_ + list.size_) > capacity_) {
    resize(size_ + list.size_);
  }

  for (i=0; i<list.size_; ++i) {
    data_[pos++] = list.data_[i];
  }
  size_ += list.size_;
  return *this;
}
```

The `operator+=` appears straightforward, but if you are not careful, subtle errors can be introduced. If we replace the last few lines with the following code so that it increments the `size_` variable as it adds the items onto the array, it will work fine in most cases.

```
// this version is incorrect
for (i=0; i<list.size_; ++i) {
  data_[size_++] = list.data_[i];
}
```

What happens if we have a `List` instance `b` and execute `b += b`? In this case, `size_` and `list.size_` are two names for the same memory location (i.e., they are both bound to the same address). Since we are incrementing `size_` each time through the loop, the `for` loop will never end because `i` will always be less than `list.size_`. These types of subtle errors can be extremely difficult to track down so always consider these special cases when writing your own code and test for them.

The `append` method is straightforward except that we may need to allocate a larger array if we have already filled the existing array. We have written a separate `resize` method that the `append` method calls when necessary to perform the steps of allocating a new larger array, copying the data to it, updating the pointer, and then deallocating the old smaller array, as we discussed in section 10.3.

```cpp
void List::append(int item)
{
  if (size_ == capacity_) {
    resize(2 * capacity_);
  }
  data_[size_++] = item;
}

// should this method have a precondition? see end of chapter exercises
void List::resize(size_t new_size)
{
  int *temp;
  size_t i;

  capacity_ = new_size;
  temp = new int[capacity_];
  for (i=0; i<size_; ++i) {
    temp[i] = data_[i];
  }
  delete [] data_;
  data_ = temp;
}
```

We leave it as an exercise to add the other methods in the built-in Python list's API to this C++ dynamic memory list. As we mentioned earlier, you do need to be careful when using **unsigned int** or the equivalent **size_t** data type. As we listed in Figure 8.4, the range of the **int** type on 32-bit systems is usually from about negative two billion to about positive two billion while the **unsigned int** type ranges from zero to about four billion. With the **unsigned int** data type, there is no bit representation that corresponds to a negative number. So the question is, what happens when an operation would result in a negative number?

```cpp
// unsigned.cpp
#include <iostream>
using namespace std;
int main()
{
  unsigned int x = 0;
  x--;
  cout << x << endl;
  return 0;
}
```

The output of this operation in a program compiled for 32-bit systems is 4294967295. This is the largest possible integer that can be represented with 32 bits (the bit representation is 32 1s). We have *overflowed* the bit representation. This is like going beyond the number of digits in a car odometer. Think about what would happen if you were able to run a car odometer backwards past zero; you would get the largest value the odometer can hold. This is essentially the same thing that happens when you overflow integer values on the computer. C++ does not automatically indicate when overflow occurs. There are ways to detect it, but we will not cover these details in this book. When writing your code, you must ensure that you do not accidently overflow the range of values the data type you are using can store or you will get unexpected or incorrect results. The next code fragment demonstrates an error caused by overflow.

```
unsigned int i;
unsigned int pos=0;
for (i=5; i>=pos; --i) {
  cout << i << endl;
}
```

If you create a program with this loop and run it, you probably expect the loop to execute six times (the expression i >= pos should be true when i is five, four, three, two, one, and zero). The problem is that after setting i to zero, the next value for i will be 4294967295 and that is obviously also greater than or equal to zero so this produces an infinite loop. If pos were any positive value, this would not occur. It is always a good idea to test your code with these boundary conditions to ensure it works in all cases.

10.4.5 Reference Return Types

As we mentioned earlier, you should not return a reference to a local variable. The reason for this is that a reference effectively returns the memory location where the variable is stored, not a value. The problem with this is local variables in a function are automatically deallocated when the function ends. Using formal terminology, the *lifetime* of local variables is the time while the function is being executed. Once the function ends, the memory locations used for local variables are reclaimed and are no longer *bound* to those local variables. You can only return by reference a variable whose lifetime does not end when the function or method ends. The following example shows an example that returns a reference to a local variable and is incorrect; most compilers will generate a warning.

```
// this is incorrect
int& f()
{
  int x;
  return x;
}

int main()
{
  f() = 5;
}
```

In our section on the List class, we discussed that since the operator[] returned a reference, we can write b[0] = 5 where b is an instance of our List class. On the left-hand side of the assignment statement, we are calling the operator and it returns a reference to the memory location. That memory location is then used to store the value 5. In the previous example, the statement f() = 5 is attempting to do the same thing; the memory location for the variable x returned by the function f is being used to store the value 5. The problem is that the memory location is no longer being used for the local variable x after the function ends.

As our List code shows, it is correct to return a reference to an instance variable of a class instance. An object's instance variables have the same lifetime as the instance of the class. The statement b[0] = 5 where b is an instance of our List class is equivalent to b.data_[0] = 5, but this is not allowed since data_ is a private member of the class. The bracket operator is a public method and returns a reference to the private data, allowing us to legally access the private data directly. In many cases this is bad programming style, but for a class that encapsulates a dynamic array, one could argue it makes sense.

A precondition for the operator[] method is that the specified index is between 0 and size_ - 1. To prevent a user of the class from crashing the program by passing an index outside of the list size, we could check that the specified index is between 0 and size_ - 1 before attempting to access that position in the dynamic array. This extra overhead is not necessary if the code that uses the class always meets the precondition. A common technique is to include code that checks the precondition while testing and debugging your program, but once you are convinced your program is correct, you can remove the code that checks the precondition to get a small performance boost.

10.5   Dynamic Memory Errors

Using pointers in C++ gives your programs more flexibility and capabilities, but is also more error prone. Pointers to data objects also require extra memory since you need to store both the pointer and the data while the C++ default stack dynamic variables only need memory to store the data. Dynamic memory errors are the source of a large percentage of errors in most large programs. Because of these reasons, you should use dynamic memory only when you need the extra capabilities it gives you.

Dynamic memory errors are often difficult to track down and correct since sometimes your program may run fine, other times it may run but give incorrect results, and other times it may crash. We suggest you learn how to use the debugger that your programming environment supports to help you track down these memory errors. You can try to find the errors by putting output statements throughout your code, but learning how to use your debugger will save you a lot of time and frustration in the long run. Adding to the difficulty of tracking down these errors is that often the statement that causes the program to crash is not the statement that is incorrect so it is also important to proofread your dynamic memory code. In this section, we will discuss the different types of errors that can occur with dynamic memory.

10.5.1   Memory Leaks

We have already briefly mentioned one type of error known as a *memory leak*. A memory leak occurs when you allocate memory but never deallocate it. If your program repeatedly calls a function or method that leaks memory, your program will eventually require more memory than the computer has. This will lead the operating system to use the disk as extra memory. Since the disk is much slower than memory, your computer will slow down. Fortunately, when a program completes, the operating system reclaims any memory the program was using so a memory leak should not crash your program. If the operating system itself has a memory leak, it will eventually run out of memory. This is the reason some people recommend you reboot your computer occasionally.

The code examples with errors in this section are short examples that you would not normally write, but show the errors that can occur as part of larger sections of code. This first example executes two **new** statements, but executes only one **delete** statement.

```
// this code is incorrect
void f()
{
  int *x;
  x = new int;
  *x = 3;
  x = new int;
  *x = 4;
  delete x;
}
```

Figure 10.3 shows a pictorial representation of the memory leak code. The left part shows the result after the line *x = 3 is executed; four bytes have been dynamically allocated with x holding the address and the value 3 is stored at that address. The middle part of the figure shows the result after the second x = new int statement is executed. We no longer have any way to access the dynamic memory that was originally allocated by the first x = new int statement. The right part of the figure shows the result after the delete x statement is executed; the variable x points to a memory location that can no longer be used and the memory location containing the 3 still exists and cannot be deallocated since we do not have a variable holding its address. This is the memory leak. To fix it, we would need another delete x statement before the second x = new int statement.

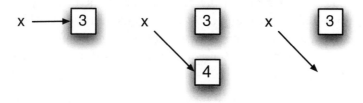

Figure 10.3: Pictorial representation of a memory leak

In many cases, the delete statement that deallocates the memory allocated by a new statement is not in the same function or method. This makes it more difficult to detect memory leaks. If you refer back to the resize method in our List class, you will notice that the delete statement in it is not deallocating the memory that was allocated by the new statement that executed earlier during the function call. The first time the resize method is called the delete statement is deallocating the memory allocated by a constructor. Each subsequent time the **resize** method is called, it is deallocating the memory allocated by the previous call to the **resize** method. This may make you think that we have a memory leak, but remember that the destructor will deallocate the memory that was allocated by the last call to the **resize** method or the memory allocated by the constructor if the **resize** method was never called.

In fact, in most cases the corresponding **new** and **delete** statements are not in the same function or method, making it difficult to be certain your code does not have any memory leaks. We will see another example of this with linked structures in Chapter 11. Proofreading and checking your code carefully is important to help prevent these errors. Some development environments provide tools to track the memory usage as your program executes so that you can watch for unexpected growth in memory usage. You may think memory leaks are not an issue to be concerned with since the operating system will reclaim any memory your program used when the program exits, but many programs run for long periods of time. A web server for a commercial site might be expected to run for months at a time without being restarted. If you do not reboot your computer regularly (letting it go into sleep or hibernate mode is not equivalent to rebooting it) and leave programs such as your email or web browser programs running all the time, you do not want these programs to have memory leaks. If these programs you leave running (or the operating system itself) have memory leaks, your computer will slow down over time until you reboot it as it starts using the disk as extra memory. Thus, it is important to get in the habit of writing code without memory leaks. The key point to remember is that each **new** statement that is executed must have a corresponding **delete** statement that is executed after your program is done using the memory allocated by the **new** statement.

10.5.2 Accessing Invalid Memory

Modern computer hardware provides checks to make certain that one program does not access memory that is used by another program. This prevents a number of problems such as one program causing another program to give incorrect data or crash. If one program could access the memory used by another program such as a web browser, it would be possible for the program to access the passwords and other sensitive information you type into a web browser. Computer hardware splits the memory into sections that are known as *pages*. On most modern computers a page is either 4KB or 8KB in size. As the amount of memory in computers continue to grow, it is likely that the page size will increase. The hardware provides protection at the page level. If a program attempts to access memory that is not in one of the pages your program is using, a hardware exception is generated and the program crashes.

Since the hardware detects errors only when a program attempts to access memory that is not one of the pages the operating system allocated for the program, a program may access memory that is one of its pages but is not a valid memory address that it should be using. In this case, your program will not crash immediately, but it can have different results each time it runs or it can crash at a later point in time.

We will start with a simple example that does not use dynamic memory, but could give unexpected results. See if you can find the error in this program before reading the paragraph after the code.

```cpp
// this program is incorrect
#include <iostream>
using namespace std;

int main()
{
  int x[10];
  int y = 0;
  int i;

  for (i=0; i<=10; ++i) {
    x[i] = i;
  }
  cout << "y=" << y << endl;
  return 0;
}
```

Unlike Python, C++ does not do any index checking when you attempt to access an element in an array (Python does check when you attempt to access an element in a list). The problem with this example is the array can be indexed using the values 0 through 9, but the `for` loop sets `x[10]`. Depending on how the memory is allocated for the local variables, this could result in the program outputting 10 for `y` even though we set `y` to zero. If the memory location used for the variable `y` is immediately after the memory location for the array, then `x[10]` and `y` correspond to the same memory address. If the memory for the variables is not allocated in this order then the program produces the expected output of 0.

Remember that pointers hold an address and dereferencing a pointer attempts to read or store data at that address. This is what can lead you to access memory you should not be using. The following simple program is almost guaranteed to crash on any computer.

```
// this program is incorrect
int main()
{
  int *p;
  p = (int*) 8;
  *p = 1;
  return 0;
}
```

This program sets the pointer variable to the memory address 8; we had to use a cast for the compiler to accept it since you should not set pointers directly to integer values (you should use the unary ampersand operator or **new** statement to set a pointer variable to a valid address). Executing the statement **p = (int*) 8** does not crash the program, but that is the incorrect line. The statement ***p = 1** attempts to store the value 1 at memory address 8 which is not part of the memory used for dynamic memory. The hardware detects this error and the program crashes. Again, you would not do this as part of a normal program, but this should show you that if you accidently set a pointer variable to an address that your program is no longer using and then later try to dereference that pointer, your program will crash. A more realistic example of the same problem is the following program.

```
// this program is incorrect
int main()
{
  int *x;
  *x = 5;
  return 0;
}
```

In this example, x is never initialized to hold a valid address so whatever address is already in the memory used for the variable x is the address in which the program will attempt to store the value 5. If that address happens to be in one of the pages the operating system gave our program, the program will not crash. This is unlikely. It is more likely that the address stored in the variable for x is not a valid address so attempting to store a 5 there will cause the hardware to generate an exception and our program will crash. Here is another example that could cause the same problem.

```
int main() // this program is incorrect
{
  int *y = new int;
  delete y;
  *y = 3;
  return 0;
}
```

In this example, we attempted to dereference the pointer y and store the value 3 at that address after we have deallocated the memory location that y points to. This again could cause our program to crash or it could run to completion. You should be starting to see why these types of errors can be difficult to track down in larger programs.

We will examine one more program with errors in this chapter, but there are lots of different ways you can have these problems. This program has two errors.

```
// this program is incorrect
int main()
{
  int *x, *y;
  x = new int;
  y = new int;
  *x = 3;
  y = x;
  *y = 3;
  delete y;
  delete x;
```

The first problem is that this program has a memory leak. The memory for two integers is allocated, but then the statement y = x causes both pointers to refer to the same memory location. This results in the memory allocated by the statement y = new int being leaked since there is no way to access it and delete it. The delete y statement deletes the memory allocated by the x = new int statement. Since x also pointed to that memory location, the statement delete x attempts to deallocate the same block of memory a second time. This will likely corrupt the dynamic memory heap. This can also cause your program to crash immediately, or at a later time, or never.

10.5.3 Memory Error Summary

Some C++ run-time environments do not show you the exact line where your program crashed or a stack trace showing the function or method calls that resulted in the program crashing at that line. Most IDEs (integrated development environments) will show you the execution traceback similar to Python indicating at what line the program crashed and the functions or methods that were called to get to that point. This information is important for determining why your program crashed. Unfortunately, as we have discussed, the line your program crashed at is not necessarily the line that is incorrect. If the line it crashes at is dereferencing a pointer, the problem is that either you forgot to give that pointer a valid address or somehow it ended up pointing to memory that is no longer valid for your program to use (for example, you already called **delete** on that memory block or it got set to a value that does not correspond to a valid address). The traceback tells you the order the functions or methods were called to the point of the crashing. This helps you determine the code that caused the problem.

Also, as we mentioned earlier, sometimes you can corrupt the dynamic heap by accessing incorrect memory locations or calling **delete** twice for the same block of memory. This will typically not result in a crash until you try to allocate memory again. These types of errors can be extremely difficult and frustrating to track down. Fortunately, while you are developing your code, you can use an IDE that provides a debugger to help track down these errors. Debuggers provide a number of features to help you find errors in your programs. Most allow you to stop execution at specific source code lines within your program, examine the values of variables at that point, and execute one line or one function at a time while you watch the values of the variables. Debuggers typically provide additional capabilities beyond the ones we listed here.

When running your program within a debugger and your program crashes, the debugger will typically show you similar information to the Python traceback. It is fairly easy to develop Python code without a debugger, but when writing dynamic memory code in C++, a debugger and good IDE will help you track down memory errors more quickly and with less frustration. Sometimes proofreading the code around the crash (or for the entire class if the crash is in a method) is the most effective way to solve the problem.

It is always a good idea to find the smallest sample input that causes your program to crash or to work incorrectly. This is especially important when dealing with dynamic memory errors. If we determined that our **List** class did not work correctly and crashed in the **append** method, we should first check if it can happen when appending fewer items than cause the **resize** method to be called. If this is the case and we have only called the **append** method and the constructor, we know that the problem is with the constructor or **append** method. If it crashes in the **append** method only after the **resize** method has been called, then the problem could be in the constructor, **append**, or **resize**, but in this case we recommend checking the **resize** method first. Try to minimize the amount of code that is executed but still causes the problem. Limiting the amount of code you have to check will enable you to find the problem faster and with less frustration.

10.6 Chapter Summary

This chapter covers the issues for using pointers and dynamic memory in C++. We summarize some of the important issues here.

- Python references and C++ pointers work similarly and essentially are the same concepts with different syntaxes.

- C++ pointers allow you to delay determining the amount of memory that is allocated until run-time when you use the `new` and `delete` statements.

- C++ pointers allow you to write classes such as a `List` that can grow in size over time; they also allow you to write linked structures as we will discuss in Chapter 11.

- Each `new` statement must have a corresponding `delete` statement that deallocates the memory allocated by the `new` statement when the program is done using that memory.

- Classes that use dynamic memory must implement a destructor that deallocates any dynamic memory a class instance is still using when the instance goes out of scope. Dynamic memory classes also must either write a copy constructor and `operator=` that make a deep copy of the dynamic memory or declare these methods private so they cannot be called.

- Using dynamic memory gives you flexibility and power, but is also error prone. Only use dynamic memory when you need its capabilities.

- Dynamic memory errors are the source of errors in many programs and can be difficult to track down and fix.

10.7 Exercises

True/False Questions

1. All C++ arrays should be created using dynamic memory.

2. Dynamic memory errors are a common source of errors in programs and are often difficult to track down.

3. Never deallocating dynamic memory will never cause problems since all the memory a program uses is reclaimed when the program ends.

4. Using dynamic memory requires more memory than using standard automatic variables.

5. Having a function return the address of a local stack dynamic variable will work correctly.

6. Functions can return the address of memory dynamically allocated within the function.

7. A method of a class can return the address of an instance variable of that class.

8. A C++ program that uses dynamic memory and runs once without crashing will never crash.

9. A C++ method that allocates dynamic memory must deallocate it before the method completes.

10. A C++ class that allocates dynamic memory does not need to have a copy constructor and `operator=`.

11. A C++ class that allocates dynamic memory for an instance variable does not need to have a destructor.

12. The following code has a memory leak.

```
int* f()
{
  int *x = new int;
  *x = 3;
  return x;
}
int main()
{
  int *y = f();
  int z = *y;
  delete y;
  return 0;
}
```

Multiple Choice Questions

1. Which of the following work the most similarly between Python and C++

   a) Python names and C++ stack dynamic variables
   b) Python names and C++ pointers
   c) C++'s pass by value and Python's parameter passing mechanism
   d) C++'s pass by reference and Python's parameter passing mechanism

2. What, if anything, is wrong with the following C++ code fragment?

```
int x, *y;
y = &x;
delete y;
```

   a) The code fragment is correct.
   b) The code fragment has a memory leak.
   c) The assignment y = &x is incorrect.
   d) The statement delete y is incorrect since the address it points to was not allocated with the new operator.

3. What, if anything, is wrong with the following C++ code fragment?

```
int *b, *c;
b = new int;
*b = 3;
c = b;
delete c;
delete b;
```

   a) The code fragment is correct.
   b) The code fragment has a memory leak.
   c) The statement delete b deletes the same memory location that was already deallocated by the statement delete c.
   d) The first statement must be delete b since the memory was allocated for the variable b.

4. What, if anything, is wrong with the following C++ code fragment?

```
int *b, *c;
b = new int;
*b = 3;
c = b;
delete c;
```

a) The code fragment is correct.

b) The code fragment has a memory leak.

c) The `delete` statement must be `delete b` since the memory was allocated for the variable b.

d) The statement `c = b` must be `*c = *b`.

5. A C++ program that has pointer variables but never calls `new` or `delete`

a) will never crash.

b) will not have memory leaks.

c) will have memory leaks.

d) will never attempt to access a memory location it is not allowed to access.

6. What is the output of the following C++ code fragment using the `Rational` class from the previous chapter?

```
Rational r1, *r2;
r1.set(1, 2);
r2 = &r1;
r2->set(3, 4);
cout << r1 << " " << r2;
```

a) 1/2 1/2

b) 1/2 3/4

c) 3/4 1/2

d) 3/4 3/4

7. If you are writing a class that uses dynamic memory, which of the methods must you declare within the class definition?

a) destructor

b) copy constructor

c) assignment operator

d) all of the above

8. What will happen if you have a class that uses dynamic memory and assign one instance of it to another instance of the class?

a) You will have a memory leak.

b) You will create a deep copy.

c) You will create a shallow copy leading to the dynamic memory being deallocated twice.

d) Everything will work properly.

9. Which of the following are true of the **this** pointer in C++ classes?

   a) You must declare the **this** pointer as a parameter for methods that want to access it.
   b) You can use the **this** pointer in static/class methods.
   c) The **this** pointer stores the address of the instance of the class with which the method was called
   d) You must always use the **this** pointer to access private data.

10. What will happen if your dynamic memory code is not quite correct?

    a) Your program may run correctly each time you run it.
    b) Your program may run correctly some times and give incorrect results other times.
    c) Your program may run correctly some times and crash other times.
    d) All of the above are possible.

Short-Answer Questions

1. Is there a potential problem with the **resize** method for the **List** class? If so, what precondition would solve the problem? Could a user of our **List** class have a problem because of this issue given that the method is declared **private**?

2. What are the benefits of using dynamic memory?

3. What are the drawbacks of using dynamic memory?

4. When should you use dynamic memory?

5. Write a C++ code fragment that has a memory leak.

6. Write a C++ code fragment that accesses memory it should not.

7. Do any of the potential, subtle issues we discussed regarding the **operator+=** method apply to writing an **operator+** method? Why or why not?

8. Why is it not legal for a function or method to return a reference to a local stack-dynamic variable?

9. When is it legal to return a reference to a variable?

10. How many memory accesses are required to access the data (do not count the memory access necessary to access the program instructions themselves) in the following code fragment? Explain how you arrived at your answer.

```
int *b, *c, x, y;
x = 3;
y = 4;
b = &x;
c = b;
*c = 2;
cout << *b << " " << *d << " " << x << " " << y << endl;
```

Programming Exercises

1. Complete the C++ **List** class with the same semantics and API as Python's built-in list using a dynamically allocated array (add the **extend**, **index**, **insert**, **pop**, and **remove** methods). Also add a method named **len** that returns the number of items in the list and an **operator+** method or function. Whenever you need to make the array larger, double its current capacity. Include **append**, the copy constructor, **operator=**, **operator+=**, **operator[]**, and the destructor. Also write a program to test your list that checks all the methods including boundary cases such as insertion at the beginning or end of the list.

2. Write a C++ **LongInt** class that allows integers to be arbitrarily large. Implement it by storing an array with each element in the array being a single digit (0–9) that makes up the number (for example, the number 678 would have 8 in position 0 of the array, 7 in position 1 of the array, and 6 in position 2 of the array). Use a dynamic array of **unsigned char** to implement this since only a single byte is necessary to hold the numbers zero through nine. Overload the appropriate operators so you can add, subtract, multiply, assign, and input/output instances of your class. Also write a program to test your class.

3. Implement a polynomial class where each element in a dynamic array of doubles stores the coefficients for the polynomial. Overload the appropriate operators so you can add, subtract, multiply, assign, and input/output instances of your class. Also write a program to test your class.

4. Write your own implementation of a **string** class by using a dynamic array of characters. Overload the appropriate operators so you can concatenate two

strings, access the element at a specific position, and input/output instances of your string class. Also add some of the methods that the Python or C++ string class support such as slicing/substrings, searching for an element, reversing a string, and so on. Name your class MyString to avoid confusion with the name of the existing string class.

5. Research how to dynamically allocate and deallocate multi-dimensional arrays (it is not covered in this book). Write a program that dynamically allocates a two-dimensional array of a size input by the user, fills it with entries, outputs the contents, and then deallocates it.

Chapter 11

C++ Linked Structures

Objectives

- To learn how to write linked structures in C++.

- To reinforce C++ dynamic memory concepts and how to write dynamic memory classes.

11.1 Introduction

As with Python, linked structures can be used to implement a number of data structures in C++ including lists and tree structures. We learned in section 10.2 that Python references and C++ pointers are essentially the same concept so to implement a linked structure in C++ you need to use dynamic memory and pointers. The main differences between writing Python and C++ linked structure classes is the need to write a destructor, copy constructor, and assignment operator for the class (or as we discussed in section 10.4, you may declare the copy constructor and assignment operator private, but not implement them). Your C++ class must also explicitly deallocate memory which is not required in Python. You will need to fully understand the low-level details of C++ memory allocation and deallocation that we discussed in the previous chapters; we will reinforce the dynamic memory topics in this chapter.

As you may have discovered when working with linked structures in Python, Python does not prevent you from making semantic errors such as setting a reference to the wrong linked object (for example, when inserting a node you might mix up the `link` that points to the next node so that you skip a node or end up with a circular linked structure such as a node's `link` pointing to itself or an earlier node). The C++ environment also does not automatically catch these types of semantic errors. The best method for finding these types of errors is to test your code extensively. Python does catch an error that the C++ compiler and run-time environment may not always catch. Python does not let you use a name to access data at a reference that does not point to a valid object (for example, a name that has not been defined or is the value `None`). If the name `node` refers to `None` and you attempt to execute `node.link` or `node.item`, the Python interpreter will always catch this problem and generate an exception and traceback if you do not catch the exception. In C++ if you try to dereference an uninitialized pointer or a pointer that refers to an object that has been deallocated, the run-time environment will attempt to access the memory location, resulting in garbage data or a memory fault that crashes your program as we discussed in the previous chapter.

C++ does not allow you to directly assign a pointer of one type to a pointer of a different type (for example, if x is a pointer to an `int` and y is a pointer to a `double`, you cannot write `y = x`). It is possible to cast a pointer of one type to another type using `reinterpret_cast` (the syntax is similar to `static_cast` discussed in section 8.9), but it is not intended for this type of use nor is `reinterpret_cast` commonly used. The C++ compiler checks that the data types match, but the C++ run-time environment does not check that the pointer actually points to a valid memory location that holds a value of that type. When you dereference a pointer that does not point to a valid memory location, sometimes your program will crash and other times it will continue running even though your program is not correct, as we discussed in section 10.5.

As you will see later in this chapter, the code for a linked structure in C++ is not much longer than the Python version and you can generally make a line by line translation of Python linked structure code to C++ code. However, writing C++ dynamic memory and linked structure code from scratch is more difficult than writing Python linked structures because Python prevents you from making some types of errors and makes it easier to find and fix other types of errors. After we discuss a few additional issues with linked structures in C++, we will translate one of our Python linked structure examples to C++.

11.2 A C++ Linked Structure Class

In Python, we used a `ListNode` class that contained two data elements: the data value and a reference to the next `ListNode` in our linked list. We can use the same technique in C++ with a class to hold the data element and a pointer to the next node in the list. A significant difference between the C++ version and the Python version is that our C++ `ListNode` can only hold an item of one type (an `int` in our examples) since all C++ variables must have a specific type. We will learn about templates in Chapter 12 and they will allow us to write one `ListNode` class that can hold any type. The following is a simple version of a C++ `ListNode` class that we will expand later in this section.

```
class ListNode {
public:
  int item_;
  ListNode *link_;
};
```

An easy typographical error for beginners to make is to forget the asterisk for the pointer in front of the `link_` instance variable. Your C++ compiler will not allow this because you are including a `ListNode` in your definition of the `ListNode`. This is essentially infinite recursion that would require the `ListNode` to use an infinite amount of memory since each `ListNode` would contain a `ListNode` as one of its data members. A pointer to any data type requires four bytes on 32-bit systems since it is to hold the address where an object of that type is stored, not the actual object. Thus, the `ListNode` requires four bytes in addition to the memory for the data type you want to store.

Usually we do not make instance variables public in C++ classes, but as we discussed when presenting the Python `ListNode` classes, allowing direct access to these instance variables makes sense since the `ListNode` class is only used directly by one other class that needs to access the data element and link (the `LList` class in our Python example). Another option is to make the `LList` class a friend of the `ListNode` class. We looked at declaring functions as friends when writing the input and output operators for our `Rational` class in section 9.4. As we mentioned in that section, you can also declare a class to be a friend. Our next version of the `ListNode` class demonstrates this and also contains a constructor so we can use it just as we used our Python `ListNode` class.

```
#ifndef _LISTNODE_H
#define _LISTNODE_H

#include <cstdlib>

class ListNode {
  friend class LList;
```

```
public:
  ListNode(int item=0, ListNode* link=NULL);

private:
  int item_;
  ListNode *link_;
};

inline ListNode::ListNode(int item, ListNode *link)
{
  item_ = item;
  link_ = link;
}


#endif // _LISTNODE_H
```

The `ListNode` constructor allows us to call the constructor with zero, one, or two parameters. We have used the default value zero for the `int` so that we have a default constructor that does not require any parameters. The default value for the `link` parameter is `NULL`. Just as the Python `None` value evaluates to false, the `NULL` value (which is zero) evaluates to false and is used to indicate an uninitialized or invalid pointer. We can write code such as `if (node != NULL)` or the shorthand version `if (node)` to check for a valid pointer since `NULL` is false and any valid pointer address evaluates to true. We discussed in the Python chapter covering linked structures that using the `is` operator in code such as `if node is not None` is the best way to do this in Python. C++ does not have an `is` operator so we use either `if (node)` or `if (node != NULL)`. It does not make any difference as far as performance in C++. For readability, some programmers prefer `if (node != NULL)`, although many programmers use the shorthand `if (node)`.

Since the constructor is only two lines long, we have defined it inline to avoid the overhead of a function call. Note that we are following the convention of using an underscore after the names of the instance variables. This allows us to use the same name for the instance variables and the formal parameters except for the addition of the underscore.

Since C++ provides explicit protection for instance members, we use that in our `ListNode` class. We have declared `item_` and `link_` as private instance variables, but made the `LList` class a friend of our `ListNode` class. At this point, the compiler does not know that there is a `LList` class since it is not referenced in this file. We cannot include the LList.h file in this header file because the LList.h file needs to include this header file (otherwise we have a circular reference). To indicate that there will be a class named `LList`, we can put the line `class LList;` before the `class ListNode {` line. This is known as a *forward declaration*, but most, if not all, compilers do not require the forward declaration when declaring a friend. Our other option is to declare the instance variables in the public section as we did initially, but then any class could access them as is possible in Python.

Recall from our **Rational** example in section 10.2 that we cannot dereference a pointer and use the dot operator without parentheses because of a precedence issue. Recall that the common usage is to use the **->**. But as the following example shows, there are two correct ways to do it.

```
ListNode *node;
node = new ListNode(2); // item parameter is required
node->item_ = 3; // this is correct
*node.item_ = 3; // this is not correct
(*node).item_ = 3; // this is correct
```

11.3 A C++ Linked List

Using our C++ **ListNode** class we can create a linked implementation of a list just as we did in Python in Chapter 4. Recall that we wrote a linked implementation of a list with the same API as the built-in Python list. In this section, we will write a C++ version of a linked implementation of a list that again matches the API of the built-in Python list. The syntax will be different, but the only semantic difference we need to make is that we need to explicitly deallocate **ListNode** instances when they are removed from the list; Python handles this automatically via its reference counting mechanism. As we did with the dynamic memory classes in the previous chapter, we must write a destructor to do the final memory deallocation. You also need to write a copy constructor and assignment operator (**operator=**) or prevent them from being called as you need to do for any class that allocates dynamic memory using its instance variables. You can prevent the copy constructor and assignment operator from being used by declaring them in a **private** section; when you declare the methods private, you do not need to provide an implementation for them. If there is not an implementation of a private method, the compiler will generate an error if the method is called. The following LList.h header file shows the interface for the **LList** class we are implementing.

```
#ifndef _LLIST_H
#define _LLIST_H

#include "ListNode.h"

class LList {
```

```
public:
  LList();
  LList(const LList& source);
  ~LList();

  LList& operator=(const LList& source);
  int size() { return size_; }
  void append(const ItemType &x);
  void insert(int i, const ItemType &x);
  ItemType pop(int i=-1);
  ItemType& operator[](int position);

private:
  // methods
  void copy(const LList &source);
  void dealloc();
  ListNode* _find(int position);
  ItemType _delete(int position);

  // data elements
  ListNode *head_;
  int size_;
};

#endif // _LLIST_H
```

As you may have noticed, we have more methods than our Python implementation of the LList class; this is because we need to properly allocate and deallocate memory. Since the copy constructor and assignment operator share some functionality, we have declared a private copy method that both methods will use. The destructor and assignment operator also share some functionality so we have declared a dealloc method that both methods will use.

A drawback of our ListNode and List classes are that they can contain only one data type (integers in our examples). For now, we will make an incremental improvement and use the C/C++ keyword typedef which allows us to define a new type name. In the following example, we have created the type name ItemType that is now a synonym for int. We can now update both our ListNode and List classes to use the type ItemType instead of int in the places that correspond to the value stored in the list. Note that we did not change all occurrences of int to ItemType; the size of an LList of any data type is still an integer. Now if we want to make an LList of a different type such as double or Rational, all we need to do is change the one typedef line in the ListNode.h file (and include the appropriate header file if it is not a built-in type).

The `typedef` statement does not allow us to store different types in the same program. Every `ListNode` in a single program will have to use whatever type we specify with the `typedef` command. A single program can only have a `LList` for one type since there can only be one class named `LList` and one named `ListNode` in a program. We could copy the code and create a `ListNodeInt`/`LListInt` and `ListNodeDouble`/`LListDouble` and change the `typedef` line in each file so it is not too difficult to reuse the code for different types in one program. In Chapter 12, we will discuss templates which will allow us to have lists of different types in one program without having to copy the class files for each type. The use of the `typedef` statement now will make it easier to convert our program to a template-based version. The following is the `typedef` version of our `ListNode` and `LList` class header files.

```
// ListNode.h
#ifndef _LISTNODE_H
#define _LISTNODE_H

#include <cstdlib>
typedef int ItemType;

class ListNode {
  friend class LList;
public:
  ListNode(ItemType item, ListNode* link=NULL);
private:
  ItemType item_;
  ListNode *link_;
};
inline ListNode::ListNode(ItemType item, ListNode *link)
{
  item_ = item;
  link_ = link;
}
#endif // _LISTNODE_H
```

```
// LList.h
#ifndef _LLIST_H
#define _LLIST_H

#include "ListNode.h"

class LList {
public:
```

```
  LList();
  LList(const LList& source);
  ~LList();

  LList& operator=(const LList& source);
  int size() { return size_; }
  void append(ItemType x);
  void insert(size_t i, ItemType x);
  ItemType pop(int i=-1);
  ItemType& operator[](size_t position);

private:
  // methods
  void copy(const LList &source);
  void dealloc();
  ListNode* _find(size_t position);
  ItemType _delete(size_t position);

  // data elements
  ListNode *head_;
  int size_;
};

#endif // _LLIST_H
```

We will now look at the C++ implementation file for our LList class. We will start with the methods that are similar to their Python versions. After examining these methods, we will look at the extra methods for properly handling memory. Our LList.cpp file needs to include the LList.h header file containing the class definition. The LList methods are the same as their corresponding Python methods except for the need to declare variables, the use of pointers, the need to deallocate nodes when they are removed from the list, and the other syntax differences between Python and C++. We include the Python version followed by the corresponding C++ version for the constructor, _find, _delete, insert, and pop so you can compare them. We have removed some of the assert statements, documentation strings, and comments from the Python version to keep the code shorter.

The purpose of the constructor is to initialize the instance variables. We will use the NULL value for a pointer variable to indicate that it does not point to a valid node. The default constructor is simple since we have only two instance variables to initialize.

```
    def __init__(self):
        self.head = None
        self.size = 0

// LList.cpp
#include "LList.h"

LList::LList()
{
  head_ = NULL;
  size_ = 0;
}
```

The `_find` method is essentially the same other than the obvious syntax differences.

```
    def _find(self, position):

        node = self.head
        for i in range(position):
            node = node.link
        return node

ListNode* LList::_find(size_t position)
{
  ListNode *node = head_;
  size_t i;

  for (i=0; i<position; i++) {
    node = node->link_;
  }
  return node;
}
```

The `_delete` method has some differences since we are removing an item from the list. In the C++ version, it is necessary to use the `delete` statement to deallocate the memory for the `ListNode` being removed.

```
    def _delete(self, position):
        if position == 0:
            item = self.head.item
            self.head = self.head.link
        else:
            node = self._find(position - 1)
            item = node.link.item
            node.link = node.link.link
        self.size -= 1
        return item
```

```
ItemType LList::_delete(size_t position)
{
  ListNode *node, *dnode;
  ItemType item;

  if (position == 0) {
    dnode = head_;
    head_ = head_->link_;
    item = dnode->item_;
    delete dnode;
  }
  else {
    node = _find(position - 1);
    if (node != NULL) {
      dnode = node->link_;
      node->link_ = dnode->link_;
      item = dnode->item_;
      delete dnode;
    }
  }
  size_ -= 1;
  return item;
}
```

Python does have a `del` statement that removes the name from the current namespace by deleting the identifier from the dictionary of accessible names (see section 4.2 if you need a brief refresher on Python's dictionary of names). As you should expect, when you remove a name, the object that the name referred to has its reference count decremented by one. When the reference count of an object is decreased to zero, Python deallocates the memory for the object. The following Python version shows the use of the `del` statement.

```python
def _delete(self, position):
    if position == 0:
        dnode = self.head
        self.head = self.head.link
        x = dnode.item
        del dnode # not necessary in Python
    else:
        node = self._find(position - 1)
        if node is not None:
            dnode = node.link
            node.link = dnode.link
            x = dnode.item
            del dnode # not necessary in Python
    self.size -= 1
    return x
```

As the comments indicate, the `del` statement is unnecessary; however, it will not cause any problems. The name `dnode` is likely the only name that refers to the object unless another Python name in a different function that is in the call chain of functions/methods that called the `_delete` method refers to it. Unless another name does refer to the object, the `del` statement will reduce the `ListNode` object's reference count to zero and Python will deallocate it. If no other names refer to the object, the reference count will change to zero when the function ends and the `dnode` name is removed from the dictionary of local names. In our original Python version, the reference count for the `ListNode` object being removed is decreased by the statement `self.head = self.head.link` or the statement `node.link = node.link.link` so both the original version and this new version with the `del` statement have the same end result.

Even though the Python `del` and C++ `delete` keywords look similar and work similarly in this example, they do not perform the same operation. The Python `del` statement removes a name from the current namespace and the C++ `delete` statement always deallocates memory. The C++ `delete` statement is required in this example or your code will have a memory leak. A key concept to make note of is that the `delete` statement deallocates the memory for the object whether or not other pointer variables point to the same object. If any other pointers do point to it, dereferencing those pointers after the `delete` statement executes is an error. We discussed this in subsection 10.5.3.

A common mistake Python programmers make when learning C++ is forgetting to use the `new` keyword when they want to allocate a node (i.e., they write `node->link_ = ListNode(x)`). The compiler will generate an error if you forget the `new` statement. You only use the `new` statement when you want to allocate a node and only use the `delete` statement when you want to deallocate a node. The allocation issue is the same in Python: you only call the constructor (e.g., `node = ListNode(x)`) when you want to allocate a node. The `append` and `insert` methods are essentially the same in both Python and C++.

```python
def append(self, x):

    newNode = ListNode(x);
    if self.head is not None:
        node = self._find(self.size - 1)
        node.link = newNode
    else:
        self.head = newNode
    self.size += 1
```

```
void LList::append(ItemType x)
{
  ListNode *node, *newNode = new ListNode(x);

  if (head_ != NULL) {
    node = _find(size_ - 1);
    node->link_ = newNode;
  }
  else {
    head_ = newNode;
  }
  size_ += 1;
}
```

```
    def insert(self, i, x):

        if i == 0:
            self.head = ListNode(x, self.head)
        else:
            node = self._find(i - 1)
            node.link = ListNode(x, node.link)
        self.size += 1

void LList::insert(size_t i, ItemType x)
{
  ListNode *node;

  if (i == 0) {
    head_ = new ListNode(x, head_);
  }
  else {
    node = _find(i - 1);
    node->link_ = new ListNode(x, node->link_);
  }
  size_ += 1;
}
```

The pop method is a little different because in Python we used the default parameter value None to indicate we wanted to remove the last item in the list. Since C++ does not have dynamic typing or a special value None, we must use a specific integer to indicate the default value. We have chosen the value -1 to indicate we want to remove the last item. Other than that, the pop method is the same except that again we did not test that the parameter i holds a valid value between 0 and size_ - 1.

```
    def pop(self, i=None):

        if i is None:
            i = self.size - 1

        return self._delete(i)
ItemType LList::pop(int i)
{
  if (i == -1) {
    i = size_ - 1;
  }
  return _delete(i);
}
```

To allow access to the list elements using the square brackets as we can with Python sequences and C++ arrays, we use operator overloading. This example also shows the use of reference return types in C++. This allows us to write the equivalent of the Python __getitem__ and __setitem__ in one method. We have only included the Python __getitem__ here for comparison.

```
    def __getitem__(self, position):

        node = self._find(position)
        return node.item

ItemType& LList::operator[](size_t position)
{
  ListNode *node;

  node = _find(position);
  return node->item_;
}
```

The next example shows usage of the method. The statement x = a[1] would work if the return type was not a reference, but the statement a[2] = 40 would not work if the method did not return a reference. Just as with Python, the element on the left-hand side of an assignment statement must be a location where a value can be stored. The technical term used for this in computer science is an *l-value*. The element on the right-hand side of an assignment statement can be a variable, a constant, or an expression. By returning a reference we are essentially returning the memory location that is the item_ at the second ListNode. When a reference return type is used on the left side of the assignment operator, the result of the assignment statement (the value of the expression on the right-hand side of the statement) is stored in the memory location for the variable returned by the function or method. When a reference return type is used on the right-hand side or as part of an expression, the actual data value is used instead of the address of the returned variable. We also covered the issues of returning a reference in subsection 10.4.5.

```
#include "LList.h"

int main()
{
  LList a;
  int x;

  a.append(10);
  a.append(20);
  a.append(30);

  // both of these methods cause the operator[] method to be called
  x = a[1]; // returns 20 which is stored in x
  a[2] = 40; // changes the 30 at the last ListNode's item to 40

  return 0;
}
```

We will now look at the additional methods for properly handling the dynamic memory for the linked list. Since Python handles memory deallocation automatically, there is no corresponding Python code to compare to these methods. The copy constructor makes a deep copy of an LList object; it needs to create a new ListNode for each existing ListNode in the original source LList it is copying. Remember that the copy constructor is called when we pass an object of this type by value. Since we will need to copy a list in the assignment operator, we are writing a copy method that both methods will call. We create the deep copy by iterating over the ListNode objects in the source list, create the new ListNode objects for the new list inside this loop, and connect the link_ links appropriately. We could write the copy method more simply by iterating over the items and using the append method to add them to the new LList object, but that would be inefficient without a tail_ instance variable.

Remember, we do not write an assignment operator in Python because assignment in Python only binds another name to the same object (i.e., makes the name a reference to the same object). The C++ assignment operator first needs to deallocate the existing ListNode objects storing its items or we will have a memory leak. We call the dealloc method, which we will look at next, to deallocate the existing ListNode objects.

```
LList::LList(const LList& source)
{
  copy(source);
}

void LList::copy(const LList &source)
{
  ListNode *snode, *node;

  snode = source.head_;
  if (snode) {
    node = head_ = new ListNode(snode->item_);
    snode = snode->link_;
  }
  while (snode) {
    node->link_ = new ListNode(snode->item_);
    node = node->link_;
    snode = snode->link_;
  }
  size_ = source.size_;
}

LList& LList::operator=(const LList& source)
{
  dealloc();
  copy(source);
  return *this;
}
```

The class destructor needs to deallocate every `ListNode` currently in the list since these are the `ListNode` instances that have not been deallocated yet. This ensures that any dynamically allocated memory is deallocated whenever a `LList` object is deallocated. As a reminder, the destructor is called automatically when a non-pointer instance goes out of scope or when the `delete` statement is used with a pointer to an `LList` object. Since our assignment operator also needs to deallocate the `ListNode` instances, we write that code once in a `dealloc` method and have both the assignment operator and destructor call it. We could write the code for our `dealloc` method using the `pop` method or using the `_delete` method by repeatedly calling one of the methods to remove one item at a time from the list. But for efficiency reasons, we will implement it directly. The code traverses each `ListNode` and deallocates the memory for it using the `delete` statement. Notice that we have to advance to the next `ListNode` before we deallocate the current `ListNode`. Once we deallocate a `ListNode` we cannot access it so we would not have any way to get to the next node. Keeping track of two pointers, one for the current node and one for the previous node, is is a common technique used in single linked structures since we often need access to both the current node and the node before it for the list operations.

```
LList::~LList()
{
  dealloc();
}

void LList::dealloc()
{
  ListNode *node, *dnode;

  node = head_;
  while (node) {
    dnode = node;
    node = node->link_;
    delete dnode;
  }
}
```

As you looked at the code for the methods, you may have wondered how we can be certain that each **new** statement has a corresponding **delete** statement that deallocates the **ListNode** object the **new** statement allocated. We will use the following simple program to discuss it. See if you can determine how many **new** and **delete** statements are executed by this code and when they are are executed before reading the paragraph after the code.

```
#include "LList.h"

int main()
{
  LList b, c;
  int x;

  b.append(1);
  b.append(2);
  b.append(3);
  c.append(4);
  c.append(5);
  c = b;
  x = b.pop();
}
```

The constructor is called once for each variable, but that does not cause any **new** or **delete** statements to be executed. The five calls to the **append** method cause five new statements to be executed. The c = b statement causes two delete statements to be executed since operator= calls the dealloc method with the instance c that deletes the ListNode objects containing 4 and 5. It then calls the copy method causing three new statements to be executed so we now have a total of six ListNode objects. The variable b has three ListNode objects containing the numbers one, two, and three and the variable c has three ListNode objects containing 1, 2, and 3. The statement x = b.pop() executes a delete statement to deallocate the ListNode containing the 3 in the b LList. When the function ends, the LList destructor is automatically called twice: once for the variable b and once for the variable c. When the destructor for b is called, it calls the dealloc method which deletes the ListNode objects containing 1 and 2. When the destructor for c is called, it deletes the three ListNode objects containing 1, 2, and 3.

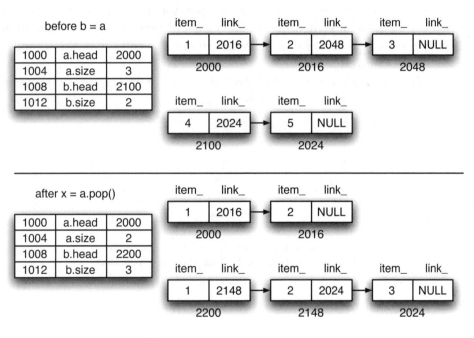

Figure 11.1: Pictorial representation of LList example

Figure 11.1 shows a pictorial representation of the execution at two points in time. The top part shows a representation before the statement c = b and the bottom part shows a representation at the end of the statements. We chose to use the memory addresses starting at 1000 for the stack dynamic variables, and the dynamic heap starts at 2000. The memory addresses we used could be anywhere in memory. In our example, we reused some of the addresses after they were deallocated by the call to `dealloc` in the `operator=` method. Again, the actual addresses used would vary and the addresses may or may not be reused immediately after they are deallocated.

The methods that add elements to the list allocate `ListNode` objects, and the methods that remove elements from the list deallocate `ListNode` objects. As long as all the methods are implemented correctly, the `ListNode` objects will remain linked together. When the variable for the `LList` instance goes out of scope, any remaining `ListNode` objects in the `LList` are deallocated. The assignment operator, copy constructor, and destructor must all be implemented correctly to ensure that all `ListNode` objects are properly allocated and deallocated when we use these methods. The other option is to declare the assignment operator and copy constructor as private methods without implementing them. This will prevent the compiler from generating any code for them and if other code attempts to call them, the compiler will generate a syntax error.

As a reminder about when destructors are called with pointers, we will show an example and discuss when the destructor is called.

```
LList* f()
{
  LList b;
  LList *c;

  b.append(1);
  c = new LList;
  c->append(2);
  return c; // the function returns a pointer to an LList instance
  // destructor is automatically called for b when the function ends
}

int main()
{
  LList *p;

  p = f();
  p->append(3);
  delete p; // delete statement causes destructor to be called
}
```

The destructor is called for the variable `b` at the end of the function `f` since `b` is a local variable whose lifetime ends when the function completes execution. This causes the `ListNode` containing the value 1 to be deallocated. The variable `c` goes out of scope at the end of function f, but since it is a pointer variable, only the four bytes storing the address of the LList object are deallocated. The LList object with its ListNode containing the value 2 continues to exist. The destructor is not called for the variable c when the function ends; if we wanted the destructor to be called in the function f, we would need to add the statement delete c to the function code. The function f returns the LList object created by the c = new LList statement. The main function then appends the integer 3 onto the list. When the delete p statement is executed, the LList destructor is called. This deallocates the LList object created by the c = new LList statement in the function f. The destructor deletes the two ListNode objects it contained. The four bytes for the pointer p are automatically deallocated when the function completes, as are the bytes for all local stack dynamic variables.

11.4 C++ Linked Dynamic Memory Errors

The same dynamic memory issues we discussed in section 10.5 apply to linked structures using dynamic memory so reviewing that section is a good idea. If you have a ListNode variable *node, it is important to remember that node->item_ and node->link_ are both dereferencing the pointer. So if node does not hold a valid address of a ListNode, those statements are incorrect and will likely cause a crash or incorrect results. If we incorrectly update the link_ instance variables when connecting ListNode instances we could end up losing access to a portion of a list. One example of this is changing our insert method to

```
// this code is incorrect
void LList::insert(size_t i, ItemType x)
{
  ListNode *node;

  if (i == 0) {
    head_ = new ListNode(x, head_);
  }
  else {
    node = _find(i - 1);
    node->link_ = new ListNode(x); // incorrect
  }
  size_ += 1;
}
```

In this case, the link_ instance variable of the newly created ListNode instance is set to NULL since that is the default value for the second parameter. This disconnects our list since we no longer have any way to access the items after the newly inserted node. In C++ we both lose access to a portion of the list and cause a memory leak, so it is extremely important to fully test your C++ code to make certain you do not have memory errors. In Python, the comparable code would disconnect our list, but would not have a memory leak since Python does its own memory deallocation using reference counting.

11.5 Chapter Summary

This chapter covers the issues for using pointers and dynamic memory to implement linked structures in C++. We summarize some of the important issues here.

- Since Python references and C++ pointers are essentially the same, the code for linked structures is similar in Python and C++. In C++ you must explicitly deallocate the link nodes when they are no longer needed.

- A linked structure class contains a pointer of its type (for example, our `ListNode` class contains an instance variable that is a `ListNode` pointer).

- The linked structure class typically declares the class that is going to use the linked structure as a friend so it can directly access the data and link in the structure.

- Classes that use dynamic memory must implement a destructor that deallocates any dynamic memory a class instance is still using when the instance goes out of scope. Dynamic memory classes also must either write a copy constructor and `operator=` that make a deep copy of the dynamic memory or declare these methods private so they cannot be called.

11.6 Exercises

True/False Questions

1. If you declare a pointer to a `ListNode`, you must use the `new` operator to give the pointer a valid address.

2. If class `A` declares that class `B` is its friend, methods of class `B` can access class `A`'s private methods and data.

3. If class `A` declares that class `B` is its friend, methods of class `A` can access class `B`'s private methods and data.

4. To create a copy of an LList, we must create separate copies of each ListNode it contains.

5. The item_ instance variable of a ListNode can be a pointer.

Multiple Choice Questions

1. A linked implementation of a list

   a) will always require more memory than an array version of the same list.

   b) will always require less memory than an array version of the same list.

   c) may require less memory than an array version of the list depending on the data type (both store the same data type).

   d) may require more memory than an array version of the list depending on the data type (both store the same data type).

2. The running time of our copy method for a LList with n items is

   a) $\Theta(1)$.

   b) $\Theta(log_2 n)$.

   c) $\Theta(n)$.

   d) $\Theta(n^2)$.

3. The most efficient possible running time of a copy method for a LList with n items is

   a) $\Theta(1)$.

   b) $\Theta(log_2 n)$.

   c) $\Theta(n)$.

   d) $\Theta(n^2)$.

4. The running time of the destructor for a LList with n items is

   a) $\Theta(1)$.

   b) $\Theta(log_2 n)$.

   c) $\Theta(n)$.

   d) $\Theta(n^2)$.

5. The most efficient possible running time of a destructor for a LList with n items is

   a) $\Theta(1)$.

   b) $\Theta(log_2 n)$.

   c) $\Theta(n)$.

   d) $\Theta(n^2)$.

Short-Answer Questions

1. How much total memory does the dynamic array `List` class in the previous chapter require for a list of **n** integers?

2. How much total memory does the `LList` class in this chapter require for a list of **n** integers?

3. How should you decide whether your program should use the dynamic array `List` class or the linked implementation `LList` class if you need to store a list of integers?

4. What potential issues are there if the `item_` instance variable of the `ListNode` is a pointer to dynamically allocated memory?

5. Why is it legal for a class to contain a pointer to an instance of the same class, but not an instance of the same class (for example, why can a `ListNode` contain a pointer to a `ListNode`, but not a `ListNode`)?

Programming Exercises

1. Complete the linked implementation by adding a `tail_` instance variable and an external iterator class. Also write code to test all your list methods. There is no automatic iteration so you will need to write the external iterator so that it can be called using code such as

```
LList l;
LListIterator li;
int x;

li.init(l);
while (li.next(x)) {
  cout << x << endl;
}
```

2. Write a linked implementation of a list where each list node element contains pointers to both the previous and next element in the list.

3. C++ also supports inheritance. The basic syntax for inheritance is

```
class CursorLList : public LList {

};
```

There are a number of issues you will want to learn if you are going to use inheritance in C++, but for this exercise you only need to know that the constructor for the base class is called automatically before the derived class' constructor and the destructor for the base class is called automatically when the destructor for the derived class completes. Create a C++ derived cursor list and the cursor class as described in subsection 4.6.2.

4. Implement a node-based binary search tree in C++. Include a copy constructor, assignment operator, and destructor.

Chapter 12   C++ Templates

Objectives

- To understand why compiled code generally needs to know the data type for the variables it manipulates.

- To learn how to write functions using templates.

- To briefly introduce the C++ Standard Template Library (STL).

- To learn how to write classes using templates.

12.1   Introduction

We have learned that C++ variables must be defined with a fixed type so that the compiler can generate the specific machine instructions needed to manipulate the variables. Dynamic typing is possible in Python because the interpreter waits until it is ready to execute a Python statement before converting it to machine language. This allows us to write generic functions and classes in Python that work for any type. As long as an object has the attribute you are trying to use, the code will work. Some programmers refer to this as *duck typing* (i.e., if it walks like a duck and quacks like a duck, it is a duck). In this chapter, we will learn a new C++ mechanism known as *templates* that allow us to write functions and classes in C++ that will give us similar functionality to Python's duck typing.

In Python, we can write our own `maximum` function (although there is no need to since Python has built-in `max` and `min` functions) that works for all data types that support the greater-than operator (i.e., the built-in types and any classes that implement `__gt__`).

```
def maximum(a, b):
    if a > b:
        return a
    else:
        return b
```

In C++, all parameters and variables have a fixed type that cannot change during the lifetime of the variable (except when using inheritance). This means we would have to write a separate `maximum` function for each type that we want to use with our `maximum` function as the following example shows.

```
int maximum_int(int a, int b)
{
  if (a > b) {
    return a;
  }
  else {
    return b;
  }
}

double maximum_double(double a, double b)
{
  if (a > b) {
    return a;
  }
  else {
    return b;
  }
}
```

The bodies of the two C++ functions are identical, as you should expect based on the Python code that works for any types supporting the greater-than operator. We saw the use of the `typedef` statement in Chapter 11 to make it easier to write code for multiple types; however, that doesn't allow the same code to be used for multiple types since the machine language code generated must be specific for the type. C++ templates allow us to write one version of the code, and the compiler automatically generates different versions of the code for each data type as needed. Templates allow us to write one `maximum` function that will work for all types that support the greater-than operator and allow us to write container classes such as lists, stacks, and queues that can hold any type. We will examine the syntax for templates and the issues involved with them in the remaining sections of this chapter.

12.2   Template Functions

The syntax for template functions is the keyword `template` followed by `<typename Item>` in front of the name of the function. You may use any legal identifier instead of `Item`, but C++ programmers commonly use `Item` or `Type`. The `Item` name is a placeholder for any valid type. You may use the keyword `class` instead of the keyword `typename` (`template <class Item>`). There is no semantic difference between the two although the use of `class` may make someone think it works only with class objects and not built-in primitive data types even though that is not the case. No matter which version you use, the actual data type that is used when the template function is called does not need to be a class; the type can be a built-in type, an array, or a class. The next example demonstrates a template version of our `maximum` function.

```cpp
// maximum.cpp
#include <iostream>
using namespace std;

template <typename Item>
Item maximum(Item a, Item b)
{
  if (a > b) {
    return a;
  }
  else {
    return b;
  }
}

int main()
{
  int a=3, b=4;
  double x=5.5, y=2.0;

  cout << maximum(a, b) << endl;
  cout << maximum(x, y) << endl;
  return 0;
}
```

In this case, the C++ compiler generates two versions of our `maximum` function. One is for the `int` type and is used when the call `maximum(a, b)` is made; the other is for the `double` type and is used when the call `maximum(x, y)` is made. The different versions are needed since the machine language instruction for comparing two integers and two double-precision floating point numbers are not the same.

We could also use this template function with our `Rational` class that overloaded the greater-than operator. Clearly the code that compares two integers and two `Rational` objects is not the same. Comparing two integers is one machine language instruction while comparing two `Rational` objects requires executing the machine code for the `Rational` class' `operator>`.

The C++ compiler does not generate any code if you do not call a template function. Depending on your compiler, it may or may not catch syntax errors in template functions that are not called. Because of this, it is important that you test all your template functions. The term *instantiate* is used to indicate that the compiler generates the code for a specific type. In our previous example, the compiler instantiates an `int` version and a `double` version of our `maximum` function.

Since the compiler does not generate the code for a template function with a specific type until it encounters code that calls the template function with that type, the compiler needs access to the source code of the template function when compiling the file that calls the function. The reason for this is that the compiler does not know the data type it will need to generate the machine language instructions for until it encounters the call to the function. Thus, once we have the type, we also need the source code for the template function to generate the corresponding machine instructions for that data type. This is not a problem if everything is in one file as in the preceding example. If you want a template function to be accessible in multiple C++ source files, you will need to write it in a header file that each source file includes.

The `Type` template parameter can be any data type, but cannot be two different types in the same instantiation of the function code. Using our previous example, we could not call our function as `maximum(x, b)` because x is a `double` and b is an `int`. C++ does support multiple template types. It does not make sense to write our `maximum` function for multiple types, but the next example shows the syntax for a function with multiple template parameter types. It uses two template parameters, but there is not a specific limit on the number of template parameters you can use.

```
template <typename T1, typename T2>
T1 maximum(T1 a, T2 b)
{
  if (a > b) {
    return a;
  }
  else {
    return b;
  }
}
```

If we call the function as `maximum(x, b)`, our C++ compiler (g++ version 4) compiles the code without any warnings or errors. The parameter T1 is `double` and T2 is an `int` so the return type is a `double`. The compiler silently casts an `int` to a `double` if necessary. If we call the function as `maximum(b, x)`, most compilers will generate a warning, but still will produce the executable machine code. The following shows the warning generated by the g++ compiler. As usual, you should not ignore compiler warnings even though the compiler still produces an executable program.

```
maximum.cpp: In function 'T1 maximum(T1, T2) [with T1 = int, T2 = double]':
maximum.cpp:35:   instantiated from here
maximum.cpp:23: warning: converting to 'int' from 'double'
```

As we have discussed, the compiler creates separate copies of the template functions for each data type that is used when calling the function. So in effect, the compiler is doing the work of writing each of the multiple versions of the functions instead of the programmer having to write each version. As the previous example shows, you will still get warnings or errors as if you had written the same code that the compiler generates based on your template.

12.3 Template Classes

As we stated earlier, you can also write classes using templates so that you can write a container class that can hold any C++ built-in data type or user-defined class. C++ also provides a library known as the *Standard Template Library* (commonly abbreviated *STL*) that provides template classes for a number of common data structures and algorithms for manipulating those data structures. The Standard Template Library is fairly complex and entire books have been written on it so we will only cover one of the classes in the STL and some simple examples of its use. We will then show you how to write your own template classes.

12.3.1 The Standard Template Library `vector` Class

One of the simpler STL classes is the `vector` class. It provides functionality similar to the dynamic array classes we developed earlier in the book. Internally the `vector` class is implemented as a dynamic array, so its use and efficiency are similar to the C++ dynamic array class we developed and the built-in Python list. The `vector` class is defined in the `<vector>` header file and is within the `std` namespace so we will need to specify it as `std::vector` or write either `using std::vector` or `using`

namespace std in our files. If you are defining your own class that uses a vector
or are writing a function that returns or has a vector as a parameter, do not put
a using namespace std or using std::vector statement in your header file (see
section 8.13 if you need a refresher on why). Instead, refer to it using its full name
std::vector in your header file. You may then put the using namespace std
statement in your implementation file as we have done in our examples.

When you declare an instance of the vector class, you must specify the data
type that the vector will contain in its dynamic array. An example of this is
std::vector<int> iv;. You can declare vectors with two different types in the
same file, as the following example shows:

```
// vec1.cpp
#include <iostream>
#include <vector>
using namespace std;

int main()
{
  vector<int> iv;
  vector<double> dv;
  int i;

  for (i=0; i<10; ++i) {
    iv.push_back(i);
    dv.push_back(i + 0.5);
  }
  for (i=0; i< 10; ++i) {
    cout << iv[i] << " " << dv[i] << endl;
  }
  return 0;
}
```

This example also shows that the vector class supports a method named
push_back (similar to the Python list append method). The push_back method
takes one parameter that matches the type with which the vector is instantiated.
The vector class also overloads the bracket operator so that the individual items
in the vector can be accessed using the square bracket array notation.

The vector class supports a default constructor, as the previous example shows,
and also has a constructor that takes one or two default parameters. The default
constructor produces a vector with no items in it. When you specify one parameter,
it is an integer specifying the size of the initial dynamic array to create. The second
default parameter is the default value to use to initialize each of the elements in the

dynamic array, so its type is the type that you are storing in the `vector`. The next
example demonstrates this.

```
// vec2.cpp
#include <iostream>
#include <vector>
using namespace std;

int main()
{
  // creates a vector with 5 int elements, each set to 3
  vector<int> iv(5, 3);
  // creates a vector with 5 double elements, each set to 0.0
  vector<double> dv(5);
  int i;

  for (i=0; i<5; ++i) {
    cout << iv[i] << " " << dv[i] << endl;
  }
}
```

If we specify the size but do not specify a second parameter, the default constructor (for the class being stored in the `vector`) is called for each element in the
`vector`; this is yet another reason you should always provide a default constructor
for classes you write. For numeric types, the items in the `vector` will default to
zero as the comment in the example indicates.

The prototypes for some, but not all, of the methods the `vector` class provides
are listed in the next code example. We use the name `Item` to specify the data type
the `vector` instance contains. C++ defines the `typedef size_type` which is the
same as an `unsigned int` (i.e., a non-negative integer).

```
// allocates the dynamic array so the capacity of the array is n elements
void reserve(size_type n);

// appends x onto the end of the vector
void push_back(Item x);

// removes and returns the last element in the vector
Item pop_back();

// returns True if the vector has no items in it, False otherwise
bool empty() const;
```

```
// returns the number of items in the vector
size_type size() const;

// returns the largest possible size for the vector
size_type max_size() const;

// returns the size of the dynamic array (i.e., the largest number of
// elements that can be stored in the vector without resizing it)
size_type capacity() const
```

The `vector` class also overloads the assignment operator. When you assign one `vector` variable to another, each of the individual elements in the `vector` instance on the right-hand side of the assignment operator is assigned to the corresponding position in the `vector` instance on the left-hand side of the assignment operator. The `vector` instance on the left-hand side will be resized if necessary so it can hold all the elements from the right-hand side instance.

Many of the STL classes also provide support for iteration. We will show a simple example, but not cover all the details. STL classes that support iterators include the methods `begin()` and `end()` which return an `iterator` object. Some classes also support methods for iterating through the container in reverse order using the methods `rbegin()` and `rend()`. The following example shows the use of an iterator with the `vector` class.

```cpp
// vec3.cpp
#include <iostream>
#include <vector>
using namespace std;

int main()
{
  vector<int> iv;
  vector<int>::iterator iter;
  int i;

  for (i=0; i<10; ++i) {
    iv.push_back(i);
  }

  for (iter=iv.begin(); iter != iv.end(); ++iter) {
    cout << *iter << endl;
  }
  return 0;
}
```

The output of the example is the numbers 0 through 9. The example shows the declaration of an iterator variable named `iter` that can be used to iterate through a `vector` containing integers. The `begin()` method of the `vector` class is used to initialize the iterator. The `for` loop uses the `end()` method to determine if the iterator has processed all the items, and the prefix increment operator (`++iter`) is used to move the iterator to the next item; this is the reason we used the prefix version of the increment operator in all our `for` loop examples. Inside the loop, each item can be accessed using the pointer deference notation (`*iter`).

In addition to the `vector` template class, the Standard Template Library also provides template class implementations of a queue, list, set, and hash table along with algorithms and iterators for use with a number of the classes. If you are interested in learning more about the STL, you can find complete books dedicated to discussing the details of the STL.

12.3.2 User-defined Template Classes

If the STL does not define the data structure you need to use or you are using an old compiler that does not fully support the STL, you can write your own template classes. As is common with non-template classes, template classes are typically split into two files: a header file and an implementation file. As we discussed earlier, a template function does not actually cause any code to be generated unless it is used. The same is true of template classes and the methods they define. As we also explained, the compiler needs to have access to the template function/method code when compiling the file that calls that template function/method. Some programmers place the entire code for all the functions and methods in the header file. You cannot do this for non-template functions and classes since it will produce multiple definitions of the functions and classes. Since template declarations do not actually produce any code, having them included in multiple files is not a problem.

Some programmers place the function or method code in a file with the suffix .template and then have the header file include the .template file at the bottom of the header file. This has the same effect of placing all the code in the header file, but allows a programmer using our class to see only the interface for the template functions and classes in the header file without seeing the details of the implementation of the functions and methods. Of course, we cannot completely hide the implementation from users since their compiler needs access to the implementation file. We will use this technique of a separate .template file in our examples.

When writing template classes, both the class definition and the implementation of each method must indicate that it is a template. The syntax for template methods is the same as it is for template functions. We will demonstrate the syntax for template classes with a template implementation of a stack class.

```
// Stack.h
#ifndef __STACK__H__
#define __STACK__H__
#include <cstdlib> // for NULL

template <typename Item>
class Stack {

public:
  Stack();
  ~Stack();

  // const member functions
  int size() const { return size_; }
  bool top(Item &item) const;

  // modification member functions
  bool push(const Item &item);
  bool pop(Item &item);

private:
  // prevent these methods from being called
  Stack(const Stack &s);
  void operator=(const Stack &s);

  void resize();
  Item *s_;
  int size_;
  int capacity_;
};

#include "Stack.template"

#endif // _STACK_H__
```

The extra syntax is to put `template <typename Item>` before the class declaration. As with functions, you can use any identifier in place of `Item`. This `Stack` class uses a dynamic array to store the elements on the stack. The declaration `Item *s_` declares the pointer to the dynamic array for the data. Since we used `template <typename Item>` before the class declaration, we need to use `Item` as the data type here so that it matches. As indicated earlier, we can either include a Stack.template file containing the implementation or put the template method implementations at the bottom of the header file. In our example, we declared the copy constructor and assignment operator private but did not provide the code for them in the following .template file. This means that these methods cannot be called as we discussed in subsection 10.4.2.

```
// Stack.template
template <typename Item>
Stack<Item>::Stack()
{
  s_ = NULL;
  size_ = 0;
  capacity_ = 0;
}

template <typename Item>
Stack<Item>::~Stack()
{
  delete [] s_;
}

template <typename Item>
bool Stack<Item>::top(Item &item) const
{
  if (size_ > 0) {
    item = s_[size_-1];
    return true;
  }
  else
    return false;
}

template <typename Item>
bool Stack<Item>::push(const Item &item)
{
  if (size_ == capacity_) {
    resize();
  }
  if (size_ != capacity_) {
    s_[size_] = item;
    size_++;
    return true;
  }
  else
    return false;
}
```

```
template <typename Item>
bool Stack<Item>::pop(Item &item)
{
  if (size_ > 0) {
    size_--;
    item = s_[size_];
    return true;
  }
  else
    return false;
}

template <typename Item>
void Stack<Item>::resize()
{
  Item *temp;
  int i;

  if (capacity_ == 0) {
    capacity_ = 4;
  }
  else {
    capacity_ = 2 * capacity_;
  }
  temp = new Item[capacity_];
  for (i=0; i<size_; i++) {
    temp[i] = s_[i];
  }
  delete [] s_;
  s_ = temp;
}
```

In this `Stack` implementation we have returned a Boolean value for many of the methods, indicating whether or not each method succeeds. Since we can return only one value in C++, we used pass by reference to send the data back from the `top` and `pop` methods. Note that we also passed the value to the `push` method as a `const` reference parameter since we do not know whether the value will be a small data type such as an `int` or a class containing many data members. We also used `if` statements in the methods that allocate dynamic memory to be certain they succeed (e.g., the `push` method makes certain there is room in the array and returns `false` if allocating a larger array when necessary failed). These extra checks will result in the implementation being slightly slower than it would be without the `if` statements. In most cases, you could write the code without these tests as the allocation will always succeed unless you are dealing with stacks that approach the size of the memory your computer can access (at least two gigabytes on most modern architectures).

To declare an instance of the template class, we specify the data type the stack will hold with the declaration just as we did with the STL `vector` class. The following code fragment demonstrates the syntax. To stay short, the example does not test all the stack methods, but remember that you need to test all the methods of a template class since some compilers do not check the syntax of methods that are not instantiated.

```
// test_Stack.cpp
#include "Stack.h"

int main()
{
  Stack<int> int_stack;
  Stack<double> double_stack;

  int_stack.push(3);
  double_stack.push(4.5);
  return 0;
}
```

In this short example, we ignored the return value from the `push` method. To be safe and check to be certain all the allocations succeed, we could write it as

```
if (!int_stack.push(3)) {
  cerr << "stack.push failed\n";
}
if (!double_stack.push(4.5)) {
  cerr << "stack.push failed\n";
}
```

Writing all these tests is tedious and probably unnecessary for a small program that only pushes a few items onto the stack since that should never result in a memory allocation failing. For a larger, mission critical program, these values should be tested. In Python, we would likely handle these issues using exception handling. C++ also supports exception handling, but it is not as commonly used as it is in Python. When using exception handling in C++, you need to be very careful when using it with dynamic memory allocation. If an exception is generated during a sequence of instructions that may have allocated memory, you need to be certain that memory is properly deallocated. You also need to be aware if the memory allocation did not happen before the exception was generated so that you do not later try to deallocate memory that was never allocated. We do not cover the details of writing C++ exception handling code in this book.

12.4   Chapter Summary

This chapter covers the basics of using C++ template functions and classes and how to write your own template functions and classes.

- Templates allow you to write functions and classes that can work with more than one type. The compiler generates separate versions of the machine code for each different type that is used.

- The compiler does not generate code unless a function or method is actually used; this means the compiler may not check the template code for syntax errors unless a function or class is used. You should fully test all template functions and classes you write to make certain they do not contain errors.

- C++ provides the Standard Template Library (STL) containing a number of classes and algorithms.

12.5   Exercises

True/False Questions

1. Templates allow you to write code once and reuse it with multiple types.

2. The compiler will always catch syntax mistakes in your C++ template functions and methods.

3. For each data type a template function is called with, the compiler generates a separate copy of the machine language instructions for the function.

4. You can place template function or method implementations in an implementation file (`.cpp`) and the linker will correctly link the code so it can be called from other implementation files.

5. Templates give you the same flexibility that Python's dynamic typing does.

Multiple Choice Questions

1. When you write a template function,

    a) the compiler generates one set of machine language instructions for all types.
    b) the compiler generates a separate set of machine language instructions for each type that you call the template function with.

c) the compiler generates a separate set of machine language instructions for every built-in type and every class your program uses whether or not the template function is called with each type.

d) the C++ run-time environment generates the machine language instructions as needed when the function is called with different types.

2. What is/are the advantages of using templates instead of a `typedef` statement and cutting and pasting the code?

a) The resulting executable program requires less memory.

b) The resulting executable program will run faster.

c) You do not have to write as much code or risk making errors when copying the code.

d) all of the above

3. Which of the following are techniques for writing C++ template classes?

a) You may write a class header file as you usually do and at the bottom of the file, include the file containing the implementation of the template methods.

b) You may write a class header as you usually do and write the implementation of the methods with the inline keyword.

c) You may write a class header as you usually do and write the implementation of the methods without the inline keyword.

d) a and b

4. Using a template class even when your program only creates an instance of the class with one data type

a) requires less memory than not using templates if you call all the methods.

b) requires more memory than not using templates if you call all the methods.

c) requires the same amount of memory than not using templates if you call all the methods.

d) will execute more slowly than not using templates.

5. Based on the example using the `vector` class, what does the `iter` variable correspond to?

a) the address of the `iv` variable

b) the address of the current element in the array

c) the value of the current element in the array

d) none of the above

Short-Answer Questions

1. Without operator overloading, would it be possible to create a template-based version of our maximum function? If not, explain why not or if so, explain how you would do it.

2. Could a template-based version of our LList from the previous chapter contain multiple types in one list? Explain why or why not.

3. How do you determine if a template class needs to write a destructor, copy constructor, and assignment operator?

4. Do the functions and methods generated from templates execute more slowly, more quickly, or the same as the same code written without templates? Why?

5. Is it possible to write template code without allowing the person using your template code to see the source code of your template code? (With non-template code, the user only needs to see the header file and the implementation can be a compiled object file or library.) Why or why not?

Programming Exercises

1. Write a template version of the mergesort algorithm and test it with multiple types.

2. Implement a queue using templates along with code to test it.

3. Implement our List dynamic array using templates along with code to test it.

4. Implement our LList linked implementation using templates along with code to test it.

5. Implement a binary search tree using templates along with code to test it.

Chapter 13

Heaps, Balanced Trees, and Hash Tables

Objectives

- To understand the binary heap data structure and how to implement it.

- To understand the AVL balanced tree data structure and how to implement it.

- To understand the hash table data structure and the basics of its implementation options.

13.1 Introduction

Now that we have covered a number of basic data structures and introduced the C++ programming language, which required us to have a better understanding of the low-level details of memory allocation and deallocation, we will examine a number of more advanced data structures and algorithms in the remainder of this book. We will discuss implementation issues for Python and C++. In most cases, we will present a Python implementation and have you implement it in C++ so you can continue to develop your C++ skills.

The data structures we have covered so far are all container objects allowing us to store and retrieve information. List objects allow us to store data in an order defined by the user. The array-based list supports efficient access by position, but does not provide efficient searching for a specific item unless we keep the list in sorted order. Inserting to and deleting from an array-based list are not efficient. We also examined a linked implementation of a list that supports efficient insertion and deletion, but requires more memory and does not support efficient access by position. Stacks and queues are also container objects, but they are not as generic as lists; they only support accessing the data in a certain order and are not intended to be used for random searching or access. Trees are useful for storing hierarchical data or for storing information so it can potentially be searched more efficiently as is the case with a binary search tree.

In this chapter, we will examine additional container data structures. Priority queues and heaps are useful for storing data and then accessing it in a sorted order efficiently. Balanced trees are an extension of the basic binary search tree that maintains a balanced structure for the tree no matter what order the elements are inserted. This ensures that searching for an item is always a $\Theta(lgn)$ operation. Hash tables are a data structure that provide very efficient inserting, deleting, and searching operations. You are already familiar with hash tables since that is what a Python dictionary is. We will examine the implementation details of heaps, priority queues, balanced trees, and hash tables in this chapter.

13.2 | Priority Queues and Heaps

In section 5.3, we studied first in, first-out queues. In some cases, we may want to prioritize the order items are processed. For example, you prioritize the order that you perform tasks. A common priority is when they are due. You likely give a higher priority to a task that is due in two days than a task that is due in a week, even if the task that is due in two days was assigned later than the task that is due in a week. If you put the tasks in a queue when they were assigned, the one that is due later would be dequeued before the one that is due earlier. Another common example is that hospital emergency rooms prioritize the order they treat patients based on the severity of the injuries or illnesses. Your computer's operating system prioritizes its execution of programs so that crucial operating system tasks and interactive programs get more frequent access to the CPU. The data structure for handling these types of situations is known as a *priority queue*. Each item in a priority queue must be assigned a priority value and these values are used to determine the highest priority item that should be dequeued next. A specification for a priority queue using Python syntax is

```
class PQueue(object):

    def enqueue(self, item, priority):
        '''post: item is inserted with specified priority in the PQ'''

    def first(self):
        '''post: returns but does not remove highest priority item from the PQ'''

    def dequeue(self):
      '''post: removes and returns the highest priority item from the PQ'''

    def size(self):
        '''post: returns the number of items in the PQ'''
```

There are a number of possible implementations of a priority queue. One is to maintain a sorted list of the items by priority order and enqueue the items in the appropriate position. As we discuss the run-time analysis, we will always state the worst-case running time unless we explicitly state we are specifying the best or average case. The enqueue operation would require $\Theta(n)$ time. If we are using an array, we can use a binary search and find the correct spot in $\Theta(lgn)$ time, but then we have to shift the items in the array to insert the new item. The worst case would be shifting all the items to insert at the beginning of the array, which requires $\Theta(n)$ time. If we use a linked list, it requires $\Theta(n)$ time to find the correct location for insertion and then the insertion can be performed in $\Theta(1)$ time. Another option is to append items onto the end of a list for the enqueue and search for the highest priority item during the dequeue; in this case, the dequeue requires $\Theta(n)$ time.

Using the data structures with which we are already familiar, either the enqueue or dequeue operation for a priority queue requires $\Theta(n)$ time. To improve on this, we will learn a new data structure known as a *binary heap*. The term *heap* is used to describe several different data structures in computer science. Computer scientists refer to the memory pool from which dynamic memory is allocated and deallocated as a heap. In this chapter, we will use the term *heap* to refer to the binary heap we are discussing here. A binary heap is a complete tree with the additional property that for every node, the item at that node is not less than the items in its children's nodes. You can also reverse this property so that the item at each node is not greater than the items at the node's children if you want to extract items in the reverse order. Remember that a *complete tree* means that at every depth level except the last level, each level has the maximum number of nodes and at the last level, the nodes are filled from the left. Figure 13.1 shows examples of complete trees that are and are not binary heaps; the tree on the right is not a heap. In these examples, we are showing only the one value that is required to indicate the position in the heap; this value corresponds to the priority for a priority queue. To actually create a priority queue, we would need to store both the priority value and the data you want to store in the priority queue.

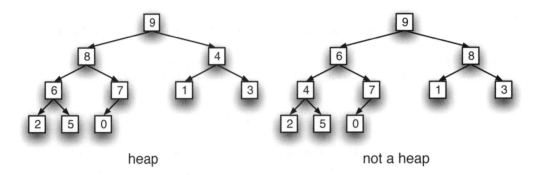

heap   not a heap

Figure 13.1: Two complete trees with only the left one satisfying the heap property

In order to make the binary heap practical for a priority queue, we must find algorithms to insert and remove an item from the binary heap in less than $\Theta(n)$ time. Given our definition of the binary heap, the highest priority item is at the root of the tree so it is easy to find and return it in $\Theta(1)$ time. Once we have done that, we need to update the heap so that the next highest priority item is at the root of the tree. Because of the heap property, the next highest priority item is one of the two children of the original root node. We could move to the root and repeat the process by moving the higher priority of its two children up to the spot in the second level. We could continue this process until we reach the bottom of the tree. The problem is that we may end up with a non-complete tree because the item we moved up from the bottom row may not have been the right-most node in the row. To prevent this from happening we can follow a slightly different process. We can temporarily move the right-most item in the bottom level of the tree to the root node and then move it down the tree by swapping it with the higher priority child. We repeat this process of moving the item down the tree until the item we originally moved to the root has moved down the tree to a location where the heap property is satisfied. Since we moved the item at the right-most spot in the bottom row, the tree will remain a complete tree.

Figure 13.2 shows the process of shifting the last item down the tree. In this example, the highest priority item 9 is removed from the heap and the last item in the heap (4) is temporarily moved to the root of the tree. We move 4 down the tree until the heap property is satisfied. We check the root's two children and find the higher priority item is 8 and that is larger than 4 so we swap the two items. Now we check the two children of the current location where 4 is and find the higher priority item is 7. We swap 7 and 4 since 7 has a higher priority. Now we check the 4 node's two children and find that both have a lower priority (2 and 0) so we are done. In practice we do not swap items; instead, we keep track of the item that was last in the tree and move the items up the tree until we find the spot the last item needs to be placed and then move it there. In this example, we would move 8 to the root, move 7 to where 8 was and then place 4 where 7 was since that is the location that satisfies the heap property.

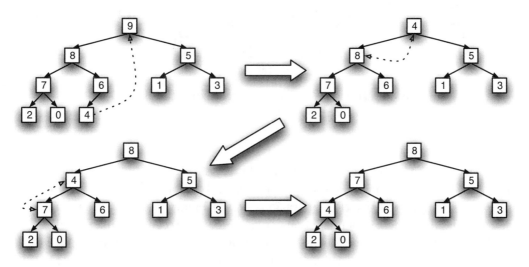

Figure 13.2: Removing 9 and reorganizing the heap

We can use a similar process for inserting an item into the heap. We place the new item at the last spot in the bottom row of the tree and then move it up the tree by swapping it with its parent until the heap property is satisfied. This will also ensure that the tree remains a complete tree. Figure 13.3 shows an example of this process. The value 8 is added to the end of the heap and then swapped with 4 and then swapped with 7. At this point, 8 is less than its parent (9) and the heap property is again satisfied. As with removing an item, in practice, we do not swap the items; instead we would move 4 to its new location, move 6 to its new location, and then place 8 in the correct location.

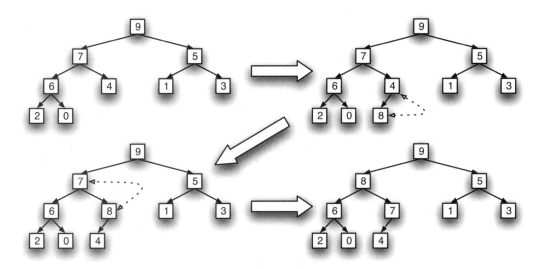

Figure 13.3: Inserting the 8 and reorganizing the heap

We indicated that to make the binary heap a better implementation for a priority queue, the enqueue and dequeue operations needed to be more efficient than $\Theta(n)$. For both the insertion and deletion operations of the binary heap, the maximum number of items moved is the height of the tree. Since the tree is complete, this is $\Theta(lgn)$ so both the enqueue and dequeue operations of the priority queue can be performed in $\Theta(lgn)$ time if we use a binary heap to implement the queue. This meets our goal of being better than $\Theta(n)$.

When we originally discussed binary trees, we indicated that an array implementation is appropriate when the tree is complete, so we use an array or list to implement the heap instead of linked nodes. As we demonstrated, the basic algorithms used in the heap are moving items up and down the tree. We will make use of the code to move items down the tree for two different heap methods, so we will write a method that performs this operation and call it from those two methods. The following Python code shows this method, commonly known as **heapify** or **percolate_down**, along with the constructor and a method to return the number of elements in the heap. These methods create a heap that is implemented as an array using an instance variable named **heap** with the root node at position one in the list. The instance variable **heap_size** indicates the number of items in the heap. Starting the tree at position one of the array results in simpler calculations for the parent, the left child, and right child than storing the root at position zero. With the root node at position one, the left child of the element at position i is 2*i, the right child is 2*i+1, and the parent is i/2 using integer division (5 // 2 is 2).

```
# Heap.py
class Heap(object):

    def __init__(self, items=None):

        '''post: a heap is created with specified items'''

        self.heap = [None]
        if items is None:
            self.heap_size = 0
        else:
            self.heap += items
            self.heap_size = len(items)
            self._build_heap()

    def size(self):

      '''post: returns number of items in the heap'''

        return self.heap_size

    def _heapify(self, position):

        '''pre: items from 0 to position - 1 satisfy the heap property
        post: heap property is satisfied for the entire heap'''

        item = self.heap[position]
        while position * 2 <= self.heap_size:
            child = position * 2
            # if right child, determine maximum of two children
            if (child != self.heap_size and
                self.heap[child+1] > self.heap[child]):
                child += 1
            if self.heap[child] > item:
                self.heap[position] = self.heap[child]
                position = child
            else:
                break
        self.heap[position] = item
```

The delete_max method returns the element at the root node of the tree and uses the _heapify method to update the heap so the heap property is maintained as we discussed. We also include the insert method here.

```
    def delete_max(self):

      '''pre: heap property is satisfied
        post: maximum element in heap is removed and returned'''

        if self.heap_size > 0:
            max_item = self.heap[1]
            self.heap[1] = self.heap[self.heap_size]
            self.heap_size -= 1
            self.heap.pop()
            if self.heap_size > 0:
                self._heapify(1)
            return max_item

    def insert(self, item):

        '''pre: heap property is satisfied
        post: item is inserted in proper location in heap'''

        self.heap_size += 1
        # extend the length of the list
        self.heap.append(None)
        position = self.heap_size
        parent = position // 2
        while parent > 0 and self.heap[parent] < item:
            # move item down
            self.heap[position] = self.heap[parent]
            position = parent
            parent = position // 2
        # put new item in correct spot
        self.heap[position] = item
```

In some cases we may have a list of values that we want to turn into a heap. We could accomplish this by inserting the items one at a time into the heap. There is a more efficient method we can use that manipulates the existing array in place using the same technique of shifting items down the tree that we used in the _heapify method. Leaf items in the complete tree cannot have children that violate the heap property and also cannot be moved down since there is no child to swap the item with. This tells us that we can start at the middle of the array since any items beyond that do not have children. We can then update the tree in a bottom-up manner so the heap property eventually holds for the entire tree. This is done by calling our _heapify method for each non-leaf node in the tree starting at the last node that has a child (which is the middle element in the array). The Python code for this is

```
def _build_heap(self):

    '''pre: self.heap has values in 1 to self.heap_size
    post: heap property is satisfied for entire heap'''

    # 1 through self.heap_size
    for i in range(self.heap_size // 2, 0, -1): # stops at 1
        self._heapify(i)
```

We know that the worst-case running time of `_heapify` is $\Theta(lgn)$ so the running time for the `_build_heap` method is no more than $\Theta(n * lgn)$. We notice that the `_heapify` method is called first with nodes at the next to last level of the tree and then with nodes closer to the root. Since we are calling it for each of these nodes, the total number of comparisons or moves performed by all the calls to `_heapify` is the sum of the heights of each of the tree nodes. For a full tree with **n** nodes and height $h = lgn$, there is one node with height h, two nodes with height $h - 1$, four nodes with height $h - 2$, and so on up to 2^{h-1} nodes with height 1. We will not go through the mathematical details, but the sum of this is $\Theta(n)$. This means that our `_build_heap` method is $\Theta(n)$.

We have written the binary heap so that we can easily extract the maximum value. We could just as easily make it so that we can efficiently extract the minimum element. For this case the heap property is that for each node, its child nodes are greater than the node. With this change, we would write a `delete_min` method instead of a `delete_max` method.

13.2.1 Heapsort

We can use the `_heapify` and `remove` methods to sort items in $\Theta(n * lgn)$ time. This algorithm is appropriately known as *heapsort*. Your first thought might be to modify the code to remove the minimum from the heap each time. You could then repeatedly call the `delete_min` method and append the items onto the end of an array or list. The drawback of this technique is that it requires a separate array or list, doubling the amount of memory required. Since the heap size decreases each time we remove an item, we can use the space at the end of the array for the removed items. To use this technique, we organize the heap so that the maximum element is removed from the heap. Each time we remove an item, we can place it at the last spot in the heap before the item was removed. After we have removed all the items except one, the resulting array will be sorted. After this process, the heap property will not be satisfied so we can no longer use it as a heap; the heap property will actually be reversed since the items are now sorted from minimum to maximum. The following Python code implements the heapsort algorithm.

```
def heapsort(self):

    '''pre: heap property is satisfied
    post: items are sorted in self.heap[1:self.sorted_size]'''

    sorted_size = self.heap_size
    for i in range(0, sorted_size - 1):
        # Since delete_max calls pop to remove an item, we need
        # to append a dummy value to avoid an illegal index.
        self.heap.append(None)
        item = self.delete_max()
        self.heap[sorted_size - i] = item
```

The `heapsort` algorithm can be used on an existing heap or we can first call `_build_heap` on an unorganized array. Since the `_build_heap` method is $\Theta(n)$ and each `delete_max` call is no worse than $\Theta(lgn)$, the overall running time for the `heapsort` is $\Theta(n*lgn)$. Also note that we need to call `delete_max` only $n-1$ times since after the last call, the final remaining element in the heap is the minimum item which is at the root of the tree (the first position of the array). After these $n-1$ calls, the array is sorted.

13.2.2 Notes on Heap and Priority Queue Implementations

As mentioned earlier, since the heap is a complete tree, it makes sense to implement it as an array. This provides the efficient access to both the parent and the children that is needed for moving items up and down the tree. The formulas for accessing the parent and children are simpler if the root is at position one in the array instead of position zero. This means the array size must be one larger than the number of items in the tree. In Python you must explicitly store a value in position zero of the list; it is common to store `None` as the placeholder. In languages where you explicitly allocate space in the array, you will need to resize the array in the `insert` method if the array is already full. This means you need an instance variable to indicate the number of items in the tree and the maximum size of the array. It is common to double the size of the array when resizing it. This means that no more than 50% of memory is wasted and that the amortized cost of the resizing operation is $\Theta(1)$ per insertion.

As we discussed at the beginning of this chapter, if you have a binary heap then it is easy to implement a priority queue. A priority queue class is typically implemented with a binary heap as an instance variable. The `enqueue` and `dequeue` methods of the priority queue call the `insert` and `delete` methods using the binary heap instance variable. The priority is typically an integer value while the item can be of any data type. In C++ we will want to use templates to implement both the binary heap and priority queue classes. In languages that provide operator overloading, the data type you insert into the binary heap needs to support the comparison operators. In Python you can simply store the items in the queue as a tuple of the form (priority, item) since the tuples will be compared first by the priority part of the tuple. In C++, you can create a class containing two instance variables: the integer priority and the data element being inserted in the heap and priority queue. You will need to write the comparison operators for this class so that elements are compared by the integer priority and the other data element is ignored.

13.3 Balanced Trees

Earlier we studied binary search trees and noticed that the worst case search time was the height of the tree. Ordinary binary search trees can have height n for n items in the tree. Consider what happens if you insert the items in sorted order; each node has only a right child, making the height n. If the tree is approximately balanced then the height of the tree is closer to lgn than n. This means that if the tree is balanced, both insertions and searches run in $\Theta(lgn)$ time. A straightforward method for maintaining a balanced tree is to update the tree structure as needed as we insert the items. To make this a good solution, the balancing operation must be able to be performed efficiently.

The first issue we need to discuss is what we mean by the tree being *balanced*. A perfectly balanced tree is a full tree. That is obviously not possible unless the number of items in the tree is exactly one less than a power of two (1, 3, 7, 15, 31, 63, and so on). A complete tree would have the same worst-case search time of $\Theta(lgn)$ as a full tree since the height of a complete tree is lgn. The problem is that it would be computationally expensive to rearrange the tree at each insertion to maintain a complete tree. To convince yourself of this, think about what you would do to maintain a complete tree if the elements were inserted in order.

We need to be less restrictive on the balancing requirement at the expense of the tree having more levels. We could start with requiring the height of the left and right subtrees of the root node to be the same. As Figure 13.4 shows, this is not sufficient. The height of the tree is $n/2$, and thus the search time would be $\Theta(n)$.

This should lead you to realize that we need to enforce the balancing at every node but cannot require exact balancing or we would have a full tree. A reasonable solution is to require that the heights of the left and right subtrees of each and every node differ by at most one. This is the solution developed by G. M. Adelson-Velskii

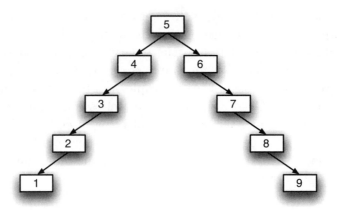

Figure 13.4: Only requiring root node to have subtrees of same height allows for trees of height $n/2$

and E. M. Landis in the 1960s and is known as an *AVL tree*. Figure 13.5 shows an example of an AVL tree and a non-AVL tree. The tree on the right is not an AVL tree because the height of the 5 node's left subtree is one and the height of its right subtree is three. The height of the root node's subtrees also differ by more than one.

The next question you should be asking yourself is what is the worst-case height of an AVL tree? Your intuition might make you think that the height can be no worse than twice that of a full tree with the same number of nodes since at every node the height of the subtrees differ by at most one. This tells us that at most half the spots in a full tree could be empty while still maintaining the balancing property. If the height is at most twice that of the best possible case (which is lgn), the height of an AVL tree is at most $2 * lgn$. This tells us that the worst-case search time is $\Theta(lgn)$ and this is what we want. To convince us that this intuition is correct, let's look at some examples. Figure 13.6 shows the worst possible cases for AVL trees (i.e., the configuration that achieves the maximum height for a specified number of nodes). As it turns out the worst case is closer to $1.44 * lgn$, but this improvement over $2 * lgn$ does not affect our calculation of the worst-case running time of the search function.

Now that we have convinced ourselves that AVL trees will provide the $\Theta(lgn)$ search time we want, we need to determine an efficient algorithm that maintains the balancing property as we insert items into the binary search tree. Adelson-Velskii

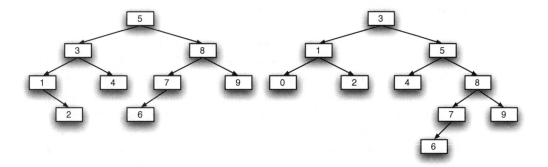

Figure 13.5: An AVL tree on the left and a non-AVL tree on the right

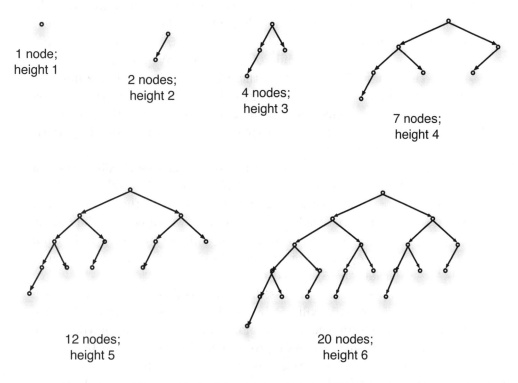

Figure 13.6: Worst-case height AVL trees

and Landis developed these algorithms for rebalancing the tree that we will look at next.

In order for the balancing property to be violated, we must be inserting a node into an existing leaf node (if a node already has one child, adding a second child does not violate the balancing property for any node in the tree). As you might suspect, there will be some symmetries in the cases depending on whether we are inserting a new node in a left or right subtree of the node whose balancing property will be violated. For the AVL property to be violated at a node, that node must have a subtree with a depth of at least two since the height of the node's two subtrees must differ by two and the newly inserted node must be at least two levels deeper in the tree than the node at which the AVL tree property is violated. Since each node has at most two children, this gives us four cases.

Figure 13.7 shows two of the symmetric cases. In the first case, the value 3 was just inserted. We know this because that is the node that causes the AVL property to be violated. The left subtree of the 8 node has a height of three and its right subtree has a height of one. This is an insertion into the left subtree of the left child of the 8 node. We rearrange the tree by shifting the 5 node to the root and making the original root node the right child of the 5 node. We then need to figure out where to place the 7 node. We know that the original root node containing the 8 will not have a left child after the rotation since its left child before the rotation (5) moved up a level. We can place the 7 node as the left child of the 8 node. It is important to note that the binary search tree ordering is maintained by these changes made to the tree structure.

The second example in Figure 13.7 shows the mirror image of the first case. In this case it is an insertion into the right subtree of the right child of the node at which the AVL tree property is violated. The right subtree of the 3 node has a height of three and the left subtree has a height of one so we know that the 8 node was just inserted. We shift the 6 node up to the root and move 5 to the right child of 3. Again, we know the 3 node will not have a right child after the rotation since its right child before the rotation (6) moved up a level.

In the rotation examples we just discussed, we replaced the root node in both cases. In many cases, the root node will not be the deepest node at which the AVL property of the tree is violated and the root will not change. The rotation will always occur at the deepest node at which the AVL property is violated. Figure 13.8 shows an example similar to the first single rotation we discussed. In this case the subtree rooted at the 8 node is the left child of a root node with a right subtree. When we insert the 3 node, the AVL property is violated at the 8 node and we make the same changes as before (not shown in Figure 13.8). The key point to realize is that the

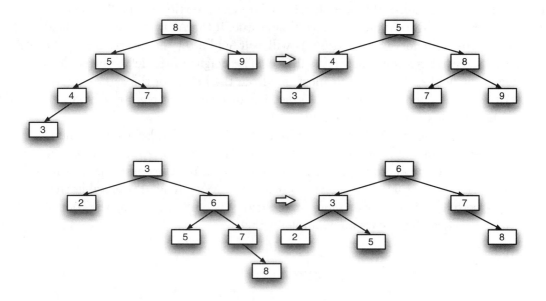

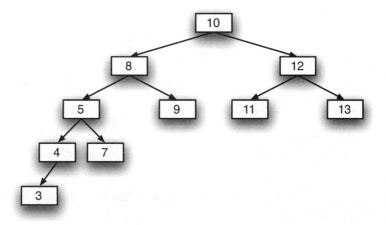

Figure 13.7: Two mirror image AVL single rotations

Figure 13.8: A case where the AVL single rotation does not replace the root node

subtree with the root 8 has the same height before the insertion of the 3 as it does after the insertion and rotation fix. Since this is true, if the AVL tree property held at the root node 10 before the insertion, it will still hold after the insertion and the rotation that rearranges the root's left subtree. The height of the left subtree does not change so it will still differ by at most one from the height of the right subtree. This tells us that at most one rotation is needed to return the tree to a balanced state no matter where the rotation occurs.

In the examples so far, the newly inserted node is three levels below the node that is at the root of the rotation. If we insert the numbers 3, 2, and 1 then the 3 is the root of the rotation and the 2 is the new root after the rotation. In that case, the newly inserted node is two levels below the root. It is also possible that the newly inserted node is four or more levels below the node that is at the root of the rotation. Figure 13.9 shows an example of this.

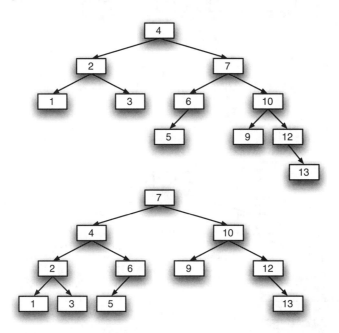

Figure 13.9: AVL single rotation in which the newly inserted node is four levels below the root of the rotation

In this example, the 13 node is the newly inserted node. The AVL property holds at each node except the root node (4) so the rotation happens at that level. If you are thinking about the implementation of the insertion and rotation, this may cause you to realize that an iterative solution will be difficult since once we find the location to insert at the bottom of the tree, we may need to move all the way back up the tree to find the node for which the AVL tree property is violated. Since most tree implementations do not have a pointer to the parent we do not have an easy way to do this. A recursive solution will make this much simpler. As it returns from each level of recursion, it is essentially moving back up the tree. We will discuss the implementation details later in this section.

We have examined two cases in which the AVL property is violated for a specific node: inserting into the left subtree of the left child of the node and inserting into the right subtree of the right child. The other two cases are inserting into the right subtree of the left child and inserting into left subtree of the right child. A single rotation cannot update the tree so that the AVL property is maintained for these two cases. Fortunately, in these cases, two rotations will update the tree so the AVL property is maintained.

Figure 13.10 shows an AVL tree that just had the value 4 inserted into the tree. The AVL property no longer holds for the root node since the height of its left subtree is now three and the height of its right subtree is one. This figure shows the case of inserting into the right subtree of the left child. None of the single rotations we examined earlier will fix this case; however, performing two single rotations will. Figure 13.11 shows the intermediate result after the first rotation on the left and then the final result on the right after the second rotation. After the two rotations, the tree again meets the AVL property. We will leave drawing the case of inserting into the left subtree of the right child as an exercise. As is the case with single rotations, the node at which the property is violated after an insertion does not have to be the root node. The root node 6 in Figure 13.10 could be part of a left or right subtree with a tree of an appropriate height on the other side of the tree that maintains the AVL property.

In order to implement an AVL tree we must keep track of a node's height which is defined as the maximum of the height of its two subtrees plus one. This means our `TreeNode` class must contain an additional instance variable to store this. We also need an algorithm to compute the height of a node. Since the height of a node is defined in terms of the heights of its subtrees, we will need to compute the heights starting at the bottom of the tree as we insert new items and update the heights as we move up the tree. The height of a node will be one plus the maximum of the heights of its left subtree and its right subtree. We will use the following `TreeNode` class and `get_height` function in our sample tree node.

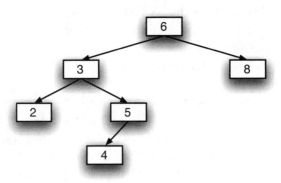

Figure 13.10: Insertion of the value 4 into an AVL tree

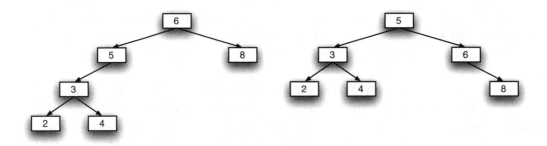

Figure 13.11: Result after the first rotation and result after the second rotation

```
# TreeNode.py
class TreeNode(object):

    def __init__(self, data=None, left=None, right=None, height=0):

        '''post: TreeNode with specified data and left/right subtrees is created'''

        self.item = data
        self.left = left
        self.right = right
        self.height = height

def get_height(t):

    '''post: returns height of a subtree at node t, empty tree has height -1'''

    if t is None:
        return -1
    else:
        return t.height
```

It is important to note that `TreeNode` has an instance variable named `height` and that the `get_height` function is not a method of the class; it is a standalone function. We can determine this by the fact that `get_height` is not indented as the `TreeNode` method is. The `get_height` function allows us to easily determine the height of a node's two subtrees. If we use it to determine the height of the left subtree of the node and that node does not have a left subtree (i.e., its `left` instance variable is `None`), it will return `-1`. This will result in a leaf node having a height of zero since the height of each of its two subtrees is `-1` and we add `1` to that. We cannot make the `get_height` function a method in the `TreeNode` class and still be able to call it with a non-existent node (`None`) as we can with `get_height` being a standalone function. This is necessary when we want to determine the height of the left or right subtree of a node that may be empty (the left or right child is `None`).

The following code fragment contains a partial Python implementation of an AVL tree. The tree has one instance variable containing the `root` node. The value `None` for `root` indicates an empty tree. A recursive implementation of the `insert` method is much simpler than an iterative method since we need to move back up the tree and adjust the heights and possibly perform a single or double rotation at one of the ancestors of the newly inserted node. The recursive calls to insert the node in a left or right subtree of a node return and move back up the tree, allowing us to make the appropriate updates after the recursive call. To allow a programmer using our tree to call the `insert` method without specifying the `root` instance variable in the call, we use the technique of having the `insert` method call a helper method that does all the work with the **root** instance variable as a parameter. The code fragment includes the calls for inserting into the left subtree; the similar code for the right subtree is left as an exercise.

```python
# AVLTree.py
from TreeNode import *

class AVLTree(object):

    def __init__(self):

        '''post: creates empty AVL tree'''

        self.root = None

    def insert(self, value):

        '''post: insert value into proper location in AVL tree'''

        self.root = self._insert_help(self.root, value)

    def _insert_help(self, t, value):

        '''private helper method to insert value into AVL (sub)tree with
        root node t'''

        if t is None:
            t = TreeNode(value)

        elif value < t.item:
            t.left = self._insert_help(t.left, value)
            # left subtree height may be now larger than right subtree
            if get_height(t.left) - get_height(t.right) == 2:
                # determine which subtree the new value was inserted
                if value < t.left.item:
                    # insertion into left subtree of left child
                    t = self._left_single_rotate(t)
                else:
                    # insertion into right subtree of left child
                    t = self._right_left_rotate(t)

        else:
            # exercise for reader

        # update height of tree rooted at t
        t.height = max(get_height(t.left), get_height(t.right)) + 1
        return t
```

The `insert` method passes `root` as the parameter to the `_insert_help` function. When the tree is empty, the `root` must be changed to the newly created node, thus the `_insert_help` method needs to change the parameter that is passed to it. When the tree is not empty, the `_insert_help` method makes recursive calls with `t.left` or `t.right` as the parameter. When we get to the bottom of the tree where the new node will be created, the value of the parameter that is passed to `_insert_help` is `None`. When the new node is created, we need to change the `left` or `right` instance variable of the node that is above it in the tree. That is the node whose `left` or `right` instance variable is the parameter that is passed to the `_insert_help` function so you might think this does what we want. The key point to remember is that the formal parameter `t` is being set to a new object so that does not change the actual parameter (`t.left` or `t.right`) that was passed. To solve this issue in Python, we must pass the parameter and return the new value of the parameter (i.e., we must call it as `t = self._insert_help(t.left)` and the `_insert_help` method needs to end with a `return t` statement). The same issue occurs with the rotation methods so those methods need to be called in a similar manner. In C++, we may use pass by reference to accomplish this. We will discuss it at the end of this section.

As each recursive call to `_insert_help` returns, the code checks the heights of the left and right subtrees. Thus, the code will check the heights of the subtrees at each node along the path from the inserted node to the root. If the heights of the subtrees of any node differ by two, the code performs the appropriate single or double rotation. The following code is the single and double rotations that are used by the `_insert_help` fragment. The mirror image rotations are needed by the section of `_insert_help` that you are to write. The `_left_single_rotate` implements the first case in Figure 13.7. The methods are named based on where the insertion occurs. The `_left_single_rotate` method is called when an insertion into the left subtree of the left child occurs. The `_left_single_rotate` method performs a clockwise rotation that you may be tempted to think of as a right rotation even though it is named `_left_single_rotate`. Obviously, the names of the methods do not matter as long as the code calls the method that correctly updates the tree.

```
def _right_left_rotate(self, t):

    '''private rotation method for inserting into right subtree of
    left child of t'''

    t.left = self._right_single_rotate(t.left)
    t = self._left_single_rotate(t)
    return t
```

```
def _left_single_rotate(self, t):

    '''private rotation method for inserting into left subtree of
    left child of t'''

    grandparent = t
    parent = t.left

    grandparent.left = parent.right
    parent.right = grandparent
    t = parent

    grandparent.height = max(get_height(grandparent.left),
                             get_height(grandparent.right)) + 1
    parent.height = max(get_height(parent.left),
                        get_height(parent.right)) + 1
    return t
```

Although it is not clear from the **_insert_help** code, at most one single rotation or one double rotation fixes the AVL balancing property when a new item is inserted in the tree. The reason for this is the height of each subtree is the same after the insertion and rotation as before the insertion. The height of the tree only increases when we insert an item that does not require a rotation. As the recursive calls return, at most one rotation fix will occur. The rotation code executes in $\Theta(1)$ time since it is updating a few references or pointers. Because the height of the tree is $\Theta(lgn)$, the insertion process will require at most $\Theta(lgn)$ steps to find the correct spot, $\Theta(lgn)$ steps to recurse back up the tree, and a constant number of steps for the zero, one, or two rotations. This makes the running time for the overall algorithm of inserting and maintaining the AVL property $\Theta(lgn)$. Implementing a **search** method will also be $\Theta(lgn)$ since the height of the tree is $\Theta(lgn)$.

Maintaining the balancing property when deleting an arbitrary node from an AVL tree is much more complicated and we will not look at the details of an algorithm for it in this book. If deletion is required, possible solutions are to mark nodes as inactive and periodically build a new tree without these items if the tree becomes unbalanced. For a theoretical computer scientist, this is not an ideal solution, but in practice it might be better than developing and debugging a complicated algorithm that will not result in significant computation time savings. Since developer time is relatively expensive and computational time is relatively cheap, the choice of a simpler, but less efficient, algorithm is sometimes made. This does not mean that we should not study the best algorithms and data structures since we may need them at times, but it does mean there are cases where it is not worth the effort to implement more complicated algorithms and data structures. The best possible case is having a well-designed, tested library of efficiently implemented data structures and algorithms that you can reuse for many applications.

We noted that the `_insert_help` method of the `AVLTree` needs to change the parameter that is passed to it. In Python when we want to change a parameter, we need to write code such as `x = f(x)` and have the function return the formal parameter that corresponds to the actual parameter `x`. In C++, we can accomplish this using pass by reference as we discussed in subsection 8.12.3. Using our same example, the prototype would be `void f(int &x)` and we could call it as `f(x)` without needing the function to return `x`.

In a C++ implementation of the `AVLTree` class, the parameter that is passed to the `_insert_help` and rotation methods is a pointer to a `TreeNode`. This may be the first time you have attempted to pass a pointer by reference in C++. The syntax for this is to place the ampersand after the asterisk that indicates we are passing a pointer. For example, a prototype for the `_insert_help` function when we are storing `int` variables in the tree is `void _insert_help(BinaryTreeNode *&node, int item)`. A way to remember the order of the asterisk and the ampersand is to recall the statement: passing a pointer by reference. The pointer symbol (the asterisk) is placed before the reference symbol (the ampersand).

13.4 Other Tree Structures

There are a number of additional tree data structures such as other implementations of balanced binary trees and non-binary trees. We will not discuss the details of these data structures in this book. Some of these other tree structures are used in the implementations of databases. If you are interested in learning more about these topics, search for information on *red black trees*, *B-trees*, and *splay trees*.

13.5 Hash Tables

With our balanced binary tree implementation, the worst-case running time to find or insert an item is $\Theta(log n)$ time. Hash tables are a data structure that improve the lookup time to $\Theta(1)$ in most cases, although the worst case can be $\Theta(n)$. As mentioned in the introductory section of this chapter, Python's built-in dictionary data type is implemented as a *hash table*. Hash tables are also known as dictionaries or as *associative arrays*. As the "associative array" name implies, a hash table associates a key with a value as Python's dictionary does. The standard array data structure allows us to look up a value based on the position in the array while associative arrays allow us to look up a value based on a key. The goal of a hash table implementation is to provide efficient methods for inserting, deleting, and searching; we want the typical case for each of these methods to be $\Theta(1)$.

We will begin our explanation of the implementation of hash tables by looking at a simplified example in which the set of all possible keys is small and known in advance. The set of capital letters A through Z meets that requirement. Hash tables use an array to store the data. This means we can quickly look up an element by position. What we want to do is look up the key based on its value, so we need a function to map the key to a position in the array storing the key and value. In our example we need to be able to map each letter to a corresponding position in the array. The term for this mapping is a *hash function* or *hashing function*. In our example we know that the array size needs to be 26 and that a simple hash function would map the letter A to position 0 and the letter Z to position 25. The following Python function is an implementation of such a hash function.

```python
def hash_letter(c):
    '''pre: c is a one character string of a capital letter A-Z'''
    return ord(c) - ord('A')
```

The `hash_letter` function uses the Python `ord` function to convert a letter to its ASCII code and then subtracts the ASCII code for the letter A to give us a value between 0 and 25. We could use this function with an array or list of size 26. The hash function maps a key to the corresponding position in the array or list where the key's value is stored. If a key is not in the hash table, we must use a special value to indicate that position is not in use; in Python, we could use the value `None`, assuming that is not a valid value to be stored in the hash table. We do not need to store the key in the array since there is only one key that can map to each location in the array or list. The following is a complete Python implementation of a hash table (without using the built-in Python dictionary) that only allows capital letters as the keys; the running time for each method is $\Theta(1)$.

```python
# HashLetter.py
class HashLetter(object):

    def __init__(self):
        '''post: initializes simplified hash table'''

        self.table = 26 * [None,]
```

```
    def __getitem__(self, key):
        '''post: returns value for specified key'''

        assert 'A' <= key <= 'Z'
        pos = ord(key) - ord('A')
        if self.table[pos] == None:
            raise KeyError(key)
        else:
            return self.table[pos]

    def __setitem__(self, key, value):
        '''post: value for specified key is inserted into hash table'''

        assert 'A' <= key <= 'Z'
        pos = ord(key) - ord('A')
        self.table[pos] = value

    def __delitem__(self, key):
        '''specified key is removed from hash table'''

        assert 'A' <= key <= 'Z'
        pos = ord(key) - ord('A')
        self.table[pos] = None
```

The `HashLetter` class contains a single instance variable that is a list with 26 items. We store the value `None` in each position to indicate that the hash table does not contain a value at that location. We add a key/value pair to the hash table by mapping the letter key to the corresponding position in the list using the hash function and then store the value at that position in the list. Hash tables do not support storing multiple values for the same key (attempting to store a second value for a key overwrites the first value). When we attempt to look up a letter key, we use the hash function to map to a position in the Python list. If the value at that position in the list is `None`, that letter key is not in the hash table and the code raises a `KeyError` as the built-in Python dictionary does. If the value at the position in the list is not `None`, that is the value associated with the letter key and it is returned.

Since we have overloaded the various bracket operators, we can use the `HashLetter` class just as we would a Python dictionary for the key values A–Z. The following example using the interactive Python interpreter shows a sample use of our `HashLetter` class.

```
>>> d = HashLetter()
>>> d['a'] = 4
Traceback (most recent call last):
  File "<stdin>", line 1, in ?
  File "HashLetter.py", line 19, in __setitem__
    assert 'A' <= key <= 'Z'
AssertionError
>>> d['A'] = 4
>>> d['B'] = 5
>>> d['A']
4
>>> d['C']
Traceback (most recent call last):
  File "<stdin>", line 1, in ?
  File "HashLetter.py", line 13, in __getitem__
    raise KeyError, key
KeyError: 'C'
>>> d['A']
4
>>> d['B']
5
>>> del d['B']
>>> d['B']
Traceback (most recent call last):
  File "<stdin>", line 1, in ?
  File "HashLetter.py", line 13, in __getitem__
    raise KeyError, key
KeyError: 'B'
>>> d['A']
4
```

The strategy used in our simple example works fine when we know the possible key values in advance, but that is typically not the case. It also does not work well when the set of possible key values is large, but many of the key values will not be used. If our set of possible key values was all the integers from 0 to 2 billion, our array would need to be huge and take up more memory than a typical computer has. What if the possible key values were English words? What hash function should we use and how big should our array be? What do we do if two keys hash to the same position in the array? These are the implementation issues we will discuss in the remainder of this section.

The first step is to convert a key to a number so that we can then apply a mathematical function to map it to a position in the array. Hash tables are not limited to using numbers and strings as keys; we can take any data, whether it is a number, string, or class with various data members and use the data values to map to a number. In our simple example, we used the **ord** function to map the letter to a number based on its ASCII value. In the case of words, we could use some or all of the characters. We could pick the first two characters and add their ASCII values together or apply a function that multiplies each of them by a constant and adds the results together. Unfortunately, certain sequences of two characters occur often in the English language so a number of words would hash to the same position in the array. This problem is known as a *collision*. We can make this less likely to happen by using more letters and using a multiple based on the position; but we cannot prevent the problem from happening in some cases. We could generate a unique hash value for four unique letters using the following Python function for a string `w`.

```
def hash(w, array_size):

    '''pre: w is an ASCII string
    post: returns a value between 0 and array_size - 1'''

    v = 0
    for i in range(min(len(w), 4)):
        v = 128 * v + ord(w[i])
    return v % array_size
```

Before we apply the modulus operation, this hash function produces a unique number for all the unique sequences of four letters since the ASCII code for characters is less than 128. Obviously words that start out with the same first four letters (e.g., `friend` and `friendship`) will still produce the same value. The hash value may be a fairly large number, so to make certain the hash value is within the array size we compute the hash value modulus the array size. This produces a value between 0 and one less than the size of the array. Once we apply the modulus function, different four-letter words in our example may map to the same position if the size of the array is less than 128^4. We could use more than four letters, but that will take longer to compute the hash function, and once we apply the modulus operation to make certain we do not map beyond the end of our list, we can still end up with multiple words mapping to the same position in the list.

In our simple example, the letters map to the array in order (`A` mapped to position 0, `B` mapped to position 1, and so on), but it is not important that the mapping is in order. When the set of possible keys is larger than the typical number of keys that will be in the hash table (as is the case with storing a number of English words), you typically will not want the words to map in order; all that matters is that the hash function is a fast calculation that maps to the position where we expect to find the key and its value. With our hash function for words, the items certainly do not map in order unless the array size is very large.

As mentioned before, no matter what hash function we use, we can end up with multiple key values mapping to the same array position, and this is known as a collision. In fact, if we know the hash function, we can usually determine many keys that map to the same position. There are two common solutions to the collision problem, known as *chaining* and *open addressing*. With chaining, each array position stores a list of the key and item values whose keys map to that position. In the worst case all the keys we are storing would be in one position. With open addressing, if a key maps to a position that already has a key/value, we repeatedly apply another function until we find the key or find an empty position in the array. Using either method, we will have to store both the key and the value in the array so we can determine if we have found an existing key in the array. We did not need to do this with our simple `HashLetter` example because each key could map to only one location in the array.

The simplest form of open addressing is known as *linear probing*. In this case, our new hash function is $f(key, i) = (hash(key) + i) \bmod size$ for each i from 0 to $size - 1$ where $size$ is the size of the array for the hash table. What this effectively says is if the key is not found in $hash(key)$ with $i = 0$ then we start with $i = 1$ and see if the next position in the array has the key or is empty. We keep looking at the next position in the array, wrapping around from the end to the beginning, until we find either the key or an empty spot or get back to the original hash location. Obviously, if we find the key, we have found its key/value. If we reach an empty position in the array before finding the key, we know the key is not in the hash table. We should not get back to the original spot unless the hash table is full; for any practical hash table, it is necessary to resize the array before it gets full to make the hash table useful.

There are more complex open addressing functions than linear probing. One is known as *quadratic probing*. It uses the hash function $f(key, i) = (hash(key) + a * i^2 + b * i) \bmod size$ where a and b are integer constants and i plays the same role as it does in linear probing. Instead of looking in consecutive locations, this function will jump ahead a number of positions each time it finds a location that is not empty and does not match the key. This produces less clustering of key/value pairs in consecutive locations, but two keys with the same result for the $hash(key)$ function will search the same set of positions.

Another approach is known as *double hashing*. It uses two hash functions $h1$ and $h2$. If the first hash function $h1$ does not map to the key or an empty location, we repeatedly compute $h1(key) + i * h2(key) \bmod size$ with the values 0 to $size - 1$ for i until we find the key or an empty position. For any of the open addressing methods, the worst case requires that every array position be examined. For double hashing to work well (i.e., the entire hash table is not examined), the value produced by $h2(key)$ must be relatively prime (i.e., it cannot share any prime factors) with the size of the array. This can easily be done by having the size of the hash table be a power of 2 and having $h2(key)$ produce an odd number. In practice double hashing works better than linear probing or quadratic probing.

The following Python code example demonstrates a hash table using chaining. The constructor creates a list of the specified size. Each position in the list is initialized to an empty list. As items are added to the hash table, they will be appended to the inner list at the appropriate position in the outer list. The `_hash` function is not necessarily a good hash function, but it does incorporate the size of the array into the calculation, allowing it to continue working after we resize the array. The list `self.coef` is used to hold a multiplier to apply to each letter in the string. For example, with the list [11, 2, 5] and the word "cat", we calculate 11 * ord('c') + 2 * ord('a') + 5 * ord('t') and then take that result modulus the array size. If your hash table becomes nearly full and you resize the list, you will want to use larger values for the `self.coef` list of coefficients. Each of the other methods uses the hash function to map the key to a position in the array. We have included a `__str__` method so we can view the details of the internal data members of the hash table.

```python
# HashTable.py
class HashTable(object):
    def __init__(self, size=11):
        self.array_size = size
        self.table = []
        for i in range(self.array_size):
            self.table.append([])
        self.size = 0
        self.coef = [self.array_size, 2, 3, 7, 5, 13]

    def _hash(self, key):
        pos = 0
        for i in range(min(len(key), 6)):
            pos += self.coef[i] * ord(key[i])
        return pos % self.array_size

    def __setitem__(self, key, value):
        pos = self._hash(key)
        for i, (k, v) in enumerate(self.table[pos]):
            if key == k:
                self.table[pos][i] = (key, value)
                return
        self.table[pos].append((key, value))
        self.size += 1
```

```
    def __getitem__(self, key):

        pos = self._hash(key)
        for k, v in self.table[pos]:
            if key == k:
                return v
        raise KeyError(key)

    def __delitem__(self, key):

        pos = self._hash(key)
        for i, (k, v) in enumerate(self.table[pos]):
            if key == k:
                del self.table[pos][i]
                self.size -= 1
                return
        raise KeyError(key)

    def __str__(self):

        s = []
        for line in self.table:
            s.append(' ' + str(line))
        return '[\n' + '\n'.join(s) + '\n]'
```

We will use the following code fragment to demonstrate our hash table. It uses
words as the keys and the numbers as the values they map to (for example, the key
"quick" has value 1).

```
# test_HashTable.py
from HashTable import HashTable
h = HashTable()
i = 0
for s in 'the quick brown fox jumps over the lazy dog'.split():
    h[s] = i
    i += 1
print h
print h.size
print h['jumps']
del h['jumps']
print h
print h.size
```

```
try:
    print h['jumps']
except KeyError:
    print 'key error raised as expected'
else:
    print 'key error should have been raised'
```

The output of this example using our chaining hash table is the following. Make certain you understand where each key mapped to and when collisions occurred.

```
[
 []
 []
 []
 [('dog', 8)]
 []
 [('the', 6)]
 [('quick', 1), ('jumps', 4), ('over', 5)]
 []
 [('brown', 2)]
 []
 [('fox', 3), ('lazy', 7)]
]
8
4
[
 []
 []
 []
```

```
 [('dog', 8)]
 []
 [('the', 6)]
 [('quick', 1), ('over', 5)]
 []
 [('brown', 2)]
 []
 [('fox', 3), ('lazy', 7)]
]
7
key error raised as expected
```

The following Python code example demonstrates a hash table using open addressing with linear probing. This code will not work if you try to insert more key/value pairs than the array holds. One of the exercises asks you to extend this code to solve that problem. The constructor creates a list of the specified size and initializes each position to None. We use the same hash function as before. The methods to get, set, and delete a key must search for the specified key starting at the position returned by the hash function. When searching, we must continue until we find the key or find None. We use the modulus function when incrementing pos so it wraps from the end of the list to position 0.

```python
# HashTable2.py
class HashTable(object):

    def __init__(self, size=11):
        self.array_size = size
        self.table = self.array_size * [None]
        self.size = 0
        self.coef = [self.array_size, 2, 3, 7, 5, 13]

    def _hash(self, key):

        pos = 0
        for i in range(min(len(key), 6)):
            pos += self.coef[i] * ord(key[i])
        return pos % self.array_size

    def __setitem__(self, key, value):
        pos = self._hash(key)
        while True:
            if self.table[pos] is not None:
                if self.table[pos][0] == key:
                    self.table[pos] = (key, value)
                    return
            else:
                self.table[pos] = (key, value)
                self.size += 1
                return

            pos = (pos + 1) % self.array_size

    def __getitem__(self, key):
        pos = self._hash(key)
        start = pos
        while True:
            if self.table[pos] is not None:
                if self.table[pos][0] == key:
                    return self.table[pos][1]
            pos = (pos + 1) % self.array_size
            if pos == start:
                raise KeyError(key)
```

```
    def __delitem__(self, key):

        # this method is incorrect, see the Exercises
        pos = self._hash(key)
        start = pos
        while True:
            if self.table[pos] is not None:
                if self.table[pos][0] == key:
                    self.table[pos] = None
                    self.size -= 1
                    return
            pos = (pos + 1) % self.array_size
            if pos == start:
                raise KeyError(key)
```

We will demonstrate our open addressing hash table using a similar example:

```
# test_HashTable2.py
from HashTable2 import HashTable

h = HashTable()
i = 0
for s in 'the quick brown fox jumps over the lazy dog'.split():
    h[s] = i
    i += 1
print '['
for item in h.table:
    print str(item)
print ']'
print h.size
print h['lazy']
del h['lazy']
print '['
for item in h.table:
    print str(item)
print ']'
print h.size
try:
    print h['lazy']
except KeyError:
    print 'key error raised as expected'
else:
    print 'key error should have been raised'
```

The output of this example using our open addressing with linear probing hash table is the following.

```
[
('lazy', 7)
None
None
('dog', 8)
None
('the', 6)
('quick', 1)
('jumps', 4)
('brown', 2)
('over', 5)
('fox', 3)
]
8
7
[
None
None
None
('dog', 8)
None
('the', 6)
('quick', 1)
('jumps', 4)
('brown', 2)
('over', 5)
('fox', 3)
]
7
key error raised as expected
```

Since we used the same hash function as our chaining example, we know that quick, jumps, and over all hash to the same position in the list as do fox and lazy. From the output, you can see that the open addressing stored them at the first open position in the list and wrapped around to the beginning of the list for lazy as it needed to.

It should be clear that for a hash table implementation to work well, the hash function must not generate collisions often. To prevent collisions, we need to make certain that the array has a reasonable number of empty positions at all times and the hash function must distribute the possible keys across all the array positions fairly evenly (i.e., we do not want many of the possible keys mapping to a small number of array positions). Designing such a hash function without prior knowledge of the keys is not an easy task.

When the hash table array becomes nearly full, we need to make a larger array to maintain good performance. The steps for doing this are create a new larger array, create a new hash function that maps the keys to the larger array, and then remap each key/value in the old array to the new larger array. Creating a new hash function is not as simple as modifying the modulus value (although that is one modification that needs to be made) for the new array size, since the hash values may always be less than the new larger array size using the current hash function. We may need to modify the hash function so it produces larger values. In our example the `hash` function for a word used four letters; we could use more letters to result in a larger value. Another option is to use larger coefficients. With the new hash function, the keys should map to different positions in the new array and some should map to index locations that are higher than the length of the original smaller array; if they do not, we have not solved our problem of reducing collisions. Just as we discussed when resizing a dynamic array in Chapter 10, the resizing operation is expensive; the running time of resizing our hash table is $\Theta(n)$. If we make the array twice as large so that we do not need to do another resizing until we insert n more items, we can amortize the cost of the resizing over n inserts, resulting in only a constant amount of time being added to the cost of each insert.

As we mentioned, the worst case is when all keys map to the same array position resulting in $\Theta(n)$ time for each of the methods the hash table supports (`insert`, `search`, and `delete`). It does not matter whether we use chaining or open addressing in this case; the result is still $\Theta(n)$. In practice, if we keep the number of elements in the hash table proportional to the size of the array (for example, we could make certain that the array size is always 50% larger than the number of items in the hash table) and use a good hash function, the number of items in each chain or the number of items before an empty position when using open addressing will be a relatively small constant. When this is true, each of the methods will be $\Theta(1)$ in most cases.

As we mentioned before, creating a good hash function is the key to making the hash table efficient. Randomly picking the coefficients as we did in this chapter will generally not work well. If your language provides a built-in hash table (as Python does with its dictionary), you should likely use it, as the developers of the language have spent considerable time developing a good implementation. If you must write your own hash table, we recommend you research hash tables in more detail before attempting to implement one for use in a real-world application.

13.6 Chapter Summary

This chapter introduces three advanced data structures and discusses the algorithms for implementing them efficiently. The following is a summary of the concepts discussed in this chapter.

- A binary heap is a complete tree with the property that at each node in the tree, its children are not less than it. This makes it efficient to remove items from smallest to largest. The property can be reversed if you want larger items to be removed first.

- Priority queues allows items to be removed by highest priority instead of first in, first out. A binary heap is typically used to efficiently implement a priority queue.

- A binary heap can also be used to sort a list in $\Theta(n*lgn)$ time, but in practice other sorting algorithms are typically used.

- By updating the tree structure as elements are inserted into a binary search tree, we can ensure that the tree remains approximately balanced. With an approximately balanced tree, the insert and search operations can be performed in $\Theta(lgn)$ time. The AVL tree is one implementation of a balanced tree.

- Hash tables are a data structure that maps keys to a value. They typically provide $\Theta(1)$ running time for insert, delete, and lookup operations although the worst case can be $\Theta(n)$. Python's built-in dictionary is implemented using a hash table.

- A collision happens when two keys in a hash table map to the same location in the list or array that stores the key/value pairs. The solutions to collisions are chaining and open addressing. When writing a hash function, it is important to try to minimize the number of collisions that will likely occur.

13.7 Exercises

True/False Questions

1. A binary heap always stores the elements as an array in sorted order.

2. The `_build_heap` method for our heap implementation places the elements in an array in sorted order.

3. An AVL tree is always a complete tree.

4. An AVL tree may be a complete tree.

5. The running time of the `insert` method for the AVL tree will always be $\Theta(log_2 n)$.

6. The `insert` method for the AVL tree may require more than one single or one double rotation to maintain the AVL property.

7. Inserting an element into a hash table may require $\Theta(1)$ time.

8. Inserting an element into a hash table may require $\Theta(n)$ time.

9. Inserting an element into a hash table may require $\Theta(n^2)$ time.

10. A hash table could be implemented using an AVL tree.

Multiple Choice Questions

1. Assuming a binary heap is arranged for efficient removal of the largest item, what is the running time to find the largest element but not remove it (like the stack method `top`)?

   a) $\Theta(1)$
   b) $\Theta(log_2 n)$
   c) $\Theta(n)$
   d) $\Theta(n^2)$

2. Assuming a binary heap is arranged for efficient removal of the maximum item, what is the running time to remove the maximum element and maintain the heap property?

   a) $\Theta(1)$
   b) $\Theta(log_2 n)$
   c) $\Theta(n)$
   d) $\Theta(n^2)$

3. If you have an implementation of a binary heap, how should you implement a priority queue?

   a) Copy the sections of code from the heap implementation into the priority queue implementation.
   b) In the priority queue, create an instance of a binary heap.

c) Have the priority queue be a subclass of the binary heap class.

d) none of the above

4. When implemented using a binary heap, the running time of a priority queue's `enqueue` method is

a) $\Theta(1)$.

b) $\Theta(log_2 n)$.

c) $\Theta(n)$.

d) $\Theta(n^2)$.

5. When implemented using a binary heap, the running time of a priority queue's `dequeue` method is

a) $\Theta(1)$.

b) $\Theta(log_2 n)$.

c) $\Theta(n)$.

d) $\Theta(n^2)$.

6. The worst-case height of a binary search tree is

a) $\Theta(1)$.

b) $\Theta(log_2 n)$.

c) $\Theta(n)$.

d) $\Theta(n^2)$.

7. The worst-case height of an AVL tree is

a) $\Theta(1)$.

b) $\Theta(log_2 n)$.

c) $\Theta(n)$.

d) $\Theta(n^2)$.

8. The worst-case running time of inserting an element into a hash table is

a) $\Theta(1)$.

b) $\Theta(log_2 n)$.

c) $\Theta(n)$.

d) $\Theta(n^2)$.

9. The best-case running time of inserting an element into a hash table is

a) $\Theta(1)$.

b) $\Theta(log_2 n)$.

c) $\Theta(n)$.

d) $\Theta(n^2)$.

10. If your application needs to repeatedly insert data elements into a data structure and occasionally (intermixed with the **insert** operations) output the
elements in sorted order, which data structure should you use?

a) binary heap

b) priority queue

c) AVL tree

d) hash table

Short-Answer Questions

1. Given the following array representation of a binary heap (where we want to be
able to efficiently extract the smallest element), draw the tree representation
and also draw the resulting tree after one elment is removed from the heap.

5, 21, 8, 27, 22, 10, 12, 28

2. Draw the tree representation of a binary heap (where we want to be able to
efficiently extract the largest element) after inserting each of the following
numbers in this order (i.e., draw eight trees).

2, 43, 25, 10, 6, 12, 55, 4

3. Draw an AVL tree where an item was just inserted into the left subtree of a
right child that causes the AVL tree property to now be violated.

4. For the following AVL tree, which node was just inserted?

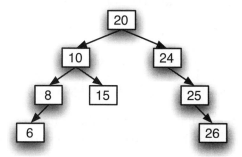

5. For the AVL tree in question 4, which of the four rotation methods (`left_single_rotate`, `right_single_rotate`, `right_left_rotate`, and `left_right_rotate`) must be called to maintain the AVL tree property?

6. For the AVL tree in question 4, which tree node is passed as the parameter to the rotation method?

7. For the AVL tree in question 4, draw the tree after the rotation(s).

8. For the following AVL tree, which node was just inserted?

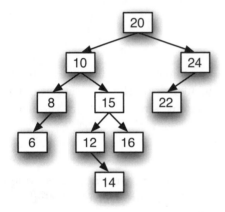

9. For the AVL tree in question 8, which of the four rotation methods (`left_single_rotate`, `right_single_rotate`, `right_left_rotate`, and `left_right_rotate`) must be called to maintain the AVL tree property?

10. For the AVL tree in question 8, which tree node is passed as the parameter to the rotation method?

11. For the AVL tree in question 8, draw the tree after the rotation(s).

12. What Python class is implemented as a hash table?

13. What is the best-case lookup (in Θ notation) for a hash table with **n** items?

14. What is the worst-case lookup (in Θ notation) for a hash table with **n** items?

15. What is wrong with setting the array element to `None` in the `__delitem__` method of the open addressing version of the `HashTable` class? How could we solve this problem?

16. What would happen if you attempted to insert another key/value pair into the open addressing hash table example when the number of items in the hash table matches the capacity of the list?

17. What are the drawbacks of using an AVL tree to implement a hash table and what would the worst-case running time of each method be?

18. Describe how you could use a hash table to efficiently implement an algorithm that would remove duplicate elements (or create a new list without the duplicates) from a list without changing the order of the elements in the list. What would the running time of your algorithm be? Why?

Programming Exercises

1. Write a priority queue class in Python using a binary heap.

2. Write a binary heap class in C++.

3. Write a priority queue class in C++ using a binary heap.

4. Complete the AVL tree class using Python.

5. Write an AVL tree class using C++.

6. Modify the Python chaining example so it doubles the size of the array whenever the number of items in the hash table reaches 70% of the array size.

7. Modify the Python open addressing example so that it doubles the size of the array whenever the number of items in the hash table reaches 70% of the array size.

8. Implement a hash table class in C++ using chaining.

9. Implement a hash table in C++ using open addressing.

Chapter 14   Graphs

Objectives

- To understand the matrix and adjacency list graph data structures and the trade-offs between them.

- To implement the adjacency list graph data structure.

- To implement various graph algorithms including breadth-first and depth-first searches and understand how these fundamental graph traversals can be used to solve a number of graph problems.

- To understand the minimum spanning tree problem and two algorithms to solve it.

- To understand how to analyze the efficiency of various graph algorithms.

14.1   Introduction

Graphs are used to model a wide variety of problems in many different application areas. A graph is a set of vertices and the set of edges that connect the vertices. A simple example of a graph is our system of roads; the roads are edges and the intersections are vertices. We may want to classify the edges as *directed* or *undirected*. A directed edge is a one-way street and an undirected edge is a bidirectional street. In addition to naming the vertices and edges, we may want to assign attributes to the edges and vertices such as a *weight* to an edge. In our road example, the weight could be the length of the road.

We will refer to a graph G as the set V of vertices and the set E of edges. Formally, mathematicians use the cardinality notation (for example, $|V|$) to indicate the number of elements in the set. In most cases it is clear when we are referring to the number of vertices instead of the set of vertices and we will just use V to indicate the number of vertices and E to indicate the number of edges. The term *degree* refers to the number of edges connected to a vertex. For a directed graph, a vertex has both an *in-degree* and an *out-degree* referring to the number of incoming edges and outgoing edges, respectively. Many problems and questions related to graphs require finding paths between vertices. A *path* from one vertex to another is a sequence of vertices such that there is an edge between each pair of consecutive vertices in the sequence. In our road example, we can ask questions such as is there a path from one intersection to another, what is the shortest number of edges to traverse from one intersection to another, and what is the shortest weighted path.

Most graphs with V vertices have at least V-1 edges or the graph is not connected. Formally, a graph is *connected* if for every pair of vertices, there is a path between those two vertices. The maximum number of edges in a graph is $\Theta(V^2)$ when there is an edge between every pair of vertices. There can be more than $\Theta(V^2)$ edges if you allow multiple edges between two vertices; this is an uncommon situation since there is generally no reason to have two edges between the same vertices, but it is possible in a weighted graph where the different edges between the same two vertices could have different weights. A graph with edges between every pair of vertices is known as a *complete graph*. For many applications, the number of edges is usually much smaller than the maximum and is typically a fairly small multiple of the number of vertices.

Another property of a graph that is often useful to know is whether or not it has a cycle. A *cycle* is a path with a length of at least one that starts and ends at the same vertex. In many cases it only makes sense to discuss cycles in directed graphs since by definition an undirected edge between two vertices forms a cycle. The term *acyclic* refers to a graph without any cycles. The acronym *DAG* is commonly used to refer to a *directed acyclic graph*.

We will start by covering the two common data structures for representing graphs. We will then cover the fundamental graph algorithms used in many applications. We cannot cover all the the graph algorithms or all the applications of these algorithms in one chapter as entire books are written on the subject. We will focus on the two fundamental graph algorithms known as the *breadth-first search* and *depth-first search* and their uses in common graph problems. As we always do, we will examine the efficiency of the algorithms.

14.2   Graph Data Structures

The two different data structures commonly used to represent graphs are an *adjacency matrix* and an *adjacency list*. In general, the matrix representation is appropriate when there are edges between many pairs of vertices; this is referred to as a *dense graph*. For most applications the graph is *sparse* (i.e., the number of edges is much smaller than the maximum number of possible edges); in these cases the adjacency list representation is usually more appropriate. The efficiency of many of the graph algorithms is affected by the data structure you use to represent the graph.

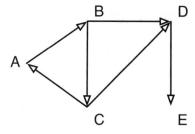

Figure 14.1: Sample directed graph

We will use the graph in Figure 14.1 to describe the two different graph representations. The adjacency matrix representation of a graph is a square matrix of the size V by V. Each row and column corresponds to a vertex. The entries in a row indicate the vertices that have an edge originating from the vertex that corresponds to the row. A 1 in the matrix indicates there is an edge from the vertex corresponding to the row to the vertex corresponding to the column. For our sample graph, the matrix representation is the following assuming the rows and columns correspond to the vertices in alphabetical order.

$$\begin{bmatrix} 0 & 1 & 0 & 0 & 0 \\ 0 & 0 & 1 & 1 & 0 \\ 1 & 0 & 0 & 1 & 0 \\ 0 & 0 & 0 & 0 & 1 \\ 0 & 0 & 0 & 0 & 0 \end{bmatrix}$$

We will follow the convention that matrix entries are referred to first by row and then by column and that we number the rows and columns starting at zero. Using the letter g to denote our matrix representation of the graph, the entry g[0][0] is the upper left entry and the remaining elements in the row are g[0][1], g[0][2], g[0][3], and g[0][4]. Using alphabetical order for the vertices, the entry g[2][3] corresponds to the edge from vertex C to vertex D. If you need to store additional information about an edge (such as a weight or a name), you could store that as the matrix entry with a special value indicating that there is not an edge (such as None or 0). You could also use a separate data structure to represent this information since the basic matrix of 1s and 0s supports a useful property. If the matrix uses a 1 to indicate an edge between two vertices and a 0 to indicate the lack of an edge between two vertices, the result of multiplying the matrix by itself results in another matrix of size V by V and the entry at row i, column j in this product corresponds to the number of paths of length 2 from vertex i to vertex j. Matrix multiplication is not performed by multiplying the corresponding entries in the two matrices; instead the value for the product g * g at row i, column j is the dot product or row i of g with column j of g. We will not cover the additional details of this, but if you are familiar with matrix multiplication, you should be able to determine why the product indicates paths of length 2. Calculating g * g * g will tell you the number of paths of length 3 for the same reason.

If the graph edges are not directed then the matrix will be *symmetric*. In a symmetric matrix, the entry at row i, column j is the same as the entry at row j, column i for every position in the matrix; this means we only need to represent half the matrix (using the diagonal to split it). As you may have figured out for yourself, a matrix is easily represented by a two-dimensional array in C++. In Python, you could use nested lists, but to use matrices in Python, we recommend you download and install the numarray module for Python. It provides many matrix operations via a module implemented in the C programming language, but accessible from Python. This is equivalent to the Python interpreter supporting matrix operations directly since the Python interpreter is implemented in C.

The adjacency list representation is more commonly used since most graphs in real-world applications are sparse. For the matrix representation this means we have lots of 0s. In the adjacency list representation we do not explicitly indicate the lack of an edge, only where there is an edge. This makes the representation more compact for sparse graphs and also means the graph processing algorithms do not have to examine entries where there are not edges as they would in the matrix representation. Using the matrix representation to find all the edges from a vertex, you have to examine V entries, but in the adjacency list representation, you examine only the actual edges originating from the vertex. A pictorial representation of the adjacency list data structure for our sample graph in Figure 14.1 is shown in

Figure 14.2. As the figure shows, we have a list of the five vertices and each vertex has a list of the vertices adjacent to it. In addition to the name of the adjacent vertex, we could stored additional information such as a label or weight for the edge. Based on this, you should be able to determine that examining all the edges in a graph using the adjacency matrix representation requires V^2 operations, but only $V + E$ operations are required to examine all the edges in a graph using the adjacency list representation. This observation will be useful when we examine the efficiency of many of the graph algorithms.

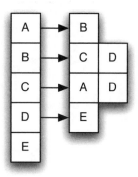

Figure 14.2: Adjacency list representation for sample directed graph

Using the built-in list data type, the following example shows a possible Python representation of the graph using a weight of one for each edge. The example also shows how to access the vertices and edges.

```
>>> g = [
...     ['A', [('B', 1)]],
...     ['B', [('C', 1), ('D', 1)]],
...     ['C', [('A', 1), ('D', 1)]],
...     ['D', [('E', 1)]],
...     ['E', []]]
>>> g[0]
['A', [('B', 1)]]
>>> g[0][0]
'A'
>>> g[0][1]
[('B', 1)]
>>> g[1][1]
[('C', 1), ('D', 1)]
```

As we discussed earlier in this book, Python's built-in dictionary is highly optimized and is generally a good choice to use for implementing your own data structures. The common way to implement a graph using a dictionary is to use the vertices as keys with each vertex key mapping to another dictionary that has the adjacent vertices as its keys. In the nested dictionary, each adjacent vertex key maps to the information about the edge (e.g., we could store the weight or a name for the edge as the value). For our sample graph, the dictionary representation and the results of accessing some of the items is the following:

```
>>> g = {
...     'A': {'B': 1},
...     'B': {'C': 1, 'D': 1},
...     'C': {'A': 1, 'D': 1},
...     'D': {'E': 1},
...     'E': {}}
>>> g['A']
{'B': 1}
>>> g['B']
{'C': 1, 'D': 1}
>>> g['B']['D']
1
```

The Python dictionary implementation also makes it easy to iterate over the vertices and over the adjacent vertices for a given vertex as the following code fragment shows.

```
# for each vertex
for v in g:
    print 'vertex', v
    # for each vertex adjacent to v
    for adj in g[v]:
        print adj, g[v][adj]
```

The output of the code fragment is

```
vertex A
B 1
vertex C
A 1
D 1
vertex B
C 1
D 1
vertex E
vertex D
E 1
```

In C++, the adjacency list representation is commonly implemented as a list of lists. If the number of edges and vertices is known ahead of time, arrays or dynamic arrays can be used, but often a linked implementation of a list is used. As you will see when we examine a number of graph algorithms later in this chapter, the common operations needed for a graph data structure are the ability to iterate over the vertices and to iterate over the adjacent vertices for a given vertex as we demonstrated with our Python dictionary code fragment.

14.3   Shortest Path Algorithms

Determining the shortest path between two vertices is a very common problem for many applications. As we mentioned in the introductory section for this chapter, maps of roads can easily be represented using a graph. You may have used a web site to find directions for a trip. These driving direction web sites represent roads and intersections as a graph and use shortest path algorithms to find the directions for your query. For some shortest path applications, we may only care about the number of edges traversed while for other applications with weighted graphs, we may care about the sum of the weights for the edges traversed. We will refer to the problem in which we care only about the number of edges as the *unweighted shortest path* problem and the problem in which we want to minimize the sum of the edges' weights as the *weighted shortest path problem*. The unweighted shortest path problem is a simplified case of the weighted shortest path problem in which all the edges have the same weight. This means we could use the same algorithm to solve both problems, but the simplified case allows us to use a simpler and more efficient algorithm for unweighted graphs.

If you have used a web site to find driving directions, you may remember that they typically find the quickest route, which is not necessarily the shortest route. For longer trips, the quickest route is often not the shortest route since highways typically provide the fastest routes even though they may not be the shortest routes. Some of these web sites also provide an option to find the shortest path and in this case the length of the roads can be used as the weight for the edges. To find the quickest route, the weights must be a function of the length and the average speed at which the roads can be traversed.

As you can imagine, determining the shortest or fastest route is a problem that must be solved every day by shipping and delivery companies. In addition to driving directions, determining the shortest path is also useful for routing traffic on the Internet and for determining how to connect traditional circuit switched phone calls. Because of the many applications of shortest path algorithms, they are some of the most common and widely studied graph algorithms. We will examine algorithms for both the unweighted and weighted shortest path problems.

14.3.1   The Unweighted Shortest Path

We will use the graph in Figure 14.3 to develop the unweighted shortest path algorithm. This graph is undirected, although the algorithm we are developing works on both directed and undirected graphs. When using the adjacency list representation with undirected graphs, each edge must appear in two lists. For our sample graph, the adjacency list for vertex A must indicate there is an edge to vertex B and the adjacency list for vertex B must indicate there is an edge to vertex A. Since the adjacency matrix for an undirected graph is symmetric, we only need to store each edge once in the matrix (i.e., we can store half the matrix split on the diagonal).

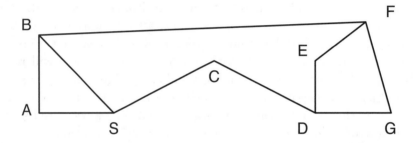

Figure 14.3: Sample graph for unweighted shortest path problem

One of the nice properties of the algorithm we are developing is that it is just as easy to find the shortest path from one vertex to another as it is to find the shortest path from one vertex to all the other vertices. We will use the vertex labeled S in Figure 14.3 as the starting vertex from which we find the shortest path to all the other vertices. As you may have determined by now, in order to find the shortest path we must follow edges starting at the specified starting vertex. From vertex S we can move to vertex A and indicate that the distance to it is one; we also could have started by moving to vertex B or vertex C. Since we are now at vertex A, we have two choices; we could return to vertex S or we could move to vertex B. There is no reason to return to vertex S since we have already been there. If we move to vertex B then we are effectively indicating the shortest path from vertex S is to move to vertex A and then to vertex B. This is a path of length two. As you can see from the graph there is a path directly from vertex S to vertex B with a length one. This tells us that we cannot just move from the starting vertex along a path and expect to find the shortest path to each vertex.

One key point to realize is that a shortest path from one vertex to another contains a shortest path to each of the vertices along the path between the original two vertices. Using our sample graph, if the shortest path from vertex S to vertex G includes the edge from vertex D to vertex G then the path it uses from vertex S to vertex D must be a shortest path from vertex S to vertex D; otherwise, we could find a shorter path from vertex S to vertex G by following a shorter path from vertex S to vertex D and then traversing the edge from vertex D to vertex G. What this tells us is that we must move outward from the starting vertex following the shortest paths. This corresponds to moving from the starting vertex to all the vertices that have an edge from the starting vertex. Once we have discovered all vertices of distance one from the starting vertex, we can then follow the edges from each of those vertices to find all vertices that have distance two from the starting vertex. This order of processing the vertices is known as *breadth first*. The algorithm is referred to as a *breadth first search* and abbreviated *BFS*. As we move outwards we do not want to revisit vertices that we have already discovered. It may be easier to visualize this if we redraw the same graph using concentric circles to indicate the distance from the starting vertex S. Figure 14.4 shows the graph in this form.

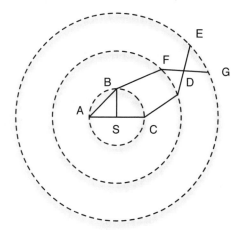

Figure 14.4: Graph from Figure 14.3 drawn with vertices on concentric circles showing the distance from vertex S

From the starting vertex S, we first want to discover the vertices that are directly connected to S (vertices A, B, and C) and thus have distance one. Once we have discovered those, we want to examine the vertices that are adjacent to A, B, and C that we have not already found (D and F) as these are the vertices with distance two, and so on. The key point is that each time we first visit a vertex, we are finding the shortest path to it since we are moving outwards from the starting vertex one level at a time from the concentric circle point of view. In order to be able to list the shortest path to any given vertex, we must keep track of the previous vertex used to reach each vertex; this is commonly referred to as the *parent* vertex. To find the shortest path from our source vertex to any given vertex, we start at the specified vertex and move backward by following the parent vertices until we reach the source vertex. This gives us a list of the vertices on the shortest path from the source vertex to the specified vertex.

Once we have convinced ourselves that these ideas will work, we need to determine how to convert these ideas to a precise, detailed algorithm. The part you may have difficulty with is figuring out how to move outwards in concentric circles. Once we have moved out one step from the source vertex along each of its edges, we need to figure out how to move outwards one step from each of those vertices. It may seem difficult to keep track of the order we need to process the vertices and their edges, but if you try it out with some simple graphs you may see that processing the vertices in the order they are discovered will work. We already have learned about a simple data structure that allows us to process items in order: a queue. Each time we come across a vertex that we have not already seen, we can insert it into the queue and keep track of the vertex used to find it (its parent). The pseudocode for our algorithm is the following:

```
set parent of each vertex to a default value such as None/NULL
set distance for source vertex to 0
insert source vertex into queue
while queue is not empty
    remove a vertex v from queue
    for each vertex w adjacent to v
        if w's parent is None/NULL
            set w's parent to v
            set w's distance to 1 + v's distance
            insert vertex w into queue
```

We will show how the preceding pseudocode works using our sample graph in Figure 14.3. A view of the parent and distance for each vertex is shown in the following table:

	S	A	B	C	D	E	F	G
parent	-	None	None	None	None	None	None	None
distance	0							

We insert vertex S into the queue and start the `while` loop. The `for` loop will process the three adjacent vertices, A, B, and C. The actual order they are processed will not affect the correctness of the algorithm as far as finding the shortest path for each vertex, but the algorithm may find a different path with the same length depending on the order the vertices are processed. For this example, we will always process the adjacent vertices in alphabetical order. After processing the three adjacent vertices, the queue contains the three vertices, A, B, and C. The table is:

	S	A	B	C	D	E	F	G
parent	-	S	S	S	None	None	None	None
distance	0	1	1	1				

The `while` loop executes again and we remove A from the queue and process its adjacent vertices B and S. Since both of those already have a parent vertex, we do not add them to the queue or change their distance. The `while` loop executes again and we remove B from the queue. We process its adjacent vertices A and F. Since A already has a parent, we move on to F. We set F's parent to B, set its distance to 2, and insert it into the queue. The queue now contains C and F and the table is

	S	A	B	C	D	E	F	G
parent	-	S	S	S	None	None	B	None
distance	0	1	1	1			2	

Next we remove C from the queue and process the adjacent vertices which sets D's parent to C, sets D's distance to 2, and inserts D into the queue so it now contains F and D. When we remove F from the queue, we set E's and G's distances to 3 and their parents to F. The queue then contains D, E, and G and the table is

	S	A	B	C	D	E	F	G
parent	-	S	S	S	C	F	B	F
distance	0	1	1	1	2	3	2	3

The `while` loop still needs to run three more times to remove D, E, and G from the queue, but since all the vertices now have their parent and distance set, the `if` statement will be false each time we process the adjacent vertices. As we indicated earlier, the order we process adjacent vertices may affect the parents of each vertex (and thus the path), but not the shortest distance. If we had processed C before B when examining the vertices adjacent to S then D would have appeared in the queue before F. Thus E's parent would be D instead of F, but in either case E's distance is 3.

The table contains all the information necessary to find the shortest path from the vertex S to any of the other vertices. The parent information for each vertex provides a shortest path from that vertex back to the source vertex S. For example, to find the shortest path to vertex E, we start at E and its parent is F. The parent of F is B and B's parent is S. This tells us a shortest path from S to E is S, B, F, E.

As always, we should determine how efficient our algorithm is. We have two nested loops, but the number of times the inner `for` loop runs is not the same for each iteration of the `while` loop if we use the adjacency list representation, so the analysis is not simply a matter of multiplying the number of times the two loops run. If you review the previous paragraphs describing the steps of the algorithm on our sample graph, you notice that each vertex is inserted into the queue exactly once and each time through the `while` loop, one vertex is removed from the queue. This tells us that the outer loop runs V times (where V is the number of vertices). The number of times the inner loop runs varies depending on how many adjacent vertices each vertex has.

The analysis technique we can use here is to determine the total number of times the inner loop executes during all the executions of the outer loop. This is actually fairly simple since each edge is processed twice (once for each direction of the bidirectional edge) during the entire execution of the loop. If the edges are directed, each edge is processed exactly once. Since the other steps all required a constant amount of time, the running time of the algorithm is $\Theta(V + E)$. This is a common pattern for graph algorithms; any algorithm that processes each edge and each vertex a constant number of times with all other operations being constant will have this run-time.

14.3.2 The Weighted Shortest Path

Our unweighted shortest path algorithm is fairly simple and efficient. The question is will it also work if the graph is weighted? Unfortunately, the answer is no in most cases. Figure 14.5 shows a graph in which the unweighted shortest path algorithm will not produce the correct results. The reason our algorithm works correctly on unweighted graphs is that we have always found the shortest path to a vertex before we start examining the vertices adjacent to it. The problem with our unweighted algorithm when using it on the graph in Figure 14.5 starting at vertex S is that we first discover vertex A with the distance 3 and vertex B with the distance 1 placing them in the queue. When we remove A from the queue, we set C's distance to 5. The problem is there is a shorter path to A by moving from S to B and then to A. Our unweighted shortest path algorithm does not provide a mechanism for finding this improved path to A and then adjusting the path to C.

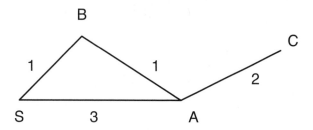

Figure 14.5: Weighted graph

If a graph has negative weights then we cannot always find a shortest path. If there is a cycle whose weights add up to a value less than zero, we could repeatedly take that cycle to produce shorter paths. The algorithm we will discuss in this section will only work on graphs with non-negative weights; for most practical applications the weights will always be positive. The key concept needed to create a correct algorithm for the non-negative weighted shortest path is to always move outwards along shortest paths. In other words, we must always look at the edges off of a discovered vertex with the shortest distance of all the discovered vertices. When we do this, we may find a shorter path to a vertex that we have already discovered. Fortunately, we will not have examined the edges off this already discovered vertex since it had a larger distance than the vertex used to find the new shorter distance to this vertex. The result is we may need to adjust the distance to an already discovered vertex; however we have not yet examined its edges so we will not have to adjust any additional vertex distances because of the new shorter path found to this vertex. This algorithm was initially developed by Edgar Dijkstra and is appropriately named *Dijkstra's algorithm*.

We will examine how this algorithm works on the graph in Figure 14.6 before developing pseudocode for our algorithm and discussing the necessary data structures. The graph is directed and we will start at vertex S. As with the unweighted algorithm, the process described here will work on both directed and undirected graphs as long as the graph data structure properly indicates the type of edges.

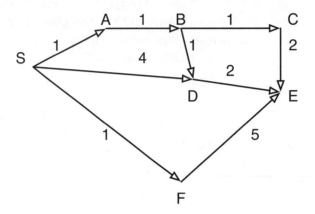

Figure 14.6: Graph for demonstrating Dijkstra's algorithm

We start with vertex S and examine its adjacent vertices, after which the table of parent and distance values is

	S	A	B	C	D	E	F
parent	-	S			S		S
distance	0	1			4		1

We are done processing the vertex S and need to process a vertex with the smallest distance value. We can choose either A or F since both have a distance of one. If we choose the vertex A and process its adjacent vertices, the table is

	S	A	B	C	D	E	F
parent	-	S	A		S		S
distance	0	1	2		4		1

Now we are done processing the vertices S and A and need to choose a vertex with the smallest distance from the remaining vertices. This means we must choose the vertex F. After processing the vertices adjacent to F, the table is

	S	A	B	C	D	E	F
parent	-	S	A		S	F	S
distance	0	1	2		4	6	1

We have now processed the vertices S, A, and F and must choose vertex B as it is the remaining vertex with the smallest distance. When we examine the edge from B to D, we notice that D already has a parent, but this new path to D using the vertex B is smaller than the previously discovered path so we need to change the parent and the distance for the vertex D. The table is now

	S	A	B	C	D	E	F
parent	-	S	A	B	B	F	S
distance	0	1	2	3	3	6	1

After processing the vertices S, A, F, and B, we can choose either vertex C or D since both have a distance of three. If we choose the vertex C, we will change the parent and distance for the vertex E since reaching the vertex E from the vertex C is better than the previous path from the vertex D. The table is now

	S	A	B	C	D	E	F
parent	-	S	A	B	B	C	S
distance	0	1	2	3	3	5	1

We now choose the smaller distance from the two remaining vertices D and E, and that is D. When we examine the edge from D to E, we find that path is worse than the previously discovered path so we do not update the parent or distance for the vertex E. Finally, we examine the vertex E and it does not have any edges to process so we are done and the table is

	S	A	B	C	D	E	F
parent	-	S	A	B	B	C	S
distance	0	1	2	3	3	5	1

This algorithm is similar to the unweighted shortest path algorithm, but the weights do add some complications. The main differences are that we need a priority queue to process the vertices in distance order. As we process the adjacent vertices, we also may need to update a vertex's parent and distance if this new path is shorter, as we saw in our example. The following pseudocode matches the steps we used in our example.

```
set parent of each vertex to a default value such as None/NULL
set distance of each vertex to infinity
set distance for source vertex to 0
insert all vertices into a priority queue (distance is priority)
while priority queue is not empty
    remove vertex v with smallest distance from priority queue
    for each vertex w adjacent to v
        if w's distance > (v's distance + weight of edge v to w)
            set w's parent to v
            set w's distance to v's distance + weight of edge v to w
```

This does not seem too difficult, but the priority queue described in section 13.2 using a binary heap will not work. The problem is that since the distance for a vertex may change after it is inserted into the priority queue, we may need to adjust its position in the heap. With the binary heap we described, there is no efficient way to find a given vertex in the binary heap. Once we do find it, we can use the same technique of moving it up or down the tree until we find a position where it can be placed without violating the heap property. One solution is to use a hash table to map the vertex to its position in the binary heap array/list allowing us to quickly find it, move the item up or down the tree, and then update the hash table to indicate the new position in the heap.

Analyzing the efficiency of Dijkstra's algorithm is a little more difficult. Each vertex is removed once from the priority queue and each edge is processed once during the entire execution of the algorithm, so this part is the same as the unweighted shortest path algorithm. What is different here is that we must extract the vertices from the priority queue and the priorities will change after the vertices are inserted into the priority queue. If we use a standard list for the priority queue and search for the smallest item each time we remove an item from the priority queue, it will require V steps. If we use a linked list, after we find the vertex we can then remove it in $\Theta(1)$ time. But if we are using an array-based list, we should just mark it as removed since the removal requires shifting the elements. If we mark it as removed, the `while` loop requires V*V steps plus the E total steps the `for` loop executes. Even if we use a linked implementation of a list and remove the vertex, the worst-case number of steps is V*(V-1)/2 so the overall algorithm is $\Theta(V^2 + E)$.

If we use the binary heap implementation along with a hash table to track where each item is located in the heap, the amount of time required to remove each item from the priority queue and readjust the binary heap is $\Theta(lgV)$. As each edge is processed, the vertex it leads to may have its distance adjusted, requiring that it be moved up or down the binary heap. Since the binary heap is a complete tree, $\Theta(lgV)$ steps may be required to move the vertex up or down the tree. This gives us an overall running time of $\Theta((V + E)lgV)$. There is a data structure known as a *Fibonacci heap* that can be used to implement a priority queue that supports a method for changing the priority of an item more efficiently, but we will not cover the details of its implementation in this book.

14.4 Depth First Algorithms

In the previous section we examined the breadth first search algorithm that moves out in concentric circles from the starting vertex. Now, we will examine the *depth first search (DFS)* algorithm and look at several graph problems it can be used to solve. As you may be able to determine from the name, the depth first search moves along one path as far as possible before backtracking and examining other paths off the earlier discovered vertices.

During the depth first search execution, each vertex goes through three phases. In the first phase the vertex has not yet been discovered. In the second phase the vertex has been discovered, but the algorithm has not completed processing all the undiscovered vertices that are reachable from this vertex. In the third phase we are done processing the vertex and all the vertices that are reachable from the vertex. One technique used to keep track of these phases is to assign each vertex a starting time when the vertex is first discovered and an ending time when the vertex and all its reachable vertices have been completely processed. Each time we assign a number to a vertex we increase the number by one so if we start with the number one, we use the numbers from 1 to 2*V since each vertex has a starting and ending time. A vertex that does not have a starting or ending time is in the first phase. A vertex that has a starting time but not an ending time is in the second phase. A vertex with both a starting and ending time is in the third phase. As with the breadth first algorithm, we will assign each vertex a parent indicating the vertex that was used to discover this vertex.

We will use the graph in Figure 14.7 to demonstrate the depth first search. As in our previous examples, we will start at the vertex S and always choose vertices in alphabetical order when we have a choice between two or more vertices. Starting at the vertex S, we assign 1 as its starting time and move to the vertex A and assign 2 as its starting time and S as its parent. Next we move to the vertex C and set its starting time to 3 and A as its parent. There are no outgoing edges from the vertex C so we set its ending time to 4 and backtrack to the vertex A. The vertex A does not have any more outgoing edges to undiscovered vertices so we set its ending time to 5 and backtrack to the vertex S. At this point our table of information for the DFS is

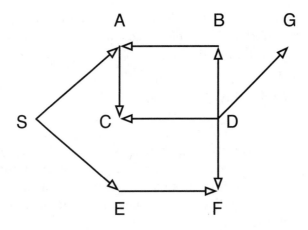

Figure 14.7: Graph for depth first search example

	S	A	B	C	D	E	F	G
parent	-	S		A				
start time	1	2		3				
end time		5		4				

The vertex S still has additional edges to undiscovered vertices so we move to the vertex E and set its starting time to 6 and its parent to S. Next we move to the vertex F and assign 7 as its starting time and E as its parent. The vertex F does not have any outgoing edges to undiscovered vertices so we set its ending time to 8 and backtrack to the vertex E. The vertex E does not have any outgoing edges to undiscovered vertices so we backtrack to the vertex E setting its ending time to 9 and then backtrack to the vertex S and set its ending time to 10. Our table is now

	S	A	B	C	D	E	F	G
parent	-	S		A		S	E	
start time	1	2		3		6	7	
end time	10	5		4		9	8	

At this point we have visited every vertex that is reachable from the vertex S so if we still have undiscovered vertices, we need to start our algorithm from another vertex. We will pick the vertex B and set its starting time to 11. It does not have any outgoing edges to undiscovered vertices so we set its ending time to 12. The next undiscovered vertex is D so we set its starting time to 13. We examine its outgoing edges and find C which has already been discovered and F which has already been discovered. Next we find G which has not been discovered so we set the starting time for G to 14 and its parent to D. G does not have any outgoing edges so we set its ending time to 15 and backtrack to D. D does not have any other outgoing vertices so we set its ending time to 16. At this point, there are no undiscovered vertices so we are done and our final table of information is

	S	A	B	C	D	E	F	G
parent	-	S	-	A	-	S	E	D
start time	1	2	11	3	13	6	7	14
end time	10	5	12	4	16	9	8	15

The DFS process should remind you of the binary tree traversals, specifically the preorder traversal. The differences are that with graphs, each vertex can have any number of children and because there can be multiple paths to a vertex and cycles, we need to determine if we have already visited a vertex. We can use the starting time to determine whether or not a vertex has already been visited. Based on the similarity to the tree traversal algorithms, you should realize that a recursive algorithm will be useful to support the backtracking. Our pseudocode will use two functions. The first function is not recursive and makes certain that we eventually process all the vertices and calls the recursive function for each undiscovered vertex.

```
dfs(g)
    for each vertex v in graph g:
        set v's starting time to 0
    t = 0
    for each vertex v in g:
        if v's start time is 0:
            dfs_traverse(g, v)

dfs_traverse(g, v)
    t += 1
    set v's start time to t
    for each vertex u adjacent to v:
        if u's start time is 0:
            set u's parent to v
            dfs_traverse(g, u)
    t += 1
    set v's end time to t
```

The variable t needs to have its old value remembered each time the dfs_traverse function is called. There are a number of ways to achieve this. One is to make

t a local variable in dfs and pass it by reference to dfs_traverse and have
dfs_traverse also pass it to itself during each recursive call. Another option is
to make it a global variable and not pass it as a parameter. A common technique
used to solve this in object-oriented programming is to make the variable t an
instance variable in a class and define dfs and dfs_traverse as methods of the
class. You could also make the parent, start, and end information for the vertices
members of the class (e.g., in Python, you could use dictionaries that map a vertex
to its parent, starting time, and ending time).

The run-time analysis for the depth first search is similar to the breadth first
search. The dfs function processes each vertex a constant number of times, and the
dfs_traverse function processes each edge once and performs a constant number
of operations as it processes each edge, so the overall run-time is $\Theta(V + E)$.

As we mentioned earlier, the DFS algorithm is similar to tree traversals. We can
view each call from dfs to dfs_traverse as producing a separate tree. Figure 14.8
shows the trees produced when we execute the DFS algorithm on our sample graph.
This graph produced three trees, one of which is the single vertex B. If you examine
the starting and ending times, you will notice that the time intervals for each tree do
not overlap. This tree representation only includes edges that were used to discover
a vertex.

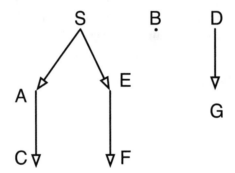

Figure 14.8: Graph for depth first search example

Now we examine a graph problem known as *topological sort* and see how it can
be solved using a depth first search. A topological sort is an ordering of the vertices
such that if there is an edge from the vertex u to the vertex v, then u appears
before v in the ordering. As the definition implies, the topological sort can only be
performed on directed graphs and there cannot be any cycles in the graph. Since an

undirected edge between two vertices u and v is equivalent to a directed edge from u to v and a directed edge from v to u, it is impossible to order the vertices u and v so that the topological sort definition is satisfied. A cycle causes the same problem since for any two vertices u and v that are part of the cycle, there is a path from u to v and a path from v to u.

A topological sort can be used to find an ordering for a set of tasks in which some tasks must be completed before other tasks can be performed. The process for generating the graph is straightforward. Each task corresponds to a vertex in the graph and a directed edge from u to v indicates that the task corresponding to u must be performed before the task corresponding to v. In order for there to be a solution, the resulting graph must be a directed acyclic graph.

A simple example of a problem that can be solved with a topological sort is the order in which you can take college courses. A course may have prerequisites that must be taken before you can take that course. You can create a graph in which each course is a vertex and directed edges are drawn to courses from their prerequisites. A topological sort of this graph will give you an order in which you can take courses that satisfies the prerequisites. As is the case in many topological sort problems, there is likely more than one order in which you can take courses.

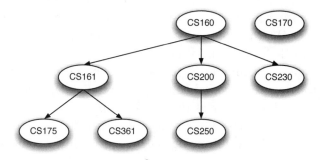

Figure 14.9: Graph showing course prerequisites

Figure 14.9 shows a graph of course prerequisites. The only courses we can take first are those with no prerequisites, corresponding to vertices with no incoming edges. In the sample graph, we can start with either CS160 or CS170. Once we take CS160, we can then take any course for which it is a prerequisite. Another way to look at this is that once we take a course, we can remove all the outgoing edges from that course. This idea should lead you to a simple algorithm for solving the topological sort problem. As we just mentioned, you must start with a vertex that has no incoming edges. We then remove the outgoing edges for that vertex, indicating that we have met that prerequisite. We can now again look for a vertex with in-degree zero. These steps can be repeated until we have processed each vertex. The question is how efficient is this algorithm?

If we use the adjacency matrix representation, finding a vertex with in-degree zero can take V steps. Removing the outgoing edges will then take another V steps. We have to do this V times, resulting in an algorithm of $\Theta(V^3)$. This is not a particularly efficient algorithm, but it always a good idea to check the possibilities for both the matrix and adjacency list before implementing an algorithm so you can pick the data structure that is more efficient for the algorithm.

Our adjacency list representation does not make it easy to find a vertex with in-degree zero, but as we remove the outgoing edges, we are decreasing the in-degree of the vertices to which they connect. So a way to solve this more efficiently is to calculate and store the initial in-degree of each vertex and place the vertices that initially have in-degree zero in a queue. As we process a vertex from the queue, we can decrease the in-degree count of its adjacent vertices and if a vertex's in-degree reaches zero, insert it into the queue. The efficiency analysis is not too difficult. We need to calculate the in-degree of each vertex which we can do by using the common nested loops that process each vertex and then each edge/adjacent vertex. As we execute these loops, we build up a count of the in-degree for each vertex. This requires $\Theta(V + E)$ time. We then process each vertex and the edges again which is also $\Theta(V + E)$ and thus the overall run-time.

As we mentioned at the beginning of the section, the DFS algorithm can also be used to solve the topological sort problem. Before reading the rest of the section that describes how, go back and look at our DFS sample graph (it is a DAG) and the table of parents, starting times, and ending times and try to determine how to use the DFS algorithm to solve the topological sort problem. A hint is to look at the ending times.

As you may have discovered on your own, if you order the vertices by decreasing the ending time, you get a valid topological sort order. This can easily be done by inserting the vertices at the beginning of a list as we set their ending time. If we use a linked list, each of these inserts can be performed in $\Theta(1)$ time so the running time of DFS, $\Theta(V + E)$, is the running time of this topological sort algorithm. The question is why does this work. They key point to remember is that there cannot be a path from u to v if v comes before u in the topological sort. Based on how the ending times are computed, we know that if there is a path from u to v, then u has a higher ending time and thus would appear earlier in our topological sort.

To convince ourselves that this is correct, there are three possible situations we need to look at. One is that we discovered v on a path from u. In this case, v's starting and ending times are between u's starting and ending times and thus v's ending time is less than u's ending time. This is the case with the vertices S and F in our DFS example. Another possibility is that we first discovered v on a path from another vertex that does not reach u and then we later found the already discovered v from another path that includes u. In this case there is a path from u to v, but u will have a higher ending time and thus appear before v in the topological sort. An example of this from our graph is vertex C and vertex D. The vertex C was first discovered on a path from the vertex S and then later found on a path starting at the vertex D; thus D has a higher ending time than C. The third possibility is that there is no path between two vertices and thus the relative order of the two vertices in the topological sort does not matter.

14.5   Minimum Spanning Trees

The *minimum spanning tree* problem is to find a subset of edges in a weighted undirected graph (in which all the weights are non-negative) that connects all the vertices and minimizes the sum of the weights of the chosen edges. The subset of edges is a tree since there cannot be a cycle in the set of edges that minimizes the weights. The reason there cannot be a cycle is that removing an edge that is part of the cycle would reduce the sum of the weights and the graph would still be connected; thus, we know there cannot be a cycle in a minimum spanning tree. A minimum spanning tree for a graph with V vertices must have V-1 edges. This is easy to see if you consider a straight line of vertices and how many edges it would take to connect them. It does not make sense to add additional edges since this would increase the weight and form a cycle. We will now discuss two different algorithms for finding a minimum spanning tree of a graph.

14.5.1   Kruskal's Algorithm

Combining the ideas of wanting to minimize weights and not having a cycle should lead you to a possible algorithm. We want to repeatedly add the edge with the minimum weight as long as adding that edge does not form a cycle until we have V-1 edges. This algorithm does work and is known as *Kruskal's algorithm* after the person who first discovered it.

Figure 14.10 shows a graph that we will use to discuss the minimum spanning tree problem. The first step in Kruskal's algorithm is to sort the edges by weight

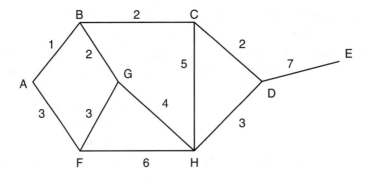

Figure 14.10: Minimum spanning tree graph

since we need to process the edges by weight. In the figure, the first edge we should add is AB since it has the minimum weight. Next we can attempt to add any of the edges with weight 2. For this example, we will pick edge BC. Adding it does not form a cycle. We continue with one of the other edges with weight 2 and pick edge CD. Adding it does not form a cycle. The last edge with weight 2 is edge BG and adding it does not form a cycle. There are three edges with weight 3. If we pick edge AF first, adding it does not form a cycle. Attempting to add edge FG would form a cycle so we cannot add it. Adding edge DH does not form a cycle so we include it. The next lowest weight is edge GH, but adding it would form a cycle. We then examine edge CH which also would form a cycle so we cannot add it. Next we look at edge FH which also would form a cycle. The last edge in sorted order is DE and adding it does not form a cycle so it is included; it is needed to connect vertex E.

This gives us the set of edges (AB, BC, CD, BG, AF, DH, DE). Our guidelines state that there must be V-1 edges and our set fits since there are eight vertices and seven edges. As we can determine from this example, there is not necessarily a unique solution to the minimum spanning tree problem. In our example, we can include either AF or GF; both of these edges allow us to connect to the vertex F and have the same weight.

The difficult step to implement in the algorithm is determining if adding an edge forms a cycle. We can use the DFS algorithm to determine if an undirected graph has a cycle (we leave that as an exercise), but we will examine a data structure known as a *disjoint set* that you can use to easily determine if adding a single edge to a set of edges results in a cycle. Once you have a disjoint set, implementing Kruskal's algorithm is fairly easy.

14.5.2 | The Disjoint Set Data Structure

A *disjoint set* data structure is a group of sets that do not contain any elements in common. The common operations that it supports are make_set(x), find(x), and union(x, y). The make_set(x) method adds a new set to the group of sets with the single element x; none of the other methods in the set may contain the element x. The find(x) method returns an identifier that indicates the set that contains x. The common technique is to have the find(x) method return a specific item in the set. The key point that must be true is that if you call find(x) and find(y) and they are in the same set, then both must return the same identifier. The union(x, y) method joins the set that contains x with the set that contains y; the precondition for the union method is that the two parameters are not in the same set. The union method decreases the number of sets in the group by one. The following is a Python implementation of a DisjointSet class.

```python
# DisjointSet.py
class DisjointSet(object):

    def __init__(self):

        self.sets = {}

    def make_set(self, x):
        '''post: adds a set to the group of sets for the single element x
        raises KeyError if already a set containing x'''

        # check if set for this item already exists
        if x in self.sets:
            raise KeyError, '%s already in DisjointSet' % str(x)
        # map element to the set/list containing it
        self.sets[x] = [x]

    def find(self, x):
        '''post: returns set/list containing x
        raises KeyError if there is not a set containing x;
        for efficiency use the "is" operator to determine if two
        elements are in the same set by making two calls to find
        (e.g., if dj.find(x) is dj.find(y):)'''

        return self.sets[x]
```

```
    def union(self, x, y):
        '''post: the sets containing x and y are merged/joined
        raises KeyError if the two sets are already the same'''

        if self.sets[x] is self.sets[y]:
            raise KeyError, '%s and %s are in the same set' % (
            str(x), str(y))

        # determine smaller list so we are adding fewer items to the
        # existing list
        if len(self.sets[x]) > len(self.sets[y]):
            # save list of elements in smaller set
            temp = self.sets[y]
            # for each element in smaller set, map it to the larger list
            for k in self.sets[y]:
                self.sets[k] = self.sets[x]
            # add all elements in smaller set/list to larger set/list
            self.sets[x].extend(temp)
        else:
            # save elements in smaller set
            temp = self.sets[x]
            # for each element in smaller set, map it to the larger list
            for k in self.sets[x]:
                self.sets[k] = self.sets[y]
            # add all elements in smaller set/list to larger set/list
            self.sets[y].extend(temp)
```

This Python implementation of a disjoint set works by using a dictionary to map each element to the list containing all the elements that are in the set. The make_set(x) method checks that x is not already in one of the sets and then creates a list containing x and maps x to that list. The find method returns the list containing the set. Since Python uses references and all the elements in the set refer to the same list, we can use the is operator to determine if the two sets are the same. By checking if find(x) is find(y) we check if the dictionary maps x and y to the same list in memory. This can be performed in $\Theta(1)$ time since it only needs to check if the two addresses are the same. Note that this is not the same as using the == operator; it checks to see if the two lists contain the same elements and would require $\Theta(n)$ time to determine if two lists of length n are the same.

The union(x, y) method works by saving a reference to the shorter list. It then goes through each element in the shorter list and maps them to the longer list. Finally, we add each method in the shorter list onto the end of the longer list using the extend method of the built-in list. Assuming that each dictionary mapping can be performed in $\Theta(1)$ time and the extend method requires an average $\Theta(1)$ per each element added, each union call requires on average $\Theta(min(m,n))$ where m and n are the lengths of the two lists being joined.

If you are implementing a disjoint set in C++, it can be implemented using a modified linked list. Each `make_set` method creates a separate linked list. Each node in the list needs both a pointer to the next element in the linked list and to the first element in the list. The `union` method then needs to set the next link of the last element in the longer list to the first node in the shorter list and then run through the nodes that were in the shorter list and set their pointer to the first node to the first node of the new combined list. The analysis for this is the same as our Python `union` method. The `find` method can then use the pointer to the first node to return the first element as the identifier. Using an array or list of linked lists still requires our `find` method to search through all the elements to find the list containing the element. You could also use the hash table technique used in our Python implementation. There are other techniques for implementing disjoint sets, but we will not cover them in this book.

The disjoint set class can be used in Kruskal's algorithm to help us determine if adding an edge forms a cycle. The first step is to form a set for each vertex (the disjoint set contains `V` sets, each with one element). When we check if we should add an edge, we check if the two edges are in the same set. If they are not, we add the edge and join the two sets. As we do this, each set corresponds to the vertices that are connected by the edges we have added. If we attempt to add an edge whose two vertices are in the same set, we know there is already a path between those edges and adding this new edge would create a cycle.

Using the disjoint set in Kruskal's algorithm requires performing V-1 `union` operations. The worst case is that we are joining sets of equal size since we then have to update the most pointers or entries in the hash table. One way to analyze this is to compare it to the merge steps of the mergesort algorithm. We start by merging/joining `V` sets with one element into `V/2` sets with two elements. Next we join those into `V/4` sets with four elements. We continue this until we have one set with `V` elements. The total number of steps required for this is $\Theta(VlgV)$. The overall running time of Kruskal's algorithm is then dominated by the sorting of the `E` edges that requires $\Theta(ElgE)$ time.

14.5.3 Prim's Algorithm

Kruskal's algorithm creates a set of trees that eventually are connected together. In this section we will describe another algorithm that was developed by Robert Prim for solving the minimum spanning tree problem that repeatedly adds edges to one connected tree until V-1 edges have been added. Using this algorithm, one connected tree is maintained during the algorithm.

The basic idea is to pick a starting vertex and add the adjacent edge with the smallest weight. These two vertices are now part of the tree. We continue by choosing the edge with the smallest weight such that of one of its vertices is in the tree and one is not. Since we are always choosing an edge with one endpoint in the tree we have formed so far, we will never have multiple trees as Kruskal's algorithm may during its intermediate steps. Using the graph in Figure 14.10 and starting at the vertex A, the following is one possible ordering of the addition of the edges using Prim's algorithm: AB, BC, CD, BG, AF, DH, DE. The algorithm is very similar to Dijkstra's algorithm for the weighted shortest path problem. We leave the exact algorithm and the analysis of it as an exercise.

14.6   Chapter Summary

This chapter only scratches the surface of the many graph problems and applications. If you are interested in learning more about graph problems, we suggest you search for information on strongly connected components, Euler tours, Hamiltonian cycles, all pairs shortest paths, and network flow problems. The following is a summary of the topics discussed in this chapter.

- A graph is a set of vertices and the edges that connect the vertices.

- Graph edges may be directed (one-way) or undirected (two-ways).

- The two common data structures for a graph are an adjacency matrix that has the size V by V and an adjacency list. An adjacency list has a list of V vertices and each vertex contains a list of the adjacent vertices, including information about the edge.

- The running time of graph algorithms is given in terms of the number of vertices (V) and the number of edges (E).

- When using Python, a dictionary of dictionaries is the common method for representing a graph in adjacency list form.

- Many graph algorithms use either a breadth first search or a depth first search.

- A minimum spanning tree is a set of edges with the minimum weight sum that completely connects the vertices. An MST has V-1 edges.

14.7 Exercises

True/False Questions

1. A matrix representation of a graph always requires more memory than an adjacency list for the same graph.

2. The weighted shortest path algorithm can be used on a graph that does not have weights.

3. The unweighted shortest path algorithm will work on a directed graph that has a cycle.

4. The weighted shortest path algorithm will never work on a directed graph that has a negative weight and a cycle.

5. The breadth first algorithm is commonly implemented using recursion.

6. The depth first algorithm is commonly implemented using recursion.

7. If each vertex is reachable from a starting vertex in a graph that does not have any cycles, the starting vertex will have the largest ending time for the depth first search.

8. If a graph has cycles, the starting vertex will never have the largest ending time for the depth first search.

9. Only a graph without cycles can be topologically sorted.

10. The number of edges in a minimum spanning tree for a graph may vary depending on which edges are chosen.

Multiple Choice Questions

1. If you calculate M^{20} where M is the adjacency matrix representing a connected graph with 10 vertices, which of the following statements is true.

   a) There will be at least one 0 in M^{20}.
   b) There will not be any 0s in M^{20}.
   c) The entries will all be 1 in M^{20}.
   d) none of the above

2. If you calculate M^{20} where M is the adjacency matrix representing an unconnected graph with 10 vertices, which of the following statements is true.

   a) There will be at least one 0 in M^{20}.
   b) There will not be any 0s in M^{20}.
   c) The entries will all be 1 in M^{20}.
   d) none of the above

3. If a graph has $2 * V$ edges, what is the running time of the unweighted shortest
   path algorithm if you use an adjacency matrix?

   a) $\Theta(V)$
   b) $\Theta(V + E)$
   c) $\Theta(V^2)$
   d) none of the above

4. If a graph has $2 * V$ edges, what is the running time of the unweighted shortest
   path algorithm if you use an adjacency list?

   a) $\Theta(V)$
   b) $\Theta(V + E)$
   c) $\Theta(V^2)$
   d) none of the above

5. If a graph has $0.5 * V^2$ edges, what is the running time of the unweighted
   shortest path algorithm if you use an adjacency matrix?

   a) $\Theta(V)$
   b) $\Theta(V + E)$
   c) $\Theta(E)$
   d) none of the above

6. If a graph has $0.5 * V^2$ edges, what is the running time of the unweighted
   shortest path algorithm if you use an adjacency list?

   a) $\Theta(V)$
   b) $\Theta(V + E)$
   c) $\Theta(V^2)$
   d) b or c are equivalent

7. When running the depth first search, which of the following are possible for
   the ending time of the starting vertex:

   a) It may have the smallest ending time.
   b) It may have the largest ending time.

c) neither a or b

d) both a and b

8. When running the depth first search on a connected graph, which of the following are possible for the ending time of the starting vertex:

a) It may have the smallest ending time.

b) It will have the largest ending time.

c) neither a or b

d) both a and b

9. The number of edges in a minimum spanning tree for a graph with V vertices and E edges is

a) V-1.

b) V.

c) E-1.

d) E.

10. Which of the following are a possible number of topological sort orderings for a directed acyclic graph with five vertices?

a) 0

b) 1

c) 120

d) b and c

e) all of the above

Short-Answer Questions

1. Exactly how many edges are in a complete graph with V vertices?

2. Write the matrix representation for the graph in Figure 14.3.

3. Draw the adjacency list representation for the graph in Figure 14.3.

4. Write the Python dictionary representation of the graph in Figure 14.6.

5. What is the run-time of the unweighted shortest path algorithm if an adjacency matrix is used instead of an adjacency list to represent the graph?

6. Does removing the corresponding row and column from the adjacency matrix as we find a vertex with incoming degree zero improve the asymptotic efficiency of our first topological sort algorithm?

7. What is the asymptotic efficiency of the second topological sort algorithm presented in this chapter that tracks the in-degree of each vertex?

8. Describe how to use the DFS algorithm to determine if a graph has a cycle.

9. Write an exact set of steps (pseudocode) for Prim's algorithm. What is the running time of your steps?

Programming Exercises

1. Implement the unweighted shortest path algorithm in Python.

2. Use the unweighted shortest path algorithm to write a program that solves the Kevin Bacon game.

3. Implement a priority queue that supports changing the priority of items already in the priority queue.

4. Using your priority queue from the previous question, implement Dijkstra's algorithm for finding the weighted shortest path.

5. Implement the topological sort algorithm that keeps track of the current in-degree of each vertex and adjusts it as we process a vertex.

6. Implement a disjoint set class in C++ using linked lists.

7. Implement Kruskal's algorithm using a disjoint set class.

8. Use the DFS algorithm to determine if an undirected graph has a cycle in $\Theta(V)$ time.

9. Implement Prim's algorithm.

Chapter 15   Algorithm Techniques

━━━━━━━━━━━━━━━━━━━━━━━

Objectives

- To understand, implement, and analyze the efficiency of the quicksort algorithm.

- To review divide-and-conquer algorithms and learn a technique for analyzing the efficiency of recursive algorithms.

- To understand the greedy algorithm and dynamic programming techniques and when they can be used.

- To understand the implementation of the Huffman compression algorithm and the longest common subsequence algorithm.

- To introduce the topic of NP-complete problems.

15.1   Introduction

Most of this book has focused on data structures and algorithms for manipulating those data structures. In this chapter we will not learn new data structures, but instead we will focus on learning a few algorithm techniques that can be applied to many different problems. You have already used some of these techniques, but in this chapter we will categorize them. This will help you tackle new problems by thinking about which categories of techniques can be applied to new problems you encounter. As you have likely noticed by now, your programming skills improve by using the knowledge and experience you have gained from solving problems in the past. This chapter will add new tools to your toolbox of knowledge.

15.2　Divide and Conquer

Divide and conquer is the name given to the strategy we have seen the most often in this book. The mergesort algorithm we examined is a classic example of divide and conquer. As the name implies, the basic idea of divide-and-conquer algorithms is to split a problem into smaller subproblems. As we saw with the mergesort algorithm in subsection 6.5.1, divide-and-conquer algorithms commonly have a step where the solutions to the smaller problems are combined to form the solution to the original problem. Many of the algorithms for processing trees can be viewed as divide-and-conquer algorithms since they process subtrees. The binary search algorithm for finding an item in a sorted list is also a divide-and-conquer algorithm since we keep dividing the list in half to find the item for which we are searching. The binary search algorithm does not need a step to combine the solutions to the subproblems as most of the other divide-and-conquer algorithms do.

Many divide-and conquer algorithms are written as recursive functions and each recursive call is made with a smaller subproblem. However, divide-and-conquer algorithms do not have to be written as recursive functions. The binary search algorithm can be written recursively or iteratively. As we discussed in Chapter 6, iteration is typically better than recursion if the iterative algorithm is simple since the function call overhead of recursion makes it less efficient than an iterative algorithm with the same asymptotic running time. Analyzing the running time of recursive functions is often more difficult than analyzing iterative solutions. Since many of the divide-and-conquer algorithms are recursive, we will discuss techniques for analyzing the running time of recursive functions before examining another divide-and-conquer algorithm.

15.2.1　Analyzing Recursive Functions

You may recall that when analyzing the mergesort algorithm, we graphically looked at the steps of the recursive calls and how much work was done at each level. When analyzing the tree algorithms, we discussed how many times each tree node was traversed and how much work was required per node to determine the running time. Drawing pictures of what happens as each recursive call is made is a common method for determining the amount of work the algorithm performs. We also used this technique to help analyze the running time of the recursive Fibonacci function; we can determine from Figure 6.2 in Chapter 6 that the amount of work to calculate the nth recursive Fibonacci number is almost twice as much work as the work required to find the n-1st Fibonacci number. The diagrams can provide some intuition, but it is easy to make mistakes when using the diagrams since they are not a formal mathematical method. As you can see, analyzing recursive functions is more difficult than analyzing iterative code.

In some limited cases of recursive functions, we can use a simple equation or algorithm to determine the running time of the code. The main restrictions required to use this algorithmic formula are that the code makes the same fixed number of recursive calls each time the function is called and each call is made with the same fixed fraction of the problem. To understand these restrictions we will discuss the topic of *recurrence relations*. A recurrence relation is an equation that is defined recursively. You may have seen a form of recurrence relations known as difference equations in your math studies.

An example of a recurrence relation is $T(n) = T(n/2) + c$. This recurrence relation states that the time to solve a problem of size n is the time to solve a problem of size $n/2$ plus some fixed constant c. The running time of the binary search algorithm can be written as that recurrence relation. Solving a recurrence relation means finding a closed form solution without the recursive reference. This can be difficult, but most recurrence relations that meet the criteria discussed in the previous paragraph can be solved fairly easily. We already know that the solution to the recurrence relation $T(n) = T(n/2) + c$ is $\Theta(lgn)$ since that is the running time of the binary search algorithm. The recurrence relation that corresponds to the mergesort algorithm is $T(n) = 2T(n/2) + c*n$ since the algorithm makes two recursive calls, each with a list half the size of the original list, and then has a loop that runs n times where n is the size of the list made for that recursive call. We know the answer to this recurrence relation is $\Theta(n*lgn)$.

There is an algorithmic formula commonly referred to as the *master theorem* for solving most, but not quite all, recurrence relations that are of the form $T(n) = a * T(n/b) + f(n)$. This corresponds to our restrictions of the fixed number of recursive calls (a times in this formula) and the fixed fraction (n/b) of the problem. We can use the master theorem to find the asymptotic running time of recursive algorithms that have recurrence relations that fit this form.[1] The master theorem has three cases:

1. if $f(n) = O(n^{log_b a - e})$ for a constant $e > 0$ then $T(n) = \Theta(n^{log_b a})$

2. if $f(n) = \Theta(n^{log_b a})$ then $T(n) = \Theta(n^{log_b a} * log_2 n)$

3. if $f(n) = \Omega(n^{log_b a + e})$ for a constant $e > 0$ and if $a * f(n/b) <= c * f(n)$ for a constant $c < 1$ and all $n >= n_0$ for a constant $n_0 > 0$ then $T(n) = \Theta(f(n))$

---

[1]For the full details of the theorem and a proof of the theorem, see Thomas Cormen, Charles Leiserson, Ronald Rivest, and Clifford Stein, *Introduction to Algorithms*, (Cambridge, Massachusetts: McGraw-Hill Book Company, 2001), 2nd ed. 76–84.

We defined the difference between big O and theta notation earlier, but have not seen the omega (Ω) notation before. Recall that big O means "less than or equal to" and that theta means "equal to." As you may be able to guess, the omega notation means greater than or equal to. As the three cases in the formula indicate, we need to compare $n^{log_b a}$ and $f(n)$ for the recurrence relation $T(n) = a * T(n/b) + f(n)$. If $f(n) < n^{log_b a}$, then the solution is $\Theta(n^{log_b a})$. If $f(n) = n^{log_b a}$ then the solution is $\Theta(n^{log_b a} * log_2 n)$. And if $f(n) > n^{log_b a}$ then the solution is $\Theta(f(n))$ if the extra condition is also met. This extra condition means the formula cannot be applied to all recurrence relations of the form $T(n) = a * T(n/b) + f(n)$, but it does work for most of them. In summary, the answer is the larger of $n^{log_b a}$ and $f(n)$ (assuming the extra condition is met when $f(n)$ is larger). If they are the same, you multiply them by $log_2 n$ to get the solution.

We will now look at a couple examples. The mergesort algorithm has the recurrence relation: $T(n) = 2T(n/2) + n$. We first need to calculate $log_b a$ which is 1 since both a and b are 2. So we now compare n^1 to n and they are the same so that tells us we need to use the second case of the formula and the answer is $\Theta(n * log_2 n)$. The binary search algorithm has the recurrence relation: $T(n) = T(n/2) + 1$. We calculate $log_b a$ which is 0. We now compare n^0 and 1 which are the same so we again use the second case of the theorem and the answer is $\Theta(log_2 n)$.

We will now examine simple, but useless, Python functions to see examples of the other two cases of the formula. The first one is

```
# recursive.py
def f1(n):
    if n > 1:
        a = f1(n // 3)
        b = f1(n // 3)
        c = a + b
    else:
        c = 0
    for i in range(n):
        c += i
    return c

print f1(20)
```

The function f1 has the recurrence relation $T(n) = 2T(n/3) + n$. We calculate $log_3 2$ which is less than one so we know $n^{log_b a}$ is less than n^1 so this is case three of the formula. We also need to show that $2 * n/3 <= c * n$ for some positive constant and large values of n. We can easily pick $c = 1$ and $n_0 = 2$ to meet the requirement. Thus, the answer is $\Theta(n)$.

Our second example is

```
# recursive.py
def f2(n):
    if n > 1:
        a = f2(n // 3)
        b = f2(n // 3)
        return a+b
    else:
        return 1

print f2(20)
```

The function f2 has the recurrence relation $T(n) = 2T(n/3) + 1$. We calculate $log_3 2$ which is less than one so we know $n^{log_b a}$ is greater than n^0 so this is case one of the formula and the answer is $\Theta(n^{log_3 2})$; this is $\Theta(n^{0.631})$, accurate to three decimal places.

Unfortunately, the formula cannot be applied to all recursive functions; we can apply it only to those whose recurrence relation fits the pattern $T(n) = aT(n/b) + f(n)$. The recurrence relation for the recursive Fibonacci function is $T(n) = T(n-1) + T(n-2)$ so we cannot use the formula. If we change our sample function f1 so one, but not both, of the recursive calls is f1(n/2), the formula cannot be applied. In these cases, you must use other techniques to find the run-time analysis as we discussed earlier in this section.

15.2.2 Quicksort

Since we have examined a number of divide-and-conquer algorithms (binary search, mergesort, tree algorithms), we will examine only one more divide-and-conquer algorithm in this chapter. The *quicksort* algorithm is a divide-and-conquer algorithm for sorting and is appropriately named as it is typically the fastest general purpose sorting algorithm even though its worst-case running time can be $\Theta(n^2)$. The basic idea of the quicksort algorithm is straightforward, but creating an algorithm that is correct in all cases and efficient in most cases requires skill and attention to special cases.

A drawback of the mergesort algorithm is that it requires an extra temporary array that is the same size as the array you are sorting. The quicksort algorithm has the advantage that it sorts the algorithm in place (i.e., it does not require a second array). The basic idea of quicksort is similar to mergesort: split the list into two parts and recursively sort each part, but the details of how this is done are different. The quicksort algorithm starts by picking an element known as the *pivot* from the list. It then moves the elements less than the pivot to the left side of the list and elements greater than the pivot to the right side of the list. The pivot element is then placed between the two lists; this is the correct position for the pivot when the entire list is sorted. The next step is to recursively sort the two smaller arrays on either side of the pivot. When the recursive call has an array of size 0 or 1, the recursion ends. It should be clear that a merge step is not needed since the partitioning step of moving small elements to the left and large elements to the right with the pivot in the middle places the elements in sorted order.

Before we try to write code to implement the algorithm, we will look at an example of how the algorithm works using the array 7, 6, 1, 3, 2, 5, 4. If we pick the last element (4) as the pivot and follow the algorithm of moving small elements to the left and large elements to the right and placing the pivot in the middle, one possible result is 1, 3, 2 followed by the pivot 4 followed by 7, 6, 5. Note that 4 is now in the correct location for the final sorted array. We now recursively sort the left array. If we again pick the last element (2) as the pivot and move small elements to the left and large elements to the right, we now have the sorted section 1, 2, 3. Even if we still make recursive calls with the left array 1 and the right array 3, the calls would immediately return since the arrays have length one. It could be the case where one side has length one and the other side may have more, so the code will be simpler if we make the recursive calls. We now recursively sort the right array 7, 6, 5 of the original problem. If we again pick the last element as the pivot (5), we could end up with 5, 7, 6. In this case there are no smaller elements so the pivot is moved to the left. Again, note that the pivot is in the correct location as it will always be after placing the elements less than it to the left and elements greater than it to the right. We now recursively sort the array 6, 7 and pick 7 as the pivot. This small array is now sorted and the entire original array is also sorted.

The implementation details we have not discussed yet are how to effectively pick the pivot so the algorithm is efficient and how to move small elements to the left and large elements to the right. We will now look at our first, but not final, implementation of the quicksort algorithm which shows how to move smaller elements to the left and larger elements to the right.

```
# qswrong.py
# this has a subtle bug
# it will not work if all the elements are equal
```

```
def quicksort(a, left, right):
    if left < right:
        pivot = a[right]
        i = left
        j = right - 1
        while True:
            while a[i] < pivot:
                i += 1;
            while pivot < a[j]:
                j = j - 1
            if i < j:
                # swap
                a[i], a[j] = a[j], a[i]
            else:
                break
        # swap
        a[i], a[right] = a[right], a[i]
        quicksort(a, left, i-1)
        quicksort(a, i+1, right)

a = range(15, -1, -1)
quicksort(a, 0, len(a)-1)
print a
```

Assuming the list size is greater than one, this implementation picks the last element in the list as the pivot. It then starts at the left and moves forward in the list until it finds an element larger than the pivot. Once it does, it starts at the right end of the array, just to the left of the last element which is the pivot, and moves backwards until it finds an element smaller than the pivot. Once it does, it then swaps the two elements it found so the element smaller than the pivot is moved to the left and the larger element is moved to the right. It then continues the process starting again where it left off on the left side moving forward in the list until it finds an element larger than the pivot and then repeats the process moving backwards from where it left off on the right side. Once those two inner **while** loops meet, the outer **while** loop stops. Thus, the code in the **while True** loop will run $n - 1$ times since it examines each element except the pivot once while the index variables i and j move towards each other. When the two indices cross, the pivot is placed at that location which is the correct location in the final sorted list. The code then recursively sorts the section of the list to the left of the pivot and the section of the list to the right of the pivot. Note that at no point is an extra copy of the list created; the elements are swapped within the original list.

Our question, of course, is how efficient is this algorithm. The analysis is not as easy as mergesort since the size of the two lists with which the recursive calls are made will vary depending on the input and which element is picked as the pivot. The experience you have developed should lead you to know that we want the two lists to be of equal size. This will give us the recurrence relation $T(n) = 2T(n/2)+n$ since we make two recursive calls with lists half the size and the steps to move the smaller elements to the left and larger elements to the right require $\Theta(n)$ time. This is the common recurrence relation for many divide-and-conquer algorithms and the answer is $\Theta(n * log_2 n)$. This matches the mergesort algorithm, but the constants that the Θ notation hides are smaller for the quicksort algorithm since we are not copying the elements to and from a second list. This is a significant benefit for large lists; with mergesort, recall that we need an extra array that is the same size as the array we are sorting. Thus, in practice, the quicksort will be faster than mergesort if we can split the list in two approximately equal halves.

Unfortunately, the quicksort algorithm may not necessarily split the list in half each time. What happens with our first implementation if the list is already sorted? In this case, the pivot will be the largest element in the list section we are sorting each time it makes a recursive call and we will be splitting the list into two lists, one of zero elements and one with only one element less than the original list, since the pivot element is not included in the recursive call. A similar partition into zero and $n - 1$ elements will happen if the list is in reverse order. These cases correspond to the recurrence relation $T(n) = T(n - 1) + n$. This does not meet the pattern that can be solved with the master theorem, so we must try a different technique. One way to look at this is to keep expanding the recurrence relation.

```
T(n) = n + T(n-1)
     = n + (n-1) + T(n-2)
     = n + (n-1) + (n-2) + T(n-3)
     = n + (n-1) + (n-2) + (n-3) + T(n-4)
     ...
     = n + (n-1) + (n-2) + (n-3) + ... + 1
```

As we just showed, this will result in the sum of the first n integers and we know that is $\Theta(n^2)$. Thus, the worst case for quicksort is worse than mergesort and equivalent to the original iterative sorting algorithms we examined in Chapter 3.

Unfortunately, in addition to being inefficient for these two cases, this implementation is not quite correct. If all the elements in the list are the same, the code will not work correctly. We leave it as an exercise to determine what happens and how to fix it. This is an example of how difficult it is to get the implementation of the quicksort algorithm correct.

Based on what we learned in the previous paragraphs, it should be clear that the choice of pivot is crucial to the performance of the algorithm. One possible choice to avoid the worst-case behavior when the list is already sorted is to randomly choose the pivot. This would mean that no specific input would be more likely to produce the worst-case running time. Another common option is to examine three elements and pick the median of those three as the pivot; this increases the likelihood that the pivot will be closer to the median element of the list.[2] We will now look at the quicksort algorithm implemented using this as the pivot strategy. This algorithm is also correct for all input cases, unlike our first algorithm.

```python
# quicksort.py

def quicksort(a, left, right):

    '''post: sorts a[left:right+1] (i.e., a[left] through a[right])'''

    if left < right-1:
        pivot = median3(a, left, right)
        i = left
        j = right - 1

        while True:
            i += 1
            while a[i] < pivot:
                i += 1
            j -= 1
            while a[j] > pivot:
                j -= 1
            if i < j:
                # swap
                a[i], a[j] = a[j], a[i]
            else:
                break

        # swap
        a[i], a[right-1] = a[right-1], a[i]
        quicksort(a, left, i-1)
        quicksort(a, i+1, right)

    elif left < right:
        if a[left] > a[right]:
            a[left], a[right] = a[right], a[left]
```

---

[2] An exercise in Thomas Cormen, Charles Leiserson, Ronald Rivest, and Clifford Stein, *Introduction to Algorithms*, (Cambridge, Massachusetts: McGraw-Hill Book Company, 2001), 2nd ed. discusses this approach.

```
def median3(a, left, right):

    center = (left + right) // 2
    if a[center] < a[left]:
        a[left], a[center] = a[center], a[left]
    if a[right] < a[left]:
        a[left], a[right] = a[right], a[left]
    if a[right] < a[center]:
        a[center], a[right] = a[right], a[center]
    a[center], a[right-1] = a[right-1], a[center]
    return a[right-1]
```

If there are at least three elements in the list, the quicksort function uses the median3 function to pick the pivot element. It examines the first, middle, and last elements and places the smallest element in the first position, the largest element in the last position, and the pivot in the next to last position. The quicksort function then works basically the same as our original algorithm. Note that we can start the index i at the second element in the section of the list since we know the element the median3 function placed in the first position is less than or equal to the pivot. Similarly, we can start the index j to the left of where we placed the pivot since we know the pivot and the element in the last position are greater than or equal to the pivot. Other than these minor changes, the code inside the while True loop works exactly the same as our original implementation. The last else statement handles the case where we have fewer than three elements in the section of the list we are sorting.

To further improve the speed of the implementation, we could write the original if statement as if (right - left < 10) and then have the else case use the selection sort or insertion sort algorithm to handle small lists. These iterative algorithms will be faster than a recursive algorithm for small lists. Since the recursive calls will eventually be sorting small lists, this change can increase the speed a significant amount.

In practice this improved implementation of the quicksort algorithm will have an average running time of $\Theta(n * lgn)$ and be faster than mergesort and other $\Theta(n * lgn)$ sorting algorithms even though the worst case running time of the quicksort algorithm is $\Theta(n^2)$. Note that using the median3 function, the algorithm will partition a sorted list or a list in reverse order into equal halves and thus will have a run-time of $\Theta(n * lgn)$ with this improved implementation. As long as the algorithm does not repeatedly split the list into two sections that are very uneven, quicksort will be faster than mergesort. In fact, if the algorithm splits the list into sizes that are fixed percentages such as 1/4 and 3/4, the $\Theta(n * lgn)$ running time will still be achieved. Proving this is beyond the scope of this book. Even though we typically analyze the worst-case running time, studying the quicksort algorithm has shown us that sometimes the average case analysis is more important (but also more difficult to do).

15.3 Greedy Algorithms

The *greedy algorithm* strategy, like most computer science terminology, is appropriately named. The common pattern in algorithms classified as greedy is that when making a choice, they always pick the choice that looks best at the moment. The greedy strategy is typically applied to optimization problems. Optimization problems usually contain one of these phrases: what is the best, what is the minimum, or what is the maximum. An example of an optimization problem is what is the minimum number of coins needed to total 42 cents? In the United States, you would choose one quarter worth 25 cents, one dime worth 10 cents, one nickel worth 5 cents, and two pennies worth 2 cents. This is a problem in which the greedy strategy can be applied. The greedy choice is to always choose the largest coin possible. Starting at 42 cents, we choose a quarter leaving us with 17 more cents. The largest possible coin we can use now is a dime leaving us with 7 cents. The largest possible coin we can use now is a nickel leaving us with 2 cents that we form using two pennies.

Using a greedy strategy involves two main steps. The first is to determine how a greedy choice can be applied to the problem. In the case of our coin problem the greedy choice we determined is to always use the largest possible coin. The second step is to prove that the greedy choice will in fact lead to the optimal solution. In our example of United States coins, the greedy choice works because all the coins are multiples of five. These coin values make it easy to determine that the greedy algorithm will work for all possible totals.

Unfortunately, the greedy strategy cannot be applied to all optimization problems. Consider the widely studied problem known as the traveling salesman problem. Given a group of cities with straight line distances between them, determine the order to visit all the cities that minimizes the total distance traveled. A greedy choice could be to choose the closest city from your current location, then choose the closest city to it that has not been visited, and so on until all the cities have been visited. This strategy will not result in the shortest path being found in all cases. We will discuss this problem again in section 15.5.

Greedy algorithms can be used in compression algorithms. The basic idea of compression is to reduce the amount of storage needed for data. There are two categories of compression: *lossy* and *lossless*. As the name implies, when you use lossy compression, you lose some of the data and cannot reproduce the original data exactly; lossless compression allows you to uncompress the data and get back the exact original data. You have likely used compressed data whether you realize it or not. Most audio formats, such as MP3 and AAC, use compression to reduce the amount of data required to store and play audio files. Similarly, most video is stored and transmitted in compressed format. Digital television is broadcast in a lossy compression format (typically the MPEG-2 compression format); other common video compression formats you may have heard of are MPEG-4 and H.264, which is a specific form of MPEG-4. Lossy compression is acceptable for audio and video applications since the exact original data is not needed. There is a trade-off between the amount of compression and the quality of the audio or video. As long as enough bits are used in the compressed version, when the data is uncompressed, the audio or video will sound or look "good enough" for most people. In the United States, different networks use different amounts of compression and in some cases, the loss of quality is noticeable in fast moving scenes such as those in sports.

For other applications, lossy compression will not work. If you compress your source code or a research paper, you need to get the original version back when you uncompress it. In this section, we will look at one of the simpler compression algorithms known as *Huffman codes* that uses a greedy strategy; it was developed by David Huffman in the 1950s. In this section, we will discuss the algorithm using examples with plain ASCII text, but the algorithm can be applied to any data that is represented using bits.

Uncompressed ASCII files use eight bits to store each letter; unicode uses 16 bits for each character. The basic idea of Huffman codes is to use fewer bits for letters that occur more frequently in the text you are compressing and more bits for letters that occur less often. We may end up using two or three bits for letters that occur frequently in our text such as a, e, and s. and more than eight bits for letters that occur less frequently such as z or q. For most files with more than a few hundred letters, the total number of bits needed when using this mixture of short and long codes will be less than the original uncompressed file. We also need to store information about the bit code for each letter so we can uncompress the file. Attempting to compress a very small file will result in a larger file because of the overhead of storing the decoding information. Of course, if the file is small, there is no need to compress it.

The technique Huffman codes use to create the compressed file generate what are known as *prefix codes* or more accurately, *prefix-free codes*; you will find both terms are used interchangeably. For codes to be considered prefix-free, no code can be a prefix of another code. The codes 10, 011, 010, and 110 form a prefix-free code set. If we assign these codes in order to the letters, a, b, c, d and have the bit sequence

0111101001010, we can easily decode the sequence by processing each bit one at a time until we find a letter that matches. In this example, we find the first three bits correspond to the letter b. We continue processing bits and find the next three bits correspond to the letter d. The next two bits then correspond to the letter a, followed by three bits for the letter c, followed by two bits for the letter a. Since no code is a prefix for any other code, this is the only way to decode the message and we can stop processing bits and output a letter as soon as the bit sequence matches one of the letters.

An easy way to visualize this and to process it is to make a tree using the codes. The bit 0 corresponds to moving left in the tree and the bit 1 corresponds to moving right in the tree. Figure 15.1 shows the codes in this example. This allows you to start at the root of the tree and move down the tree as you process each bit. When you reach a leaf node with a letter, you output that letter and start the process again at the root of the tree. As the tree representation makes it easy to see, the letters will always be at leaf nodes. If a letter was not at a leaf node, the code would not be a prefix-free code and would be ambiguous when we tried to process it a bit at a time. Consider the codes 0, 11, and 110 that are not a prefix-free code corresponding to the letters a, b, and c. If we attempt to decode 110, is it the letter c or the two-character sequence ba? With prefix-free codes, we do not have this problem.

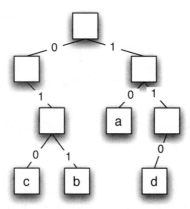

Figure 15.1: Prefix codes represented as a tree

Of course, the problem is how to form the tree that will result in the most compression. As we stated earlier, we want the more frequent letters to have shorter codes and the less frequent letters to have longer codes. That means frequent letters need to be near the root of the tree and less frequent letters need to be farther down the tree. Because of this, our first step is to process the input file, determine the frequency of each letter, and sort the letters by frequency. To demonstrate the algorithm, we will use a common palindrome "a man a plan a canal panama" since it has only a few unique letters keeping our tree fairly small. The following table shows the letter frequencies for this phrase:

Letter	Frequency
c	1
m	2
l	2
p	2
n	4
space	6
a	10

Remembering the two requirements that all characters must be at leaf nodes and we want less frequently occurring letters near the bottom of the tree, we will create tree nodes for each character and build up the tree starting at the bottom of the tree. We show this pictorially in Figure 15.2 with each node showing the character followed by its frequency. We have ordered them by increasing frequency.

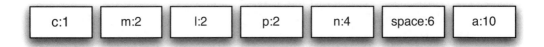

Figure 15.2: Starting trees for Huffman codes

The algorithm Huffman developed works by combining the two trees that are currently the smallest into one tree. The first step for our example selects the characters c and m and combines them into one rooted tree with a total frequency of three (the sum of the two individual frequencies). This is shown in Figure 15.3.

Next we select the characters l and p since they have the two smallest frequencies and create a new combined tree with them as shown in Figure 15.4. The two smallest frequencies now total 3 and 4 so we combine them as shown in Figure 15.5. We continue the process and combine the two trees with frequency totals 4 and 6 as

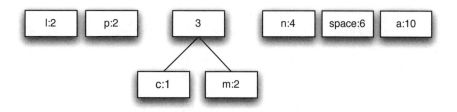

Figure 15.3: Combining the first two trees

shown in Figure 15.6. The next step combines the two trees with frequency totals 7 and 10. Finally, we combine the two remaining trees and obtain the final result shown in Figure 15.7.

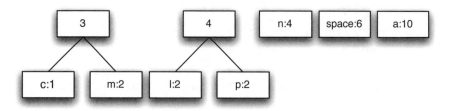

Figure 15.4: Combining the second two trees

The table after the figures shows the characters, their original frequency, their bit code, and the total number of bits required to store that letter using the bit code (the frequency multiplied by the length of the bit code). For the example string "a man a plan a canal panama," 76 bits are required. As mentioned earlier, we also have to store the letter and its code so that we can decode it. In this case, the short length of the string will likely result in the compressed file being larger because of the overhead of storing the code for each letter.

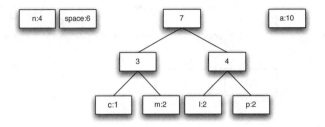

Figure 15.5: Combining the third two trees

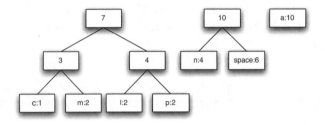

Figure 15.6: Combining the fourth two trees

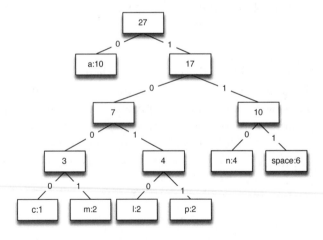

Figure 15.7: Final tree for Huffman codes

a recursive call returns, we remove the last element in the list. The running time for this is linear in terms of the number of nodes in the tree. Again, this can be considered a constant since there are at most 512 nodes in the tree. The next step is to store each unique letter and its code in a new file followed by the code for each letter in the order they appear in the original file. As you can see, for large files the running time is dominated by reading and writing the characters and is linearly related to the number of bytes in the file.

To decompress the file, we need to read the header information containing the bit code for each character in the file. You could then form the tree or create a hash table matching each code to its letter. As you then read the file a bit at a time, you use the tree to decode it as we discussed at the beginning of this section or keep building up the code until you get a code that is a key in the hash table. The time required for this is again linearly related to the number of bytes in the file.

To actually compress the file, we need to do bit-level manipulation. Most programming languages, but not all, provide operators for performing bit-level manipulation. In Python and C++, the « and » operators can be used to shift bits and the binary & and | operators can be used to perform bit-level **and** and **or** operations. The following shows an example of this using the interactive Python interpreter.

```
>>> x = 1
>>> x = (x << 1) | 1
>>> x
3
>>> x = (x << 1) | 0
>>> x
6
```

The statement x«1 shifts the bits left one position, resulting in x being 2 assuming it was initially 1. After using the | operator to do a bitwise "or" operation, x is now 3. Shifting the value 3, which is represented as 11 in base 2, left one position gives us 110. The bitwise "or" with zero does not change it, so x is now 6. This type of bit-level operations can be used in the Huffman compression algorithm to build up the bit codes for sequences of characters. Each time you reach a certain number of bits, such as 8 or 32, you can write that value out to the file and start the process again.

The final question is how good is the compression using this greedy choice. The answer is it is optimal for prefix-codes since we are using the shortest number of bits for the most frequent letters. However, if you implement the algorithm and compare the compression to compression programs such as `gzip`, `bzip2`, or `zip`, you will likely find they compress the files more than your Huffman compression program. The reason they work better is they often group multiple letters together and form codes for those. For example, the two-character sequences sh, th, and ch occur frequently in English words. If we use short bit codes for these multiple character sequences, we usually achieve more compression than compressing each single character with a bit code.

15.4 Dynamic Programming

Dynamic programming is another technique that is often applied to optimization problems and is similar to the divide-and-conquer strategy. The basic divide-and-conquer strategy works well when each subproblem appears only once as we split the problem into subproblems. Recall that the recursive Fibonacci algorithm in Chapter 6 is inefficient because it required that we recompute the same subproblems multiple times. Dynamic programming solves this problem by storing the answer to each subproblem and reusing the stored value instead of recalculating it. Our iterative Fibonacci solution can be classified as a dynamic programming algorithm. As a reminder, here is the iterative Fibonacci function from Chapter 6 that has a running time of $\Theta(n)$.

```
def loopfib(n):
    # pre: n > 0
    # returns the nth Fibonacci number

    curr = 1
    prev = 1
    for i in range(n-2):
        curr, prev = curr+prev, curr
    return curr
```

This is one of the simpler dynamic programming examples since we only need to store the answer to the two most recent subproblems and it is easy to combine the answers to the subproblems to find the answer to the current problem. As with the divide-and-conquer strategy, one key concept for dynamic programming algorithms is to determine how to combine the solution to the subproblems into the solution to the original problem. In some cases, we need to examine only one or two subproblems to solve the original problem. In other cases, we need to look at a number of subproblems. In cases that require examining a number of subproblems, dynamic programming is very common since we will often be examining the same subproblem multiple times while solving the original problem. This concept is typically referred to as *overlapping subproblems*.

Having overlapping subproblems is not the only criterion that is required to apply the dynamic programming technique. The other important criterion that an optimization problem must meet is that the solution to the original problem must contain optimal solutions to the subproblems. Determining how to combine the optimal solutions to subproblems to determine the optimal solution to the original problem is typically the most difficult task when designing a dynamic programming algorithm.

While divide-and-conquer algorithms are typically implemented recursively, dynamic programming algorithms typically start with the base case problem and use it to determine the solution to the larger problems until the solution to the original problem is reached. Because of this, dynamic programming algorithms are typically not implemented using recursion. Instead, the typical method uses an iterative solution that stores the solutions to the subproblems in a table and fills in the table with the answers to larger problems as it works to compute the answer to the original problem. We will now examine one problem in detail that dynamic programming can be applied to and give the basic algorithm for another problem that dynamic programming should be used to solve.

15.4.1 Longest Common Subsequence

The longest common subsequence problem is a fairly simple problem to understand, which makes it a nice first example for dynamic programming. For this problem, we define a *sequence* as a finite, ordered list of items. A Python tuple, list, or string qualifies as a sequence. A *subsequence* is an ordered subset of the original sequence; in other words, you may remove some (possibly none) of the items from the original sequence, but not change the order of the sequence. The longest common subsequence problem is, given two sequences, what is the maximum length sequence that is a subsequence of the two sequences. For example, consider the two words `abracadabra` and `batter` as sequences of letters; a longest common subsequence for these two sequences is `bar`. There may be more than one common sequence with the same maximum length, but in this case, `bar` is the only subsequence of length three.

A brute force algorithm is to determine all the subsequences for one of the sequences and then check if it is a subsequence of the other sequence and keep track of the longest subsequence found. For a sequence of length n, the number of subsequences is 2^n. This is easy to picture by viewing each item in the sequence as an item that can be selected or not selected. This allows us to count the number of subsequences by treating the sequence as n binary digits. Given n bits, the number of items that can be represented is 2^n so this results in an algorithm that is $\Theta(2^n)$

just to compute all the subsequences. We then need to find the longest subsequence that is a subsequence of the other sequence.

It is likely not intuitively obvious to you that dynamic programming can be applied to this problem. This is why we study examples of the various algorithm techniques. The experience of seeing techniques for solving various problems can help you determine when these techniques might be applied to new problems. To use dynamic programming for this problem, we need to determine how we can find the optimal solution to larger problems given the solution to smaller problems. This is where intuition and experience will help you.

Our first step is to examine small problems, so we will start with sequences of length one (i.e., the base case for the problem). If the two sequences contain the same element, the common subsequence length is one, otherwise it is zero. A possible next step is to see what happens if we add a letter to two sequences for which we know the longest common subsequence. If we have two sequences and add the same character to each sequence, the length of the longest common subsequence between the two longer sequences is one more than the longest common subsequence of the two original sequences. For example, consider the sequences `abcd` and `cabe`; the longest common subsequence of these two sequences is `ab`. If we add the letter `f` onto the end of each sequence, the longest common subsequence is `abf`.

Now that we have some initial ideas, let's draw a table to see if that can help us determine a complete set of steps for the problem. Since we have two sequences, we will make a two-dimensional table using our first sample sequences. We will let the entry $[i, j]$ in the table refer to the length of the longest common subsequence for the sequence of letters 1 through i of the one sequence and 1 through j of the other sequence. We have filled in the first row and column in the following table.

	a	b	r	a	c	a	d	a	b	r	a
b	0	1	1	1	1	1	1	1	1	1	1
a	1										
t	1										
t	1										
e	1										
r	1										

The upper left zero corresponds to the longest common subsequence between the letter `a` in `abracadbra` and the letter `b` in `batter`. The one in the next position to the right corresponds to the longest common subsequence between the sequence `ab` of `abracadbra` and the letter `b` of `batter`. Once you have a one in the first row, the rest of the entries in the first row must be a one based on how the entries in the table are defined. The first column is filled out in exactly the same manner. Once the first row and first column in the table have been calculated and stored, the rows or columns can be computed in order. We have filled out the second row of numbers in the next updated copy of the table.

	a	b	r	a	c	a	d	a	b	r	a
b	0	1	1	1	1	1	1	1	1	1	1
a	1	1	1	2	2	2	2	2	2	2	2
t	1										
t	1										
e	1										
r	1										

If we now think about what each table entry means, we can determine how to compute each entry based on the entries above it, to the left of it, and diagonally up and to the left. As discussed earlier when developing some intuition for the algorithm, if the element at position i in the one sequence matches the element at position j in the other sequence, we can add one to the longest common subsequence between the first $i - 1$ entries of the one sequence and the first $j - 1$ entries in the other sequence. An example of this is the first two in the second row of numbers. This corresponds to the longest common subsequence of abra and ba. We have already determined that the length of the longest common subsequence between abr and b is one. When we add the letter a to each of those two sequences, we can add one to the length of the common subsequence, giving us two. In our table, this corresponds to adding one to the entry diagonally above it to the left when the elements match.

We also have to determine what to do if the letters do not match. An example of this is adding the letter c to abrac. We want to know the length of the longest common subsequence between it and ba. Since the letter c does not match the last letter of ba we cannot increase the length of the longest common subsequence. Instead, the longest common subsequence of abrac and ba must be the maximum of the longest common subsequence of abrac and b and the longest common subsequence of abra and ba. This corresponds to the maximum of the entries in the table above and to the left of the entry we are computing. The final table for the example is the following.

	a	b	r	a	c	a	d	a	b	r	a
b	0	1D	1L	1L	1L	1L	1L	1L	1L	1L	1L
a	1D	1L	1L	2D	2L	2L	2L	2L	2L	2L	2L
t	1U	1L	1L	2U	2L	2L	2L	2L	2L	2L	2L
t	1U	1L	1L	2U	2L	2L	2L	2L	2L	2L	2L
e	1U	1L	1L	2U	2L	2L	2L	2L	2L	2L	2L
r	1U	1L	2D	2L	2L	2L	2L	2L	2L	3D	3L

Given this table, we likely also want to determine what the longest common subsequence is. The key point to realize is that when we added one to the diagonal entry, we were adding a letter to the common subsequence. By keeping track of which entry we used to compute an entry, we can determine the actual common subsequence. We can picture an arrow in addition to the number indicating which entry we used to determine the value for each entry. For our table we have used the letter D to indicate a diagonal entry, the letter L to indicate a left arrow, and the letter U to indicate an up arrow. Starting at the lower right corner of the table, we chose the three to the left when picking the maximum of the left and above entries. From there we chose the diagonal entry so the last letter in our common subsequence is r. We continue following the arrows, inserting letters at the beginning of our common subsequence when we follow a diagonal arrow. When an arrow moves us out of the numeric entries, we are done and have determined the longest common subsequence.

Continuing our example, we will insert the letter a when we reach the entry in the table corresponding to abra and ba. We finally insert the letter b when we reach the entry in the table corresponding to ab and b. That diagonal entry moves us off the table, indicating that our common subsequence is bar. In our example, we broke all ties when choosing the maximum of the left and above entries by choosing the left entry. Choosing the above entry could result in a different common subsequence with the same maximum length.

The run-time analysis of this algorithm is fairly simple. We have to fill in the table. Computing each entry requires a constant amount of time. Given sequences of length m and n, the running time is $\Theta(m * n)$. The running time for our brute force algorithm of creating all subsequences of the shorter sequence and then checking if they are subsequences of the other sequence is at least $\Theta(2^n)$ where n is the length of the shorter sequence. Clearly, the dynamic programming algorithm is much more efficient.

One drawback to our algorithm is that it requires $\Theta(m * n)$ space to compute the result. A common application for the longest common subsequence problem is DNA matching, which uses long strings of letters. Fortunately Dan Hirschberg, a computer science professor, developed an algorithm that requires only a linear amount of space, making it much more efficient for long sequences.

15.4.2 Memoization

As we mentioned before, the iterative approach of storing and computing table entries in fixed order is the common technique used to implement dynamic programming algorithms; however, it is possible to implement them using recursion. The term *memoization* refers to using the recursive formula for the divide-and-conquer strategy, but storing results as they are calculated so that we do not need to calculate them multiple times. Before a recursive call is made to compute an entry, the code first checks to see if that result has already been computed and stored. If so there is no need to make the recursive call to compute it and we can simply use the stored value. This gives us a running time equivalent to our iterative solution, but retains the recursive form of divide and conquer. One possible method to store the calculated values in a hash table. This is easy to implement in Python using its dictionary. An array or list could also be used to store the previously computed values. A memoized implementation of the Fibonacci function is the following:

```
# fibm.py
def fibm(n, d=None):
    if n < 2:
        return n
    if d is None:
        d = {0:1, 1:1}
    if n-1 not in d:
        d[n-1] = fibm(n-1, d)
    if n-2 not in d:
        d[n-2] = fibm(n-2, d)
    return d[n-1] + d[n-2]
```

If you execute it, you will find its actual running time is similar to the iterative Fibonacci function whereas the pure recursive Fibonacci function is much slower for values greater than 25. Generally the iterative implementation will be slightly faster than a memoized recursive implementation due to the overhead of the numerous function calls made in a recursive algorithm.

15.4.3 Matrix Chain Multiplication

Determining the most efficient way to multiply a number of matrices together is another problem that dynamic programming can be used to solve. We will first provide some brief background on matrices before discussing how dynamic programming relates to the problem. A *matrix* is a two-dimensional array of numbers. In order to multiply two matrices together, the number of columns in the first matrix must match the number of rows in the second matrix. For example, a 6 by 8 matrix can be multiplied by an 8 by 4 matrix, but the 8 by 4 matrix cannot be multiplied by a 6 by 8 matrix. The size of the resulting matrix is the number of rows in the first matrix by the number of columns in the second matrix; the result of multiplying the 6 by 8 matrix by the 8 by 4 matrix is a 6 by 4 matrix. The amount of work required to perform the calculation is the product of the number of rows in the first matrix, the number of columns in the first matrix (which is the same as the number of rows in the second matrix), and the number of columns in the second matrix. To multiply the 6 by 8 matrix by the 8 by 4 matrix requires 6*8*4=192 steps. If you are not familiar with how to multiply two matrices, do a quick Internet search or ask your instructor.

Matrix multiplication is not commutative even when the sizes of the matrices allow the order of the two operands to be reversed. However, matrix multiplication is associative. Consider the amount of work to multiply three matrices A, B, and C with the sizes 2 by 10, 10 by 4, and 4 by 3, respectively. If we calculate (AB)C, by first multiplying the 2 by 10 and 10 by 4 matrices together, we get a 2 by 4 matrix that requires 80 steps. Multiplying the resulting 2 by 4 matrix by the 4 by 3 matrix requires 24 steps for a total of 104 steps to calculate the final 2 by 3 matrix. If we instead calculate A(BC) by first multiplying the 10 by 4 matrix with the 4 by 3 matrix, we get a 10 by 3 matrix that requires 120 steps. We then multiply the 2 by 10 matrix by the 10 by 3 matrix to obtain the same 2 by 3 matrix, but this requires 60 more steps for a total of 180 steps. This means we want to parenthesize the matrices as (AB)C instead of A(BC) to produce the result with fewer calculations.

For three matrices, there are only two choices on how to parenthesize the calculation as we showed in the previous paragraph. If we have four matrices ABCD, our choices are A((BC)D), A(B(CD)), (AB)(CD), ((AB)C)D, and (A(BC))D. The question is how can we apply dynamic programming to this problem. The key point to realize is that if the optimal way to parenthesize the product is to multiply ABC together and then multiply that by the matrix D, then we will need the optimal way to multiply ABC which is either (AB)C or A(BC). This is what allows dynamic programming to be applied to this problem; the optimal solution to the original problem contains optimal solutions to the subproblems. If we have five matrices, ABCDE, the optimal way to multiply them together might be (ABC)(DE). If it is, we will want the optimal way to multiply ABC together.

If we have a large number of matrices to multiply together, the different parenthesizations can result in widely different amounts of required calculations. Determining the optimal order is commonly known as the *matrix chain multiplication* problem. We saw the number was significantly different with just three matrices in our initial example. With more matrices, the differences can be even more dramatic, so if you have a large number of matrices to multiply together, it is likely worth it to first determine the optimal parenthesization.

The dynamic programming solution to this problem starts with calculating the optimal way to multiply each group of three consecutive matrices together. The next step is to determine the optimal way to multiply each group of four consecutive matrices together, and so on. This will require an n-by-n table if we have n matrices labeled $A_0, A_1, \ldots, A_{n-1}$ to multiply together. The entry in the table at the position $[i][j]$ indicates the optimal number of steps for multiplying matrices A_i through A_j. We only need to compute half the table since it is symmetric (i.e., entry $[i][j]$ will be the same as $[j][i]$). Unlike the longest common subsequence problem where a constant amount of work is required to compute each table entry, the amount of work to compute this table is the difference between i and j. We will leave the remaining details of this algorithm as an exercise.

Some dynamic programming algorithms require a one-dimensional table, while others require a two-dimensional table as we have seen in our examples here. It is possible that some problems could require even higher dimension tables. Some algorithms will require a constant amount of steps to compute each entry in the table and others require more calculations to compute an entry in the table. As an algorithm designer, your job is to determine if dynamic programming can be applied to the problem, and if so, what is the least amount of work required to calculate the final result.

15.5 NP-Complete Problems

Since this is an introductory book, we will cover only the basic details of *NP-complete* problems. "NP" stands for "non-deterministic polynomial" time. NP problems have the property that you can verify a solution in polynomial time; we will discuss what this means shortly. The category P of problems corresponds to all problems that can be solved in polynomial time. Thus, P is a subset of NP. The open question is does P equal NP or is P a proper subset of NP. NP-complete problems are a category of problems for which no polynomial time algorithms are known. The interesting point is that if one NP-complete problem could be solved in polynomial time, then all NP-complete problems could be solved in polynomial time.

The traveling salesman problem mentioned earlier in this chapter is an NP-complete problem. The only known algorithm to solve the traveling salesman problem exactly is to measure all the possible paths and pick the shortest. Unfortunately, there are 2^n possible paths if you have n cities so this algorithm is extremely inefficient. If someone tells you that a certain path has a length of 1,000, we can verify in polynomial time (linear time in fact) that the path has a length of 1,000. Because of this, the problem qualifies as an NP problem. And since there is no known polynomial time algorithm to solve it, it is NP-complete.

Graduate computer science students typically study how to prove that a problem is NP-complete. The process of proving a problem is NP-complete is known as *reducing* or *reduction*. The basic idea is to create a transformation between the problems that can be performed in polynomial time. Thus, if we could solve our problem in polynomial time, we could apply the polynomial transformation and solve the known NP-complete problem in polynomial time. This is why if we could solve one NP-complete problem in polynomial time, we could solve all of them in polynomial time.

It is important to know if a problem you are attempting to solve is NP-complete since that means no polynomial time algorithm is known to solve it. This can prevent you from wasting time trying to find an efficient algorithm. Of course, if your problem is NP-complete and you find a polynomial algorithm then you have just solved one of the open problems in computer science. Knowing that your problem is NP-complete also tells you that if you have a large problem to solve, you will unlikely be able to solve it in a reasonable amount of time. Instead, you might search for algorithms that approximate an optimal solution. In some cases you might be able to show that your approximation algorithm produces a solution that is within a certain percentage of the optimal solution. For example, we might be able to find an algorithm that produces a path for the traveling salesman problem that is no worse than twice the length of the optimal solution.

As we mentioned, proving an algorithm is NP-complete is an advanced topic and we will not cover it in any detail in this book. Fortunately, other mathematicians and computer scientists have proven a number of problems are NP-complete. An entire book[3] was written categorizing a number of NP-complete problems and how they can be reduced. If you are struggling with coming up with an efficient algorithm for your problem, a first step would be to check a list of known NP-complete problems to see if your problem is already known to be NP-complete.

---

[3]Michael Garey and David Johnson, *Computers and Intractability: A Guide to the Theory of NP-Completeness*, (New York: Freeman, 1979).

15.6 Chapter Summary

This chapter formalizes a categorization of some of the algorithm strategies we have used throughout this book and when each strategy can be applied. Understanding these techniques and when to apply them will help you develop algorithms to solve new problems you encounter. The following summarizes the specific concepts presented in this chapter.

- Divide-and-conquer algorithms break problems into subproblems and then combine the solutions to the subproblems to solve the original problem.

- Divide-and-conquer algorithms typically are written using recursion; the master theorem can be used to analyze the running time of many recursive algorithms.

- The quicksort algorithm is commonly used for sorting. In practice, a good implementation of it is fast, but it can be slow depending on the initial order of elements to be sorted and the choice of the pivot element.

- Greedy algorithms are typically applied to optimization problems and work correctly when making the choice that looks best at the moment leads to the optimal solution to the original problem. Prefix codes for compression are an example of a greedy algorithm.

- Dynamic programming is an algorithm strategy similar to divide and conquer. It is often applied to optimization problems. It should be used when a divide-and-conquer strategy would attempt to solve the same subproblem multiple times. Instead of resolving the subproblems each time, we solve it once and store the answer so it can be used the next time that subproblem would be solved.

- There are a number of problems for which no known polynomial time algorithm exists. The category of NP-complete problems is a subset of these problems with the interesting property that if one NP-complete problem could be solved in polynomial time then all the NP-complete problems could be solved in polynomial time.

15.7   Exercises

True/False Questions

1. Quicksort is always the most efficient algorithm for sorting.

2. Quicksort is a divide-and-conquer algorithm.

3. The quicksort algorithm requires less memory than the mergesort algorithm.

4. The choice of the pivot element affects the running time of the quicksort algorithm.

5. All recurrence relations can be solved using the master theorem.

6. Greedy algorithms will work correctly for all optimization problems.

7. Dynamic programming should be used for all divide-and-conquer problems.

8. Dynamic programming algorithms store the results of the subproblem solutions so they can be reused without recalculating them.

9. There is always a unique answer to the longest common subsequence problem.

10. Any dynamic programming algorithm can be implemented recursively using memoization.

11. If we could solve one NP-complete problem in polynomial time, we could solve all NP-complete problems in polynomial time.

Multiple Choice Questions

1. Using the master theorem, what is the answer to the recurrence relation $T(n) = 3T(n/2) + n$?

    a) $\Theta(n)$
    b) $\Theta(n^{log_2 3})$
    c) $\Theta(n^{log_2 3} * log_2 n)$
    d) It cannot be solved with the master theorem.

2. Using the master theorem, what is the answer to the recurrence relation $T(n) = 4T(n/2) + n^2$?

    a) $\Theta(n)$
    b) $\Theta(n^2)$

c) $\Theta(n^2 * log_2 n)$

d) It cannot be solved with the master theorem.

3. Using the master theorem, what is the answer to the recurrence relation $T(n) = 2T(n/3) + 2T(n/4) + n$?

a) $\Theta(n^{log_3 2})$

b) $\Theta(n^{0.5})$

c) $\Theta(n^{0.5} * log_2 n)$

d) It cannot be solved with the master theorem.

4. When is it acceptable to use lossy compression instead of lossless compression?

a) in all cases

b) to compress the source code for your programs

c) to compress an executable program

d) when you do not need to reproduce the exact original version

5. When should dynamic programming be used with a divide-and-conquer algorithm?

a) for all divide-and-conquer problems

b) when the divide-and-conquer algorithm's running time is not $\Theta(n * log_2 n)$

c) when there are overlapping subproblems

d) only for optimization problems

Short-Answer Questions

1. What happens with our original quicksort implementation if all the elements in the list are the same? How could we correct the code?

2. Give the denomination of three coins and a total value for which using the greedy strategy does not result in the minimum number of coins being used.

3. Show your work and the final prefix codes using the Huffman coding algorithm for the following letters and their frequencies: {a: 2, b: 3, c: 6, d: 12, e: 24, f: 9}.

4. What is the total number of different parenthesizations for a product of five matrices?

5. What is the running time of the matrix chain dynamic programming algorithm for n matrices (for determining the optimal order, but not computing the matrix products)?

Programming Exercises

1. Search for a divide-and-conquer algorithm that finds the two closest points in a plane. Implement this algorithm.

2. Using Huffman codes, write programs to compress and uncompress a file.

3. Implement the longest common subsequence algorithm described in this chapter.

4. Search for Dan Hirschberg's algorithm and use it to solve the longest common subsequence problem.

5. Implement the matrix chain multiplication problem using dynamic programming.

Glossary

abstract data type A description of a data type that is independent of any particular implementation.

abstraction The purposeful hiding or ignoring of some details in order to concentrate on those that are relevant.

actual parameter An argument that appears in the call to a function.

acyclic graph A graph that does not contain any cycles.

adjacency list A technique for implementing graphs. It is a list of nodes that are connected to a given node via an edge.

adjacency matrix A technique for implementing graphs. It is a matrix where each entry (r,c) represents information about the edge (or lack thereof) from node r to node c.

algorithm analysis Using mathematical techniques to determine the computing resources (e.g., time and space) required by an algorithm.

aliasing Describes the situation where there are multiple live references to the same data. Changes to the data through one reference will be visible to the other references as well.

API Application programming interface.

application programming interface The set of values, operations, and objects provided by a code library or framework.

array A collection implemented as a sequence of identical "cells" in a contiguous block of memory.

ASCII American Standard Code for Information Interchange. A standard for encoding text where each character is represented by a number 0–127.

assembly code A low-level programming language whose structures have a direct correspondence to the underlying machine language of a particular computer architecture.

associative array A container type that implements a mapping from keys to values.

asymptotic notation Big-O notation. A way of describing an upper bound on the resources required by an algorithm for an input of a given size.

attribute A component of an object. Sometimes it is used to mean the data in an object, as opposed to its operations.

AVL tree A technique for maintaining a binary search tree in a (nearly) balanced fashion for efficient lookup.

balanced tree A tree where the all the nodes at each level have (nearly) the same number of descendants.

base case In recursive functions or problem-solving, this is a small version of the problem that does not require recursive decomposition.

big-O notation A way of describing an upper bound on the resources required by an algorithm for an input of a given size.

binary heap A heap data structure implemented as a binary tree.

binary search A very efficient searching algorithm for finding items in a sorted collection. Requires time proportional to $\log_2 n$ where n is the size of the collection.

binary search tree A binary tree with the binary search property. For every node, the data in its left subtree is smaller than the data and the node, and the data in its right subtree is larger.

binary tree A tree in which each node has at most two children. The two children are traditionally named "left" and "right."

binding A binding is an association between two things. A variable is a binding of an identifier (name) with a memory location.

bit Binary digit, fundamental unit of information. It is usually represented using 0 and 1.

breadth first traversal An algorithm that explores a tree or graph in a fashion that guarantees that every node's immediate children are examined before its other descendants.

byte A group of eight bits. It is the smallest addressable unit of storage on most modern computers.

byte code An intermediate form between high-level source code and machine language. Byte code can execute on a virtual machine interpreter or be further compiled to machine code.

chaining A technique for maintaining multiple items in a single "slot" of some container structure. A chain of items is typically maintained as a linked list.

class A class describes a set of related objects. In object-oriented languages, the `class` mechanism is used as a "factory" to produce objects.

class variable A variable that "lives" in a class and whose value is shared by all instances of the class.

client In programming, a module that uses another component is called a client for the component.

collision Occurs when two or more distinct items hash to the same location in a hash table.

compiler A program that translates a program written in a high-level language into the machine language that can be executed by a particular computer.

complete graph A graph in which every pair of nodes is connected by an edge.

complete tree A tree where every node except at the deepest level has the maximum possible number of children.

connected graph A graph in which there is a path from every node to every other node.

const method In C++, a method declared with the `const` designation cannot change any of the instance variables.

constructor The method that creates a new instance of a class.

container class A class of objects whose primary function is to store a collection of objects.

copy constructor A C++ constructor that takes an object of the type being constructed as a parameter and creates a new copy of it.

cycle A path in a graph that starts and ends on the same node.

data compression A technique for representing information more compactly (using fewer bits) for the purpose of storage or transmission.

data structure A way of storing data so that it can be effectively used for some application.

data type A particular way of representing data. The data type of an item determines what values it can have and what operations it supports.

debugging The process of finding and eliminating errors in a program.

decision statement A control structure that allows different parts of a program to execute depending on the exact situation. Usually decisions are controlled by Boolean expressions.

declaration A statement that states properties of a variable or function (such as its type) to the underlying compiler or interpreter.

deep copy A complete copy of some data such that no mutable structure is shared between the two copies.

definition A statement that provides the implementation of a variable or function.

degree In an undirected graph, it is the number of edges incident to a particular node.

depth first traversal An algorithm that explores a tree or graph by following a single path of descendants to the maximum depth before backing up and considering alternative paths.

dequeue The operation that removes an item from a FIFO queue.

dereference The process of retrieving the item that is referred to by a pointer (an address).

destructor The method that is called to "clean-up" an object that is no longer needed. In C++, for example, a destructor is used to deallocate dynamic memory.

dictionary A mapping from keys to values, also called an associative array.

Dijkstra's algorithm An efficient algorithm for finding the shortest paths in a graph.

directed acyclic graph A graph having directed (one-way) edges and no cycles when paths are followed in the directed fashion.

directed graph A graph in which edges have a distinguished direction. Each edge has a from-node and a to-node.

disjoint set structure A data structure for keeping track of the partitioning of a set into disjoint subsets.

disjoint sets Sets that have no elements in common.

divide-and-conquer algorithm An algorithm design technique that breaks a problem into smaller versions of the original.

duck typing Refers to the method of type equivalence used in dynamic programming languages. Any type object can be passed to a function or method provided the object implements all of the operations that the function or method requires. The name refers to the quip "If it quacks like a duck and waddles like a duck, then it's a duck."

dummy node A special node at the front or rear of a linked list that is used as a marker rather than to contain data.

dynamic memory Memory that is allocated and deallocated to a program at run-time.

dynamic programming A technique for developing efficient algorithms involving problems that can be decomposed into a series of overlapping subproblems.

dynamic typing A programming language mechanism where data types are attached to values rather than variables, and the actual data type stored in a particular variable can change over time.

encapsulation Hiding the details of something. Usually this is the term used to describe the distinction between the implementation and use of an object or function. Details are encapsulated in the definition.

event-driven simulation A technique for programming simulations that relies on probabilistic generation of events and adjusts a global "clock" to when the next even happens. Compare to time-driven simulation.

explicit heap dynamic The situation in C++ where memory can be allocated and deallocated at run-time directly under programmer control.

exponential algorithm An algorithm with resource requirements that grow as an exponential function of the size of the input.

formal parameter A parameter that appears in a function definition (as opposed to a function call).

forward declaration A partial description of some program element that is used to inform the compiler of something that will be completely defined later in the program. In statically typed languages, it is often necessary for defining recursive data structures.

full tree A tree where every non-leaf node has the maximum possible number of children.

global variable A variable that is accessible to all parts of a program.

graph An abstract data type comprising a set of nodes and a set of edges that relate pairs of nodes.

greedy algorithm An algorithm design technique wherein each step of a multi-step strategy is chosen to make the maximum possible immediate progress toward the final goal.

hash function An operation for turning some data into a relatively small integer, often for the purpose of locating that data in an array.

hash table A container data structure that implements a mapping and uses hashing (mapping keys into numbers) to support efficient insertion and retrieval.

head The traditional name for the first node in a linked list.

header node A dummy node at the front of a linked list.

heap (data structure) An ordered container data structure that supports efficient insertion of items and removal of a minimum (or maximum) item.

heap (memory allocation) The area of memory from which objects can be dynamically allocated at run-time.

heap sort An $n \log n$ sorting algorithm that relies on the heap data structure.

Huffman coding A data compression algorithm based on a tree data structure.

implementation independence The ability to change the implementation of a service without affecting the clients of the service.

implicit heap dynamic Allocation of memory for objects at run-time that is managed automatically by the run-time system of the programming language. Garbage-collected languages such as Python provide implicit heap dynamic storage.

in-degree For a directed graph node, it is the count of incoming edges.

inheritance Defining a new class as a specialization of another class.

inline function/method A mechanism to tell a compiler that the body of a function/method should be directly inserted at each point in the program where the function/method is called, thus avoiding the run-time overhead of the function/method call.

instance variable A piece of data stored inside an object.

instantiation In C++, the process of creating a specific instance of a templated function or class.

interface The connection between two components. For a function or method, the interface consists of the name of the function or method, its parameters, and its return values. For an object, it is the set of methods (and their interfaces) that are used to manipulate the object. The term "user interface" is used to describe how a person interacts with a computer application.

interpreter A computer program that simulates the behavior of a computer that understands a high-level language. It executes the lines of source code one by one and carries out the operations.

invariant A precondition and postcondition for a function, method, loop, or class. For a class, an invariant is a precondition and postcondition for each method. For a loop, an invariant is a value that is true before each iteration and true when the loop completes.

iterator An object that encapsulates the position of a traversal through a collection. An iterator is used to loop through a collection in an implementation independent fashion.

Kruskal's algorithm An algorithm to find a minimal spanning tree of a weighted graph.

l-value The "meaning" of an identifier when it appears on the left-hand side of an assignment statement.

library A collection of useful functions or classes that can be imported and used in a program.

lifetime (of a variable) The time during execution of a program when a variable is bound to a storage location.

linear algorithm An algorithm with running time that is directly proportional to the size of the input.

linker A program that assembles separately compiled program units into an executable whole.

list A general Python data type for representing sequential collections. Lists are heterogeneous and can grow and shrink as needed. Items are accessed through subscripting.

literal A way of writing a specific value in a programming language. For example, 3 is an `int` literal and `"Hello"` is a `string` literal.

local variable A variable inside a function or method whose scope is limited to that function or method.

lossless compression Any compression technique in which all information is preserved, thus guaranteeing accurate reconstruction of the original data.

lossy compression Any compression technique in which some information may be lost, thus leading to imperfect reconstruction of the original data.

machine code A program in the machine language of a specific computer.

macro In C++, it is analogous to a function definition, but when "called" it results in a textual expansion by the C++ preprocessor prior to compilation of the program.

memoization An algorithmic technique for automatically "caching" previously computed results so that they can be returned without requiring additional computation when needed again later.

memory leak A program error in which memory is allocated but not deallocated when it is no longer in use.

method A function that lives inside an object. Objects are manipulated by calling their methods.

minimum spanning tree A subgraph that is a tree connecting all the nodes of a graph and having the least total cost as measured by the sum of the weights of the included edges.

mutable Changeable. An object whose state can be changed is said to be mutable. For example, Python `int`s and `string`s are not mutable, but lists are.

mutator method A method that changes the state of an object (i.e., modifies one or more of the instance variables).

namespace The set of identifiers that are defined in a given scope. Python uses an inspectable dictionary to represent namespaces.

non-local variable A variable that is accessible in, but not defined within, some given scope. Global variables are non-local.

NP The class of problems that is solvable by non-deterministic polynomial time algorithms. Intuitively, these are problems whose solutions can be checked for correctness in polynomial time, but the generation of the solution is done in exponential time.

NP-complete A problem known to be as hard as any problem in NP. Every NP problem can be reduced to it.

object A program entity that has some data and a set of operations to manipulate that data.

object-based Describes design and programming that use objects as the principle form of abstraction.

object-oriented Describes object-based design or programming that includes characteristics of polymorphism and inheritance.

open addressing The process of finding an alternative slot in a hash table to avoid a collision. Compare it to chaining.

operator overloading Attaching more than one method or function to a particular syntactic operator.

out-degree In a directed graph, the count of the number of edges leaving a node.

overflow Occurs when the number of bits required to store a value exceeds the number of bits allocated for it.

P The class of problems that can be solved deterministically in polynomial time.

parameter A special variable in a function that is initialized at the time of call with information passed from the caller.

pass by reference A parameter passing technique used in some computer languages that allows the value of a variable used as an actual parameter to be changed by the called function.

pass by value A parameter passing technique in which the formal parameters are assigned the values from the actual parameters. The function cannot change which object an actual parameter variable refers to.

path In a graph, a sequence of nodes such that there are edges connecting successive nodes in the sequence.

pointer A value that is the address in memory of some data.

polymorphism Literally "many forms." In object-oriented programming, the ability for a particular line of code to be implemented by different methods depending on the data type of the object involved.

prefix code An encoding scheme in which no code word is a prefix of any other code word.

prefix-free code A prefix code.

Prim's algorithm An algorithm to find a minimum cost spanning tree of a graph.

priority queue A container abstract data type that includes operations for inserting items and removing the maximum (or minimum) item.

pseudocode The writing of algorithms using precise natural language, instead of computer language.

quadratic algorithm An algorithm whose resource needs vary with the square of the size of the input.

queue A container abstract data type with first in, first out access.

quicksort An $n \log n$ average case sorting algorithm.

r-value The meaning of an identifier when it appears on the right-hand side of an assignment statement.

recurrence relation An equation that defines the terms of a sequence using operations on previous terms in the sequence.

recursion A technique of defining something in terms of itself.

reference count A field associated with an object that counts how many variables refer to it. Python does automatic reference counting and performs garbage collection when the reference count goes to 0.

reference semantics When the variables of a language always store references to heap-allocated data objects rather than storing the objects themselves.

regression testing Running a set of previously passed tests over again when a program has been changed.

reserved word An identifier that is part of the built-in syntax of a language.

row-major order Storing a multi-dimensional array linearly into memory one row after the next.

scope The textual area of a program where a particular variable may be referenced.

semantics The meaning of a construct.

shallow copy A copy of a data structure where only the upper level of references are duplicated and the copy shares lower-level structures with the original.

short-circuit evaluation An evaluation process that returns an answer as soon as the result is known, without necessarily evaluating all of its subexpressions. In the expression (`True or isover()`) the `isover()` function will not be called.

signature Another term for the interface of a function. The signature includes the name, parameter(s), and return value(s).

simulation A program designed to abstractly mimic some real-world process.

specification A precise description of what some component does, as opposed to how it works.

stack dynamic A term to describe variables that are allocated on the run-time stack. When a function or method begins, stack-dynamic variables are given memory on the run-time stack. When a function or method ends, the run-time stack shrinks, effectively deallocating the memory used for the stack-dynamic variables.

static typing A programming language technique in which data types are attached to variables and variables may only be assigned values having the declared type.

static variable In C++ a static variable is a local variable that maintains its value from one function invocation to the next.

symmetric matrix A square matrix that is the same as its transposition.

syntax The form of a language.

template A C++ mechanism for writing generic functions or classes that are parameterized by data types and automatically specialized (instantiated) by the compiler.

test-driven development A method for incremental program development where each new component of functionality is identified by writing an automated test before writing production code that passes the test.

theta notation An algorithm analysis that provides a tight bound on the resources needed as a function of input size.

topological sort A total linear ordering of the nodes in a directed acyclic graph such that no node appears after one of its descendants.

traversal The process of sequentially visiting each item in a data structure.

tree A hierarchical data structure consisting of a root node and its descendants.

tuple A Python sequence type that acts like an immutable list.

undirected graph A graph in which an edge represents a symmetric pairing of nodes.

unit testing Trying out a component of a program independent of other pieces.

value semantics In an assignment statement, the value of an expression is actually copied into the variable. Compare it to reference semantics in which the variable would store another reference to the same value.

variable In programming languages, an abstraction of a named storage location.

weighted graph A graph in which the edges have associated numeric values.

Index